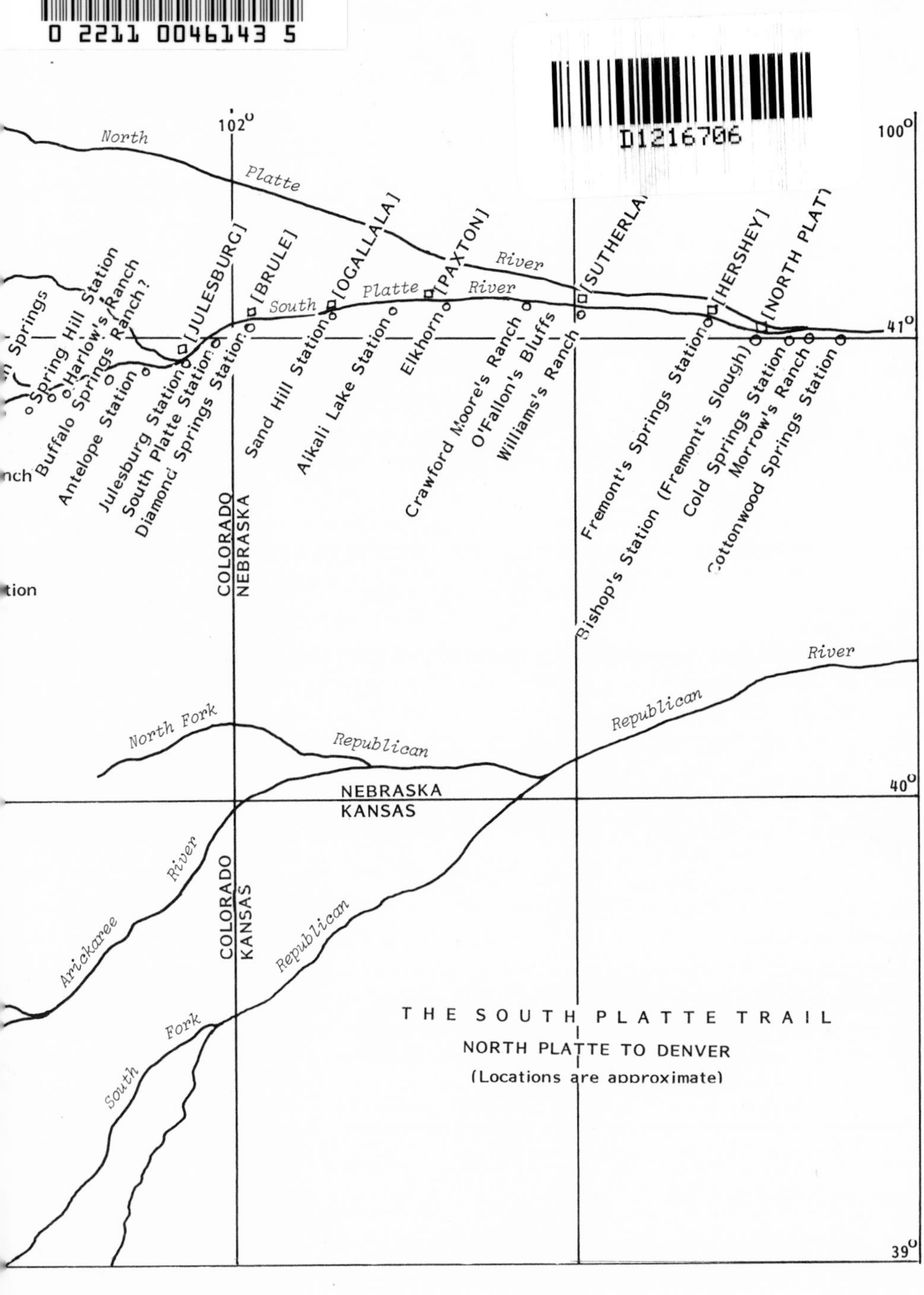

THE SOUTH PLATTE TRAIL
NORTH PLATTE TO DENVER
(Locations are approximate)

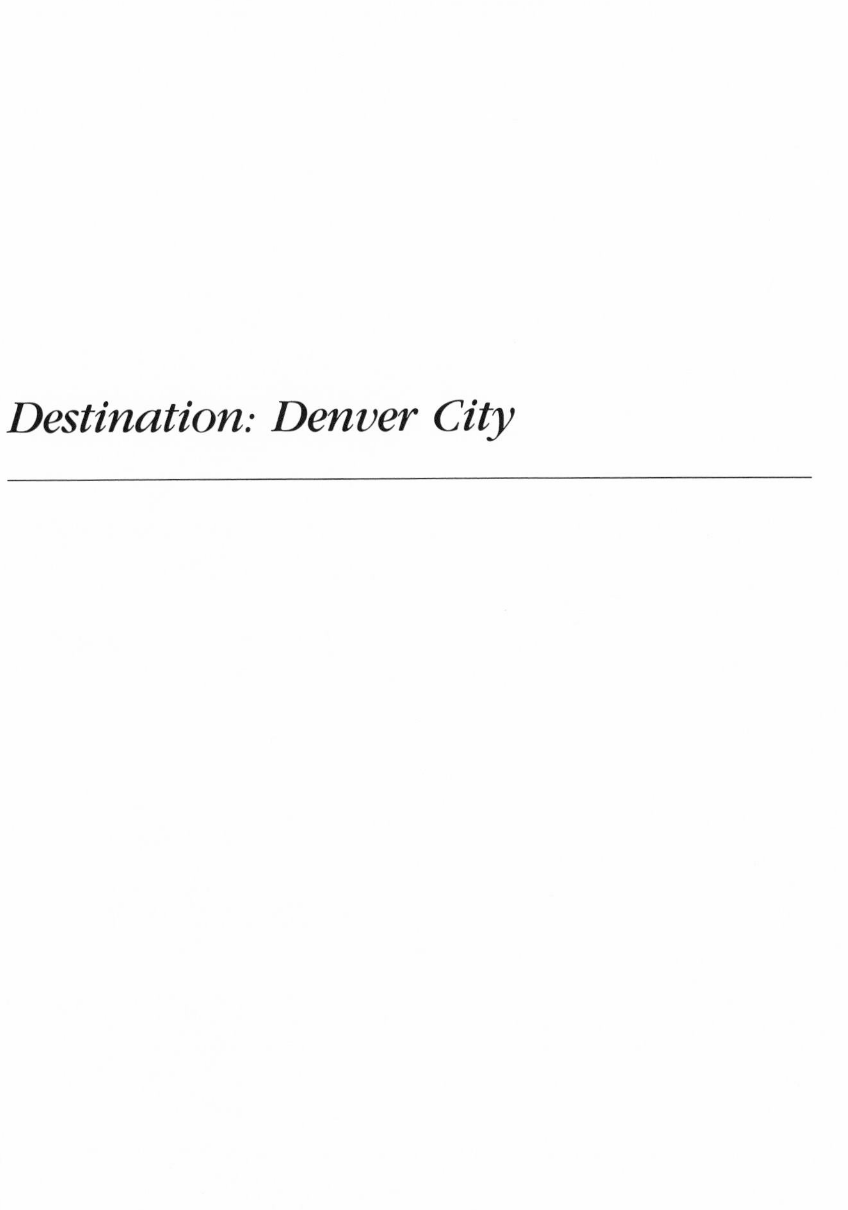

Destination: Denver City

Destination:

Doris Monahan

Denver City

The South Platte Trail

Swallow Press / OHIO UNIVERSITY PRESS
Athens Ohio Chicago London

A Sage Book of Swallow Press

Swallow Press Books are published by
Ohio University Press, Athens, Ohio 45701

Library of Congress Cataloging in Publication Data

Monahan, Doris.
Destination, Denver City.

"A Sage book of Swallow Press"—
Bibliography: p.
Includes index.
1. South Platte River Valley (Colo. and Neb.)—History. 2. Trails—South Platte River Valley (Colo. and Neb.)—History. 3. South Platte River Valley (Colo. and Neb.)—Description and travel. 4. Frontier and pioneer life—South Platte River Valley (Colo. and Neb.) I. Title.
F672.S7M66 1985 978.8'7 84-24060

ISBN 0-8040-0859-0
ISBN 0-8040-0860-4 (pbk.)

To my husband Rex and to all of my children—but by priority, to Susan, Kathie, Melissa and Bill—with much love.

Contents

Illustrations

Preface

The story of northeastern Colorado in the 1860s has never been fully told. Buried under a century of legend, it has been distorted, embellished, exaggerated, or simply ignored. It deserves better treatment. Where else can you find, packed into one ten-year period, a gold rush, covered wagons, stagecoaches, and an Indian war? The seeds for the Indian war of the 1860s were sown and nurtured in northeastern Colorado, and climactic events occurred there. These have been overlooked in many accounts of the war because of an emphasis on the Massacre of Sand Creek in southern Colorado; but the revenge exacted by red men in the northeastern section was equally dramatic. The whole story has a momentum and inevitability that made it seem necessary to be more fully revealed.

Eyewitness accounts, such as those of Morse Coffin, Irving Howbert, John Smith (the interpreter), and officers of both the First Regiment and the Third, provided a new perspective on Sand Creek, a personal view which is a powerful force in story-telling. The accounts are found in government publications: the three reports of the investigation of the Sand Creek Massacre and the Official Records of the Civil War, which include the correspondence of the military forces in

Colorado during the period. These letters, though they are official reports, are quite revealing about the writers (often *because* they are official). They were a help in examining motives as well as facts.

During my research I grew to know the people involved, though they were faded by time. Letters and reminiscences provided characterization. In this background material there was enough detail to make four men, especially, live again in my imagination: Edward Wynkoop, one of the founders and the first sheriff of Denver City; Jim Moore, a pioneer rancher who was also a Pony Express rider with a record ride; George Bent, halfbreed white-Indian with a special grasp of history; and Eugene Ware, an exceptionally observant soldier. These four came to exemplify the participants in the conflicts of that time and place, which arose when the culture of the white newcomer threatened the very different life of the Indian, when a settler population was brought up against nomad wanderers—conflicts which culminated in bloody battles between white and red.

I wish to acknowledge special gratitude to the following people: Elizabeth Sharp for valuable criticism and advice; the late Paul Riley of the Nebraska Historical Society Library for exceptional generosity; the late Otto Unfug for encouragement; Lydia Vandemoer for kind assistance; Mildred Eliott Renquist, Nina Pilkington and Isabel Blair of the Overland Trail Museum for many privileges and cups of coffee; Jean Swift Amelang of the Muncie, Indiana, Public Library for tiresome research; Jean Afton of Denver for the use of her microfilm; Andrew Martin of LaJunta, Colorado, for a glimpse of history; Marne Jurgemeyer of the Fort Morgan Museum; the staff of the Denver Public Library Western History Department (especially Pam Patrick and Bonnie Hartwick); Kay Engels and staff of the Colorado Historical Society Library; members of the Nebraska Historical Society Library; and most especially my husband Rex Monahan, for discriminating criticism as well as constant encouragement.

Destination: Denver City

Chapter

1

The Tangled Threads of Destiny

It was a bitter cold day in January of 1865, and the brittle snow crackled underfoot. Toward a protecting arc of the South Platte River which shielded the Washington Ranch a swarm of Cheyenne Indian warriors descended from the sand hills and rode with grim intensity toward the adobe walls of the ranch corral.

Among the warriors was a young man with a Caucasian complexion, awkwardly painted with war colors to which he was not accustomed. He confidently raised his rifle and aimed toward an opening in the mud brick wall. He fired and hit a trifle wide of his mark; the bullet embedded itself harmlessly in the hardened earth.

On the other side of the wall a light-haired, blue-eyed westerner positioned his rifle through an opening between the bricks. He aimed at the light-skinned Indian and pulled the trigger. He missed. The Indians circled but did not approach the wall again. Instead they concentrated on driving off the herd of cattle grazing in the valley. It had been a brief encounter.

George Bent, the young man with the warriors, was a half-breed: his mother was a Cheyenne Indian, his father a pioneer fur trader. George was fundamentally a gentle person, and as a result of having been involved in a number of bloody battles in the Civil War, he had no taste for warfare. James Moore, the westerner in the corral, came from a peaceful farming family in Ravenna, Ohio. At the age of nineteen he had followed the swell of expansion to the West, and now, at twenty-five, having made a name for himself as a Pony Express rider, he was trying to raise cattle in the South Platte Valley. Jim Moore was a genial, pleasant, good-natured person who wished no harm to anyone. Both men were involved in the story of the South Platte Trail from beginning to end.

Why were they here?

One could not say that the South Platte River was responsible for the confrontation between two peace-loving men; but the fact remains that without the river there would not have been a South Platte Trail. Today the body of the river squirms almost imperceptibly from southwest to northeast, following a dilatory and unhurried course from the Rocky Mountains above Denver, across the plains of northeastern Colorado, to join the North Platte near the present town of that name in Nebraska. Between Denver and the town of North Platte was the location of the trail which developed—and disappeared—along the south bank of the southern fork of the Platte during the decade of the 1860s.

As rivers go, The South Platte is poorly arranged. It is usually shallow and lazy in movement. It sprawls aimlessly into undisciplined streams becoming a tangled skein of muddied channels. It may have seemed unimpressive and useless to the early arrivals from the east, but it provided man and beast with a necessary water supply. The trail existed because of the river.

The river watered the innumerable masses of American bison which roamed the prairie for countless years, thriving and multiplying almost uncontested. It is not likely that the Plains Indians would have come to the area if the strange-looking shaggy beasts had not preceded them, for the Indians were dependent on the bison for their livelihood. Nevertheless, the exchange of lead between the half-breed Indian, George Bent, and the frontiersman Jim Moore was not caused by the buffalo.

The Indian War which germinated and bore fruit during the 1860s was not the consequence of anything so simple as the water, the food supply and the influx of easterners. The cause was more complex than this. As imperfect man spins the tenuous strands of history from a random selection of incompatible fibers, so the story of the South Platte Trail is woven from scattered unrelated ravelings. The story was shaped by the larger influence which encompasses the history of Colorado and western Nebraska and the events and personalities which contributed to the area over a long period of time. True, the Indian War was aggravated by the existence of the trail, and the expression of hostility was finally concentrated on the inhabitants of the river valley. The South Platte reaches only from North Platte, Nebraska, to Denver, Colorado—but its history encompasses an expanse as wide as the entire High Plains.

Among the personalities who formed the first impressions of the South Platte Valley were the explorer Stephen Long, in 1820, and mapmaker John C. Fremont in 1842. Stephen Long and his party left the most intriguing glimpses of life along the western base of the Rockies before the wave of immigration began. John R. Bell, the journalist who accompanied Long's expedition, was fascinated by the bison. He described the unwieldy creatures that he watched from one of the camps located on the South Platte. He said that in the early morning, as the herds came into view from among the swells and hollows of the sand hills, the animals going to the river moved compactly with a measured pace, "like columns of a large army, concentrating for a general engagement."[1]

When the herds were less crowded it could be seen that individual animals habitually formed a line following an older animal in the lead—usually a bull or an experienced cow—and in this manner they forded a river or moved across the prairie. When a calf strayed from the line, the mother would call to it, making a deep throaty sound like the "muttering of distant thunder." As these throngs of huge animals crossed the grasslands they left their mark in great networks of aimless trails, crooked meandering paths, curving and intersecting. These incisions were cut deeply into the sod, three or four inches deep, from the successive hoofs of the long procession of heavy beasts, each behind the tail of the next, proceeding from water to grass and back again by another route. These were the first trails beside the river; there were more to come.[2]

The panoramic openness of the prairie was another evidence of the passage of the herds of bison.

Most of the trees along the trail had been nibbled away or trampled underfoot in the seedling stage. From time to time a few cottonwoods survived, but they were so scarce, their presence was noted. When Bell passed along the South Platte he noted on June twenty-ninth (by which date his party had passed Beaver Creek) that clusters of cottonwood trees on the banks of the river were growing at intervals of three or four miles. Later, when Fremont led his mapping expedition through this area in 1842, his only mention of trees was a group of cottonwoods on an island, which provided shade from the July sun for his camp. Occasionally a tough seedling must have survived in a protected place among rocks or on the precipitous side of a bluff, because by 1859 traders and trappers were using various "lone-tree" landmarks along the route. There was one entire grove which was still in existence in 1859, and this became the location called "Fremont's Orchard."[3]

But even more than by buffalo and cottonwoods, the explorers were delighted by the Plains Indians. In July of 1820 a detached group from Long's expedition encountered a trading party of Indians camped on the Arkansas River. From a council with four of the chiefs, Dr. Thomas Say, the entomologist of Long's party, wrote about the Indian tribes.

Among the group of chiefs there was one who could speak the Pawnee language with Bijeaux, one of Long's guides. It was discovered that the chiefs represented four tribes, the Kiowas, Kaskias (Kiowa-Apaches), Shiennes (Cheyennes) and Arapahoes. About the Cheyennes Dr. Say wrote:

> The Shiennes, or Shawhays, who had united their destiny with these wanderers, are a band of seceders from their own nation and sometime since, on the occurrence of a serious dispute with their kindred on Shienne River of the Missouri, flew their country and placed themselves under the protection of Bear Tooth [a southern Arapahoe chief]. These nations have been, for the past three years, wandering on the headwaters and tributaries of Red River, having returned to the Arkansas only the day which preceded our first interview with them, on their way to the mountains at the source of the Platte River. They have no permanent town but constantly roam as necessity urges them in pursuit of the herds of bison in the vicinity of the Platte, Arkansas and Red River.[4]

The course of migration which was so briefly described by Dr. Say has since been traced to a beginning with the Kiowas, who must have crossed the plains from the south to north in the very early part of the eighteenth century. The Kiowas were related linguistically to the Pueblos of the Rio Grande area, but the memory of their origins was apparently lost, since tribal tradition went no further into the past than their residence on the headwaters of the Missouri River far to the north. The Kiowas are credited with bringing horses from the south to the northern Indian tribes.

The Cheyennes and the Arapahoes, two Algonquin-speaking tribes, came from the north. Originally, these were agricultural sedentary people. Both tribes were first noted in the area of Minnesota and the Great Lakes. In stories passed from generation to generation the Cheyennes remembered living in earth-covered log houses, planting corn and vegetables and making pottery. Although the Cheyenne traditions deny it, they probably gave up their location in this area in deference to pressure from the invading Sioux tribes. After crossing the Missouri River, the Cheyennes and Arapahoes remained for several generations in the Black Hills, where they gradually adopted a different life style. They gave up stationary houses and began to live in lodges made of skins and poles, fastened down only by rings of stones so that they could easily be made portable. A nomadic existence necessitated the abandonment of agriculture, and eventually, dependence on small game and the buffalo for their food supply.

After migrating by degrees, a number of Cheyenne bands and most of the Arapahoes crossed the South Platte River about 1820 and then ranged progressively farther south and east. The Cheyennes first began to cross the High Plains to carry trade goods acquired from the Missouri River Indians to exchange for horses from the southern Kiowas and Comanches.[5]

As Fremont and his group were traveling up the South Platte in 1842 they met a party of Arapahoes who were out hunting buffalo. Fremont provides a first-hand account of the spectacle. The headman of the hunters politely explained to Fremont's interpreter that the herd had been sighted on the other side of the river in the early morning. Since that time the Indians had been moving in a wide circle, traveling stealthily with the wind in order to surprise their prey. The chief asked Fremont and his companions to halt in order to avoid alarming the herd and frightening them away. Fremont and his men unsaddled their horses and sat down to enjoy the show. A few minutes later a purposeful group of Indian women, riding astride and "naked from the knees down and the hips up" came galloping along the river bank prepared to skin and dress the kill.

Fremont said that as soon as the Indians reached the opposite bank, they separated into two groups: one group went directly ahead while the other moved upriver to flank the herd. The buffalo now had the smell of man, and they struck out in every direction as the chase commenced. Unfortunately the hoofs of so many animals threw up so much dust that very little could be seen from Fremont's point of vision. Fremont watched through his field glass, and he described the scene as having a "kind of dreamy effect." The distance obliterated all sound, and the flickering glimpses of a particular brave with a spear chasing two or three buffalo faded in and out among the luminous dust clouds. Apparently the hunt was successful; as the map-making expedition remounted and progressed toward the Indian camp, they were followed by a long procession of Arapahoes, each pony carrying a dripping load of meat.[6]

The buffalo robe played an important part in the early development of a road long the South Platte River. The precious hide of the bison was the raw material of dozens of necessities for the Indian, ranging from lodge covers to moccasin laces. The preparation of the hides by the Indian women was laborious and time-consuming. The buffalo skins were staked to the ground with pegs in order to dry. After the skins had dried to unyielding stiffness the hair was removed from the skin either with natural caustics or by shearing, and then the squaws patiently reduced the density of the hide by a painstaking process of shaving with a chipping tool until the thick flesh was less than half its former thickness. In order to restore pliability the skin was rubbed with a paste of fat, soapweed and buffalo brains, a smooth stone being used as a tool. Sometimes the skin was softened by pulling it many times through the hole of a buffalo shoulder blade. When a fur robe was produced the steps of the process were nearly similar except, of course, the hair was not removed. The carefully finished buffalo robe, when new and clean, was highly marketable in the eastern United States, and it proved to be one of the major factors contributing to the early betrayal of the Plains Indians.[7]

In the early days of occupation of the plain by the Cheyennes, the white population in the Rocky Mountains was an uncertain number of fur trappers, mostly French-Canadians, who seldom made their presence noticeable. They lived a solitary life in the wilderness trapping beaver, and made contact with their fellow trappers only at the times of the famed rendezvous in order to market their furs. The quantity of these mountain men was already decreasing steadily by the time the Cheyennes had established themselves in the new territory. There were two reasons for the departure of the fur men; besides the dwindling supply of beaver, another factor developed. Not long after the War of 1812 the silk stovepipe hat was introduced in Europe and the classic soft hat of beaver felt began to decline in popularity. Consequently the price for beaver pelts in the Rocky Mountains declined proportionately. Among these fur men, William Bent, his brother Charles and Ceran St. Vrain were latecomers in pursuit of the vanishing beaver.

William Bent, best known as a trader, and spokesman as well as friend, of the Cheyenne Indians, was born on a farm near St. Louis in 1809, the son of Silas Bent, a surveyor. There were already four children in the family, headed by Charles, born in 1799. Silas Bent was appointed to the Supreme Court of Missouri Territory during the year in which William was born, so the family enjoyed considerable prestige. However, as six more children were born in the following years it became evident that prestige alone was not sufficient for the support of a large family.

First Charles entered the employ of the Missouri Fur Company on the upper Missouri River, and sometime after 1825 William is said to have followed his brother into the company. It was probably during these years that William learned to speak the Cheyenne language, and during this decade the brothers met Ceran St. Vrain, who was also from St. Louis. Reinforced by mutual enthusiasm, the three young men decided to go south to the foothills of the Rockies and undertake a trapping and fur-trading business of their own. At some date near 1830 they established a stockade at the mouth of Fountain Creek on the Arkansas and formed the company of Bent and St. Vrain.

The young trappers from St. Louis were too late for the beaver but a little ahead of the demand for the warm buffalo-fur robes produced by the patient Indian squaws. These robes, which were accepted from the Indians as an alternative to beaver pelts, provided good cargo to fill empty wagons bound for the Missouri River. It was soon discovered that this trading for robes proved to be more profitable than trapping, so around 1832 the Bent brothers and St. Vrain built a new adobe stockade on the north bank of the Arkansas about ten miles upstream from the mouth of Purgatory River. The trading post was christened Fort William, but it later came to be known as Bent's Fort, and then, still later, as Bent's Old Fort. This became an important center of operations for the partners, since in the meantime Charles Bent and Ceran St. Vrain (and later, others of the Bent brothers) had established a regular freighting business along the Santa Fe Trail, and the Bent–St. Vrain wagons creaked and groaned back and forth along the Arkansas River on a regular schedule.[8]

William Bent had a sturdy appearance; he was not tall, and had a squarish body. His face was wide and flat, with a beaked nose. He was intelligent (though not especially literate), and he soon acquired a deep understanding of the culture and social structure of the Cheyenne people. When it came time for marriage, William went to the Cheyenne village where he was trading for robes (which may have been on the South Platte River), and negotiated for one or both of the daughters of an important man of the tribe, Gray Thunder, Keeper of the Medicine Arrows.[9]

These young women whom William Bent admired, Owl Woman and Yellow Woman, enjoyed their special position in the tribe because of the religious–magical properties of the Medicine Arrows which were entrusted to their father. Along with his wife, Gray Thunder was considered to be a sacred person by the tribe, and the couple wore random splotches of red paint on their faces to accentuate their importance.

Both daughters of Gray Thunder were desirable brides, but apparently William married the elder, Owl Woman, probably in 1837. The ceremony would not have involved much more than the exchange of a few ponies for the bride, and the wedding date was not recorded. At the time the practices of the Cheyennes were still matrilinear in that the bridegroom usually became a member of his wife's family; but William Bent took his wife to live at Bent's Fort, where the birth date of their first child, Mary, was recorded as January 22, 1838. Other children followed: Robert was born about 1841, and George, who was to become one of the principal persons responsible for the preservation of the history of the Cheyenne Indians, was born July 7, 1843. It is not known when Yellow Woman came to live with her sister and William Bent, but it was probably shortly after her father was killed in 1838. It cannot be determined when William's household became a polygamous unit, but Yellow Woman gave birth to William's son, Charley, around 1845. Owl Woman died in 1846, some say at the birth of her second daughter Julia.[10]

In the meantime white men had come to the South Platte Valley. At the foot of the mountains where the river runs north were "forts" being built by traders who had discovered the profits to be gained from the trade of buffalo robes. These were not forts in any military sense, but merely establishments containing numerous rooms built inside of strong adobe walls. The large area was necessary to protect the trade goods which seems to have included a large quantity of whiskey that required safekeeping.

Good buffalo robes brought from three to five dollars each in St. Louis, and there was an exceptional grade which sold for almost eight. This was called a "silk" robe, meaning that the texture of the fur was finer and the color was lighter. The traders bought whiskey in St. Louis for as little as forty-eight cents a gallon, and after transporting it to their forts in the West, they diluted it with five times as much water and traded it to the Indians at the rate of one or two pints for one buffalo robe.[11]

The dubious distinction of being the first man to teach the Indians to drink is attributed to John Gantt, a fur trader, trapper and military guide who was familiar with the foothills and rivers of the Rocky Mountain area as early as 1835. It is said that Gantt mixed sugar with the alcohol which he offered to the Indians. They had not been tempted before because they disliked the taste, but they could not resist the sweetness of the sugar, and later could not adjust to the effect of the alcohol. William Bent and his brother Charles were aware of this practice and opposed it vehemently. It was observed by a military officer in 1835 that there was a high rate of alcohol addiction among the Cheyenne on the Arkansas River. Very soon after this the traders on the South Platte decided that with the application of hard work and strict economy—plus a barrel of whiskey—a young man could make a fortune in the West.[12]

The first of the trading posts in this area was Fort Vasquez, which was built and operated by experienced mountaineers, Andrew Sublette and Louis Vasquez. After obtaining a trading license in St. Louis from the Superintendent of Indian Affairs, the partners built their fort in 1835 on the South Platte several miles above the mouth of St. Vrain Creek. An old fur trader of intriguing racial origin, a mulatto named James Beckwourth, worked for them here in 1838.

The location was a level space beside a cliff overlooking the river. The road ran north and south on the west side of the fort, but it is not known whether the main gate faced on the road or toward the south. The walls extended about 125 by 105 feet, and they were reported to have been twelve feet high and two feet thick. It was said that the walls had openings with embrasures at intervals, but in the ruins on the west side no evidence of openings remained below the height of eight feet. Perhaps they were placed high on the walls, above the roofs of the enclosed buildings. There may have been two observation towers originally, but ruins remained of only one, a round tower which was said to project five feet above the walls. The fort was built of adobe bricks laid with mud mortar, mud which was probably mixed by oxen driven in a circular ditch to blend the heavy clay with a binder such as straw.[13]

Lt. Lancaster Lupton, a West Point graduate, had traveled up the South Platte River with a military expedition headed by Col. Henry Dodge, sent by the Secretary of War to restore order among warring Indian tribes in 1835. This expedition passed before Sublette and Vasquez had begun their fort, but Lupton was aware of the possibilities for trade in this area, having been informed about it by the guide, John Gantt. When Lupton received his discharge in 1826 he came directly to the South Platte. Undeterred by the proximity of Fort Vasquez, he built his own trading post, which he called Fort Lancaster, about ten miles farther up the river. The size of Fort Lancaster was larger than its predecessor, being about 150 by 125 feet. The walls of adobe brick were reported (perhaps unreliably) to have been fifteen feet high and four feet thick at the bottom. A rectangular bastion, twenty feet square, which projected from the southwest corner, was provided with embrasures on three sides. A large watchtower rose from the northeast corner.[14]

Lancaster Lupton brought a youngster with him from the east, an eighteen-year-old adventurer named Seth E. Ward who soon became a permanent member of the trading network which extended from Fort Laramie in the north to the South Platte Valley along the foothills. Ward was genial and adapted to the life of the forts with remarkable ease. He was an asset to Fort Lancaster and soon learned the fundamentals of Indian trading.[15]

The following spring, in 1837, a third fort was built on the South Platte very near to the other two. This new trading post, built by Peter Sarpy and Henry Fraeb, was called Fort Jackson. Since this fort was demolished after it was sold, there are no remains by which to judge its dimensions or architectural plan.

When the news of the South Platte forts traveled to the Arkansas, William Bent and Ceran St. Vrain became alarmed about the three competitors in the north. Without delay Bent and St. Vrain moved a stock of trade goods to the foothills on the South Platte. They established yet another fort called Fort Lookout, about a mile and a half below St. Vrain's Creek. It was constructed on high level ground east of the bend in the river. In dimensions, Fort Lookout was about equal to Fort Lancaster, perhaps 150 feet square. The walls were of adobe brick, ten to fifteen feet high. In a description of this fort from almost contemporary sources, the height of the wall is described as being sufficiently above the one-story rooms of the ground floor to provide an adequate breastwork over the rooftops for defense.[16]

With affectionate detail, George Bent wrote a vivid description of Fort Lookout. "I had been there several times with my father," he wrote, ". . . I remember it well. The double gate was east side down next to the river. . . . Small gate was north side, another gate was on west side going into the adobe corral. . . . Corral gate was facing south towards the river. Lots of prickle pear were planted on top of the walls of this corral clear around so no one could climb over it."

Bent said that the gates were covered with iron sheets to prevent their being battered down from outside. He went on to describe the towers.

> The towers of [this] fort were around, one tower was built northeast corner and one southwest corner. These towers were built to protect the outside walls from Indians or other enemies. . . . From these towers, one on northeast protected north and east walls, one on southwest protected south and west walls. . . The towers had small windows to shoot out from. . . . It was planned to run [to] these towers first thing when attacked. Another tower was built over the big gate for a watchtower. They had fine telescope in this tower. Many times this saved surprise during daytime. The rooms were all built inside, of course, there were many good rooms. Storehouses, blacksmith shop and carpenter shop. There was [a] billiard hall also when the fort was in its prime.

In addition to the fort, Bent described the fall gathering of the Indians.

> There was flagpole and flags, of course, and one cannon. When the Cheyennes and Arapahoes came to the fort in fall for winter camps near [to] it to trade, when [the Bent-St. Vrain Company] moved inside the fort, they fired this cannon. This meant for everybody to come to the fort for their big feast which was customary. The men eat first. The women had to unpack their ponies. . . and then the women and children would come next. Same time the Company made presents to them, knives to skin buffalo, paints, combs, and powder and bullets.[17]

The new fort was in business by the spring of 1838, but apparently there was something arithmetically wrong with the ratio between the number of Indian women who produced buffalo robes and the amount of whiskey which their husbands and fathers could drink. Sarpy and Fraeb of Fort Jackson soon decided that the valley was becoming entirely too crowded. They sold their fort and stock of goods to Bent and St. Vrain in July of 1838, and the new owners pulled down the entire structure. Sublette and Vasquez operated several more seasons but finally sold their trading post to traders named Lock and Randolph. The new owners were not able to compete, and they abandoned Fort Vasquez in 1842. Lancaster Lupton switched from the buffalo-robe business to farming and livestock sometime before 1843, but discontinued his occupation of Fort Lancaster (later to be known as Fort Lupton) before 1845.[18]

Fort Lookout continued to be operated by Bent and St. Vrain, and it survived under several names for some time. Before 1842 the name of the fort was changed to Fort George. The management of Fort George was handled by Marcellin St. Vrain, the younger brother of Ceran. By this time Seth Ward, who had gone trapping on the western slope for three years, had come to work at Fort George, where he soon achieved the title of Chief Trader. When Fremont's party passed along the South Platte in 1842 they stopped at Fort George and noted that it was now called Fort St. Vrain, but probably in connection with Marcellin rather than Ceran.[19]

By 1845 the Company of Bent and St. Vrain no longer operated the fort during the summer when the Indians were away on the plains. Marcellin St. Vrain spent the winter of 1844–45 at the fort, but after that he and his six-foot wife, Tall Pawnee Woman, moved to a tributary of the Arkansas River where he set up a ranch. William Bent continued to take parties with trade goods to Fort St. Vrain during the winters until after 1852, and he also continued to operate a winter trading post east of the present location of Denver on a periodic basis. But in actuality, the short era of the fur-trading forts on the South Platte had ended.[20]

During his stay at Fort St. Vrain, Seth Ward had become acquainted with a trader named William Guerrier, who also worked for Bent and St. Vrain. When the staff of Fort St. Vrain was disbanded, Ward and Guerrier moved north to the area of Fort Laramie, where they established a trading post. Guerrier married a Cheyenne girl, and they had a son whom they named Edmond. After William Guerrier was accidentally killed in 1859 by the explosion of a keg of powder, an unknown guardian ensured Edmond's education by sending him to Kansas where he attended school at St. Mary's Mission. Edmund later became a lifelong friend of George Bent, and eventually married George's sister Julia. Seth Ward, too, formed an alliance with an Indian girl. His choice was a voluptuous Brule Sioux named Wasna, who was obtained by the usual method of presenting ponies—not to her father in this case, but to her brothers. Wasna and Seth had four children before she died of tuberculosis. One of these was a boy, also named Seth Ward. When the pretentious biography of Seth Ward (senior) was published in 1901, it mentioned his marriage in Laramie in 1860 to Mary McCarty of Westport, Missouri, but it made no mention of Wasna and her half-breed children of the High Plains.[21]

William Bent continued to trade with the Cheyennes and Arapahoes at Bent's Fort on the Arkansas until the tragic year of 1849, when the Indians were more than decimated by a cholera epidemic. Annually each spring it was usual for William to take his accumulation of hides to Westport, a prosperous frontier town located just below the bend of the Missouri River. He owned a farm there where he left his men and wagons while he took the winter's produce downriver to St. Louis by boat. In the spring of 1849 William set out with his eldest son Robert and twenty wagons laden with fur robes. Owl Woman was now dead and Yellow Woman was Bent's wife. During his absence, Yellow Woman took the three children, Mary, George and Charley, to the Cheyenne village to visit her mother and their grandmother, and during their visit cholera broke out. The children's grandmother died and George remembered that they put her in a tree, as was customary. Yellow Woman packed the two boys onto a travois and, mounting Mary on a pony like herself, Yellow Woman fled in panic, riding all night away from the Cheyenne village.

Trade was ruined and William became very discouraged. The government offered to buy Bent's Fort but would not meet William's price. William told Yellow Woman that he could not bear to look around the rooms where there had been happier times. He recalled that four of his brothers had lived there with him; three of them were now dead, and Owl Woman had died there. It made him feel bad. He loaded his family and all of his portable possessions onto wagons and set up temporary camp down the river. The following day he rode back to the fort and set a fuse to the powder magazine, which had not been emptied. He touched a match and blew up the old fort. Bent took his family to the South Platte fort for two years, but in 1852 he began to build a new trading post, constructed of stone, in the Big Timbers, a sparsely wooded area on the Arkansas River.[22]

In Westport William Bent had many friends with whom he traded and also maintained close social relations. One of these friends, Albert G. Boone, assumed the guardianship of Bent's children when they came to Westport to be educated: Mary and Robert first, certainly, and George and Charley later. Julia was not mentioned. George first started to school in 1853, and after finishing the elementary school in Westport, he moved on to St. Louis in 1857, where he was put under the guardianship of Robert Campbell, another business associate and good friend of William Bent. While George attended an academy in St. Louis he probably lived at the school, spending his vacations in Westport, which he called home. Whether or not the other children went to school in St. Louis, George did not say.[23]

If there had not been an Oregon Trail, perhaps there would have been no need for soldiers on the Platte Rivers until the Gold Rush of 1849 made army posts necessary for the protection of the emigrants traveling to the west coast. Cross-country travel began in 1841, and each succeeding year brought more and more intruders into the Indians' way of life. It was true that the emigrants used the scarce and precious wood along the rivers, and they may have had an adverse effect on the ordinarily unperturbed buffalo; but it is also true that the Indians had no compunctions about appropriating horses, tobacco, and sugar wherever they were left unguarded. It is said that the Indians did not steal cattle in the early years because they did not care for the taste of "tame" meat, but if wild game was scarce, an occasional emigrant lost a cow to the Indians' campfires. And then too, there were more serious resentments.

The emigrants complained to Congress, and in 1845 Colonel Stephen W. Kearny, guided by Thomas Fitzpatrick, led a body of troops into the Platte Valley to hold councils with the Indians about the harassment of the travelers on the Oregon Trail. The councils were seemingly successful; but nevertheless two forts were established in 1849, Fort Laramie on the North Platte and Fort Kearny on the Platte.[24]

The soldiers believed that they were there to protect the emigration from the Indians, but hampered by numerous language barriers and inadequate interpreters, the military on the Oregon Trail in the mid-nineteenth century were an inconsistent and thoroughly confused lot, with no real guidelines to follow. Like the legendary horseman who jumped on his horse and rode off in all directions, they were never exactly certain what was the correct procedure for maintaining order.

The Cheyennes and Sioux raided their respective enemies as usual, and while crossing the rivers back and forth they picked up a few "stray" horses from time to time which may or may not have belonged to emigrants. Sometimes someone would get killed while trying to retrieve the "stolen" horses, and someone had to be punished for both the theft and the killing. It is quite possible that the concept of "punishment" was entirely missing from the ethical standards of the Plains Indians at that time—but revenge they understood. The language they used to describe these incidents varied according to the sympathies of the narrator, but it seems that Indians were honor-bound to exact vengeance for the death of a tribal brother who had been "murdered" by the soldiers as a result of "punitive measures." Soldiers, on the other hand, were obliged to "punish thieves and murderers" and to "teach them a lesson."

Meanwhile, Thomas Fitzpatrick, Kearny's guide, had been appointed Indian Agent for both the Upper Platte and the Arkansas rivers in 1846. In spite of his contempt for all members of the Indian race (whom he considered to be ungrateful, low, mean, cunning, cowardly, selfish and treacherous), Fitzpatrick, a twenty-four-year veteran of the plains, made an honest and thorough effort to work out a plan for peaceful settlement of the Indians' tribal differences and to end the raiding on the Platte River Roads and the Santa Fe Trail. In an attempt to stop the expanding circle of theft, vengeance, murder and punishment, Fitzpatrick suggested that the various tribes be assigned to definite areas of their own choosing where they could be expected to stay out of trouble. He also proposed that a strong, knowledgeable body of troops be assembled to enforce this segregation, but this last suggestion was evidently ignored.[25]

In accord with the idea of apportioning lands, the Treaty of 1851 was signed on Horse Creek near Fort Laramie by a large number of persons from a number of different tribes. Their names were spelled phonetically and they signed their "X"s. The interpreters were an Arkansas River trader, John S. Smith, for the Cheyennes, and an old trapper, John Poiselle, for the Arapahoes. The Indians agreed to do exactly what they had been doing all along. The Sioux were assigned to land above the North Platte extending to the upper Missouri; the Cheyennes and Arapahoes were to have the territory from the North Platte to the Arkansas, bordered on the west by the mountains and on the east by a line which reached from the forks of the Platte straight south to a point on the Santa Fe Trail. Fitzpatrick's intended restrictions were not imposed by the treaty, which stated: "It is however, understood that making this recognition and acknowledgement, the aforesaid Indian nations do not hereby abandon or prejudice any rights or claims they may have to other lands and further that they do not surrender the privilege of hunting, fishing or passing over any of the tracts of country heretofore described." Nowhere in the treaty was anything said about denying access to the Platte rivers to either the Sioux, the Cheyennes or the Arapahoes—the river was a field of conflict between these tribes and the emigrants, and it would continue to be so. One definite change was accomplished by this treaty however. The Indians were endowed, completely and irrevocably, with lands of vast area which, some people believed, had previously belonged to the U. S. Government as a result of the Louisiana Purchase. The fact that the Treaty of 1851 was never ratified by Congress does not seem to have altered the commitment.[26]

Although the obscure Cheyennes who represented the tribe at this signing had a full understanding of its implications, they were not authorized to sign in the name of the entire tribe, and many southern Cheyennes were scarcely aware that this treaty had been signed—and even so, what did it change? Life continued on the plains much as before. In the summer of 1856 the northern Cheyennes picked up four stray horses near the Upper Platte bridge, downstream from Fort Laramie. The soldiers requested the return of the horses to their owners. Three of the horses were brought into the fort, but one stubborn Indian brave refused to surrender the fourth. Some Cheyennes were arrested; they attempted to escape and one was killed. One was recaptured and died in the guardhouse. The troops confiscated and burned Indian property as punishment. Illogically, the Cheyennes killed an innocent trapper in retaliation. At this point, all of the northern Cheyennes connected with this feud took their families and moved south to join the southern Cheyennes on the Arkansas.

During this summer other incidents occurred on the Platte. A large war party of Cheyennes heading north paused to send a member of their party to ask the driver of a mail wagon for tobacco. Frightened out of his wits, the driver fired at the Indians. The warriors shot the driver. The following day the usual punitive expedition of troops was sent out in pursuit of the war party, which had returned to the tribal encampment. The troops charged on the camp and later claimed to have killed ten Indians—or perhaps it was six. Soldiers in the West were well known for their ability to enhance the number of enemies vanquished. The troops "captured" twenty-two horses and two mules.

Shortly thereafter the Cheyennes killed two white men and a child from a wagon train and captured some property. In early September an Indian party attacked some emigrants and killed two men, a woman and a child, and abducted another woman who is said to have been gang raped by the Indians. (She was later surrendered to a surveying party.)

Sometimes during the summer a group of southern Cheyennes were detained for questioning at Fort Kearny but became frightened and ran away. The soldiers pursued them but only managed to acquire thirteen horses. A few days later another Cheyenne war party noticed the Cheyennes' animals grazing with government horses, and they recaptured the thirteen horses.[27]

These were isolated incidents—there were others. The Cheyenne view was that the war parties which were on the Platte that summer were looking for their enemies, the Pawnees. No people were killed wantonly (except for justifiable vengeance) and no horses were stolen, only "gathered up" as strays. Now that the season for warfare and the acquisition of horses was ended for the year, it was time for the fall hunt and the establishment of winter quarters. The southern Cheyennes gathered at Bent's Fort to receive their government annuities in the fall of 1856.

There were conversations in high places that autumn regarding punishment of the Cheyennes. The Commander of the Department of the West, General P. F. Smith, thought that the Indians should be severely punished, and Jefferson Davis, the Secretary of War, agreed. However, it was decided to postpone the punitive campaign until spring. When John Floyd succeeded Davis as Secretary of War the following year he received information that Colonel Edwin Vose Sumner was preparing an elaborate expedition against the Cheyennes.[28]

Colonel Sumner, old enough to have white hair and beard but young enough to maintain an impressive soldierly bearing, was loved by his men. He had a deep resonant voice which reinforced the impression of an exceptionally competent commander, and it was said that he seemed to come alive when he found himself about to engage in actual battle. His plan of 1857 for chastising the hostile Indians was based on a wide encircling maneuver in which he would lead a force from Fort Leavenworth to Fort Kearny, on to Laramie, and thence south to the South Platte. Meanwhile Major John Sedgwick would lead a similar command along the Santa Fe Trail, up the Arkansas, and thence northward to the South Platte, where the two bodies of soldiers would meet and consolidate to search out the Indians on the plains, if they had not been encountered previously.[29]

Percival G. Lowe, the wagonmaster of the expedition, accompanied Sumner on the northern route. Lowe noted in his diary that Sumner started from Fort Leavenworth on the twentieth of May, 1857, with two troops of the First Cavalry and his wagon train, which included two mountain howitzers and stock consisting of three hundred oxen besides horses and mules. The expedition proceeded to Fort Kearny where it was reinforced by two troops of Dragoons.

With great difficulty, the cavalry and train crossed the South Platte going northward at what was called the Old California Crossing. At this point the river channel was a half mile wide, usually shallow, with most of the distance relieved by sand bars; but Lowe's wagon train was faced with the "June rise," the annual swelling of the river from the melting of mountain snow. The current was three to four miles an hour over stretches of treacherous quicksand. The young wagonmaster had many anxious moments before the crossing was accomplished.

The command marched on to Fort Laramie to be further reinforced by three companies of infantry. At the fort, where supplies for the whole expedition, including Sedgwick's command, would be purchased, Lowe made the acquaintance of Seth Ward, newly appointed sutler of the post. (A sutler was a civilian whose responsibility it was to provide supplies for army personnel.) Lowe was pleased to find that Ward was well supplied. Lowe thought that Fort Laramie had never seen such activity as was required to outfit Sumner's troops for the summer campaign.

It was on the Fourth of July when Sumner's train reached the point where the Cache la Poudre joins the South Platte, and the flood of the river had not abated. Finding it impossible to cross the river here, Lowe found a campsite downstream. In honor of the day the howitzers were prepared for firing the customary 32-gun salute, one shot for each state of the Union.[30]

In the meantime, Major Sedgwick's troops, four companies of the First Cavalry, had departed from Leavenworth two days previous to the start of Sumner's command and had traveled along the Santa Fe Trail. Included in this body of men was Robert Morris Peck, who made notes of the progress of Sedgwick's force. He noted that Sedgwick had employed six Delaware Indians from that tribe's reservation near Lawrence, Kansas, the group being led by old Fall Leaf, a venerable but still powerful chieftain. The Delawares were good hunters and provided Sedgwick's men with an almost constant supply of fresh game.

Except for having been nearly trampled to death in a buffalo stampede, nothing of great importance happened to Sedgwick's troops until they reached Cherry Creek, which they intended to follow to its juncture with the South Platte. They had just begun their northward course when they met a bedraggled party of six or eight men walking southward, accompanied only by a small wagon drawn by a yoke of oxen and driven by a black slave. In the wagon was a badly wounded man who needed immediate attention from the Army surgeon who traveled with Sedgwick.

The party of men told a fascinating story. They were from Missouri, and had been prospecting for gold in the mountains between Cherry Creek and Pike's Peak all winter. They had been very successful, but all of their stock except the one pair of oxen had been stolen by Indians, and the party decided their only choice of action was to go back to Missouri, take others into their confidence, and then return to the mountains in sufficient force to resist the Indians. It certainly appeared that it was going to be a long walk. Sometime during the encounter between Sedgwick's command and the miners a small bag of nuggets seems to have been transferred from the pockets of the prospectors to those of the Delaware scout, Fall Leaf. The manner of its exchange and for what commodity—it could not have been anything but army property—the wily old Delaware never did choose to explain.

The body of troops continued northward, carrying the wounded prospector with them. Several of the soldiers deserted and disappeared into the mountains. The officers, alarmed by the desertions, insisted that the invalid miner deny the entire story of finding gold in this area, and they made certain that his statement was circulated through the entire camp. Recollections which persisted of the party of miners from Missouri were filed away for future reference.

In the early days of July, Sedgwick's command followed the east side of the swollen South Platte. They passed the old trading posts—Fort Lupton, Fort Vasquez and Fort St. Vrain—which were now deserted and slowly crumbling into ruin. On the Fourth of July the troops went into camp near the bend of the river and prepared their two howitzers for the traditional 32-gun salute. There had been no word in all of this time from Colonel Sumner, and the whereabouts of the other part of the expeditionary force was unknown. There was great excitement in Sedgwick's camp when the reverberation of the last cannon died away. From fifteen or more miles downstream on the other side of the river, Robert Peck and his fellow troopers heard the answering Independence Day salute from Sumner's guns. Immediately Sedgwick dispatched the youngest and strongest of Fall Leaf's Delawares to carry a message across the dangerous river to Colonel Sumner.[31]

On the opposite side, in Sumner's camp, Percival Lowe said that the soldiers watched in fascination while the Delaware struggled against the current. After disappearing and being given up for lost several times, the young Indian finally emerged dripping and triumphant to present Sedgwick's message to the commander.[32]

On the sixth day of July Sedgwick's men and the animals battled the river to join Sumner's command and the wagon train on the north bank. At this point, the force was stripped of wagons and oxen and limited to bare essentials and pack mules, an ambulance, and the battery of four guns. The expedition then moved down the river about eighteen miles below Sumner's first camp, where they crossed to the south, leaving the wagon train behind. They followed the south bank for three or four days before the combined Delaware and Pawnee scouts led the expedition off into the prairie, following a trail left by the lodgepoles of an Indian camp.[33]

The previous autumn, in 1856, William Bent had told the Cheyennes that it was very likely the government would send military forces to punish the Indians for the summer's depredations. The Cheyennes were disdainful. They would not stand and fight, they said; they would keep their families in a safe place and the warriors would only strike from a safe distance in small groups which could retreat and disappear quickly. They made boasts of the many women prisoners they would take and of the number of emigrants they would kill.[34]

The usual practice of Indians in warfare was to make surprise attacks and disperse rapidly, and to avoid large bodies of soldiers entirely. A strange circumstance intervened to change their tactics in the case of the conflict with Sumner. Two medicine men, Dark and Ice, somehow convinced the Cheyennes that they had precognition that in the fight the soldiers' guns would fail to fire, and the Cheyennes would have nothing to fear when the Dragoons charged on them. It was late in July of 1857, on the fork of the Solomon River, when Sumner's troops, numbering about four hundred, approached. The Cheyennes were so confident that they rode out to meet the soldiers. The Cheyennes stripped and painted for battle, mounted their ponies and calmly formed into an orderly arrangement for fighting.[35]

Sumner's official report stated that there were "about three hundred" of the Cheyennes and "most of them had rifles and revolvers." Both of these statements have been disputed by analysts of the engagement. Since military reports of Indian battles were consistently exaggerated, Sumner's assertions were no doubt as inaccurate (or accurate) as any others. Sumner was experienced in the ways of placating politicians and protecting himself and his military superiors, as well as being an exceptionally intuitive field commander.

As his cavalry faced the Cheyennes, Sumner placed his troops to cover any flanking maneuver which the Indians might attempt, but before giving an order to charge, a bit of prelude was enacted. The Delaware, Fall Leaf, rode out in advance of the troops and fired a shot at the body of Cheyennes. Sumner was very likely responsible for this incident since he turned to a nearby officer and said, "Bear witness . . . an *Indian* fired the first shot!"

For what happened next there was no precedent, and no one has conjectured about Sumner's reasons for doing so, but he made a sudden and somewhat illogical decision. Suddenly he ordered his entire force to sling their carbines and draw their sabers for the charge. As the soldiers rode toward them with gleaming weapons, the Cheyennes, who had depended solely on their magical protection against bullets, were shocked and demoralized. They halted their forward movement.

An unnamed and unremembered Cheyenne brave was leading the force of Indians. Robert Peck wrote of him with admiration, "At their first checking of speed," Peck wrote, "a fine-looking warrior mounted on a spirited horse, probably their Chief, dashed up and down in front of their line with the tail of his warbonnet flowing behind, brandishing his lance, shouting to the warriors and gesticulating wildly, evidently urging his men to stand their ground when he saw symptoms of panic among them. Many of us found time to admire his superb horsemanship for he presented a splendid sight as he wheeled his horse, charging back and forth, twirling his long lance over his head now and then."[36]

In spite of their leader's bravery the Cheyennes broke and retreated. Sumner reported that the cavalry pursued them for seven miles but the Indian ponies were more fleet than the cavalry horses, and the enemy escaped. Sumner claimed nine Indians dead and many wounded; the Cheyennes said they lost only four men. Sumner lost two of his cavalrymen and eight or nine wounded.

The Cheyennes then abandoned their village and fled. Sumner burned about 170 lodges then marched to the Arkansas, where he found the winter annuities waiting for the Cheyennes at Bent's Fort. William Bent had withdrawn earlier when he anticipated trouble. Sumner confiscated the bulk of the annuity allotment, and after parceling it out to the Indians who lived permanently near the fort, he told the recipients that it was an advance on the 1858 annuity. He packed up the remainder and started back to Fort Leavenworth, but before he reached that post he received orders to send his troops northward to join a force going to Utah for the so-called Mormon War.

Fall Leaf, the Delaware, returned to Lawrence, Kansas, with a small bag containing nuggets of gold.

Chapter

2

Gold—The Elusive Seductress

In the early 1800s there were few names for the landmarks of the western portion of Kansas and Nebraska Territory. Zebulon Pike had no objection to correcting this deficiency, but when he conducted an expedition to the area of the central Rockies in 1806–7, he had no intention that one of these impressive mountains should become his monument. It did not occur to him that Pike's Peak would be named for him. He did not claim discovery of the mountain; when he mentioned it in his reports he called it "the Grand Peak." Nevertheless the name "Pike's Peak," proved to be irresistible to journalists and cartographers, probably because of its pleasant alliteration.

It was a cold day late in November 1806 when Pike and a few members of his exploring party decided to make the attempt to climb this mountain, which seemed, in the distance, to be "a small blue cloud." The group climbed almost to the summit of one of the front range mountains, only to discover that they were still some distance from their objective. On November twenty-seventh Pike wrote in his diary:

> Arose hungry, thirsty and extremely sore from the unevenness of the rocks on which we had lain all night but we were amply compensated for our toil by the sublimity of the prospects below. The unbounded prairie was overhung with clouds which appeared like the ocean in a storm, wave piled upon wave, and foamy, whilst the sky over our heads was perfectly clear. Commenced our march up the mountain and in about one hour arrived at the summit of this chain. Here we found the snow middle deep. . . . The thermometer which stood at nine degrees above zero at the foot of the mountain here fell to four degrees below. The summit of Grand

> Peak, which was entirely bare of vegetation and covered with snow, now appeared at the distance of fifteen or sixteen miles from us and as high again as we had ascended. It would have taken a whole day's march to have arrived at its base, when, I believe no human being could have ascended its summit. This, with the condition of my soldiers, who had only light overalls and no stockings and were everyway ill-provided to endure the inclemency of this region, the bad prospect of killing anything to subsist on, with the further detention of two or three days which it must occasion, determined us to return.

Pike's party continued on southwesterly across the Sangre de Cristo Mountains in an attempt to find the source of the Red River. On the other side of the mountains they found themselves in Spanish territory, where they were soon taken into custody by Mexican territorial soldiers, but since the Governor of New Mexico was uncertain what to do about the group of trespassers, they were detained in Santa Fe.[1]

While in that city Zebulon met a trader from Kentucky named James Purcell, who was also being entertained indefinitely by the Mexican government. Purcell was acquainted with the area through which Pike had just passed, and during their conversation Purcell mentioned having found some gold in the mountains where the South Platte had its source. When Pike later wrote of the meeting, he said, "[Purcell] assured me that he had found gold on the head of the Platte and had carried some of the virgin metal in his shot pouch for months, but that, being in doubt whether he should ever [return to] the civilized world—he threw the samples away." Zebulon Pike published the substance of this conversation in his *Observations of the Interior of New Spain,* but the United States was not yet ready for that phenomenon called a "gold rush."[2]

After the great migration of 1849 to California in search of gold, a few traders, hunters and some professional miners had traveled along the banks of the South Platte scarcely disturbing the grass. Even though gold had been found in Colorado during these intervening years before 1859, it had not been brought to the attention of the general public. The events which brought about the hysteria of the Pike's Peak gold rush must be traced from a number of sources.

Discounting the group of Missourians who met Sedgwick's troops in late June of 1857, the first organized and competent search for gold in the Rocky Mountains was initiated by William Green Russell of Georgia. Russell was an experienced miner, having worked in Georgia mines and in California. By association and correspondence with men who had actually found gold in the Rockies, Russell planned an expedition composed of his two brothers, six friends and a party of Cherokee Indians from the lower Arkansas River. They started from Georgia in February of 1858, met the Indian party, and in the early spring they passed Bent's Fort and entered the central Rockies, where they prospected streams along the front range, including the South Platte in the neighborhood of Cherry Creek. The pickings were slim, and when summer arrived all but a dozen of the party had given up and returned home. Russell and his brothers were among those who stayed, and in early July they finally found some gold in paying quantities at the mouth of Dry Creek. In the autumn, when the traders from Fort Laramie brought their wagons to the Missouri River, they confirmed the rumor on the frontier that William Green Russell had found gold in the Rockies.[3]

On his return to Kansas in 1857, Fall Leaf, the Delaware scout, had been presented with a "full-moon-size silver medallion" bearing the likeness of President Franklin Pierce in honor of the Indian's distinguished service to the U.S. Government. He had served as a scout for more than ten years—having traveled with Fremont in the 1840s—and he had numerous certificates signed by various important people to prove that he was of good character and ability. When Fall Leaf told his story about *finding* the gold nuggets in the sand while he stooped to drink from a stream in the foothills of the Rocky Mountains, he was readily believed. It is possible that the story was actually true. No one will ever know.

John Easter, a butcher from Lawrence, Kansas, and forty-two other men, including William Parsons who wrote about the journey, gathered together to form a prospecting expedition. They hired Fall Leaf for "six dollars a day in gold in advance" to lead them to his mountain stream. The party was almost ready to depart when Fall Leaf unfortunately had a little too much to drink one night and became involved in a fight. Several broken ribs incapacitated the old scout so that he was unable to consider leading the expedition.[4]

Parsons wrote that he and his impatient friends decided to go without the guide. They started off in the middle of May, 1858, with about ten weeks' provisions and "not the slightest knowledge of where we wished to go or how to get there and still we were happy." This group of amateur prospectors, later to be known as the Lawrence Party, traveled along the Arkansas River, over the Sangre de Cristo Pass to Fort Garland without finding any gold. Somehow a rumor reached the party about a discovery at Cherry Creek, so the group hurried back over the mountains. They camped in the angle formed between the mouth of Cherry Creek and the South Platte River on September 23, 1858. That day the son of a mountaineer had washed $2.50 worth of gold out of Cherry Creek and Parsons said, "We saw it, handled it, and tasted it . . . the gold was there."

Panning gold on Cherry Creek proved to be disappointing for the party however, and it broke up. A number of men, including Parsons, returned to Kansas. ''We had in our possession,'' Parsons wrote, ''less than half a dozen wild turkey quills, nearly all of the gold which had thus so far been taken out . . .'' Nevertheless in the tight money economy of the Missouri River arterial, the sight of actual gold was the spark that started the conflagration.[5]

The contagion and feverish activity of the gold rush of 1858–59 was spread chiefly by the printing presses of Missouri and Kansas. There were newspaper editors and merchants who remembered from the California rush of 1849 that not all of the profit from gold fields came from nuggets and shining dust. The streets of Leavenworth, Kansas, blossomed with freshly painted signs. Some were new names for old businesses, such as ''Pike's Peak Hotel,'' ''Pike's Peak Ranch'' and ''Pike's Peak Lunch.'' Other signs were raised over brand new establishments advertising ''Pike's Peak Outfits.'' Miners would need equipment and supplies, and the Missouri Valley suppliers were very willing to bolster their sagging economy by providing these commodities to anyone who had the price of a pick and a pan.[6]

Indirectly it was the financial panic of 1857 which brought about an abrupt focus on the glowing western horizon. General unemployment and lack of money in 1858 caused normally level-headed men to give credence to the irresponsible newspaper reports of gold discovery at Cherry Creek or Pike's Peak. Pike's Peak, in its lofty eminence, actually had nothing to do with the gold strike; it was ninety miles away from the first recorded gold find.

On Cherry Creek it was autumn of 1858 and it was time to bed down for the winter. Those of the Lawrence Party who stayed behind put together a collection of log cabins at a location a little north of Dry Creek and then duly christened it Montana City. The site soon proved to be unsatisfactory, so the majority of the group moved down to the junction of Cherry Creek and the South Platte, which had been their first camp in September. Here, on the east bank of Cherry Creek, the Lawrence Party founded another city called St. Charles. Taking care not to overlook anything, the town planners drew up articles in a formal manner. The corners where staked out by a surveyor member of the group, a few streets were laid out and notices of incorporation were posted. The town lacked one necessary thing; a charter, which must be obtained from the Kansas legislature. It was decided that except for one man, Charles Nichols, the entire population of St. Charles would return to Lawrence for the winter and return in the spring with the necessary charter.

There was yet another city in the area. On the west bank of Cherry Creek stood the cabin of Levi, one of the Russell brothers. This cabin became the nucleus of a settlement of log houses which the Russell brothers named Auraria (Gold City) after a similar town in Georgia. By early 1859 there were nearly fifty houses in this village—primitive houses with pole and sod roofs and dirt floors, but dwellings nevertheless.[7]

It has been said that it seemed that most of the Pike's Peak pioneers were more interested in the "manipulation of real estate" than the "drudgery of prospecting and placer mining." Even the most reclusive miner must have been aware of the excess of planners who were peddling lots in paper cities from the Missouri River to the Rocky Mountains. A contemporary journalist, Albert D. Richardson, wrote: "In old England only cathedral towns were cities, in New England only incorporated towns, but in the ambitious west anything is a city from a board pile upward." There was a ridiculous simplicity in the trick of making money by nothing more than putting a few stakes in the ground and drawing a plat, and then, with no other equipment than a sheaf of blank deeds, a pen, a bottle of ink and a smooth tongue, a promoter could create a metropolis.[8]

The western part of Kansas Territory—Arapahoe County, a vast expanse of prairie and foothills—was formed by the Kansas Territorial Legislature in 1855. It extended from the 103rd meridian on the east to the continental divide of the Rocky Mountains on the west, and from the 40th parallel on the north to the 37th parallel on the south. As this area became more important because of the gold discovery, the Governor of Kansas Territory, James W. Denver, decided to send a set of officials to the center of activity for the government of the county. He enrolled seventeen men from Lecompton, Kansas, and gave commissions as officials of Arapahoe County to members of the group. The office of Sheriff he entrusted to twenty-two-year old Edward Wanshear Wynkoop.

Wynkoop had been raised in the anthracite coal regions of Pennsylvania, but came west to Lecompton where he was able to find employment in the United States Land Office because his sister was married to General Brindle, a federal employee in charge of the office. No doubt General Brindle also had access to the ear of Governor Denver, resulting in Wynkoop's frontier commission (and accomplishing what may have been Brindle's purpose—removal of his talkative and persuasive brother-in-law from Lecompton). Ned Wynkoop was very tall and strikingly handsome. He had considerable dash and daring and a gift for verbal communication which, combined with a resolute self-confidence, was about to make its mark on the history of his time and place.[9]

The seventeen men of the Lecompton Party, complete with County

Commissioners, Probate Judge and Sheriff, gathered together at Topeka, Kansas, and set out on the Arkansas River Road in the early fall. "Not one of the party had ever crossed the plains," wrote Wynkoop; "When we cut loose from civilization we felt as though we were at sea, an inexperienced crew . . ." They traveled for more than a month, and upon arrival in Auraria, Ned Wynkoop was puzzled by the prospect of his official duties as sheriff. "The only inhabitants . . ." he wrote later, "were buffalo and Indians. My duties, I suppose, were to keep the buffalo and Indians in order, a nice crowd to summon a jury from." Consequently he became involved in the local winter pastime of city planning.[10]

Also from Kansas—Leavenworth in this case—had come a group of experienced town promoters who had no intention of working the gold fields. Among this group were William Larimer, his son Will and a friend, Dick Whitsitt. The Leavenworth group and the Lecompton group of officeholders decided to join forces and found a principal city. The best site for this city was obvious: it was already occupied by the staked-out vacant lots of St. Charles, which was inhabited by Charles Nichols. Larimer and his friends obtained possession of the constitution and bylaws of St. Charles, by the simple means of matching the number of signers and obtaining nine additional names in favor of the proposed city of Denver; St. Charles was pre-empted by the Lecompton-Leavenworth group. Nichols left for Lawrence, Kansas, to report this takeover, but he was overlong in his journey. On November seventeenth the promoters of the new city met in Auraria to organize the Denver City Town Company. The naming of the city (in honor of Governer Denver) is traditionally attributed to Wynkoop.[11]

The problem of obtaining a charter for Denver City was the greatest complicating factor the town company faced. The St. Charles group was already in Lawrence, Kansas, where the legislature was meeting. In order to secure the charter for Denver City before the St. Charles group obtained theirs, delegates must be sent immediately to Lawrence with the application. It was already late in November, and crossing the plains in dead winter was not only risky, it was foolhardy. Wynkoop, already bored with keeping buffalo and Indians in order, volunteered to make the trip. Albert Steinberger, another Pennsylvanian, agreed to accompany him. They were appointed General Agents of the town company.

On the third of December, in below-zero weather, the two rash young men started out with a spring wagon, two mules and necessary supplies. They decided to travel along the banks of the South Platte River across four hundred miles of inhospitable country to Fort Kearny in Nebraska Territory and from there to Omaha. Why they chose this route to Lawrence, Kansas, is not entirely clear. It may have been on the advice of a group of prospectors who had arrived in Auraria in October after traveling the Platte River Road. For some reason, Ned and Albert believed that this was a better way than the Arkansas River Route, so they headed northeast in spite of bitter winter weather. On the first day of their trip Wynkoop froze his feet and was taken in and treated by a camp of hunters. The second night they were sheltered by a local character known as Big Phil the Cannibal, in an Arapahoe village. The following day their host sent two Indians with them in order to show them a good place to camp the following night. Briefly, Wynkoop described the remainder of the trip:

> Our journey thence to Omaha was accomplished without any particular incident but upon our arrival. . . we created an immense sensation, we were the first to have returned from the new gold regions and just at that time, the whole frontier was in a state of excitment in regard to reports of that country. . . As we walked into the Herndon House at Omaha, I saw my full figure displayed in a mirror and I must confess, it was as horrible-looking a specimen of humanity as ever I gazed upon. Dressed in buckskin from head to foot, an otter-skin cap and Indian mocassins, long matted hair falling below the shoulders, unshaven and dirty face, belt around the waist with pistols and Bowie knife attached, I seemed to be a cross between a Malay pirate and a Digger Indian. My companion bore the same appearance with the elegant addition of a red and white striped Indian blanket coat with peaked hood, the latter drawn over his head. How we found admission into a respectable hotel is a mystery to me.[12]

In the middle of January in Atchison, Kansas, Ned and Albert were interviewed by the Atchison *Champion,* and possibly in order to hide the real reason for the trip, they told the reporter that they had come to petition the legislature for a "charter for a company who intend digging a canal from the mountain streams through the 'dry diggings' for the purpose of supplying the miners with water. . . They estimate the canal will cost a million dollars and the dirt taken from it will pay for the work." The newspaper reporter did not indicate that he doubted the story even in the slightest degree.[13]

The charter for Denver City was granted. Wynkoop arranged for lithographed plates and printed certificates of stock for the town company. In the spring of 1859 Ned Wynkoop, in company with his older brother George and a party from Lecompton, returned to Denver City. On their way they met the tardy petitioners to the legislature from the Auraria Town Company who were just now traveling to Lawrence.[14]

Along the Missouri River frontier the rumors were spreading and igniting susceptible imagination. It was the treasure hunters who cut the first wagon tracks along the southern bank of the South Platte. In 1859, thousands of would-be prospectors came surging across the Kansas–Nebraska territories. There were three routes available, all originating on the Missouri River in the area from St. Joseph through Leavenworth to Kansas City. One of these trails ran southward along the Arkansas River and thence north to Cherry Creek. The northern route followed the west bank of the Missouri, or along the Little Blue River, to the Platte River then westward along the Platte Valley to branch at the South Platte and follow this river to the site of present Denver. The central route, which was new and scarcely cut, was called the Smoky Hill Trail. This uncertain path vaguely followed the meandering Smoky Hill River through Kansas and crossed the present border of Colorado opposite Pike's Peak. From this point the untried route passed through long stretches of waterless country. Even though this was the shortest way to the rainbow's end, wiser men preferred the longest and safest route, the much-traveled Oregon Trail along the Platte. The South Platte Trail was therefore born.

One traveler observed that along the Platte in Nebraska there was a hierarchy in the ranks of emigrants who moved slowly westward. Among the long lines of dust-clouded wagons, the aristocrats were the through traffic to California. Sometimes these sturdy wagons had their destination emblazoned on the canvas superstructure, but even without this identification they were recognized by their well-planned equipment and easy measured pace. The Mormons occupied second place in the apparent class distinction, only because, even if they were not so well stocked or so carefully prepared, they were still serenely confident and self-sufficient. The Rocky Mountain gold rushers, on the other hand, could be distinguished because they were more often than not inadequately provided, and the main body was "without discipline or discretion." They were regarded with suspicion by the other travelers, and for good cause, since the majority of Pike's Peakers had no conception of what life in the wilderness would provide, not to mention what it would require.[15]

Frequently the gold rushers traveled in small wagons and even two-wheeled carts. Especially notable was one tall, thin-face prospector with muttonchop whiskers named A. O. McGrew, who gained fame as the "Wheelbarrow Man" because it is said that he had "trundled his entire outfit across the plains with just ten cents in his pocket." A later source of information reports that, though McGrew had started out trundling, he was picked up by a passing wagon after about two hundred miles. As the tale was told to the tenderfoot on the streets of Denver, however, it picked up a little embroidery, and there was one staunch witness who claimed that, not only did McGrew push that loaded wheel barrow all the way to Denver, he also took on a passenger to help defray expenses.[16]

Among those who traveled in one of these small wagons was a young man from Ohio named Jared (or Judd) Brush. Accompanied by a friend named Bates in 1859 Judd traveled to Sioux City, Iowa, where they joined a wagon train which was setting out for the mountains. Brush and Bates invested in a strong wagon, two pairs of oxen, a load of provisions and what Judd called "small traps."

The train crossed Nebraska from the Missouri River to Fort Laramie in sixty days; from this point Judd and his partner turned south on the old trail along the foothills heading towards Denver City. Suddenly it became apparent that the partners differed in their ideas of destination. Judd preferred Central City while Bates intended to go farther south. At LaPorte their routes separated and here they were faced with the complicated business of dividing their property. The two teams of oxen were no problem, and their provisions could be portioned easily, but there was only one wagon, and it was indispensable to both of the young men. For either of them to sell his half to the other was out of the question because there was no place to buy another. They gave the situation a great deal of thought while they camped at LaPorte, until finally a Solomon-like idea came to Judd—they would cut the wagon in two and each would take half!

The only drawback to this plan was that a certain inequality would result: each would have a pair of wheels and an axle but there was only one operative end of the wagon. It was decided that they would cut a deck of cards to see which of them would get the front and which the back. Judd drew the back wheels. With cheerful acceptance of his fate, he cut a pole and fashioned a new wagon tongue, closed up the open front of the box with branches and set off with his half-wagon for Russell Gulch in the mountains.[17]

On the Platte Road, the westbound wagons were traveling billboards with their white canvas covers bearing various legends, many of them warmed-over from the California gold rush of '49. The freight carriers, their occupation firmly bound to their ox-drawn wagons, honored their prairie schooners with names similar to those of water-going vessels: dignified names like Constitution, Excelsior and Republic. There were simple business notices on some of the emigrant wagons such as "FAMILY EXPRESS—Milk for sale" and "Old Bourbon Whiskey Sold Here." One particular inscription must have caused five hundred miles of strained neck muscles as it advertised "Cold Cuts and Pickled Eel's Feet."

Most wagons carried the name of their destination, further elaborated by the individual variations which depended on the frame of mind of the owner when he painted the letters across the new white surface. There was optimism in "Ho For California," grimness in "Oregon or Death." A slight deficiency of confidence was probably the motive for the well-worn slogan, "Pike's Peak or Bust." More imagination was employed in "From Pike Country to Pike's Peak." Friendly cameraderie may have inspired "I am off for the Peak, Are You?" and lusty bravado proclaimed "Hell-Roaring Bill from Bitter Creek." In any case, there is no explanation except downright unfriendliness in the pithy comment, "The Eleventh Commandment: Mind your own business."[18]

The number of wagons which traveled across Nebraska has been reported variously and unreliably. Most witnesses agreed that during the good weather there was an endless stream of wagons going west. The much lamented drudgery of the pioneer woman is somewhat tempered by the report of a lady who seemed to have had nothing better to do than sit in front of her cabin in central Nebraska on a sunny day in the early sixties. At one sitting she counted 900 wagons passing before her. Lt. Eugene Ware, who recorded this feat of endurance, said that he observed that it took two minutes for an ox-drawn wagon to cross his line of vision; at this rate 900 wagons would have taken thirty-six hours if they passed one at a time. Lt. Ware assumed that the lady was counting the wagons which were coming as well as those going. It is well known, however, that wagons did not necessarily travel one at a time in single file; frequently as many a three or four trains would move along side by side.

Of course this was transcontinental traffic, and not all of these wagons were going to Denver country. For those who did intend to turn south, heading for that area, there were two possible routes. Some would turn to the south bank of the South Platte; others would go on to Fort Laramie in present Wyoming, then turn south along the foothills of the Rockies. An exact count of the number of vehicles cannot be determined; only estimates are available—60,000, 80,000 and either more or less. There were certainly enough to make their presence obvious. They deepened the ruts beneath them, stirred up stifling shrouds of dust, and frightened the buffalo away from their watering places.[19]

This was not an entirely spontaneous migration. Actually, there were many people who came to believe that one man alone was responsible for the entire movement to the Rockies. This man had been accustomed to moving westward throughout his life, from Maine to Iowa to California. Daniel C. Oakes had responded to the California gold rush in '49 and by the time he was twenty-four years old he had four years of profitable mining experience behind him. When he returned to his home in Iowa in 1853, he had over $5000 worth of gold. He then married, settled down and invested his money in a contracting and building business. Unfortunately the recession of 1857 affected his income to the point that he turned his ear toward the siren song of the waters of Cherry Creek. Consequently, in October of 1858 Oakes gathered four friends together to form a party which traveled to the Rocky Mountains from Glenwood, Iowa. During the autumn of that year the weather in Colorado was especially mild, and in a short time D. C. Oakes and his friends were well satisfied with their results, each of them finding as much as ten dollars worth of gold per day. Oakes soon became convinced of the potential wealth of the foothills.

Soon afterward, while washing gold on the upper South Platte, Daniel met and became friends with an experienced miner named Luke Tierney, who had also prospected in California. Tierney had been in Colorado for six months and had become familiar with Cherry Creek and portions of the headwaters of the South Platte. He had also kept a diary and had written a guide for the other gold seekers which he called the "History of the Gold Discoveries of the South Platte River."

Oakes was very enthusiastic about Tierney's "history" and could see the likely possibility of profit to be made by providing first-hand information to eastern prospectors. When the party from Iowa packed up to return home for the winter, Luke Tierney was persuaded to allow Oakes to take the diary back to the States with the hope that a publisher might be found. On the trip east Oakes made observations and notes about the trail along the South Platte, and when he arrived home he soon found a partner, Stephen W. Smith, for the publication of the guidebook. Oakes worked up the guidebook section from his notes, recommending the South Platte Route, the only one with which he was familiar. With a scope of vision that was typical of him he also remarked that the country was suitable for cultivation—an alien thought in a guidebook to the gold fields.

Early in 1859 the booklet was published and widely distributed at the outfitting stations along the Missouri River. The book had been put together with a healthy optimism, but the effect of the printed page on the average reader was more of a metallic gleam than a rosy glow.[20] Nearly every Pikes-Peaker who started across Nebraska Territory in 1859 carried a copy of the *History of the Gold Discoveries in the South Platte River* by Luke Tierney. The title further stated "To which is appended a Guide to the route by Smith and Oaks." Perhaps it was fortunate for D. C. Oakes that his name was misspelled; there were times when he would wish that it had been omitted altogether.

Having seen the possibilities for development at the foot of the Rocky Mountains, Oakes decided that his conventional business of con-

tracting and constructing would be more profitable than prospecting in the long run. He found a partner and bought a sawmill, which was loaded on several wagons in segments. Proceeding slowly westward in the spring of 1859, Oakes and his partner had plenty of time to talk with fellow travelers. Those who were headed in the same direction as Oakes were pleased and proud to be in the company of the man who wrote the guidebook. Those who confronted him as they returned along the trail were grimly hostile. Already, there were disappointed would-be miners going home with empty pockets. Poorly prepared and expecting miracles, most had become disillusioned. With no other ready target for anger, these bitter and thwarted gold seekers converged on the hapless writer of the guidebook. No amount of argument could persuade the complainers that the actual fault lay in their lack of vision. After nursing their resentment day after weary day, they had come to the conclusion that D. C. Oakes was to blame; he had cheated them all and he alone was responsible—the worst fate they could wish for him was better than he deserved.

In later years, Oakes wrote about his ultimate punishment:

> It happens sometimes when talking of the early days of '59 that some of the old-timers will mention having seen my grave in the spring of that year, on the banks of the Platte River near the town of Julesburg. That the old-timers spoke the truth and did really see my grave . . . I know to be so, for I, too, saw it myself, and at the same time and place.
>
> The grave was a lonely little mound, near the river bank and close beside the main traveled road of the emigrant trail, in a position where it might readily be seen, and the epitaphs easily read by all the emigrants that traveled that way. It was marked with buffalo bones for tombstones, and inscribed with epitaphs of various degrees of sentiment and feeling, crudely written with a mixture of charcoal and axle-grease.
>
> The epitaphs inscribed thereon were of a character not so much of sorrow as of wrath. One epitaph was as follows: "Here lies D. C. Oakes, dead, buried and in Hell!"
>
> Another, more poetical, bore these lines: "Here lie the remains of D. C. Oakes, who was the starter of this damned hoax."[21]

The writing of guidebooks to Pike's Peak soon became a lucrative business, judging from the number of them which have survived, and among those written was one by a man who had not yet set foot in what would become Colorado Territory. This man, William N. Byers, had been born in Madison County, Ohio, where he spent his childhood on a farm. At nineteen, he drove team and wagon to Iowa where he was hired as a surveyor by the government, and he subsequently worked westward toward Oregon and Washington. In 1852, on the way to Oregon, his crew stopped at Fort Laramie for repairs and provisions. During this stopover, Byers first learned of the dribble of gold which hunters and trappers of the Pike's Peak area sometimes brought into the fort. It seemed an intriguing bit of gossip but had nothing to do with Byers or with his occupation at that time.

W. N. Byers proceeded with his surveying crew across Wyoming to Oregon; then in 1852–54 he went to California and soon returned to Nebraska. When that state opened for settlement, Byers went to Omaha, which he said consisted of one log cabin. Apparently he made a living there, working as a surveyor, until 1859 when a memory of the trickle of gold he had seen at Fort Laramie and visions of unmeasured land inspired Byers to sponsor the second of the most famous of the guidebooks. Early in 1859, William N. Byers and John H. Kellom published *A Handbook to the Gold Fields of Nebraska and Kansas.* Whether written by Byers or Kellom, this book contained this statement that it was "Compiled from the notes of William N. Byers, who traveled the route in 1852." Almost true, yes, he traveled over part of the route, but had not yet seen the latter half, the more difficult and less-known part of the trail, along the South Platte. Although Byers had interviewed Ned Wynkoop and Albert Steinberger when they arrived in Omaha in January of 1858, the boys had been more interested in writing about the colorful mountain men than offering any useful advice for the guidebook.

Like that of D. C. Oakes, this book also received more blame than was justified, and it too became immortalized by the poetic souls of frustrated miners. The graffiti of the trail was the chief source of reading material for the bored emigrants who waited for oxen to graze and rest, and there was an abundance of authentic grave markers memorializing the many who did not survive to see the mountains. These improvised headstones were read carefully and sometimes mentioned in diaries. Any sort of sign post was systematically noted. It is not surprising that Byer's name was added to that of D. C. Oakes, and soon a string of graves of guidebook writers reached from the mouth of Cherry Creek to Fort Kearny. The inscriptions were seldom original, and the sentiments were in agreement: "Hang Byers and Oaks—for starting the Pike's Peak Hoax."

That other reading matter, the wagon-cover inscriptions, became mournful in tone when borne eastward on dirty and bedraggled canvas: "Pike's Peak, Not For Me," "Pike's Peak—Over the left," and "Pike's Peak Not for Joseph, No, No!" There was a phrase used by the pioneers which though carefully researched, has not yet been adequately explained. This phrase, "seeing the elephant," was in 1849 an expression of hope and excitement, but now it had become a common euphemism for giving-up-and-going-home. It had a sad significance for the returning emigrants. One wagon-cover in 1859 bore a large charcoal drawing of an elephant, with the inscription under it "What We Saw at Pike's Peak."[23]

The road home was harder and dustier, and much much longer. The mosquitoes penetrated heavy woolen shirts and drew blood. The nights were cold, the days were intensely hot. There was no shade and no shelter, and stomachs were empty. This desperate struggle to reach civilization—before starvation—even caused many ex-Pike's Peakers to attempt the navigation of the shallow South Platte River downstream in skiffs, the first of many unsuccessful attempts. The mood of the departing miners was nasty, and in some cases disappointed gold seekers nurtured accumulated rage amounting to violence by the time they reached the Missouri River. The meager population of Omaha was so concerned by their past relationship with the merchants who sold gold-mining equipment and with William Byers and his guidebook that panic set in, and weapons from the territorial arsenal were made available to all persons who felt that they were in danger of retaliation from the vengeful miners.[24]

Meanwhile, Byers had departed for Denver. In the fall of 1858, in his real estate office in Omaha, Byers confided to a group of friends talking about the promise of the West, that he believed "it would be a good enterprise to put in a newspaper and printing plant in Denver." His friends agreed and were willing to help finance it, if it would not be too expensive. Within six months, Byers found a printing press in a defunct village in Nebraska, and almost immediately, on March 8, 1859, he and his friend John L. Dailey left Omaha.

The trip was extremely difficult; the ground was soft from a long wet period and traveling with the press was slow. Byers recalled that "It was discouraging to work all day and then camp in sight of the camp of the previous night." After arriving in Denver, the wagon bearing the press became stuck while crossing Cherry Creek. With the help of passersby, the wagon was finally dislodged, and the press was carried up an outside stairway to the second floor of the only buildings in town with a wooden roof and a wooden floor. This roof, of split clapboards, was less effective shelter than the roofs of the other building in town, which consisted of either sod or canvas. Byers cleaned the previous snow out of the loft before the paper went to press, but while the small crew was printing the first edition on a Saturday night it began to snow again, and it was necessary to erect a canvas awning over the press to keep the paper dry.[25]

William Byers and his associates managed to put out the first weekly issue of the *Rocky Mountain News* on April 23, within three days after the arrival of the press. This was the first newspaper published within the boundaries of present Colorado, and although he was apparently inexperienced in the publishing business, Byers proved to be a faithful and persistent advocate of his newly adopted home territory. In the early days the *Rocky Mountain News* made an admirable effort to present accurate reporting, and very rarely did the newspaper resort to sensationalism, although the news was frequently politically slanted. Still, a newspaper is a powerful force for the influence of the public mind, and Byers was not so idealistic that he would not use his writing for this purpose. His concept of the future of the area included a settled community, a town—a city—a state—complete with agriculture and industry.

The growing number of emigrants returning to the States caused Byers a great deal of anxiety. This evaporation of the gold-seeking population disturbed the ambitious editor because among those who were leaving was a large number of young and adventurous farm boys who conceivably might be the raw material from which communities are made. Byers's answer to the ebbtide was published in a crude but shaming editorial of June 18, 1859, titled "The Gobacks" in which he scolded: "We hope this class are again safely at home to their Ma's and Pa's, their sweetheart, or 'Nancy and the babies': there may they dwell in sweet seclusion, retirement and repose . . . Farewell to the 'gobacks,' they have had their day and soon will be forgotten. Whilst they are following the plow or swinging the scythe at fifty cents per day they can sing the words and keep step to the music of 'Our trials and tribulations over the plains . . .' "[26]

Among the motley crowd of emigrants to Denver City during the summer of 1859 was Colonel Charles R. Thorne and the "Thorne Star Company," which included the three Brown sisters, Rose, Flora and Louisa. A reporter from the *Missouri Republican* of March 23, 1859, had described just such a group which he saw on the South Platte trail going toward Denver. "I have seen five beautiful girls," he wrote, "all dressed in bloomer costumes hitched to one of these carts and trudging along with song and laughter." These were not members of the Colonel Thorne's theatrical company, of course, but the situation could have been similar. Borne in London, Rose Brown, known professionally as Mlle. Haydee, was a talented dancer. Her sister, Louisa, was a graceful and attractive actress, and Flora, who sang competently, also performed with the group in a lesser capacity. Other members of the group included Colonel Thorne's two sons William and Tom, beside the "walking gentlemen" of the troupe, Jared Carter, and an actor-technician named Sam Hunter. Not involved in acting, but traveling with the company, were Mr. and Mrs. George Wakely. Mrs. Wakely was the mother of the three Brown girls. Apparently this family had not been associated with Colonel Thorne for very long because Wakely, a professional photographer, was listed in the Chicago directory as late as 1858.

After six nights of performance at the Apollo Theatre in Denver during early October of 1859, Colonel Thorne and his son William abruptly disappeared with the cash receipts, leaving brother Tom, the entire cast of actors, and all of the equipment behind. The situation was far from hopeless however. Mr. Wakely went into business producing ambrotypes (photographs printed on leather) and he bought or rented a house for his family directly across the street from the theatre. Under the name of the "Haydee Star Company" the theatrical company continued to function at the Apollo theatre.

In the meantime, Ned Wynkoop and Albert Steinberger, both back in the Rocky Mountains, had spent the summer mining gold, and Ned had acquired a rather large stake on which he placer-mined. In December he ran officially and formally for the job of Sheriff and was elected. Ned and Albert decided to spend the winter in town.

In a very short time their attention was drawn to the attractive and unattached Brown sisters at the Apollo Theatre. Albert devoted himself to play-writing and he soon composed an exercise in romantic nonsense titled *Skatara, The Mountain Chief.* Albert was easily persuaded to play the title role and Ned assumed that of "Hardicamp, a mountaineer," who was probably the romantic lead. Ned, being tall and dashing, was very likely matched with Miss Louisa as his leading lady and one thing led to another. The play was such a resounding flop that it was not even mentioned by the newspaper, but its production accomplished a definite purpose. Sometime during 1860 the Sheriff of Arapahoe County, Ned Wynkoop, and the attractive English actress, Louisa Brown, were married.[27]

The Gobacks continued to go east, and the dreamers continued to travel west. On the return trip to the States in the summer of 1859, one party of men counted all of the wagons going and coming for thirty days. They determined that the combined number would provide a continuous line of wagons, four abreast, from Pike's Peak to St. Joseph, Missouri, a distance of seven hundred miles. The concept of an orderly row of wagons traveling along a clearly defined path however is merely hypothetical. Groups of vehicles and animals usually met and passed in a more or less disorderly manner. The wide swath cut in the prairie by the South Platte Trail was still clearly visible near Fremont's Orchard in 1875; an observer reported that the average width of the trail was about seventy-five feet.[28]

Since the South Platte road was a thoroughfare, a large part of the traffic which passed over its sandy stretches consisted of freight wagons. Freighting to Pike's Peak country soon became a much more profitable business than mining. Wagon trains of all types and sizes originated on the Missouri River, at St. Joseph, Leavenworth, Atchison, Nebraska City, Omaha, and lesser known places. Steamboats unloaded their cargo on the docks, where it was loaded into the massive wagons designed for the long hauls of prairie transportation. These wagons were named either Murphy or Espanshied, made in St. Louis, or the Studebaker, manufactured in South Bend, Indiana. This type of vehicle was "made of the best timber, wide-tracked, strong and tight, high double box and heavy-tired, covered with heavy canvas over the bows." The Murphys were used most commonly; however, some believed that the Studebaker was easiest to run. A wagon like this could carry three to five tons of freight if skillfully packed. To allow for crossing rivers and streams the cargo was balanced with all perishable items stowed at the very top of the load. The wagons were piled full, and the canvas was drawn so tightly and fastened down so securely that it was difficult for anyone to steal anything from the cargo without attracting attention.[29]

The wheels of the wagon were mounted on wooden axles terminated by metal caps called thimbles. In the wooden-spoked wheel there was a similar thimble called a skein, and the wheel was attached by fitting the thimble into the skein and securing it by a linchpin. This metal-on-metal arrangement was lubricated with tar, and the tar bucket hung conveniently on the rear axle. At every camp the joints required fresh tar, and at every supply station on the road there was a lift-jack to support the wagon while the wheels were removed so the axles could be lubricated. Most wagons carried spare axles, extra tongues and also extra yokes for the oxen.[30]

Far from being the complacent plodding beasts which one imagines, the cattle, or oxen, were wild, unbroken, savage long-horned animals. They were usually wild steers brought to the Missouri River terminals from the Cherokee country or from Texas. One old-time freighter described the Texas steer affectionately: ". . . holding his head high with his long horns and soft wild eyes like those of a deer, quick on his feet, quarters light and tapering, limbs clean-cut, could run like a horse and quite as fast when alarmed"[31]

The process of subduing them or "breaking" them to the yoke, was a spectacle that drew audiences from a large radius. When the yoke was first put on a rambunctious steer, it took ten or twelve men with lariats to accomplish it. Unlike the horse, which pulls with its chest, the ox pulls with its shoulders, so the harnessing of a steer differed from that of a horse. The yoke, the wooden part over the animal's shoulders, pulled the load. Attaching this yoke to the unbroken steer was the difficult part. When the animal's neck was finally enclosed by a loop, or bow, the two ends of the loop were fastened temporarily, perilously close to the lethal horns, by a key. The steer was then chained to a firm object while another steer was roped and tied. When the second steer had his bow in place behind his horns and the ends were joined by the key, he was dragged unwillingly to join his future partner.

The next process was that of removing the key from the bow of the first animal, inserting the ends of the bow through the holes at one end of the yoke, and then resetting the key. This operation was then repeated with the second animal at very close quarters to two sets of tossing horns. It was not unlikely that a particularly stubborn creature might twist himself in such a way that the yoke would be under his neck while still over the shoulders of his team-mate. Once two cattle were pinned into their yoke, they wore it for several days until they became accustomed to the strange encumbrance and learned to tolerate the close association with, and proximity to, one another.[32]

Five pairs of average steers could draw seven thousand pounds of freight, but six pairs were required if the steers were lightweight. For an average wagon load, six yokes—twelve oxen—were employed; when two wagons were hitched one behind the other, ten or twelve pair of oxen were chained into one unit. The order in which the oxen were arranged depended on individual characteristics of the animals themselves. Next to the wagon would be a team of submissive heavy stock called wheelers; in front of these would be a yoke of "second best." In the center would be one or more yokes of untrained recruits—the swing teams—and in front, a team of trained leaders.[33]

The crew of a train consisted chiefly of drivers, called bullwhackers, who walked beside their teams and controlled them with a long whip which the driver learned to manipulate so expertly that he could make the tip crack just over the ears of a particularly recalcitrant steer. The bullwhackers walked the entire route on the left side of the team unless the wind was blowing from the right, in which case the driver moved to the other side in order to avoid the dust. When the bullwhacker's shoes wore out, he would usually switch to Indian moccasins, which over a period of time proved more comfortable and practical.

The train was headed by a wagon-boss and his assistant, who both rode on mules since horses were not durable enough for the rigors of prairie travel, except for Indians ponies born and bred on the plains. The wagon-boss rode at the head of the train, giving commands, while his assistant rode at the end of the column, lonely and alert, always wary. Eugene Ware compared the wagon-master to a king and said that "his altercations with the whackers were very frequent."

A train of wagons and oxen, known as a bull-outfit, was usually limited to about twenty-five wagons, but could include as many as a hundred. A mess wagon was supplied for each group of twenty-five, and this wagon carried food as well as spare parts for wheels and possibly a blacksmith's forge. In addition, the train usually included several extra ponies for herding and a number of extra oxen for replacements.[34]

The appearance of a wagon train as it moved out from the Missouri River outfitting post presented a spectacle as moving as the launching of a fleet of ships. Wind-rippled wagon covers of shining white over majestic hulls decorated with red and blue inched in sinuous lines as far as the horizon. Dots of men were visible in their bright-colored flannel overshirts, moving beside their unruly teams. Here and there at the end of a line a herder moved more rapidly on his pony to control the extra cattle, mules and ponies. As the train disappeared in the cloud of its own dust, another outfit would be forming itself ready for the command to move out. "Civilization" was headed for the South Platte Valley.

Chapter

3

The Cradle on Wheels

On May 7, 1858, the first stagecoach of the Leavenworth & Pike's Peak Express Company arrived in Denver City. Actually, there were two of them—spanking new Concord coaches, the bright paint still gleaming in spite of a generous coating of dust. When the driver pulled up the team of four tired mules in front of the Denver House, the first coach was still swaying on its leather-band suspension as the occupants got out. Beverley D. Williams, the Division Superintendent of the new stage line, hopped down, accompanied by Dr. John Fox, who was to become the Resident Agent. Then from the two coaches twelve other passengers alighted in a somewhat dazed condition, extremely grateful to be able to put this great experience behind them. Since this was an especially exciting moment, a crowd soon collected. More interesting than the passengers was the fact that the stagecoach had brought express packages, letters that were still readable and newspapers bearing information that was still current. Even though this shiny vehicle was travel-stained and grimy, it had brought the smell of civilization. Mark Twain called the stagecoach a "cradle on wheels" because of the rocking motion of its body, but for this incipient community, the symbolism was richer. Now that the carriage had arrived, the infant Denver City could be brought up from the bulrushes and nurtured with propriety.[1]

The credit for this advancement in western transportation belonged to William Hepburn Russell, a tightly wound promoter who operated on the Missouri frontier. He was the product of a tiresomely aristocratic line of English gentry who had fostered in him the firm—but mistaken—conviction that he could do no wrong. Russell was forty-seven years old in 1859 and he was no self-made man; fortunately for him he had partners who advanced the wherewithal for his schemes and followed him to pick up the pieces of his disasters.

His career had begun when he came with his family to the Missouri River Valley in the 1820s. At the age of sixteen Russell was introduced to western trade by a spotty career of apprenticeship to, and later management of, various mercantile businesses, as well as posts in public service, which provided a shaky basis for his future. He experienced his first bankruptcy in 1845, but since his real-estate holdings seemed to be profitable, he decided, characteristically, to build a twenty-room mansion for himself in Lexington, Missouri.

Russell went into the freighting business from Westport, Missouri, in 1847; then in 1849, with an experienced and competent partner, he began to finance military freighting for the government, sending trains to Santa Fe and later to other military posts in New Mexico. It was through various partnerships and financial associations in the freighting business that he met William B. Waddell, and in 1854 the two men formed a partnership with Alexander Majors, a capable freighter, to start a line of shipping across the continent by the northern route. In 1858 Russell, Majors and Waddell began operating the famous freight line from a base at Nebraska City, and conveniently, this freighting firm provided a more or less stable foundation for Russell's future exploits.[2]

Meanwhile, William Russell was preoccupied with a new toy. In partnership with an old associate named John S. Jones, Russell set out to launch a line of stagecoaches from Leavenworth to Denver to capitalize on the gold rush. In spite of very logical opposition from his other partners in the freighting business, Majors and Waddell, who advised strongly against the plan, Russell borrowed heavily on ninety-day notes to finance the Leavenworth and Pike's Peak Express Company stage line. He would be content with nothing but the best. He ordered fifty-two new Concord coaches and a thousand mules with which he intended to institute a daily service from Leavenworth to Denver. Part of Russell's plan involved the radically conceived route to Denver which the coaches would travel, a new road which would be shorter than any of those previously attempted.

From Leavenworth the stage line would proceed along the Santa Fe–Arkansas route as far as Fort Riley, where it would branch off northwesterly into new and untried country along the divide between the Republican and Solomon Rivers, crossing the "heads of Prairie Dog, Sappa and Cramner Creeks." It would then continue westward to "Rock Creek, between 101 and 102 degrees, where the road would follow the Republican River to a point near its source." Then, striking due west, it would "cross the heads of Beaver, Bijou and Kiowa Creeks, passing through a beautiful pine country for sixty miles and striking Cherry Creek twenty miles above its mouth." This road would be 687 miles long, but cutoffs were planned to shorten it.[3]

On March 28 a large train of wagons was dispatched to the new route past Fort Riley to build the new stations. Another train of supplies and personnel departed from Leavenworth on April first. The stations were planned for twenty-five-mile intervals until reaching Junction City, which was 135 miles from Denver. At first the stations were established in tents, but plans were made to build houses for the stationkeepers and their families. A six-man crew was planned for each station, four drivers and two stocktenders. Nelson Sargent was the Route Agent of the 150-mile section nearest to Denver, but this section apparently had no stations in operation by the time the first coaches passed on May 7. Perhaps none were ever built, because the coach which left Leavenworth on May 25 was the last to travel on this route.[4]

The reason for Russell's abrupt abandonment of his new stage route lies in the history of the mail service by the northern route to Salt Lake City and the west coast. Government-sponsored mail to Salt Lake City was initiated in 1849 by establishing a post office in that city and authorizing bimonthly service, with the contracts let successively to two private individuals, both of whom proved unsatisfactory. In 1850 a new contract was made with Samuel Woodson of Independence, Missouri, to carry the mail to Salt Lake City monthly for payment of $19,500 annually. No stations were built along the way and the same teams and wagons were employed for the entire trip. In 1854 the contract was granted to William Magraw for the reduced rate of $14,000 a year. Magraw's contract was made for four years, but he was obliged to discontinue operation of the mail route in 1856 because of financial loss brought about by Indian attacks on the mail wagon.

Hiram Kimball of Salt Lake City assumed the contract for the mail delivery after Magraw, but with an increase in the remuneration to $23,000 per year. The Mormons planned to establish stations along the route, not only for the convenience of the mail carriers but also for emigrants on their way to Salt Lake City. A few stations were built, but they were halted by the progress of the military force headed by Col. Albert Johnston which marched to Salt Lake City in 1857 to suppress the so-called Mormon War.[5]

S. B. Miles obtained the contract for the mail service in 1857 for $32,000 a year, but this arrangement was cancelled in April of 1858. John M. Hockaday, a twenty-one-year-old law student and a partner named William Liggett then acquired the mail contract for the lucrative sum of $190,000 a year. There were stipulations, however, which established definite points on the route: first, that the point of origin be St. Joseph, Missouri, and second, that mail be delivered to both Fort Kearny and Fort Laramie. In the way of performance, the contract required that there be weekly service on a twenty-two day schedule each way to Salt Lake City. The Post Office Department added a clause which would permit the reduction of this service to semimonthly if it seemed advisable to do so.[6]

In 1857 Hockaday's company listed assets of seven stations, ten coaches, and ninety-two mules; they employed eighteen men. The divisions of the line were headed by some well-known names in the history of the northern route: Charles W. Wiley, Superintendent of the Division from St. Joseph to Morrell's Crossing (Upper Crossing of the South Platte River), and Joseph A. Slade, Superintendent from South Pass to Salt Lake City. A different evaluation of the company was made by Alexander Majors in his memoirs. He recalled that "Messrs. Hockaday and Liggett had a few stages, light cheap vehicles, and but a few mules, and no stations along the route. They traveled the team for several hundred of miles before changing, stopping every few hours and turning them loose to graze, and then hitching them up again and going along."[7]

Before the advent of the Leavenworth & Pike's Peak Express Company, mail service to Denver was haphazard. Hockaday and Company had delivered the Denver mail to Fort Laramie, two hundred miles from the mining town. William Byers recalled that it was delivered once a month at the fort, and the people of Denver hired Jim Saunders, a mountaineer with a pack mule, to go to Laramie to pick up the mail. Another of these mail-carriers was Charles Gardiner, called Big Phil the Cannibal. After the Leavenworth & Pike's Peak stage line began service in May of 1859 the coaches unofficially delivered the Denver mail back and forth to and from Leavenworth for ten cents a letter and twenty-five cents a paper. However, they delivered newspapers to and from the *Rocky Mountain News* free of charge.[8]

In the first months of 1859 the Postmaster General reviewed the Salt Lake mail situation and decided to reduce the service to semimonthly, with a reduction in subsidy to $125,000 starting in July of that year. Hockaday and Liggett were evidently ruined, judging from the emotional language which was used in their claims for damages against the government. Liggett's family was reported to be "beggared" and Hockaday was so distraught that he was in a "state of mental and physical disability which disqualifies him from bestowing any attention whatever to his business."[9]

The freighting firm of Russell, Majors and Waddell was not making enough to do more than meet their financial obligations when it became obvious that the Leavenworth & Pike's Peak stage line would not be able to pay off the ninety-day notes which Russell had negotiated. The partners of the freighting firm felt that they were obliged to pay them, and by assuming control of the stage line the partnership consequently became even more deeply involved. An offer was made by Russell, Majors and Waddell to buy the facilities of Hockaday and Company if the mail contract could be included in the purchase. Majors wrote about it this way: ". . . we bought the line of Hockaday and Liggett . . . thinking that by blending the two lines we might bring the business up to where it would pay expenses if nothing more." On May 11, Russell bought the contract for the Salt Lake mail service from Hockaday and Company for $50,000; and the appraised value of Hockaday's equipment, which Majors had regarded so contemptuously, brought the sale price to $144,000, to be paid from the quarterly subsidy payment from the government.[11]

There could be no argument with the terms of the original contract as to route. Hockaday's agreement was to carry the mail from St. Joseph, Missouri, by Fort Kearny and Fort Laramie to Salt Lake City; consequently it was necessary for Russell to change his stage route to the Platte Road. It was conceded that the line might be extended through Atchison, Kansas, however, to Leavenworth, where the stages would continue to originate."

Beverley Williams, the Division Superintendent in Denver, was put in charge of changing the stock and personnel of the Leavenworth & Pike's Peak company from the unfinished Solomon–Republican route to the Platte Road. Williams was instructed on May 31 to reserve stock and equipment to build three stations between Morrell's Crossing (Upper Crossing of the Platte) and Denver. On the sixth of June the last coach over the Solomon–Republican trail arrived in Denver, and Byers was informed that the stage route had been changed; the South Platte Road would now become a branch line from Morrell's Crossing. The first coach to be sent from Denver on the northern route was on June 9; the first coach to return arrived in Denver on July 9.

During this month, transfer of the main route and coordination with the branch line encountered numerous problems at Morrell's Crossing. In the absence of any means of communication the coach from Denver would arrive at the crossing and wait patiently for the coach from Salt Lake in order to connect mail, gold shipments and passengers with the main line. The eastbound stage drivers had no instructions for the commerce with the Denver branch and refused to take the mail and passengers. The gold shipments presented another difficulty. In order to ship gold, it was necessary that it be accompanied all the way by a specially qualified messenger, and now there was a shortage of such persons in

Denver. After enough time had elapsed for messages to be delivered back and forth from Leavenworth, the snarls were gradually untangled and the coaches began to run on a weekly schedule to both Salt Lake City and to Denver.[12]

The new stations of the Platte Route were not built rapidly. They were said to be sixteen to forty miles apart, often established at ranches or supply stores which were already in existence. The passengers who arrived with the first stage to Denver on July 9 said they were very pleased with the service. It would seem that they must have been very easy to please. On the upper South Platte Road, no actual stations were mentioned by travelers in the first part of 1859. There was a trading post at O'Fallon's Bluffs, and there must have been some kind of supply store at Morrell's Crossing. It is probable that a French-Canadian trader named Jules located near this crossing before the summer ended. Beyond that there was only a hastily installed station in the ruins of Fort Lupton, but accommodations for men and animals in this area must have been in tents or rudimentary shelters.

When William Byers went east to bring his wife and children to Denver, they made the return trip in a buggy, and Byers noted the progress made by the stage company. In late July, he observed that: ". . . we found their stations on the South Platte fitted up *in the best style possible*. Several new stations have also been made below the Crossing in addition to the old Salt Lake Mail Company's stations. Houses have been erected, wells dug, and the conveniences of life are rapidly being gathered around points along a distance of hundreds of miles, where two months ago there was not a fixed habitation. Passengers by this line get their regular meals, on a table and smoking hot. . . ." (Emphasis added.) Byers comments must be regarded with some suspicion, however, since he had received many favors from the stage line.[13]

In the *Leavenworth Times* of August, 1859, the reporter remarked: "At each of the express stations, *with the exception of the division from the South Platte crossing to Denver City*, comfortable buildings have been erected. . . . From the South Platte Crossing to Denver, *efforts are perceptible* at each of the points selected for stations to erect permanent improvements in the shape of sod houses, mule guards, stables etc. and in less than a month, everything will be as comfortable on the [opposite] end as on [this] end of the route." (Emphasis added.)[14]

During the summer a new western headquarters for the overland stage line and also for the branch line was established at Box Elder station, which was situated about five miles upstream from Cottonwood Springs, near the junction of the North and South forks of the Platte. Here, B. J. Ficklin, as General Superintendent, made his headquarters, and Nelson Sargent, who had been the Western Route Agent for some time, was also located at Box Elder. Early in September there was a change of personnel in Denver. Dr. J. M. Fox, the former Resident Agent, departed for the States and Beverley Williams, the former Division Superintendent, took charge of the mercantile business of Jones and Cartwright, a freighting firm. Reasons for the replacement of these officials were not stated in the newspaper, and those who took their places were not named.[15]

This was the situation when John J. Thomas came to work for the stage line in the summer of 1859. Thomas was a freighter who had hauled supplies to Salt Lake City in 1857 and had managed a wagon train loaded with corn which traveled from Atchison to O'Fallon's Bluffs for the Hockaday Company in 1858. He said that there was a supply station for the Hockaday Company at that point which was managed by Ike Hockaday, a cousin of John Hockaday. Having made the trip twice before, Thomas was hired again to freight corn and other supplies for the Leavenworth & Pike's Peak Express Company. Having reached his destination, which was Box Elder Station, Thomas did not return to Kansas but went to work for the stage company on the crew that was building stations. "We built fifteen cabins in all," he recalled, "including Plum Creek and Midway, stations down the river from Box Elder, and Lillian Springs and Alkali Station up the river."[16]

By August 27, 1859, the *Rocky Mountain News* was advertising a table of distances for the South Platte Route which included stations from Cottonwood Springs at the confluence of the two forks of the Platte. The stations from this point west were: Cottonwood Springs, O'Fallon's Bluffs, Lower Crossing of the Platte, Morrell's Crossing, Lillian Springs, Beaver Creek, Fremont's Orchard, St. Vrain's Fort and Denver City. In recognition of the new cities in Colorado, a correspondent to the *Missouri Democrat* touched wryly on the founding of these new stage stops: "Auraria, Denver City, December 1, 1859. . . Let me mention first a list of our substantial cities (the towns I will give another time). . ." The correspondent then made a list of the most recent wide-places in the road, concluding: ". . . and Fremont's Orchard precinct which will be duly hooped and skirted under the cognomen of 'city' just as soon as a corner grocery store, a billiard room and tenpin alley are established in the municipality."[17]

Now that it was hopelessly encumbered with debt, the Leavenworth & Pike's Peak Express Company was taken over by Russell, Majors and Waddell in October of 1859, but it was not until early March, 1860, that a new combined company was formed and chartered by the Territorial Legislature of Kansas. The stage line was now to be called by the excessively long name of "Central Overland California and Pike's Peak Express Company," a name which evidently covered all the possibilities Russell desired.

On the seventh of March the new stage company, the COC&PP, announced plans to the *Rocky Mountain News* for the construction of a shorter route between Denver and Beaver Creek which would subtract forty-five miles from the former distance. A train of wagons departed from Denver at that time to build the new stations along the road, which was to be called the Cut-Off.[18]

On January 13, 1860, the Kansas–Nebraska Legislature had granted a charter to the Beaver Creek Road and Bridge Company, consisting of John Colman, John Anthony and John A. Nye besides others, to construct the road, and the charter also granted the privilege of collecting toll from all persons using the road. This toll was to be limited to fifty cents for each wagon with team attached and five cents for each head of loose stock.[19]

The road was ready for use before the stations were completed, but in June the proprietor of the road was advertising the advantages of the new route, station by station. Starting from Beaver Creek, the first station was two miles away at Platte Junction; at Bijou Creek—thirteen miles farther—the operators advertised wood and water; at Cottonwood Springs—after thirteen more miles—more water was promised. An unnamed station could be reached after three miles, and Living Springs, the most important station on the route, was fifteen miles farther. After five more miles, at Kiowa Station, wood and water were expected to be available; nine miles from there was Box Elder Station, also with wood and water. Another nine miles reached Cold Creek, which promised only wood, no water. Here the toll gate was located, and by the date of this publication—June, 1860—the toll had risen: "One wagon, drawn by two animals, $1.00; one wagon drawn by four animals, $1.50, and loose stock per head, 5¢." It would seem that confusion must have been caused by the duplication of two names, Cottonwood Springs and Box Elder, with stations on the lower South Platte. The repetition is even more puzzling since the COC&PP used all four stations.

Another writer described the route in August of 1860. The writer said that at the beginning of the toll road, at Bijou Ranch on Bijou Creek, the proprietor of the road, N. D. Morris, offered general accommodations, wood, water and grass. The traveler was warned to expect "one mile of sand" after leaving Bijou Ranch; fifteen miles farther down the road was the unnamed station kept by V. Wood who promised water and grass (apparently the new Cottonwood Springs station had disappeared). After Wood's station a high bluff would be encountered, followed by a rolling road to Living Springs, fifteen miles farther. After Living Springs, the road continued to roll for five miles to Kiowa Ranch, kept by H. Conant. Box Elder Station (#2), nine miles farther, was also kept by H. Conant and was not the COC&PP stage station.

Thirteen miles from Box Elder Station was Eight Mile Creek, where the toll gate was still located, and another eight miles brought the traveler to Denver City.[20]

Many of the emigrants in early 1860 were extremely indignant about the deficiencies of the Cut-Off route. One traveler wrote that it was eighteen miles to Bijou Creek (from the Junction with the old road to Denver) with no water available. Rumors were passed along about the road—that "there was no water, and but little grass to be had and it was lined with the carcasses of dead bullocks." Twenty-five or more disgruntled travelers who came to Denver by the Cut-Off were so angry when they arrived that they entered an advertisement in the *Rocky Mountain News.* "Pike's Peak Humbug!" it read. "The undersigned having crossed over the so-called CUT-OFF, from Beaver Creek to Junction, take this method of warning their fellow emigrants against this road as it is a full 90 miles long, SANDY, MINUS WATER, save what is alkalied, and is in fact a nuisance and a humbug!"[21]

On May 30, 1860, William Hedges and his fellow travelers approached the Cut-Off route with apprehension. They filled every container they had with river water before starting across the barren plains. At nightfall they camped near a stage station where they could get water, but the following day brought them to Kiowa Creek where there was only a little brackish water standing in pools. On the third day they used the last of the river water since they expected to be in Denver by bedtime. It was a hot day and the promised water supply at Box Elder was exhausted, leaving only a well-tracked mud puddle which yielded no water even after they dug into it with shovels. At sundown Denver was still not in sight and the teams had had no water all day. The road was sandy, and the wagons sank almost to their axles. Hedges and his companions were becoming frightened, but since there was a full moon they decided to press on. A short time before midnight the tired and parched men and animals came over a rise in the prairie and could see the lights of Denver below them.[22]

Near Beaver Creek, at Platte Junction, written on a stump of a pole, the ubiquitous graffiti writer had left a warning: "Gentlemen and ladies will please go the old road," it read; "Damned fools will take the Cut-Off!"[23]

Many of the emigrants were opposed to paying the toll, and some of them refused to do so. Suit was brought against N. D. Morris in Denver courts, but his right to collect toll was upheld and the road continued to be used by more and more travelers. It was true that at some times of the year the streams had less water, and there was a great deal of alkali. In late summer, the grass would become eaten down and the wood supply gradually diminished; but a consensus of opinion was that there was actually much less sand on the new road than in just one difficult area on the South Platte road between Bijou and Fremont's Orchard.

From a few well-kept journals written by travelers who journeyed along the South Platte trail in 1860 fragments of observation provide almost enough information for a reasonable reconstruction of the sequence and appearance of the places along the route. Among these persons was Edward J. Lewis of Philadelphia, who had studied law and had been involved in the newspaper business until he started out with a party of gold seekers from Bloomington, Illinois, in the first part of March of that year. Another prospective miner was Jonah Girard Cisne of Antioch, Ohio, who ran away from home before he was twenty-one and was struggling to buy a farm in southern Illinois. He started toward the Rockies in April, hoping to find enough gold to finish paying for his farm. Dr. C. M. Clark of Manlius Square, New York, had just completed his medical training in 1857 and had been living in Chicago when he was bitten by the gold bug in the spring of 1860. He set out with a party of prospectors sometime in late April or early May for the Rocky Mountains.[24]

The South Platte Trail begins at the fork of the Platte where the north and south branches of that river meet. For some distance the two tributaries can be followed upstream in almost parallel lines across the flat valley above the fork. Near the place where the rivers meet was a settlement called Cottonwood Springs, and as Edward Lewis passed it in March of 1860, he found "several houses and excellent water in spring." A little farther on Edward saw the first prairie dog town he had ever seen, and he discovered the grave of a man from Michigan who had been killed recently in a hunting accident. Jonah Cisne passed Cottonwood on May 7; it was snowing and there were four or five inches of snow on the ground when he woke up in the morning. Dr. Clark merely mentioned passing this village and Box Elder Station as well. Cisne also noted passing Box Elder.

Lewis mentioned two ranches after Cottonwood Springs. He camped at the second one, where he found water and buffalo chips, the *bois de vache* of the plains. It is odd that he did not name this ranch, because it was probably the well-known Jack Morrow Ranch. Dr. Clark went into considerable detail about Jack Morrow and his ranch, which Clark said was called Junction House at the time. To Clark, Morrow's store seemed to be a wonderland of variety, considering its remote location. He said the main store was constructed of square-cut cedar timbers, and it was attached to an older building built of rough-hewn logs. Across the road was "a good corralle" walled with "hewn cedar posts." Clark also mentioned the good well at Morrow's place.

Dr. Clark found Jack Morrow to be an interesting character. Morrow,

Clark was told, had carried the mail to Fort Laramie "in years past" (Morrow was only twenty-six years old in 1860). Now, Clark suspected, Morrow might possibly be in league with the hosts of horse thieves, both white and red, who preyed on emigrant trains. Clark thought that if properly approached Morrow could probably "find" stolen property without much difficulty in a very short time. Clark described Morrow as a "small, slim personage . . . light complexion, wearing long auburn hair, his features small but regular, no beard, and withal a very social man." Clark also mentioned that Morrow had a Sioux wife and had had several before her—or concurrently.

When Clark left Jack Morrow's ranch, he described the terrain. There was a deep ravine just past the house which was bridged—but no toll was charged—and the bluffs that followed were very broken, "rising up in innumerable peaks, and assuming the proportions of mountains." He said that, except for an occasional pocket of cedars and thick buffalo grass in the hollows, the bluffs were barren. After crossing the bluffs he descended to Fremont's Slough where there was a stage station, which he said was called Bishop's Station. William Bishop of Bavaria lived here and operated a trading post.

After Cisne passed Box Elder Station he camped three miles beyond by a big cottonwood tree. Here, he said, he saw a beaver that a Frenchman had caught; Cisne mentioned that the Frenchman lived nearby and had an Indian squaw for a wife. Cisne's group made very little progress the following day. He made a gloomy comment in his journal that they were obliged to camp at Fremont's Slough, which was only about nine miles from where they had camped the night before. Here they saw the body of a young man who had frozen to death in the recent storm while he was hunting for his cattle in the hills.

It is not certain which of the three travelers—Lewis, Cisne or Clark—was mistaken, but there is confusion about the Fremont's Springs Station. Clark said that the station was at Fremont's Slough and called it Bishop's Station; Cisne mentioned passing Fremont's Springs, but did not comment about the station. Lewis, however, wrote that he watered at the slough but "drove on some four miles to Fremont's Springs, three or four weak springs eddying from sandy bank of slough. Express station here."

No one had any doubts about distinguishing O'Fallon's Bluffs; the task of crossing over the top of the steepest one with a wagon and team was formidable. One traveler described the area as follows: "It is at the bluffs that the two streams [the north and south forks of the Platte] begin to diverge from each other and in the elbow made by the rather sharp bend of the South Platte fork, the bluffs come abruptly down to the river so that the road perforce must cross them. They are high and broken enough to make a fairly rugged thoroughfare for several miles and are so exposed that the winds have a clean sweep. . . ." The stage drivers dreaded crossing the bluffs. At one point in the broken sand hills the road descended so sharply that it inclined at almost a forty-five degree angle, and "although the driver applied the brakes so tightly that they held the wheels, the team fairly flew down the steep and winding stretch."[25]

Dr. Clark spoke of the bluffs with harsh words: ". . . a high ridge, that presents a hard, even surface, covered with short stunted grass, and in some places with large fields of prickly pear. The country is sterile. . . its surface seldom watered by rains, the soil is poor, consisting of a granitic sand with a mixture of clay and the incinerating products of vegetation, and a thick incrustation of alkali may be often seen dotting the ground which is so hard-baked and destitute of moisture that it is fissured and cracked in many places."

Ed Lewis did not comment on the difficulties of the crossing; he was distracted pleasantly by the view from the top where he could see both branches of the river and an Indian camp in the distance. Another traveler, a lady, described the view as "unsurpassed." She mentions that as they climbed and descended they could see the valley between the gaps in the bluffs. In the valley the south fork of the Platte was bordered with level bottoms that "looked like the meadows of Maryland." In the distance the North Platte was like a "silver stream" winding between the bluffs which resembled "ranges of mountains in the distance."[26]

On the other side of the Bluffs, once again in the valley, was Bob Williams's Ranch. Williams, originally from Ireland, lived here with his wife Fanny, who came from Missouri. The couple had resided in Nebraska Territory for eight years; all of their four children were Nebraska-born. A few buildings stood near Williams's trading post as well as several tipis where Indian wives and children of the traders and laborers lived. Two miles farther up the valley was the trading post and blacksmith shop of Crawford Moore and his clerk, Benjamin Grimes. A post office was located here when Cisne passed on April 10, but by the time Clark came by in May, it had been moved to the Upper Crossing of the Platte. Moore and Grimes continued to operate a mail station at this location for some time however. In July of 1860 Grimes departed from this post and Crawford Moore became the sole proprietor.[27]

From these ranches there was a long stretch of upper prairie to be traveled, with a strip of sand to be struggled through, before reaching Alkali Lake Stage Station, a distance of about twenty-plus miles from Moore and Grimes' trading post. The three travelers with whom we are chiefly concerned crossed this part of the country merely noting the place names and the sighting of antelopes and Indian families moving along the riverbank. Ed Lewis mentioned a wagon powered by the wind which passed them; unfortunately he did not elaborate on a description of the vehicle.

The only ranch of note in this area, nine miles below the Lower Crossing of the Platte, was that of two French-Canadians, Louis Girioux and N. Dion, who, with their Sioux wives, Mary and Sophia, kept the "Lone Tree Ranch"—actually no more than an ordinary trading post. It is possible that N. Dion was the same person as the Sam Dion whom Eugene Ware wrote about meeting in 1864 on the North Platte. Ware remembered: "At Bordeaux Ranch I met a frontiersman whom I had heard considerable of, and whom I had met once before by the name of Sam Dion. He was one of the pioneer Frenchmen of the period, a jolly, royal, generous fellow who cared for nothing particularly, was happy everywhere, and whom the very fact of existence filled with exuberance and joy. He gave me a beautiful Indian-tanned beaver skin, one of the largest and prettiest I ever had seen. . . ."[28]

A ranch along the South Platte Trail in the 1860s was by no means the sort of organization implied by the title in later times. The word "rancho" came from the Spanish, and meant a place where a group of people could eat together; eventually the name expanded to include a group of huts where the people also lived. At the time when the word was Gallicized to "Ranche" its meaning still did not include much more than the simple group of huts of the Spanish. Dr. Clark was puzzled by the use of the title. He said, "The proprietors do not cultivate the soil, nor do they raise stock, they are merely squatters along the line of the trail." The buildings, he said, varied somewhat in size and number; the materials from which they were constructed were adobe, rough-hewn logs, or occasionally, trimmed cedar logs, like Jack Morrow's trading post. Clark considered the proprietors of these ranches to be a rough lot, dressed in "garments made from elk and deer skins, ornamented with long fringes of the same material up and down the seams." Usually they wore their hair and beards long and frequently uncombed. Many of these ranchmen had squaw wives who lived in Indian lodges erected near the main buildings.

After the Diamond Springs Stage station, which was about two miles below the Lower Crossing of the Platte, the ranch of G. P. Beauvais was situated at what is sometimes called the "Old California Crossing." Beauvais was said to have emigrated from Montreal as so many of his neighbors had done, but he had come from St. Louis to this ranch, perhaps as early as 1849. He was now almost forty years old and had lived in the west long enough to have accumulated "at least three Indian wives and a number of half-breed papooses." He operated a large and well-known store where he offered a large assortment of Indian goods and fur robes as well as groceries. Clark, Cisne and Lewis all noted that they camped in this area, and Clark also mentioned two ranches and a blacksmith shop.[29]

After leaving the Lower Crossing, the next stretch of ground (called the Devil's Dive in later years) was so difficult that it would occupy the attention of most travelers for the larger part of a day. Clark reported that "the road at times leads through deep ravines and gravel pits, and occasionally over a piece of sand, which was deep and heavy, and often times it was necessary to 'double up' our teams, in order to pull our heavy loads across." Another writer described the road from the point of view of the stage drivers. "There was a deep rugged canyon, probably washed out by floods caused by waterspouts. . . . For a short distance on either side of the road there were high and almost perpendicular banks. . . . To go through it, it was necessary for the horses to go on a run in order to give the stage a sufficient momentum to reach the top on the other side. In almost every instance the passengers would get out and walk through this bad place. . . . Parties in charge of ox and mule trains. . . always went around. . . quite a distance to the south because they could do this quicker than they could stop and hitch on double the amount of teams. . . ."[30]

The Upper crossing was reached by Ed Lewis on the ninth of April. There was a strong north wind, and it snowed and rained a little. There were about twenty-five wagons in the camp and Lewis mentioned "two or three good lumber houses at this point." Cisne reached the Upper Crossing on a Monday, May 14. It was clear and cold, but it had rained and snowed the previous day. One of his friends obtained some moccasins from a group of Indians. Another friend traded his gun to an Indian for a buffalo robe.

Clark described the Upper Crossing as follows: "At length, we reached the Upper Crossing where there is a little cluster of framed buildings together with a good well of water. . . . This point is the headquarters of Beaubien, the old Indian trader. We saw him here, seated in the store, surrounded by several stout warriors, passing the pipe and telling stories." If only Clark had obtained the correct name and verified it, one could be certain that the almost legendary character Jules Beni, or Reni (or perhaps Benoit?), for whom Julesburg is named, was the trader Clark described above. As it is, Clark may have mistaken the name of Beauvais, who lived at the Lower Crossing, for the person whom he saw at the Upper Crossing, passing the pipe and telling stories.

No one has left a record of actual acquaintance with the man Jules, but Eugene Ware said that he had been told in 1865 that Jules was a half-breed, French and Indian. Ware said that Jules was an exceedingly dangerous man who had killed two men. Ware found this amusing: it was said that the old trader had severed the ears of his victims, dried his trophies and thereafter kept them in his pockets to be displayed as a grisly conversation piece. It is quite likely that Jules had operated a trading post near the Upper Crossing for some time before the Leavenworth and Pike's Peak Express Company adopted the route. Jules probably had been trading with the Indians and emigrants, and when the stage company needed a station at the Upper Crossing, they evidently hired Jules to manage it for them at his store. It is generally agreed by most writers that Jules was probably even more dishonest than most of the traders on the Platte Road.

Besides these endearing characteristics, Jules apparently had an appetite for whiskey. Eugene Ware repeated a story as it was told to him by an old-timer who claimed to have witnessed the incident. On one occasion when Jules was more than half drunk, he decided to demonstrate to a rapt but incredulous audience a method for making mortar as Jules claimed he had seen it done in Omaha. He brought out several sacks of flour, worth a dollar a pound at the time, and a barrel of whiskey, selling at ten dollars a quart. He then poured the flour into a mortar bed, soaked it with the whiskey and proceeded to stir it to smoothness. When his audience ventured to suggest that these were expensive ingredients for mortar, Jules was quite unconcerned. It was very likely that the materials had been the property of the stage company and there would be more available when they were gone.[31]

Jules' station at the Upper Crossing must have been first named "Julesburg" in 1860. Although official postal records do not record the original post office at this location, there was one established here in May of 1860 after it was transferred from Moore and Grimes' trading post. There may still have been some doubt about the name, however, since an emigrant guidebook published in the latter part of 1860 spelled the name "Galesburg." Still the name of Julesburg caught on for some reason and stubbornly refused to be replaced.[32]

Jules himself was not present at the station when the Federal Census was taken in August of 1860. What happened to Jules? On the particular day when the census-taker passed, Jules may have been out hunting, or he may have departed from the Upper Crossing at the request of the Division Agent for the COC&PP, Jack Slade. In the latter part of the nineteenth century the story of the demise of Jules at the hands of Jack Slade became one of the most lurid—and most widely varied—tales of this part of the country. The legend which Mark Twain threaded together in *Roughing It* was a collection of different versions which the author took delight in exaggerating. Eugene Ware, who is a nearly contemporary source, said simply that Jules became so dangerous that

Slade had to kill him. Without the trimmings of a master story-teller, the story stands approximately as follows: Slade discharged Jules from the employ of the stage line and attempted to regain some of the stolen property for which Jules was probably responsible. Jules resisted and both men became angry. Slade and Jules hacked and shot at one another until both of them nearly died, and Jules disappeared into the mountains, where Slade pursued and eventually found him. According to the legend, Slade removed Jules's ears after finally dispatching him.[33]

After the transcontinental traffic crossed the South Platte at the Upper Crossing, travelers for Denver and the Rockies continued up the south side of the river over the sand hills. Cisne believed that he saw the mountains just before he reached Lillian Springs. He did not mention the new stage station, Spring Hill, which was five to seven miles downriver from Lillian Springs. Lewis, who had passed in April, mentioned the stations as coexisting but without naming either. Clark did not mention Spring Hill Station but described Lillian Springs as an adobe building used as a trading post beside an excellent spring of water. It is likely that Lillian Springs Station was located at the ranch of James A. Forbes, a trader from New York, who lived here in May of 1860; after the station was built at Spring Hill, Forbes continued to run the stage station from his ranch headquarters. All of the three traveler journalists complained about the dense and disabling sand between Lillian Springs and Valley Station. Lewis camped near Valley Station; Cisne passed it very slowly, battling the sandy ravines. Clark merely mentioned that there was a stage station located here. Apparently it was unimpressive.[34]

Lewis made a brief mention of Beaver Creek Station, which he said was about two miles downstream on the Platte below Beaver Creek. He said that the creek was a fine large stream with two fords and his party used the lower. Cisne camped here but Clark found nothing but the "ruins of two sod houses." Clark goes on to describe the road above Beaver Creek. "Leaving Beaver Creek we follow along the upper prairie some distance back from the river, for a distance of ten or twelve miles, then we again descend to the bottom of the road, having a small strip of sand to cross, we then follow up the bottom for some seven miles, and again ascend to the light land, where there is a stage station, and two miles below this, we reach a branch road leading to Denver, known as the 'Cut-Off.' " This unnamed station, which Clark said was two miles below the Cut-Off, was Junction Station, built in the spring of 1860 three miles below the mouth of Bijou Creek.[35]

At the Cut-Off junction Lewis found a signpost which declared that the distance by the old road was 116 miles to Denver, while the Cut-Off promised that destination in only sixty miles. Lewis and his party took the old road; Clark did not trust the Cut-Off so he also took the old road. Lewis remarked in passing that Bijou Creek was "mineralized" and had a swift current. Clark found Bijou Creek to be a small clear-running stream but containing too much alkali for the cattle to drink.

Cisne, on the other hand, had had good reports of the Cut-Off, so he and his party took the new road; but his description is tantalizingly brief. His party's first camp was someplace on Bijou Creek, and the following morning they traveled seven miles to a stage station near the Kansas–Nebraska line (the 40th parallel). They then camped again at a ranch about fifteen miles from Denver. They passed the toll gate and, arriving in Denver about four o-clock in the afternoon, they parked their wagon and went off to see the sights. Evidently the crowd of wagons in Denver was extensive and the spirits were plentiful. Cisne's group could not remember where they had parked and were unable to find their wagon until ten o'clock that night.

On the old road after the Cut-Off junction, it seems that there were two roads from Bijou to Fremont's Orchard. Lewis said that his group took the right-hand road—where there was no deep sand but a very steep bluff—down to the river. Clark followed the same course, following along the river bottom then crossing a large hill, where it was necessary to "descend a precipitous bank." Both Edward Lewis and Dr. Clark commented about the resemblance between the gnarled cottonwoods of Fremont's Orchard and an eastern orchard of old apple trees. Lewis said there was a good growth of cottonwood and willows on the islands above the town. In April, when Lewis visited, there was still a stage station at Fremont's Orchard. The transfer of the COC&PP stage line to the Cut-Off was accomplished two months later.

After leaving Fremont's Orchard, Clark was intrigued by the winding ravines which bordered the river on one side. He mentioned seeing many niches and caves and "isolated pillars and columns of sand" which reminded him of the ruins of an ancient city. Four miles from Fremont's Orchard was what was called Fremont's Hill, high and steep. Clark wrote that the trail was so badly cut up and the sand so deep that the party was forced to hitch four, six or eight yoke of cattle to each wagon in turn in order to pull them up the hill. On the other side of the hill the road descended again to marshy bottomland, which the trail followed for five miles before ascending again. By this time, Clark's entire group had changed their heavy boots for Indian moccasins.

Lewis found the trail easier after Fremont's Orchard—or perhaps it was just that he no longer considered the sand noteworthy. There is also the possibility that the ground was still frozen in April and provided a firmer roadway. His party rounded the great curve of the river on good road and passed the mouth of the Cache la Poudre River and a place called Smith's Ranch.

They camped at Douglas City, which he said consisted of one house with a fenced corral. The following day, Lewis passed the three old forts, and he mentioned that Fort Lupton was partly repaired and occupied. The ranches and houses became more frequent and the land more hospitable as they approached Denver City.

Clark's party passed within two miles of St. Vrain's Fort, where they turned south. Clark noted that there was a bridge here over the South Platte leading to the Laramie Road. Clark also mentioned a ranch at Fort Lupton, which was apparently no longer used by the stage line in early June. From here Clark proceeded joyfully to Denver as his predecessors had done.

The occasional sight of a stagecoach was a pleasant diversion for plodding travelers. "Here comes the stage!" someone would call out. Old-timers who wrote about stagecoaching days became very upset about the careless terminology which developed. "A stage is not a coach," they insisted; "a stage is the distance between one station and another." It was important not to offend the vehicle-loving instinct which has dwelled in the soul of the average man since the wheel was invented. It seems that accuracy about the stagecoach was an especially touchy subject. Brightly painted, shining, glowing with lamps inside and out, fitted with leather upholstery, window covers, straps and arm-slings, the coach must have seemed to the embarking traveler to be as magical as Cinderella's pumpkin.

The body of the coach was shaped somewhat like an elongated basket with slightly flaring sides and elegantly curved lid. The four yellow wheels supported a "sand board" in front and "rear bolster" in back. Between these two projections—which were rather like the head and foot of a bed—two leather straps were suspended on high metal supports which, with accompanying harness and buckles, were called "thoroughbraces." The body of the coach, the basket, was balanced on these leather straps. This contrivance protected the passengers from the grinding jolts of a rough road, but also subjected them to a constant swinging from side to side and back and forth which sometimes caused nausea.

The inside of the early Concord was divided into three seats, one facing forward, one to the back and one in the middle. The seats backing on the end walls of the coach had back rests, but the center seat had only a strap across the breadth of the coach to keep the occupants of this precarious perch from being thrown backwards into the laps of the passengers behind. For a forward thrust, there was no remedy except forgiveness. The three seats accommodated nine passengers, and the seat behind the driver being considered to be the most desirable, it was customarily offered to ladies. Such close quarters for long periods of time necessitated a new code of manners for travelers, and one of the simplest—but most misunderstood—concessions to be made was called "dovetailing." Since there was not sufficient room for the passengers in the center and the occupants of the end seats to extend their legs in front of them at the same time, a compromise was reached whereby one leg of each of the persons facing would pass between those of the person opposite him. Casual enough for men, but for Victorian females in crinolines and petticoats, not allowed by decency to admit that they had legs, dovetailing was a minor erotic experience.

The outside of the coach was utilized to a maximum efficiency. Two seats on the upper front lip of the coach were usually occupied by the driver and either an express messenger or a guard. The top of the coach had a railing around it, and at least four men could sit within this enclosure. For storage, there was a deep leather pocket, called a "boot," attached to the front of the body of the vehicle under the driver's feet. The back end supported a four-foot platform where luggage was stacked and fastened down. This platform was covered by a leather apron with straps and buckles.[36]

The coach was pulled by teams of either four or six horses or mules; the number of animals hitched to the coach depended on the weight of the load, and they, like oxen, were designated in pairs as the wheelers, the swing team and the leaders. In the early years horses were used in the east where the roads were flat and well-hardened, but as the terrain was more formidable in the west, mules were used in that rugged part of the country.

A stagecoach traveled day and night for over a week from Leavenworth to Denver, and though the remarkable adaptability of humankind to adversity is acknowledged, it should be considered again with a touch of appreciation when referring to the passengers on the stagelines of the 1860s. On the first night out "precious little sleep fell to our lot," wrote a lady passenger. But as each day passed it became easier to nod off and eventually the exhausted traveler could be awakened abruptly by a violent motion and yet would fall back into a sound sleep almost immediately.

Three times a day the coach stopped for half an hour for meals, and the starved passengers disembarked to eat an unpalatable fare. The stations where meals were served were called home stations and here a stationkeeper and his wife worked together to manage the stock and cook for the passengers as well as the stage drivers and stock tenders who boarded at such stations. The food on the South Platte Road was crude: buffalo, bacon and bread provided subsistence at some stations, but later, in 1861, the bill of fare had improved and a traveler wrote that a meal usually consisted of rabbit, antelope, or buffalo steak, soda biscuits and coffee, with dried-apple pie for dessert. No butter or milk was provided, and each person was charged a dollar and a half whether he ate or not. Mark Twain said that he was offered rancid bacon, bread the consistency of cement, and a drink called "slumgullion," which was supposed to contain tea but Twain said that dish rag, bacon rind and sand were far more in evidence. One may assume that the author stretched the truth—but not much.[37]

The stage teams were changed at fifteen- or twenty-five-mile intervals; the stations where this was accomplished were called swing stations or feed stations. Usually these outposts were manned by only two employees—a stationkeeper and his assistant—but more frequently this service was provided by a rancher who was previously established. It was planned that at each of these points the team would be replaced with fresh animals, while the retiring team would be rested and fed and then on the following day hitched to another coach going in the opposite direction. As a driver brought the coach into a swing station he would blow a bugle, and by the time he pulled up his reins the fresh team would be harnessed and waiting for him. Five minutes were allowed for changing teams and allowing the passengers to disembark. A five-minute stop might be adequate for someone like Mark Twain to "stretch his legs," but if there were women aboard the considerate stage-driver would sometimes pull up his team to rest near a clump of bushes between stations, and suggest that during the interval the ladies would have time to "pick daisies."[38]

The first stage stations on the South Platte Road were hastily thrown together, using the only material readily available: the grass roots of the prairie. For these buildings, sod was chosen from the bottomland where the grass roots were tightly interwoven and long, preferably from the soil bordering on a lagoon. Rectangular blocks of grass and adhering clay-like mud were cut from this ground, each of the blocks being twelve to fourteen inches wide and two to three feet long, the mud as thick as the roots could hold, usually from three to five inches deep. Two rows of these blocks side by side were laid lengthwise in courses, following the proposed wall; each third layer was laid crossing the others at right angles to bind the two lower rows together. Thus the walls grew, extending the length of two or three rooms, one after the other. The width of a house was from fourteen to eighteen feet wide simply because the ridgepoles, a scarce necessity, were brought for many miles, and their length was limited both by the height of the tree and the length of the wagon which transported them.

The roof was made of boards laid on low-pitched eaves and was weighted at the corners with rocks. Covered with layers of sod, these fanciful roofs sprouted cactus blossoms and other wildflowers as gaily as an Easter Bonnet—a comparison which was equally applicable in a rainstorm, since the vulnerable mesh of grass roots wilted and leaked almost as readily as the most fragile creation of straw and silk. There was a common saying about sod house living: "If it rained outside for one day, it rained inside for two days more." If at all possible the ceiling and walls were covered with coffee sacks or, in more luxurious circumstances, plastered smooth with mud and whitewashed. Then again, the walls might be left in a natural state of crumbling dirt. As one female observer noted in her diary: "The people all make their houses of sod in this country. Some look very nice and some do not. Those that have been plastered look very nice and warm."[39]

The windows were small, partly to make the interior warmer, since there was no glass, and partly as a defense measure against the possibility of Indian attack. Sometimes the more fearful house-builders made the openings no larger than porthole size, just big enough to sight along the barrel of a rifle. Storerooms and stables were built close to the main building, and all of the buildings were often joined by a common wall which extended around the enclosure for animals, also built of sod in a rectangular shape.

Augustus Wildman, who traveled by stage from St. Joseph to Denver in September of 1860, described the South Platte stations as "almost twenty-five miles apart. At some of them we could get what they call accommodations, which for eatables consist of buffalo meat, bacon and bread, and for sleeping, your length and breadth on the floor of this shanty."[40]

The average stage station consisted of only one room, furnished with a bed or two, crude benches, a table, a fireplace and little else. In his book, *Roughing It*, Mark Twain recalled just such a station, and wrote a classic description which bears repeating one more time:

> . . . you had to bend to get in the door. In place of a window there was a square hole just about large enough for a man to crawl through but this had no glass in it. There was no flooring, but the ground was packed hard. There was no stove, but the fireplace served all needful purposes. There were no shelves, no cupboards, no closets. In a corner stood an open sack of flour, and nestling against its base were a couple of black venerable tin coffeepots, a tin teapot, a little bag of salt and a side of bacon . . . in one corner of the room stood three or four rifles and muskets, together with horns and pouches of ammunition. . . . The furniture of the hut was neither gorgeous nor much in the way. The rocking chairs and sofas were not present, and never had been, but they were represented by two three-legged stools, a pineboard bench four feet long, and two empty candle

> boxes. . . . The table was a greasy board on stilts, and the tablecloth and napkins had not come—and they were not looking for them either. . . . Our breakfast was before us but our teeth were idle.

The passengers on the stagecoach reached their destination, and they usually recovered, but the unsung heroes of the South Platte Trail were those who lived in the mud hovels the year around—the traders, farmers, ranchers and station keepers who were called, collectively, the "Platte River Settlement."

Chapter

4

People of the Platte

Reaching toward the northwest from the confluence of the Platte forks there is a broad clear sweep of valley, several miles wide. Between the branches of the river, stubbornly resisting the onslaught of the merging currents of the North and South Platte Rivers, there was, in 1860, a large island adorned with a growth of willows and scrubby cottonwoods. To the south from the river, the bluffs were incised by tree-lined Cottonwood Canyon, which extended for twenty miles to the tableland; the trail through the floor of the canyon was softened and worn smooth by the moccasins, ponies and travois of generations of Indians who traveled north and south through this passageway. At the mouth of this canyon was a fresh-water source called Cottonwood Springs, so called because one large tree grew nearby. The water, though fresh and free of minerals, was not actually from a spring but was provided by seepage from the river through the gravel. A large pit had been dug out here to receive this innocent water which became a focal point for many thirsty camps, both Indian and emigrant.[1]

Near these springs, where the road made a southward turn, Izador P. Boyer and a partner named Roubidoux erected the first trading post of the settlement in 1858. (Boyer had only one leg, and this misfortune had caused him to be called "Hooksah" [meaning "Cut-Leg"] by the literal-minded Sioux.) This building was the nucleus of Cottonwood Springs village. Across the road, during the following year, Richard Darling built another store, which he sold to a Tennessee man named Charles McDonald. McDonald and Boyer conducted a very profitable exchange with passing travelers and Indians. In January of 1860 Mc-

Donald brought his wife, Orra, from Omaha, and in February their first child, James, was born. McDonald had a large fenced corral which extended out across the level ground at the mouth of the canyon. Just beyond this fence lived another trader, Washington M. Hinman, and his Indian wife, Clara, who had come east from Fort Laramie to settle at Cottonwood Springs. Hinman employed a clerk named Thomas Hays, soon to become a trader on his own at another location. Besides the usual clerks employed by the traders, these three establishments comprised the settlement in the spring of this pivotal year.[2]

Between the ranches of McDonald and Hinman was a large and well-staffed stage station kept by John S. North. Twelve employees of the stage company, including two stage drivers, two carpenters, herdsmen and laborers lived here. Another building housed the kitchen and sleeping room; a third contained a private dwelling, probably for the stationkeeper as well as being used for storage. A fourth building was used as a sleeping room for passengers, a place where exhausted travelers could "lay over." This was the original Box Elder Station as mentioned by Jonah Cisne and Dr. C. M. Clark as being "five miles above the springs" and "intervening" between Cottonwood Springs and Jack Morrow's Ranch. By the following year, 1861, this station was called Cottonwood Springs Station, at least formally, and perhaps this accounts for the apparent disappearance of the first Box Elder Station.[3]

This was certainly the station where Richard F. Burton, a discriminating tourist, and his fellow travelers arrived on the eleventh of August, 1860, at 1:35 A.M.—Burton called it Cottonwood Station. The coach had been traveling four days and nights, and the passengers would be laying over in what was called the "Pilgrim's Room" of the station. Burton described it as a "foul tenement," where the travelers threw themselves on mattresses, "averaging three to each, and ten in a small room." Burton commented on the strange notion of westerners which insisted that every window, door and airspace must be closed, even in the high temperature of August, trapping flies and mosquitoes inside. At breakfast time, the passengers found it was necessary to rent the skillet with which to cook their own breakfast which, according to Burton, was composed of "various abominations, especially cakes of flour and grease, molasses and dirt, disposed in pretty equal parts." The saving grace of these deplorable accommodations was that it cost only fifty cents total.[4]

From this beginning, the meager population crept along the banks of the South Platte and settled on the borders of the roadway which pushed its way to Denver City in 1860. A little farther along the valley lived an Indian trader who was probably the only man in the whole valley past middle-age—Joe Jewett was sixty-six—but not too old to have a twenty-eight-year-old Indian wife. Joe was commonly thought to be a half-breed, but unlike many others in the neighborhood, who were from Canada, he was a true Frenchman. Apparently he spoke the Sioux language because he was sometimes employed by the military as a scout, even though his honesty and dependability were questionable. In later years, when a new influx of soldiers came to Cottonwood Springs, a brash patrol was passing along the South Platte when they came across Joe Jewett and a few of his cronies. The soldiers summarily arrested the entire group as "suspicious characters" and sent them to Omaha under guard. The military authorities in Omaha could not actually find any concrete evidence to uphold the suspicions so they sent the prisoners back to the Springs. Within months Joe Jewett was again happily and warmly welcomed as a scout for the military camp.[5]

The Shorter County census taker in 1860 found Jack Morrow much as Dr. Clark had left him at his large and prosperous cedar-log trading post. For the U.S. Census, however, Morrow refused to admit to having the Sioux wife with which Dr. Clark had credited him. Nearby the census taker found Hugh Morgan, afterward to become Morrow's very dependable and equally unscrupulous right-hand man. In 1860 Morgan was still an independent trader with an establishment of his own and with the usual employees, a clerk and laborer.[6]

About eleven miles from Morrow's place, near a swampy part of the river called Fremont's Slough, a young Bavarian trader named William Bishop (or Bischopf) kept a trading post, previously owned by Jack Morrow, which had been used as the stage station in May of 1860. By June 9, however, nine miles farther up the valley, the stage company had almost completed a set of buildings including a station house, an eating and boarding house and another building used as quarters for stocktenders and also as a warehouse for grain storage. Two carpenters, George McKenna and James Kneen, were still at work on the station and two stage drivers boarded there. The station was called Fremont's Springs, and R. A. White was the station keeper.[7]

In August, two months later, Richard Burton dismissed both Jack Morrow's Junction House Ranch and Fremont's Slough as "whiskey shops." Burton's coach stopped for dinner (the noon meal) at Fremont's Springs. He said the spring of water was excellent, but the station was composed of two huts connected by a "roof-work of thatched timber." The stationkeeper and his wife, both of whom had been at this post only three weeks, received thirty dollars a month for their services. The stationkeeper's wife, "a comely young person, uncommonly civil and smiling," supplied the travelers with pigeons, onions and light bread. She informed them that she had hopes of starting a poultry yard.[8]

After crossing O'Fallon's Bluffs the census taker found Bob Williams and his family at their ranch. There was also a blacksmith shop where two smiths provided essential service. Two miles farther was Crawford Moore's ranch, where two more blacksmiths were in business. A carpenter and his small family, all from New England, also lived here, as well as a laborer and teamster. Richard Burton stopped here also, at the invitation of Crawford Moore, who had been a fellow traveler on the stage with Burton. Moore invited everyone in for a drink in the recently completed saloon. Burton said that Moore had lived here (in the West) for twenty years. This was an exceptionally long period of time for anyone except the old fur traders, and according to the census, Moore was only twenty-nine years old. Burton reported that Moore's business was worth $16,000 per annum, and the contents of the store ranged from "a needle to a bottle of champagne."[9]

Burton traveled on to Alkali Lake Station, which was run by some genial Irishmen who fed the passengers antelope meat, accompanied by iced drinks in the heat of August. This seemed a miracle of preservation from the frozen river of the preceding winter. Burton commented that the stage arrived later in the evening, about 9:15 P.M., at Diamond Springs, where the travelers found "whiskey and its usual accompaniment, soldiers."[10]

To complete the survey to Denver City, one must consider that the census record of the South Platte Valley from O'Fallon's Bluffs to the fortieth parallel would not be completed until the last of August of 1860 and the valley changed rapidly during that summer. The stage company was still building stations as fast as possible, and the famous Pony Express had begun in April of 1860, making it necessary for William Russell to concentrate on providing supplies and quarters for each stage of this chain of riders reaching from St. Joseph to Sacramento. Summarily, Russell gave the orders, then turned his attention to something else, not pursuing his plans to supervise their execution.

Since the South Platte Road from the Upper Crossing to Denver was now a branch line of the COC&PP, it was more or less neglected by the stage company; this condition proved to be an advantage for the independent traders who not only served the stream of gold rushers which was still pouring into the Rockies, but also functioned as makeshift stations for the Denver-bound run of the stagecoaches. The trading posts increased in size. Now that there was time and the sun was hot, the traders were making molds in which they shaped the river mud to form bricks for drying. From these they built the durable adobe buildings of the prairie settlements. The dry climate of the plains did not erode the mud brick, and in case of fire, the adobe cabin rose like a phoenix from the flames—unconsumed. Large corrals were built of the brick or of sod blocks, and the traders began to accumulate cattle. It was soon discovered that the tired and sick animals which the emigrants were forced to abandon responded after a period of grazing in the lush bottoms of the valley and very often recovered when the effect of drinking alkali water had worn off. Life was harsh on the South Platte Trail, but it was promising.

Meanwhile, far up the river across the bridge over the South Platte at St. Vrain's, beside the road which led to Fort Laramie, Joe Miravalle, a Mexican, set up a little trading post for the benefit of the miners who believed that they might find gold in Big Thompson River. Here Joe and his two daughters, Mary and Louisa, aged twenty-eight and fourteen, lived and prospered while the diminutive city of Miravalle grew around them in March of 1860. A number of long-standing Indian traders lived in this area. One of them was the pioneer Elbridge Gerry.[11]

In reference to Gerry, the title of "First Permanent Settler" of an area is a distinction difficult to define. Frequently, after the turn of the twentieth century, the honor was claimed by some gabby old-timer who had outlived his contemporaries and could then make his story stick, but occasionally it was bestowed on some person who was so unfortunate as to die before he had the opportunity to move away. If this person was buried in a recognizable grave, the local Historical Society or Boy Scouts would eventually erect a marker, and the first permanent settler is thus identified for as long as the monument lasts. Elbridge Gerry, who died in 1875, has been endowed with the prestigious label in Weld County, Colorado, but his story is much more important for the influence he exerted on the history of the South Platte Trail and the associated Indian War of the 1860s than for his residence in this particular area. His romantic legend has become an indestructible fiber of Colorado history, even though facts have dispelled much of the fantasy.

Gerry was born in Boston, Massachusetts, on July 18, 1818. This fact he noted over and over in his account books like a penmanship lesson; he wrote with a flowing style and could spell. He was an educated man for his time. In his lifetime, it was believed that he was descended from the Elbridge Gerry who was Governor of Massachusetts and also Vice-President of the United States in the 1820s. Elbridge Gerry the Colorado pioneer enjoyed the prestige of the name all his life, even though since then family genealogists have denied the later Gerry's descent from his more famous namesake.

At an early age Gerry may have gone to sea. In middle age Elbridge showed a tattoo of a ship on his arm to more than one friend and hinted darkly that it represented the secret of his life. There were many secrets of his life; very little is known about him before he settled on the South Platte River. He has been described with familiar clichés as a "stockily built person of medium height, weighing about one hundred eighty pounds" with "steely gray eyes" and "an aloofness about him." His photographic portrait presents him as an impressively handsome man.[12]

LeRoy Hafen, the eminent historian, has accepted a reference in the journal of a trapper named Osborn Russell in which Russell spoke of his friend Elbridge who was a sailor from Beverly, Massachusetts. Russell never mentioned his friend's last name, but he described him as about five feet ten inches tall, "a great easy good-natured fellow—weighing two hundred pounds." Perhaps Mr. Hafen is correct in assuming that this friend of Osborn Russell was Colorado's Elbridge Gerry. If so, the journal shows that Gerry was trapping in Idaho in 1839, a long way from the sea. Gerry's obituary also indicates that this may be the case. His actual presence in the West is not documented until April 2, 1853, when he dated his account book and named his place of residence as "South Platte."[13]

At some time around 1842 Gerry may have married some unknown woman. This may have occurred in New England, because Gerry's oldest children, Eliza (or Lizzie), born 1843, and Henry (Hogar?), born 1848, may have been born in New England. Whether these details are true or not, Gerry was in Nebraska Territory before 1850 when he married Kate Smith, a fiery half-breed girl, the daughter of a Cheyenne mother and soldier father—a father whom she did not know because he deserted her mother and herself when his term of duty expired.[14]

In 1850 Gerry and Kate had a daughter Maria, and other children followed, probably two sons, Seth and William. After moving to the South Platte trading post, Gerry developed a roving eye. When he abruptly left on a trading expedition to the Arkansas River, a young and attractive Indian maiden disappeared from the neighborhood at the same time, and when Gerry returned a year later, the young woman returned with him, carrying an infant. Kate Smith, remembering her own father, had strong emotions regarding the inconstancy of husbands, but after being dissuaded from using physical violence to express her opinion, she simply walked out—back to her people. She left five children plus a young mistress and her child, for Gerry to manage as best he could.[15]

Also living in Miravalle was a twenty-four-year-old farmer from New York named John Y. Clopper, who had the distinction of being a brother-in-law of a clerk for the Census Department of Nebraska Territory. When the decision was made to attempt the census survey of this territory in 1860, John Y. Clopper was found to be uniquely qualified to undertake the task in his part of the country. In early June, John Clopper and an associate known only as "Joe" started from Miravalle with a buggy, wagon, horses and provisions to count the inhabitants of that area north of the fortieth parallel to Fort Laramie and from the mountains east to Alkali Lake Station.

From the very start Joe was suffering from a deep involvement with a bottle, or bottles, which did not seem to improve for almost a week. Clopper was beginning to worry about the sanity of his companion when (as Clopper claimed) he found Joe sitting in a tree from which he refused to descend. After much useless persuasion, Clopper hit upon the only obvious solution. Bringing out his own private stock of strictly medicinal whiskey (called Blair and Company's Best), he put the bottle at the foot of the tree and withdrew for some distance to wait for the bait to be taken. In less time than it took Clopper to tell it (Clopper was exceptionally long-winded), Joe was on the ground "as nimbly as a squirrel," and was draining the dregs of the bottle when Clopper reached him. According to the account quoted Joe eventually recovered, but when one reads the census reports of the Settlement of the Platte it seems evident that not one but both of the census takers were somewhat distracted.[16]

In early August when Clopper and Joe interviewed their neighbor, Elbridge Gerry, they recorded facts (or total errors) that have confused Gerry's biographers irreconcilably. For instance, although Gerry's birthplace was noted correctly as Massachusetts, Eliza, the daughter, was recorded as having been born in Maine and Henry in Massachusetts, which if true seems inconsistent with the known information about Gerry's life. On the other hand, if this was an error, it provides Gerry with the mysterious past which he does not deserve.

John Clopper could not decide what to do about Indian women. The census forms of that year made allowances for whites and blacks but nothing else. Indians were not citizens. Consequently, Clopper often listed the head of the family and groups of children down to babes-in-arms without mentioning the existence of a mother. Half-breed children, however, were counted as whites. Occasionally an Indian wife was counted if her husband chose to do so, in which case the word "Indian" would be written in.

Clopper started along the South Platte Valley, traveling downstream, about the first of August, 1860, but in order to continue the order in which the emigrant guides and journals are written, the records of the census must be reversed; therefore the place where he visited last, Alkali Lake Station, will be discussed first in this narrative.

During the last days of August at desolate, lonely Alkali Lake John Clopper found a family headed by F. L. (or T. S.?) Felton, his wife Mary and their two-year-old daughter. Felton was keeping the station, and the family provided board for a stage driver. It is disappointing to discover that Clopper was not interested in the careful cataloguing of each structure, such as stores and the various buildings of the stage stations, as his counterpart in Shorter County had been, and history suffers from Clopper's negligence. Neither was he particularly interested in the names of people, often referring to them by one or two illegible initials plus surnames which were frequently misspelled.[17]

Girioux and Dion were doing well at the Lone Tree Ranch, and two or three miles below the Lower Crossing at Diamond Springs Station, P. McWearny and J. C. Mattingly were keeping the station for the stage line. Two stocktenders were employed here, and one of them, recorded by Clopper as C. Turner, was probably George Turner, who had just arrived in the West and would soon be promoted by the COC&PP to driving a stagecoach. Clopper found no inhabitants at the Beauvais Ranch, which is surprising. Just below the Upper Crossing the census taker came to Buckeye Ranch, operated by S. H. (?) Baker and H. B. Fales.

At Julesburg there was apparently a number of dwellings as well as several stage buildings. In one of these Alexander Benham, the Denver Agent for the COC&PP, was staying in a household with two laborers and a Pony Express rider named George McGee. In another building John Code (Coad?) was living with another pony rider, W. Simmons. John Coad was only eighteen years old, which was under age, nevertheless he was employed by the stage line as a stationkeeper, probably for the Pony Express. In the census it was necessary for Coad, as well as others, to give their age as twenty-one because there was a rule made by the COC&PP that their employees be of age. However, in practice, this rule was not kept among either the stationkeepers or the Pony Express riders.[18]

Also at Julesburg was L. S. Dennison, who was acting as a stationkeeper. Dennison had his family—his black-eyed wife Mary and five-year-old son Albert—with him, as well as a stock herder named John Lynn. Dennison was credited with property valued at $5,000, a significant amount at the time, and he was probably working in Julesburg while he found a location for the establishment of a ranch—which he soon accomplished at a place farther upstream.

Another house in Julesburg sheltered six teamsters who should have been on the road during the good weather but must have been delayed in Julesburg for some good reason; perhaps they were in the employ of the stage company and had just finished a delivery of materials to this station. A wagonmaker from Saxony, F. Leschky, seemed to be situated near the Lower Crossing in August but moved into the village of Julesburg very soon afterwards. Another stationkeeper, named C. Smith, was boarding two carpenters.[19]

It was likely that James Kneen was only a very ordinary carpenter, but his claim to fame is based on having appeared twice in the 1860 Census of Nebraska Territory. In April he had been working at Fremont's Springs Station, but now in August, he was working in Julesburg. As an example of the fallibility of census takers in general, James Kneen, the carpenter, had apparently aged two years in the intervening time, and though according to the April report he was born on the Isle of Man, he was recorded by Clopper in August as having been born in Georgia.[20]

In Julesburg the mysterious Jules was absent, and the principal supply store was being operated by two prominent traders named George Chrisman and G. W. Thompson. The post office was located here.

Apparently there were no settled inhabitants of the lonely stretch of road which extended up the South Platte River from Julesburg, and there were no stationkeepers listed for Spring Hill Station. Probably it was being kept by the traders at nearby Lillian Springs Ranch, which was still occupied by James A. Forbes and an associate named Arthur C. Lewis. Although Clopper recorded Lewis as having been born in New York, his wife Harriet was born in England, and Lewis no doubt came from there also. At either Lillian Springs or Julesburg—it is difficult to determine which—was the household of Martin Wright and Charles Miller, stage drivers, which included Wright's wife Rosa and his son Alfred, a baby of five months. Rosa was employed as a cook, and since the dwelling at Julesburg did not include a resident cook, it is probable that this is where Wright and Miller were stationed.

Valley Station, like Spring Hill, did not have a stationkeeper employed by the COC&PP when Clopper passed about August 23 to 27. The station was probably being kept by two traders, F. H. Armitage and E. E. Gordon, who employed a cook named Ada Cassale and boarded two stage drivers. Very shortly after this, however, Armitage seems to have moved on, and William A. Kelly was hired to keep the station with Gordon at the Valley stage stop. Previously Kelly may have been the same laborer (recorded as Wm. N. Kelly) that Clopper found upstream from Beaver Creek.[21]

There were no other inhabitants of the twenty-seven-mile distance between Valley Station and Beaver Creek in the census of 1860. The stage company had apparently based its station at the ranch of J. H. Stephens and J. A. Moore near Beaver Creek where three stage drivers, a cook and a baker were evidently residing. The cook, an Irishwoman named Mary Myers, was the wife of one of the stage drivers, John Myers, and they had a nine-year-old daughter named Catherine.

The several groups of laborers encountered by Clopper upstream from Beaver Creek were probably workers cutting hay in the river bottoms. There were two residents listed as farmers in this area, J. Valentine and B. Martin; the latter had his family with him, a wife and a seven-year-old boy. Six miles short of the Junction of the Cut-Off was Fred Lamb's ranch, where the stage line had based their station until a permanent location could be built. The station was kept by Lamb, an Englishman, and his wife Caroline with four little Lambs ranging in age from sixteen years to two years, and only the youngest of these children had been born in the United States.

After the Junction, without the landmarks provided by stage stations or familiar names, it is puzzling to decide which names from the census belonged to Fremont's Orchard. There were two trading posts which may have been in this vicinity: that of John Houston, his brother and two sons, and the post of William Roland and his wife, child and brother. There were a number of families of ranchers located in the river valley in this neighborhood, one in particular, named King Allen, was a patriarch of sixty years and had a rather large family of children and grandchildren in his household.

Not far from Fort St. Vrain, F. W. Hammett and his wife were farming near the place where a few years later a nucleus of families would form a settlement. Hammet became the teacher for a school here which must have been the first school in Weld County, and he later became a Probate Judge of this county. Twenty-two miles north of Denver, the ranch of Joel Estes Sr., was still in operation, and two of his sons, J. W. and Marion, were in charge of a crew of hired men occupied at this time with rounding up the cattle in order to move them to a new home. Joel Estes Sr. had moved to the mountains where he spread out his new ranch in the beautiful basin which was later to become known as Estes Park.[22]

Downstream from these agricultural areas the fortunes of the people of the South Platte were almost directly dependent on the prosperity of the COC&PP stage line and the emigrants in the autumn of 1860. The number of emigrants was dwindling, and the go-backs had almost passed. The mail services of the COC&PP and the Pony Express, both on the northern route, were losing money, but on the other hand, the branch line from Julesburg to Denver was profitable at last. No government provision for the mail to Denver had been made, so consequently a charge made by the stage line of twenty-five cents for a letter and ten cents for a newspaper was more than adequate to support the tri-weekly service of the coaches. Besides this income, passengers paid $100 each, and extra charges were made for express mail and the transporting of treasure boxes.

Far from Denver carefully guarded negotiations were being made to disrupt the monopoly of the COC&PP Express Company. Byers, at the newspaper office, reported what information he could get, but the plans being made for a competitive stage line remained a mystery. On February 15, 1860, Byers had reported that H. S. Clark had arrived on the stagecoach. Clark was associated with the Western Stage Company, which operated in eastern Nebraska, and also with a firm called the U. S. Express Company. Byers wrote that Clark had opened a headquarters and was planning a stage line which would run from Kansas City to Denver by the Arkansas River Route. On June 12 Byers quoted a story that the *St. Joseph Gazette* had printed, saying that the Western Stage Company had dispatched twelve four-horse stagecoaches to stock a line which would operate between Denver and the mountains.

For some unknown reason, in August of 1860 the Post Office Department awarded a mail contract from Julesburg to Denver to a man named E. F. Bruce who apparently had no connections with any stage line. Ironically, in order to fulfill his contract, Bruce was forced to employ the services of the COC&PP Express Company to deliver the mail to Denver. On Friday evening, August 12, the incoming stagecoach unloaded two mail bags with government locks on the step of the Denver postmaster, Judge McClure. No explanation was offered and no procedure was recommended. The Hinckly Express stagecoaches, which formerly delivered the mail to miners in the mountains, were unable to get these letters from the postmaster, since he had no authorization to release them. On Monday the fifteenth another COC&PP coach arrived in Denver with one small bag of mail, but the greater amount of letters and newspapers which usually arrived on this day were missing. Nothing more happened and everyone was confused. A week passed, and suddenly sixteen bags of U. S. Mail were delivered to the Denver post office; six or eight assistants were required to sort and distribute the large quantity of letters and papers. Notice was provided at last that the Post Office Department was now assuming responsibility for employing mail carriers to the various outlying districts.[23]

Either Bruce sold the mail contract to the Western Stage Company or his contract was rescinded by the Post Office Department. Byers was informed in September that the Western Stage would begin a weekly coach service from Kansas City to Denver by the Platte Route and that this line would deliver the mail. E. F. Hooker, a representative of the Western Stage Company, told Byers that almost all of the required stage stations would be arranged at trading posts along the line, and this was accomplished to a point where passenger service could be offered by August 30. The Western Stage Company would not use the Cut-Off but would follow the South Platte Route through Fremont's Orchard and St. Vrain, probably because this area was more populated and could provide services for the stage line. By November 12 all the stations were stocked, and according to Bob Willard, the Division Superintendent, the Western Stage line had built only five stations between Kansas City and Denver.[24]

The South Platte Route followed by the Western Stage began at the first station on this river, which was situated with Charles McDonald near Cottonwood Springs; a second was placed at the ranch of William Bishop at Fremont's Slough. A third stopping place was lodged with Crawford Moore at O'Fallon's Bluffs, and a fourth with S. H. Baker and H. B. Fales at their Buckeye Ranch near the Lower Crossing. Past Julesburg the Western Stage stopped at what was called the Nebraska Ranch, newly formed by George Ackley, a newcomer, and James Forbes, formerly of Lillian Springs. The old ranch of Lillian Springs, now operated by Arthur C. Lewis alone, was reinstated as a stage station for the new company. There were no more stations for the Western Stage until after Beaver Creek was crossed, where a station was located with William McMakin and Company at a recently established trading post just three or four miles downstream from the Cut-Off junction. Unfortunately no record has been discovered concerning the Western Stage Stations from the Junction through Fremont's Orchard and St. Vrain's to Denver. The hastily organized chain of the Western Stage Company stations proved to be unexpectedly satisfactory to passengers. Amos Billingsley, a missionary, was impressed by the excellent meal he obtained at Lillian Springs in April of 1861. It was probably Harriet Lewis, the Englishwoman, who cooked what Billingsley described as "good antelope, ham, eggs, good light wheat bread, custard and fine honey for seventy-five cents a meal."[25]

In the intervening time since the census count in August and the spring of '61, several new ranches had sprung up on the South Platte banks—for instance, that of Walden and Horner at Sand Creek Ranch, just below Julesburg, and Simons and Hafford at Twelve Mile Ranch above the Upper Crossing. However, the most celebrated of the new trading posts was that of Holon Godfrey.[26]

Holon Godfrey became a legend in his own time, though the force of his personality and the tedium of the plains combined to exaggerate the true facts of his exploits beyond belief. Tall and raw-boned, he wore whiskers that seemed to spread fanwise from his lean jaw, each crinkly hair pursuing an independent path into space. He loved to talk, spicing his conversation with pungent profanity. It was seldom that he told any story the same way twice, and in spite of the easy familiarity with which he met people, there seemed to be a dark reserve of coldness behind his icy-blue eyes. It was said by an acquaintance that he was not a pleasant person and when he was drunk "he was rather mean."[27]

At forty-four years Godfrey was older than most of the emigrants who came to Colorado. Originally from New Jersey, he had married Matilda Richmond, a lady of distinctive homeliness, in 1842 in Ohio, and two of their children, Martha and Allen, were born there. After four years the family had pushed west to Wisconsin, where two more children, Anna and Celia, were born. When the California gold rush of '49 attracted Holon's attention, he followed, leaving his family in Wisconsin. After five years of fairly successful mining he returned to Wisconsin. In 1859, another child, Kirby (later called Cuba), was added to the family, and the following year, 1860, Holon Godfrey was off again for the gold fields, this time to Colorado. He outfitted at Council Bluffs with an ox team and traveled cross-country to Julesburg. By this time, the reports of the gold mining in the Rockies were quite discouraging, so Godfrey, rather than return to Wisconsin empty-handed, looked around for a business opportunity near Julesburg. Sometime during the autumn of 1860 Godfrey moved along up the valley and settled on a barren river bank almost halfway between Valley Station and Beaver Creek. Apparently he had sent to Wisconsin for his family in the meantime, because besides groceries and "all kinds of vegetables," Godfrey advertised that he could provide baked goods for the emigrant trade.[28]

The typical store along the South Platte Road dealt chiefly in flour, sugar and coffee. They also stocked such things as salt, pepper, vinegar, pear ash, soda, dried apples, some canned goods and some bacon and ham. If the storekeeper kept a cow and chickens in sufficient quantity, he sold butter and eggs. Baked goods were a rare product; with one exception, Godfrey's store was the only post on the South Platte to offer it. This store was probably of the most raw and primitive sort—both stage lines had passed it by as a stage stop. It may have been the stereotype for that described by a journalist who said that very frequently the most profitable item offered for sale was whiskey. This whiskey was of such poor quality that no one ever tasted it; it was swallowed quickly to avoid its touching the tongue. Its alcoholic content was its chief virtue, and even that was sometimes lacking. It has been written that in January and February it was sometimes necessary to break the ice in the whiskey barrel before a drink could be purchased. There were two kinds of whiskey available for the connoisseur; "bust-head" or "forty-rod," so named because the former would have just that effect and the latter would so influence the feet that the drinker would be able to go no farther after imbibing. It has been said that Holon Godfrey not only dealt in this commodity but also consumed a goodly amount.[29]

The Pony Express had been in operation since April of 1860. In retrospect it is apparent that William H. Russell had never slackened his preoccupation with the government mail contract for delivery to California, a contract which was firmly held by the Butterfield Overland

Mail Company, which ran a southern route through Texas and the southwestern states. Russell, while searching for a superior way of carrying mail, a method that could not fail to attract the attention of Congress, made plans to put a fast horse relay system into operation. Plunging ahead, spending borrowed money, he bought the best horses and special saddles, while he hired picked men for riding and extra men for tending horses and express stations. Additional stations were built and clerks were hired to collect fees and to transfer messages to the lightweight tissue used for letters. The elaborate and costly plan was initiated on April 3, 1860, when the first rider left St. Joseph, Missouri, going west, and at the same time another started from Sacramento going east. The South Platte Trail experienced very little of the excitement of the pony riders, since the route of the Pony Express branched southward at Cottonwood Springs along the south fork but crossed it and proceeded northward again at Julesburg. The original plan for the Pony Express had included a branch run from Julesburg to Denver, and a Denver firm was contracted to supply all the stage stations for the ponies and riders, but apparently the equipment was never used for that route.[30]

There is a legend that the news of Lincoln's election on November 6, 1860, came to Denver by Pony Express, and it is said that the rider was so charged with excitement that he "covered the last five miles at the rate of nineteen miles an hour." Time had softened the anguish of the real story of how the election news was brought to the foot of the Rockies by the time William Byers wrote about the incident in 1934. He recalled that the authentic Pony Express riders did not come nearer to Denver than Julesburg but that the *Rocky Mountain News* hired a special rider to meet the Express rider at Julesburg and bring the news back to Denver on this special occasion. Across the country the usual impressive speed of the Pony Express was being accelerated even more to carry the election news by shortening relays and riding harder.[31]

As it happened, Byers reported on November 6 that the election was taking place and he expected to have news of the result in four days, on Friday. Friday came and went with no news, and finally on Monday the twelfth Byers explained what had happened. The news of the election was to be received at the end of the newly completed telegraph line at Fort Kearny, and here the Pony Express rider was expected to pick up the dispatch and then leave it off at Julesburg for transport to Denver. Due to a misunderstanding at Fort Kearny the pony rider was not instructed to transfer the Denver dispatch at Julesburg, and he carried it on to California. Eighteen hours later, Thursday's news, that of November 8, was sent out in due course by the Pony Express from St. Joseph. The rider from Denver was still at Julesburg. In the meantime the Western Stage, which originated in Omaha, passed through Fort Kearny on Wednesday, picked up a copy of the election news from the telegraph station and brought it to Denver, where at 12:30 A.M. on Monday, November 12, it delivered the important information to a rival newspaper, the *Mountaineer* of Golden, Colorado, which promptly and gleefully published an extra edition. The *Rocky Mountain News* was grimly chagrined to find that the coveted news story was six hours stale when it arrived by the special rider at noon on Monday, too late for publication that day. Byers published the returns on Tuesday, November 13, a week after the election—in spite of the Pony Express rather than because of it.[32]

It has been written, perhaps too often, that William F. Cody was hired by George Chrisman, the Julesburg trader, to ride the Pony Express even though Cody was only fifteen years old at the time, three years below the alleged minimum age for Pony Express riders. Cody claimed that he was expected to ride forty-five miles, at fifteen miles per hour, with three changes of horses. He said that after two months, when his mother became ill, he gave up riding and went home. William Cody was later hired by Joseph Slade to ride the Express mail from a station farther upstream along the North Platte.

George Chrisman was the stage agent for the COC&PP at Julesburg where the mail route separated and turned northwest along the North Platte Road, as did the Pony Express route. When Chrisman hired Buffalo Bill, it was to ride the regular route of the Pony Express, either northwest or east, and not the legendary route from Julesburg to Denver.[33]

The romance of the Pony Express attracted a number of young men of daring from the ranks of the stage line employees. Among these were J. J. Thomas and a former stage driver named Bill Trotter, who would later return to driving a coach on the South Platte; most important was James Moore, the rancher from Beaver Creek. It is said that there were only eight Pony Express riders hired when the service was instituted, an incredibly low number for transcontinental riding. J. J. Thomas, in his reminiscences written in 1910, said that he and Jim Moore had ridden on this first trip. Thomas said that Jim Moore rode from Box Elder Station going west to Julesburg and Thomas rode the opposite relay. This story is doubtful, since Thomas went on to say that he received his discharge from the parent COC&PP Express Company at the end of April before he moved on to the mountains. At that time, Jim Moore was probably working at the Beaver Creek trading post with his partner, J. H. Stephens, since this is where Moore was living in August when the census was taken.[34]

James Moore was the son of a stock grower from Ravenna, Ohio, and had come west in 1859 at the age of nineteen. As there is no suggestion in his biographies and interviews (of a much later date) that he ever visited the gold fields, it is likely that he went directly into the employ of the stage company. He was described, somewhat effusively, as "straight as an arrow" with "limbs like a thoroughbred." He also possessed a strong neck, which was "well set on his shoulders," an attribute which probably saved his life several years later. Moore began riding for the Pony Express sometime before June of 1861. At five feet ten inches and 160 pounds, he was exceptionally large and heavy according to the standards set up by the Express Company (the average rider weighed much less than 135 pounds), but apparently his various other talents made up for an excess of weight. His regular run was from a station called Midway (located near Cottonwood Springs) to Julesburg. The distance of Moore's ride was 140 miles, and he made the grueling trip twice a week, once to the west and once back to the east, with two or three days rest between rides. The alternate rider on this route was probably Theodore Rand, whose term of service (said to be from April 1860 to November 1861) made up in longevity what it lacked in glory.[35]

The Pony Express was only a month old when the best-remembered ride was made by a single rider. There was Indian trouble in Nevada, and "Pony Bob" Haslam made history by riding through dangerous territory into which the regular rider, who ordinarily succeeded him, refused to go. The ride was not especially noted for speed but established a record for endurance. Pony Bob rode 380 miles, spending thirty-six hours in the saddle with only eight hours rest in the middle of the run.[36]

It was in June of 1861 when Jim Moore made his spectacular ride. He was doing double duty, riding both east and west between Midway and Julesburg because his alternate was not well. Jim had managed this for some time by resting for twenty-four hours at each end of the ride. At seven o'clock on June 23, he started from Midway, and in twelve hours, with six changes of horses he rode into Julesburg. He arrived there, transferred his express matter to the westbound relay, and was just about to eat and bed down when the Express rider from the west came dashing in. There was no one available to ride east, so Jim Moore took the dispatch case and turned back to Midway. He arrived there in thirteen hours, thus establishing the record of a single trip of 280 miles in twenty-five hours, the second most famous ride in the history of the Pony Express. It is said that he received a certificate and a gold watch in recognition of his achievement.[37]

It is likely that the Pony Express would have been discontinued by the end of 1861 anyway, but the transcontinental telegraph made the extinction a certainty. After Congress passed an act in June of 1861 to encourage the building of a telegraph line from coast to coast, the contract was won by Hiram Sibley of New York, president of the Western Union Telegraph Company. Sibley brought about the consolidation of several California telegraph companies to form the Overland Telegraph Company, which could start building the line from the west coast while the Western Union Corporation was building from the east coast. A subsidiary company of the Western Union, the Pacific Telegraph Company, was to start across Nebraska from Brownsville to Salt Lake City, where it was hoped that the two lines would meet. Although the Pacific Telegraph Company was not yet incorporated, W. B. Stebbins of that company had built a line from Omaha as far as Fort Kearny in time for the news of Lincoln's election.[38]

Edward Creighton, who supervised the actual building of the telegraph, headed his crews westward from Fort Kearny in the spring of 1861. They had reached Gilman's Ranch, fifteen miles east of Cottonwood Springs, by August 21, and expected to be in Julesburg in three weeks. The two lines met at Salt Lake City and were able to transmit messages across the continent by October 24, 1861. Although the telegraph was closer to Denver than before, all news sent by wire continued to be brought by stagecoach from Julesburg. It was not until the summer of 1863 that a line was constructed from Julesburg to Denver.[39]

When the Civil War began in the spring of 1861, it became evident that it was necessary to move the California mail route from the south. The Butterfield Overland Mail Company, who still owned the mail contract, offered to negotiate with Russell and his associates to make terms for the delivery of the west coast mail by the COC&PP on the Central Overland Route. On March 12, 1861, William Russell completed contracts, one with Butterfield for the relinquishment of the mail service to the south and the other with E. S. Alford, president of the Western Stage Company. In return for $20,000 to compensate for their mail contract for service to Denver, the Western Stage agreed to suspend their stagecoach and mail service from Fort Kearny to Denver, although they retained their regular route between Fort Kearny and Omaha.[40]

In late April of 1861 Bela M. Hughes was elected President of the COC&PP to succeed William Russell, who resigned. In May, Hughes and Russell made a trip to Denver—apparently it was Russell's first visit to the area. The admiring natives were so impressed that a Grand Ball was planned at the foot of the mountains in Golden on May 31 to honor the famous William Hepburn Russell.[41]

The insurmountable financial difficulties of the Pony Express and the COC&PP were not generally known as yet, but for the preceding three years (and for another year to come) Bela Hughes had arranged for the COC&PP to borrow money from Hughes's cousin, Ben Holladay. During this period the Express Company borrowed $300,000 from Holladay and became $550,000 in debt for wages and provisions for the stage line. The employees seldom saw cash; they were paid by certificate, and when the paymaster came around, the stage driver or stocktender would draw what money he could get and then his certificate would be "adjusted" to the new amount. Deservedly, the COC&PP became known as "Clean Out of Cash and Poor Pay."[42]

A few changes were made along the stage road in 1861. New stations were built and new people arrived, but with the passing of the Western Stage Company, other people disappeared. George F. Turner, recently a stage driver, was joined by his wife and son and became the agent at Junction Station. Beaver Creek Station was finished before the first of August, and Hester and Mahlon Brown came west to keep the station. Hester wrote that there were two log houses with two rooms each. Hester cooked and served breakfasts at seventy-five cents per head, to all passengers of both east and westbound coaches as well as stray freighters who succumbed to the luxurious indulgence of eating from a table. Hester said that her husband kept the teams ready for the stagecoach, but he also bought lame cattle from the emigrants and he soon had a large herd.[43]

Of these recent arrivals to the valley in 1861 the most notable were Samuel Plummer Ashcraft and his brother Granville, who set up a ranch about two miles downstream from Junction Station. Ashcraft was no more than the typical trader dealing chiefly in "Pine-Knot," "Red Eye" and "Old Taylor" but he was said to be an honest man. His greatest asset was his Sioux wife, and surprisingly, his Sioux mother-in-law, who was described as "as wretched a specimen, so far as physical beauty is concerned, as her tribe could produce." The mutual tolerance which existed between Ashcraft and his mother-in-law was unusual because of the taboo existing among the Sioux which dictated that in-laws might not look at, or speak to, one another. Either Ashcraft ignored the old lady completely or they had agreed on a more convenient adjustment of tribal law. Being a squawman usually brought about a sympathetic understanding between the white man and his wife's culture, but this was not necessarily so in Ashcraft's case; he may have tolerated the Sioux, but he continued to have a vitriolic hatred for the Cheyennes.[44]

These people, these ghost-like individuals who built the trail from Cottonwood Springs to Denver, were its greatest contributors. History cannot usually stand still for the parade of individuals to pass; consequently in many cases all that remains is their names, and usually even those are missing. The mention of the most insignificant person may suggest to a future historian that this human being played a part in the great drama, that he is worthy of mention. The study of man, his achievements and his mistakes, is after all the most accepted reason for the recording of history.

Chapter

5

Another Kind of Enlightenment

Three hundred years ago, when the Age of Enlightenment first glimmered on the horizon of the minds of men, John Dryden wrote a charming triplet as a line in a play: "I am as free as Nature first made man," the speech declared, "Ere the base law of servitude began; when wild in woods the noble savage ran." The philosophers of the late seventeenth and early eighteenth century, searching for the cause of the evils of society, adopted a premise that "natural" man occurred in the primitive state, untroubled by the complexities enforced by the yoke of civilization. In 1762 Jean Jacques Rousseau wrote that "nothing can be more gentle than (man) in his primitive state, when placed by nature at an equal distance from the stupidity of brutes and the pernicious good sense of civilized man."[1] Cushioned by the soft swells of nineteenth-century romanticism, James Fenimore Cooper expanded the theme of the wise stoicism of natural man in the character of Uncas of the *Last of the Mohicans* and of Chingachgook of *The Pathfinder,* the latter written in 1840. Through the middle of the century the American Indian gradually gained a stature in literature comparable with that of an epic hero, until "the noble savage" eventually reached his apotheosis in Longfellow's Hiawatha in 1855.

Profoundly influenced by the philosophical predispositions of their time, the individuals of the detached party from Stephen Long's expedition in 1819–20 were pleased when they had the opportunity to observe at first hand the unspoiled natural state of the Plains Indians near the Rocky Mountains. When the party discovered representatives of several tribes—Kaskias, Kiowas, Arapahoes and Cheyennes—camped together on the Arkansas River, the scientists eagerly approached the Indian camp. The Indians welcomed their guests warmly, shaking their hands and offering hospitality. The women brought select pieces of jerked bison, a supply sufficient for several days.

The visitors were invited to sit down in the prayer circle for the passing of the ritual pipe, but the language barrier made anything but visual acquaintance with the Indians very difficult. The strangers smoked and then tried as best they could to explain from whence they had come and their reason for being there. On the following day, with the help of their interpreter, Bijeaux, who spoke English and French, another trader who spoke French and Pawnee, and an Indian who spoke Pawnee and Arapahoe, a conversation was held between four of the chiefs and the principals of the expeditionary group. It was at this conference that the botanist Edwin James and the entomologist Dr. Thomas Say got the impression that the four tribes had come together at this place for the purpose of trading horses, and it was at this same meeting that James and Say discovered that the Cheyennes were recent refugees from the main tribe of Cheyennes located in the upper Missouri area.

After the conversation was finished, the party of easterners distributed gifts to as many of the Indians as possible. Dr. Say was amused by the ingenuity of the Indian children, who satisfied their curiosity about what was happening in the center of the conference by leading their ponies to the outer fringe and then managing to stand on the backs of their mounts, three or four in a group on each animal, in order to see over the crowd.

Dr. Say was also fascinated by a squaw who had received a wooden comb and was taking full advantage of the luxury. She seated herself with a piece of skin on her lap and, leaning over, proceeded to dislodge the crawling inhabitants from her hair. As the vermin fell to her lap, a friend seated nearby picked up the fat little creatures and crunched them between her teeth as casually as she would have enjoyed a handful of nuts.

Dr. Say went into great detail as he described the appearance and dress of the Cheyennes. He believed that the average person was somewhat shorter, than the Indians of the Missouri Valley, he thought that their noses were less "Roman" and their faces were wider. While women cut their hair to shoulder length, the men allowed theirs to grow, and even added buffalo and horse hair to the two long braids which sometimes reached to the knee. These braids were decorated with ribbons and strips of colored skin. A variation of this style was an unwieldy arrangement which was described as a series of flat masses separated at intervals by a substance that seemed to be like red clay. Dr. Say mentioned one boy who had hair so light in color that it was "decidedly of a flaxen hue."

Women wore a wrapped skirt of supple skin which reached the calf of the leg. Another piece of skin covered the upper body—when the wearer chose to be covered; otherwise the garment was casually cast aside if the weather was warm or to accomodate a suckling child. Some of the more vain females had rectangular dresses of red or blue cloth with a border of blue and white beads. The hem of the dress was further ornamented by a row of bells made of sheet copper which produced a tinkling sound as the wearer walked. Usually it was only the young unmarried girls who could dress in this elaborate manner, since they frequently were excused from the heavy labor which the married women performed.

Men wore a breechcloth stretched between their legs, pulled up and over a thong belt, and allowed to hang free in front and back as far down as the knees. Sometimes a man would add leggings, moccasins and a buffalo robe for warmth. A fortunate few possessed red and blue blankets obtained from the Spanish colonists south of the Arkansas River. Ornamental discs of silver were also acquired from the Spaniards.[2]

When John C. Fremont visited the Arapahoes on the South Platte in 1842 he provided a descriptive impression of an Indian camp of a period twenty-two years later than James and Say. He said there were about 125 lodges, of which twenty belonged to Cheyennes. There was a broad street about 150 feet wide running parallel to the river which divided the camp into two divisions. The Cheyennes were camped somewhat distant from the Arapahoes. Anthropologists have since determined that, haphazard as it might have seemed, the Indian camp circle was oriented with the cardinal points sectioning it into four segments, into which the participating bands divided themselves. This preoccupation with the four directions may have been the origin of the mystical and sacred character of the number four among the Cheyennes, though not unique with this nation; the four-armed cross relating to the cardinal points is of importance among many primitive societies. The Cheyennes frequently used this cross with equal sides in their face paint, as well as on their weapons and clothing.[3]

The single thing that impressed Fremont was the mounting of weapons beside the lodges. He said that one might see beside some of the tipis a tripod frame of three smooth birch poles on which were hung the shield, spear and other weapons of the braves who lived within. The shields were of spotless cleanliness and the spears were polished and shining. The shield of a Cheyenne warrior was round, made of the toughest rawhide and decorated with some personal and magical design. From its edge would be suspended feathers, sometimes only attached around the edge of its circumference, but if the experience of the warrior warranted it the feathers might be hung on suspended strips. Lances, too, were sometimes decorated with clusters of long rows of feathers and streamers. The frightful daubing and streaks of face and body paint, combined with the large bonnet trimmed with eagle feathers varying in number from just a few to such a great quantity that they were supported by a long band which could reach to knee length, made the Cheyenne warrior an enemy of imposing appearance.[4]

Edwin James and Dr. Say described a returning war party of Cheyennes on the Arkansas in the summer of 1820. It was a large party, and they had made a raid on the Pawnee Loups where they had killed one squaw whose scalp was suspended from the lance of one of the warriors. The lance was also decorated with "strips of red and white cloth, beads and tail plumes of the war eagle." The owner of this lance and one other member of the party had decorated themselves for returning to their village. Both of these warriors were painted over their entire bodies with deep black charcoal—a mark of distinction, James learned; one of them had removed the scalp and the other had been the first to touch the dead body—thus accomplishing a coup.[5]

Evidently the body color for homecoming varied with circumstances, as demonstrated by some Cheyenne guides which Fremont had in his party. The Indians were returning to their families who were living in an Arapahoe village. Before they entered the village, the Cheyennes prepared themselves for an impressive arrival by bathing in the river, painting themselves with vermillion and dressing in new calico shirts (which they had stolen from Fremont's men). Unfortunately their triumphal entry was spoiled by the fact that while they had been bathing in the river their pack horse had run away into the hills carrying all their possessions, including their precious shields and spears.[6]

The Plains Indians raised no crops, but the Cheyennes and Arapahoes were aware of their history as a sedentary people living in the far north where the women cultivated grain and men hunted and trapped. Since the tribes had been forced onto the open plains there was almost no advance in work skills except for devising methods of utilizing every part of the bison. This lack of development was a result of a nomadic way of life made necessary by the constant pursuit of the major food supply, the buffalo herds.

As nomads, these people were almost helpless without the horse. Faced with continual traveling, the male Indian now worked primarily on the acquisition, multiplication and training of the horse herds. There were three ways to acquire horses: by trade, by capture or by taming wild horses. Since the early Cheyennes and Arapahoes possessed almost nothing for trade purposes, they were compelled to steal the animals. A man's bravery was measured by the number of horses he could capture from an enemy. The enemy—usually the Pawnees on the east or the Utes on the west—retaliated and attempted to recover their lost stock, also hoping to acquire a few extra ponies. If this reciprocal raid was successful it was then necessary for the Plains tribes to make additional forays to rebuild their herd.

Besides perfecting the fine art of horse-stealing, these reprisals provided an opportunity for the development of a specialized style of warfare aside from the motive of property acquisition. An important part of the raids was the skirmishing in which the young men of both tribes were able to prove their courage and attain the status of warriors. This was a prime requisite in the life of a male Indian on the plains—to achieve honor in battle. Without enemies and battle there could be no honor. It is said that this distinction could be acquired by merely touching an enemy with a stick or lance ("counting coup"), but since the likelihood of killing or being killed was inevitable in a battle, honor became complicated by the necessity for revenge.

If a man was killed, revenge on the enemy was required for his death. If a number of warriors were killed, the retaliation increased proportionately. The intensity of revenge which motivated each attack on the enemy varied according to the degree of humiliation which the aggressor had suffered during the last encounter. Attack on an enemy camp was usually planned as a surprise and usually conducted at dawn. The number of inhabitants who were slaughtered depended on the vindication required by the number of scores to be settled. It was not unusual for female Indians to take part in these battles; some could ride astride and shoot as well as warriors, and the more excessive cruelty of the squaw was an acknowledged fact.

When alerted to the danger, the defending warriors of a camp would hurriedly arm themselves, mount their horses and form a line of defense on open ground, away from the village if possible, while the women gathered the children and rode, or retreated on foot, as rapidly as they could to a safe place until the battle was resolved. This sort of battle was not likely to be fought for a great length of time, and if the women, children, old people and horses were safe, there was no obligation for the defenders to stand and fight. From the attackers' point of view, if there was any possibility that the two groups of warriors were equally matched, the aggressors were likely to postpone the raid until another day when a victory could be achieved at less cost.

In tribal legend, the original government of the Cheyennes had been initiated by a woman or girl (depending on a choice of three legends) who had appointed forty-four chiefs to govern the Cheyenne nation. Apparently she chose four principal chiefs; the remaining forty were supplied by the tribe in general. A chief held office for ten years and then was either re-elected or replaced by a qualified person, sometimes by a relative. As the Cheyennes dispersed over the plains, constantly separating, and kept on the move because of the need to find fresh pastures for the horse herds, the tribe divided itself into segments called bands, which were comprised of loosely interrelated family groups extended by several generations. Each band was governed by four chiefs who, besides having a religious function, made the decisions about moving the camp and fixing the time and place for the major hunts. All of the chiefs served their ten years concurrently; when the period ended a great council was called and new chiefs were appointed.

When the southern Cheyennes seceded and spread over the High Plains they may not have maintained the nation's custom of forty-four chiefs with four chiefs from each band. If they had chosen to do so, considering their scarcity of numbers, the result might have been the situation described in the saying: "too many chiefs and not enough Indians." Theoretically, the four head chiefs did not have special authority over the forty, but if they had been elected or chosen for special abilities their opinions were accorded greater importance. The actual function of a chief was that of keeping peace and caring for widows and orphans—not a very exalted position but one of extreme importance. A chief was not permitted to take part in a quarrel or exact personal vengeance. If it was necessary to enforce a particularly unpopular decision, the chiefs were obliged to ask the soldier societies for assistance.[7]

The warrior societies maintained order within the tribe and made the decisions regarding warfare. There were five different warrior societies—the Kit-Fox Men, the Bone Scrapers, the Red Shields, the Bowstring Men and the Dog Soldiers. The sixth party, the Crazy Dogs, did not have an organization among the southern Cheyennes. Almost all of the Cheyenne males over the age of thirteen belonged to one society or another. Each group had its own distinctive items of dress and particular rituals. The soldier societies were not based on family ties as were the bands, and also in contrast, the members were chosen and the leaders elected. The election was made at the same time as the selection of the forty-four chiefs. The leaders of the warrior societies were usually the bravest and most renowned, but they were not necessarily the leaders of war parties. Any man who could enlist followers could lead a party to war.[8]

Not all chiefs were great leaders and not all great leaders were chiefs. Bear Tooth, a powerful Arapahoe chief of 1820, was described by Edwin James as a man "capable of inflicting exemplary punishment upon anyone who should disobey his orders." Later in the 1860s, chiefs such as Black Kettle and White Antelope admitted freely that they could not control the warriors of their tribe. The real power of the tribe was in the hands of the warrior societies and specifically of the leaders of these organizations, who were also called chiefs—or war-chiefs for the sake of distinction. While Black Kettle and White Antelope were of the peacemaker variety of chiefs, Bear Tooth may have been a warrior.[9]

The warrior groups competed for popularity and ascendancy. If one or the other had been particularly successful in warfare over a period of time, that warrior society would enjoy domination. This arrangement prevailed until about 1830, when the Dog Soldiers broke away from the original clan system and formed a tribe of their own. Soon after, the Red Shields joined them, leaving only three of the orthodox soldier societies. The Dog Soldiers were considered outlaws by many of the more traditional tribesmen. Besides the autonomy of the government of this society, tribal customs were ignored; members brought their wives to join the Dog Soldiers rather than living with the clan of the wife as had been done previously. The Dog Soldiers also intermarried freely with the Sioux who ranged south of the Platte River. Outlaws or not, most of the strongest and most confident of the young men of the Cheyenne nation were members of the society, and they soon gained the respect, if not the approval, of their tribe.[10]

This simple social structure of the Cheyenne Indians might have continued on the High Plains for many centuries if it had not been for the invasion of civilized men with their wheels, guns and written words. After the decline of the buffalo robe traders there was little interference in the life of the people of the prairies except when the so-called natives and the so-called invaders met at the common thoroughfares of traffic—the Platte and the Arkansas rivers. Disputes and depredations on the Santa Fe Trail were not publicized in Denver, probably because there were no stage employees to pass along the news as there were on the South Platte Road. The depredations committed on both the Platte Route and the Arkansas Route were probably more numerous than have been recorded, but many of these were at the level of theft and harassment. Still it became evident that the danger was growing for the increasing number of emigrants to the West. The establishment of two forts, Fort Laramie and Fort Kearny, and the extensive research, councils and treaty-making arranged by Thomas Fitzpatrick, Indian Agent for the Upper Platte Agency, actually did not accomplish much to alleviate the growing conflict which festered all through the decade of the fifties.

In 1858 William Bent was unofficially appointed Indian Agent for the Upper Arkansas Valley. The complexity of his position weighed heavily on his shoulders. In the summer of that year he set out from St. Louis with a trainload of annuities for the Cheyennes and Arapahoes. He was accompanied by his seventeen-year-old son, Robert, who was trying his mettle in the freighting business by serving as transportation contractor for the wagon train. The Indians were reported to be hunting north of the Upper Republican, so Bent and his son traveled along the South Platte, hoping to overtake them and distribute the annuities and food supplies which were badly needed by the Indian tribes. On Beaver Creek the Bents found a camp of forty-five Cheyenne lodges. Here William Bent paused to write letters to the Superintendent of Indian Affairs, A.M. Robinson, in St. Louis and to A.B. Greenwood, the Commissioner of Indian Affairs.[11]

As Bent sat in the blazing heat of the South Platte Valley in July, he could gaze across the lazy channels of the river and evaluate the situation with the simplicity of long acquaintance with the people and the land. "The country is very equally divided into halves by the South Platte," he wrote, "A confederate band of Cheyennes and Arapahoes who are intermarried occupy and claim exclusively the half included between the South Platte and the North Platte. A similar confederated band of the same people distinctly occupy the southern half included between the South Platte and Arkansas River. Between the Arkansas River and the Raton Mountains is a territory, formerly a part of New Mexico, not occupied or claimed by any other tribe."

Here William Bent paused and stared blankly at the dusty wake of the fleet of passing wagons, "The prominent feature of this region is the recent discovery and development of gold . . ." he continued. "I estimate the number of whites traversing the plain across the center belt to have exceeded 60,000 during the present season." Sadly he reflected, "The concourse of whites is therefore swelling, and incapable of control or restraint by the government." William Bent remembered that since 1849 he had been watching emigrants pass his door on the Arkansas, and after ten years of observation he had come to the conclusion that confining the nomad Indian tribes to a reservation where they could learn to practice agriculture was the only solution to prevent their extinction. These Indians, Bent said, were surrounded by Texans, Kansans and the gold-rushers, and the influx of emigrants into the center of their territory threatened the Indians with eventual starvation.[12]

After following the Cheyennes and Arapahoes for a month, the Bents returned to their trading post on the upper Arkansas. In the autumn of 1859 Bent sold his fort to the army, which garrisoned it and christened it Fort Fauntleroy (later to become Fort Wise and still later, in 1861, Fort Lyon). William Bent moved to the south bank of the Purgatory river, where he built a new stockade for himself and his family.

In Denver City the Arapahoes camped on the bank of the South Platte were an object of curiosity to the arriving miners just as, in turn, the miners amused the Indians. Albert D. Richardson, the correspondent for the Boston *Journal,* was in Denver during the summer of 1859. He wrote "A few yards from this busy street [Blake Street], you may visit the village of the Arapahoes, where barbarism thus far maintains its ground against the advance of (nominal) civilization. But ere long it must be crowded out. In general the Arapahoes are poorer, more filthy, more wretched than most tribes of the plains; but when prepared for the warpath the braves are sometimes picturesque; and the squaws are at least rich in the number of their children playing about the lodges." This camp must have been like another group of Arapahoes which Richardson described as follows:

> Near[by] was encamped a party of Arapahoes with thirty or forty children playing upon the grass. Those under four or five years were entirely naked. The older boys wore breechclouts of buffalo skin, and the girls were wrapped in robes or blankets. . . . The boys of this company were very expert with the bow, easily hitting a silver half-dollar at sixty or seventy yards. All were inveterate beggars, asking by signs for food and drink. Their camp consisted of twenty conical lodges twelve or fifteen feet high—buffalo robes with the fur inside, stretched around a circle of poles. These dwellings ten or twelve feet in diameter, with a hole at the top for the escape of smoke, are warm in winter and cool in summer. . . . In front of each the shield and quiver of the brave rested upon a pole or tripod. The shields, worn upon the left arm, are covered with antelope skin or buffalo hide stuffed with hair, and will usually ward off any rifle ball which does not strike them perpendicularly. The bows have great force, sometimes throwing an arrow quite through the body of a buffalo. . . .
>
> Several squaws who were making moccasins fringed with beads offered me a pair for a cup of "sooker," (sugar). Others were eating soup with their fingers from a kettle, while naked children on the ground were gnawing tough buffalo meat. A dozen muscular half-naked braves lying in the sun shook hands with me, declaring themselves "Good Indians." But only yesterday they threatened to kill and scalp a station keeper unless he should leave their country.[13]

For the Denverites, the great excitement derived from the visit of the Arapahoes centered on the entertainment offered to Little Raven, the Arapahoe chief. He and several warriors were received by William Byers at the office of the *Rocky Mountain News.* Byers wrote that Little Raven "looked upon the various operations and minutiae of the office with interested wonder and astonishment, and when he had seen the movements of the press and the printed sheets therefrom and the whole operation was explained to him, he ejaculated, 'Big Medicine!'"[14]

During the week a dinner party was given by Dr. Fox at the office of the Leavenworth & Pike's Peak Stage Company to entertain Little Raven and four of his warriors. The correspondent to the *Leavenworth Times* wrote that Little Raven "is a very sensible and friendly-disposed man. He handles knife and fork and smokes his cigars like a white man. He was so well pleased with the entertainment that he invited Dr. Fox to come to his lodge and sleep with him, which invitation, however, was not as heartily received as given. . . ."[15]

On May 8, at Judge Smith's, a talk was arranged in order that General Larimer and Governor Beall (formerly of Wisconsin) could talk with Little Raven, but it is said that it was necessary to postpone the meeting because the interpreter, Dubray, was too drunk to function, and when he fell off his chair the meeting was adjourned. On May 9 the meeting was called to order at Blake and Williams Hotel. William Byers was present to record the proceedings and he watched the discourse with something of a tongue-in-cheek attitude—not because he was amused by the message conveyed, but because of the ridiculously stilted conventions of White–Indian diplomatic language.[16]

The podium was occupied by Governor Beall, who conducted the conference, General Larimer, an interpreter, and Little Raven and his braves. The Governor began by informing Little Raven that he had "nothing to say from the Great Father," (apparently meaning that he had no message from the President of the United States). Governor Beall wanted to assure the chief that all the citizens of the United States owed allegiance to "his great Father," (perhaps suggesting that even the Indians owed allegiance to some other Great Father). Would the Chief like to say a few words to the congregation present?

The Chief stood up and began by saying that all he wanted to say to his white "brethren" was that he "liked all the whites he had ever known," that he was glad to see so many here and he hoped they would find as much gold as they needed. He wanted to mention, however, that all the land in this area belonged to him and his "children," and although he did not expect the miners to buy his land, he hoped that the "Great Father" might do so. He went on to say that he and his tribe wanted to agree with the whites and he hoped that the miners would be patient with his children and would not "say anything bad to them." He also hoped that the miners would not stay around very long.

Governor Beall then took the floor again and reminded the chief that the various Indian nations in the area had agreed not to trouble the white people. He said that he hoped the Great Father would be able to do something about purchasing the land and would the Chief be so kind as to tell his children not to touch the horses and cattle that belonged to the whites?

After this, a gift of "flour, bread sugar and so forth" was presented to the Chief and his party. Little Raven said that he was very glad to receive the food since his people were starving. The meeting was disbanded. A few days later, the lodges were dismantled, belongings were gathered together, ponies were rounded up and overnight the Indian camp had moved away to hunt buffalo.[17]

The following spring, in 1860, the Arapahoes returned to Denver and Dr. C.M. Clark, who had just arrived in the city after his long trip over the South Platte Trail, wrote that his party encamped on the sixth of June on high land above the city near to "the smoky wigwams of the Aborigines, amid which could be seen the dusky forms of stalwart Indians, filthy squaws and naked children lazily basking in the warm sunlight."[18]

An early pioneer to southern Colorado, Irving Howbert, was just a boy when he arrived in Denver on June 14, 1860. His first recollection of the place was the large encampment of Indians near the Platte River. Howbert wrote that as his family approached the village "a very considerable number of Indians came from the village on horseback. Many of them were squaws and old men. The squaws . . . crying and seemed very much distressed. We could not imagine what was the matter but later learned that a war party had gone to the mountains from this Indian camp a few days before and in a battle with the Utes had suffered defeat. News of which had just been received. The squaws and old men that we had seen probably were relatives of the dead and wounded who were being brought in by the returning warriors."[19]

In the autumn of that year another raid on the Utes occurred which was described by a witness: "In the fall, a party of braves from Denver went on the warpath toward the South Park. When a short distance in the mountains they surprised a small party of Utes, killed a squaw and captured three or four boys. The Utes, being reinforced, attacked them in return, killed several and drove them out of the mountains. The captive boys were brought to Denver and were taken in charge by the citizens. One of them was adopted . . . the others, I think were subsequently returned to the Utes. When the Plains braves returned here, they proceeded to hold a grand pow-wow or scalp dance. With the scalp of the squaw tied to a spear or pole, they paraded the streets, stopping at different places to perform their dance with a peculiar singsong accompaniment and keeping this up the greater part of two days and nights. I never became entirely satisfied whether this performance was an occasion of rejoicing or mourning but concluded it partook something of the character of both."[20]

A.D. Richardson wrote to the Lawrence *Republican* of the same event: "The 500 Arapahoe and Apache Indians who went out to fight the Utes obtained more than they bargained for. At first they surprised a village, killing several squaws and papooses, taking other prisoners and stealing some sixty horses, but the Utes soon rallied and drove them away and afterwards surprised and attacked them while they were camping at night, killing six of their warriors and causing them to stampede for Denver in great haste. On the way they grossly insulted several emigrants, compelling them to supply them with provisions, and drew their cocked revolvers and rifles on a defenseless lady whom they found alone in a log house. Unless the Arapahoes very soon abandon such proceedings they will soon find a more formidable foe in the field than their Indian enemies. They have now interred their warriors and are about starting on another expedition against the Utes."[21]

Needless to say, there was great concern among the inhabitants of Denver that the white men could become involved in the quarrels of the Indians. The city lived in terror that the Utes might come down from the mountains for a retaliatory raid and massacre the white settlers.

During that summer difficulties caused by the proximity of the Arapahoes was not the only cause for concern regarding the Indians. In April a band of Cheyennes and Apaches came to Denver to trade robes, camping near an area where the old trader Jim Beckwourth lived. John Poiselle, the interpreter, and his wife camped with the Indians. On a Saturday night a group of drunken miners, which may have been led by Big Phil the Cannibal (Poiselle later testified that it was he), invaded the camp. "Drunken devils and bummers," Beckwourth wrote to the *Rocky Mountain News,* "[they] went to [the] lodges, took the women and girls forcibly out, committing acts of violence. . . . Age was not respected—the gray hairs of John Poiselle's old Indian wife could not protect her. She was taken from her husband's side in bed, but before they succeeded in their hellish work, crippled as he is, [he] compelled [them] by threats with his pistol, to release her." The miners also stole three mules, took them ten miles away and fettered them. The following morning the Indians recovered their mules but went to Jim Beckwourth with their story, threatening vengeance on the whites. Beckwourth persuaded them not to act and promised to notify the people of Denver about the outrage. Several meetings were held in Denver, the incident was investigated and a collection was taken up for the Indians as a gesture of apology.[22]

In August of 1860, at Girioux and Dion's Ranch on the lower South Platte, a man named Iler and his wife were on their way back to civilization and found it necessary to camp near a band of Indians. Iler noticed a mule in the pony herd belonging to the Indians and indicated that he wished to buy it. The Indian who owned the animal seemed willing to sell and indicated the price by spreading the fingers of both hands twice, meaning twenty dollars. In trade with the Indians of that period a half-dollar coin was considered to be one dollar, and Iler believed that he was dealing by this monetary standard; consequently he counted out twenty half-dollars. The Indian looked at it, shook his head and returned the money. Iler became angry and struck the Indian. The Indian was insulted. He went to his lodge, got his bow and quiver, mounted his pony and returned. As Iler saw him coming, he and his wife jumped into their wagon and tried to escape. The Indian began to circle the wagon and shot an arrow into it. Mrs. Iler was so badly frightened that she jumped from the wagon and as she did so, another arrow struck her in the side, penetrating deeply. The Indian was now satisfied and he rode off. Mrs. Iler was taken to O'Fallon's Bluffs where the arrow was removed, but she was obliged to stay there for several months before she was able to travel on in October. Dr. C.M. Clark, who passed Girioux and Dion's the day following the incident, went to considerable trouble to obtain facts of the case as they are related above, but the *Rocky Mountain News* published an inflammatory account of the affair which they obtained from the express messenger of the COC&PP stage line when he arrived in Denver on August 20. The News article was written as follows: "Indian Troubles. From Mr. Rogers, express messenger on Monday's evening coach, we learn that the Cheyennes have recently occasioned some trouble along the road below the Platte crossing. Two or three thousand of the tribe are moving up this way begging and stealing. In several instances they have fired into ranches and in one case wounded an emigrant woman very dangerously. She was at O'Fallon's Bluffs when Mr. Rogers came up and it was thought she would not live. We did not learn the particulars or cause of this outrage on the emigrant train."[23]

It would seem that after the summer of 1860 the Indians, and particularly the Cheyennes, had become the enemy. Travelers reacted to them with a mixture of fear and contempt. In 1859 A.D. Richardson had described a village of Cheyennes on the Republican River Route as "instinctive thieves" and he described their chiefs as having "cutthroat faces." Dr. Clark tempered condemnation with praise; "Cheyennes are tall in stature, having fair and regular features," he wrote. "They are, however, abominably lazy and sometimes disgustingly filthy."

The emigrants' lack of respect toward the Cheyennes was largely influenced by their peculiarities of dress, which the white man found to be sometimes fascinating, always amusing and occasionally hilarious. Richardson described the long queues of hair worn by the braves, braids lengthened with buffalo hair sometimes reaching the ground. He noted the ornaments of tin and silver hanging from their ears. He observed that the women painted their cheeks and foreheads with bright vermillion. Clark wrote with more detail:

> Their taste evinced in the matter of dress is peculiar, and often have we been amused at seeing a stalward Indian with a blue military coat on, adorned with innumerable brass buttons, and buttoned to the chin on the hottest days, while his nether limbs were entirely destitute of covering. Many of them are seen wearing fancy colored shirts, gaudy vests, and old felt hats, and one, I remember, had an umbrella which he carried spread above his head, which he considered as adding much to the dignity of his appearance. They all wear more or less trinkets, such as coils of brass wire and bands of silver on their arms and fingers, together with a long string of circular pieces of silver, graduated in size and attached to a leather strap, which is attached and suspended from the back hair like a queue, they term it "money," and its length is generally proportionate to their wealth. . . . The old squaws are very slovenly in appearance, wearing a loose cotton tunic, belted at the waist with a broad leather belt, studded with large brass buttons, which is bedaubed with grease and dirt; their faces corrugated with wrinkles, and their hair hanging dishevelled and matted about it—the abode of "creeping things,". . . . The young squaws are more neat in appearance, wearing broadcloth skirts, fancy colored blankets, and bead-trimmed leggings and mocassins, and sometimes an ornamental buckskin cape.[24]

It is evident that by 1860 the noble savage of the High Plains had dissolved as childish myth in the mind of the literate traveler. "Lo, the poor Indian!" Alexander Pope had written in 1833; "Lo, the poor Indian! whose untutor'd mind sees God in clouds or hears him in the wind. . . ." the work which incorporated these lines was a thesis in poetry called "An Essay on Man," in which Pope examined ideas of heaven and the hereafter. His intention was to express the simple concept of the universe which an uneducated mind might produce. Pope indicated that the unsophisticated Indian would believe that heaven was beyond the next cloud-topped hill, and as he approached the hereafter "his faithful dog shall bear him company." Out of context, Pope's lines seemed utterly silly, presenting a picture of a childlike creature in a benign pastoral setting. The western traveler soon became aware of the incongruity, and it was not long before the simple verse was altered to fit the situation. "Lo, the poor Indian!" the westerners paraphrased, "whose untutored mind, clothes him before and leaves him bare behind!"

In his capacity as Indian Agent, William Bent discussed the possibility of farming with the Cheyennes and Arapahoes with whom he came in contact in 1859. Either they did not understand what he was proposing or they thought the prospect was so remote that there was not harm in being agreeable. It is even possible that William Bent would envision how it might be accomplished, in a fertile land with good water and women doing the work as the ancestors of the Plains tribes had done in the North, and perhaps Bent was able to present the picture in an appealing way. However the agreement was reached, Bent reported that he believed the Cheyennes and Arapahoes were willing to settle in one place and raise crops. Bent wrote to St. Louis that the Indians had passed laws among themselves that they would do anything that Bent advised. During the winter of 1859–60 Bent wrote letters imploring the Commissioner of Indian Affairs, A. B. Greenwood, to make a treaty assigning permanent lands to the southern tribes. Bent went to Washington in May of 1860, but whom he saw there is not recorded; his trip was probably in relation to this treaty. Commissioner Greenwood petitioned Congress for funds to consummate the treaty, and this money, $35,000 was granted in 1860.[25]

During the summer the War Department began construction at Fort Wise, which formerly had been installed at Bent's Stone Fort but now was to be built a mile away from his post. Major John Sedgwick was sent to command the post, but due to summer hostilities among the Indians south of the Arkansas, the Comanches and Kiowas, Sedgwick was occupied by pursuit of the angry tribes. Work on the fort was begun in September, just about the time that Commissioner Greenwood arrived at Bent's Fort for treaty negotiations. With him came an entourage of relatives, friends and thirteen wagons of trade goods.[26]

Almost coincidentally, a number of Arapahoes happened to be camped near the site, although the chiefs were not present. However, Left Hand, a conciliatory Arapahoe chief, soon arrived. Two weeks later, Black Kettle and White Antelope, the most important of the pacifist Cheyenne leaders, with a few of their sub-chiefs, presented themselves; but they came without the main body of their bands, who could not travel for some time yet. It would have been inconceivable to them to come south at this time of year since this was the period of the great autumn hunt, during which meat was killed and dried for the winter supply. The northern Arapahoes and Cheyennes and representatives of the Dog Soldier bands did not come at all.

Greenwood would wait no longer, so he called a council. He showed a diagram of the restrictions imposed by the 1851 treaty and he then explained the conditions and restrictions of the new treaty. The Arapahoes present agreed too readily to the prospect of becoming farmers if teachers could be sent to instruct them. Where the Cheyennes were concerned, William Bent had assured the commissioner that this tribe was willing to do as Bent thought best, but in return he felt that he was obligated to bargain for more land than the government had proposed for the reservation. This the commissioner did not have authority to grant. It didn't matter; in either case the Cheyenne chiefs would not agree to the limits of the reservation without consulting the rest of the tribe.

Greenwood distributed part of the gifts, promising to give the rest when the treaty was signed, and departed. The revised papers of the agreement were to be sent after he reached Washington. Before leaving he accepted William Bent's resignation as Indian Agent, and at the request of the chiefs Greenwood appointed Bent's friend, Albert G. Boone, as the new agent.[27]

In February of 1861 Albert Boone returned from Washington with the treaty papers. Boone arbitrarily chose six leaders from each of the two tribes to sign the treaty. George Bent said that these leaders were of varying importance and certainly were not the representatives the tribesmen would have sent. The Cheyennes laughed and called these men "the six chiefs" as a term of derision. On the eighteenth of February the Treaty of Fort Wise was signed by Little Raven, Storm, Shave Head and Big Mouth for the Arapahoes, and for the Cheyennes were Black Kettle, White Antelope, Lean Bear, Little Wolf, Tall Bear and Left Hand. The interpreters were John S. Smith, who spoke several Indian languages, and Robert Bent, who translated for the Cheyennes. The area to which the Indians agreed to confine their people was a triangle of relatively arid land well removed from heavily traveled roads in what is now southern Colorado. In exchange for being confined here each Indian would have forty acres of land and the government would pay $15,000 to each tribe each year for fifteen years. The government would also furnish stock and tools, houses and a sawmill, as well as the services of mechanics, interpreters, millers and farmers to the limit of $5,000 per year. After the signing, the treaty was sent to Congress where it was amended and ratified. By October of 1861, Boone had returned to Fort Wise, and after some difficulties, succeeded in obtaining the same signatures again. The Arapahoes signed, and Boone reported that they seemed to be "well pleased." Despite this, it is said that later (in 1865) Little Raven, the Arapahoe chief, said at the Council of the Little Arkansas that "Boone came out and got them to sign a paper, but [they] did not know what it was. . . ."[28]

Boone wrote that the Cheyennes did not come in from their hunt until after the Arapahoes and that the Cheyennes were not so agreeable to signing. However, Boone promised to give them "thirty-six sets of uniforms, six of them to be complete with epaulets, and permission for the chiefs to visit Washington." The Cheyennes signed.[29]

During November of 1861 Albert Boone undertook a census of the Indians in his agency in order that the land apportioned to them could be distributed prior to enforcing the terms of the treaty. He reported 1380 Cheyennes (250 lodges) including only 425 men. At that time the principal chiefs of this tribe were Lean Bear, White Antelope, Little Wolf, Left Hand and Tall Bear. Black Kettle was no longer listed as a chief, but Boone believed that Black Kettle was the only Cheyenne who actually comprehended the situation and problems which the tribe faced. The military continued to deal with Black Kettle as a principal chief.[30]

S. G. Colley, having been appointed Indian Agent for the Upper Arkansas during the autumn of 1861 replacing Albert Boone, assumed his office in November. Although Colley contributed very little to the improvement of the puzzling problems of the care of the Indians, he was aware of one obvious fact—the men of the tribes of this generation would never stoop to tilling the soil, work which traditionally had always been done by women. Colley suggested that they be taught cattle-raising instead; but this sensible suggestion was lost in the general correspondence of 1861.[31]

With the beginning of the Civil War in the spring of 1861 the affairs of the Plains Indians had been shouldered aside.

Chapter

6

The Distant Sound of Cannon

In April of 1861, as the beginning of the Civil War was resounding in the far away southeast, the Western Stage Company was still operating stages to Denver from Omaha, since the contract which had been signed for its discontinuance was not yet in effect. On the coach that left Omaha on April 21, 1861, there were ten passengers: a lady, a boy, six unidentified men, and a missionary named Amos Billingsley. The tenth person was larger than life in his time; he was immense—over six feet tall and weighing nearly two hundred and fifty pounds. This was a clergyman named John Milton Chivington.[1]

Billingsley, the missionary, was a gentle man, and he was probably subdued by the bombastic and hell-fire inspired theology of his traveling companion. As they rode through the monotonous corridor of the Platte Valley, Billingsley must have been informed by the huge black-eyed man that the latter was forty years old and had been born in Ohio of Scotch-Irish descent. As the stagecoach traveled across the sandy stretches from Julesburg to Beaver Creek, Chivington undoubtedly told his fellow travelers about his childhood. He had grown up in a forested region of Ohio where he had worked hard at the lumbering business with his father and his brother Lewis. His education was chiefly self-acquired, with the help of a devoted mother—in a manner that was suspiciously similar to a well-known story of the 1860s. Since Abraham Lincoln had so recently been elected, the tales of the rail-splitting president who studied his youthful lessons by firelight lent color to Chivington's account of his own boyhood, and the coattails of the president were long enough and strong enough to sustain John M.

Chivington. Several years later during a political speech, Chivington recalled a story which had probably been told often, of how he had started felling trees at an early age, and he spoke wistfully of the "little axe" which his mother treasured. He also told of spending his small wages (thirty-seven and a half cents per day!) on books from which he learned to read and write. After he graduated from his axe-swinging days Chivington became an accomplished carpenter, and he practiced his trade until his marriage and subsequent religious conversion sometime between 1840 and 1844.[2]

In reference to his church work Chivington must have summarized his career, from his conversion to Methodism and ordination to the ministry in 1848 at Pleasant Green, Missouri. Chivington had preached in Illinois, Missouri and Nebraska, and he had been appointed Presiding Elder of the Rocky Mountain District of the Methodist Episcopal Church South on March 14, 1860.

On May 8, 1860, Chivington had first arrived in Denver. He had thrown himself into a routine of administration, but his preference was clearly preaching to the mountain camps. On July 8, 1860, a mass evangelical meeting was held at Mountain City on a hillside in the afternoon shade, and Chivington was exhilarated by the spectacle. As he remembered it, the facts were overwhelmed by his emotion as he wrote, "The first quarterly meeting held at Mountain City was one of the most extraordinary ever held in this or any other country. There were present thousands upon thousands of people from every state and territory in the Union and from almost every country of Europe, declaring the wonderful works of God."

A miner, Eliphus Rogers, at Russell Gulch, wrote to his brother in Fremont, Nebraska, to tell him that the Methodists were anticipating Chivington's arrival in August. Familiar with Chivington's style of oratory from earlier times in Nebraska, Rogers wrote that he guessed "the bones will begin to rattle when he comes."[3]

Before Chivington and Billingsley reached Denver, a crisis arose in the city; a Confederate flag was hoisted over Wallingford and Murphy's Dry Goods Store. The citizens gathered around rapidly with tempers crackling. The number of Secessionists and Unionists in the group was so evenly matched that a full-scale riot was imminent. Of the Union men who were present, Samuel M. Logan pushed forward, climbed to the roof of the building and pulled down the flag. A physical clash was averted, but dissension continued to smolder. Abraham Lincoln was aware of the need for a staunch Union sympathizer to control the new Territory of Colorado which had been formed in February of 1861, and for this opportunity a seasoned westerner, military man and lawyer was brought to the President's attention. His name was William Gilpin.[4]

When Gilpin arrived in Denver on the COC&PP on May 27, 1861, Amos Billingsley was one of the crowd who turned out to meet the first governor. Billingsley thought that Gilpin was "splendid." Splendid he may not have been, but Gilpin was extraordinary. He was educated in England, graduated from the University of Pennsylvania, and was said to have attended West Point. It was reported that he fought Seminoles in Florida. It is known that he accompanied Doniphan's expedition to Mexico during the Mexican War in 1847. He traveled with Fremont to Colorado in 1843 and then continued to Oregon, where he lived for a time in the Willamette Valley. Even before 1859 he had made numerous speeches regarding the potential of the West in general and Colorado specifically. The appointment of Gilpin to the task of governing Colorado Territory was not entirely political. It seemed that he was the ideal man for the job.[5]

His experience in military service was especially useful to Gilpin, since in the summer of 1861 the vulnerable position of the new territory in relation to both the Confederacy and the increasingly hostile Indians was beginning to cause great tension. The U. S. Troops in Colorado, stationed at Fort Wise and at Fort Garland beyond the Spanish Peaks in the San Luis Valley, were too far removed to deal with the very real danger of internal warfare in the city of Denver and the mining towns or to protect the miners from the Indians. The civil government of the territory was progressing through the necessary stages of formation, so Gilpin was able to turn his attention to defense. Since he was convinced that he could not wait for federal approval, he appointed a military staff and authorized them to organize a regiment of volunteers. To finance this military body, Gilpin issued $375,000 in drafts on the U. S. Treasury without sanction of the Treasury Department. This expeditious but unwise move was Gilpin's undoing, and it led to his removal from office in April of 1862.

The Civil War touched Colorado only indirectly, but the profound influence which it exercised over ordinary men changed their attitudes, their behavior and their lives. Since these men were to play a significant part in the future of the South Platte Trail and the Indian War, it is important to consider the effect on these individuals which was brought about by the great conflict in the eastern part of the country.

In 1861 the First Regiment of Colorado was formed. Among the earliest volunteers was Ned Wynkoop, the erstwhile sheriff, who now became Second Lieutenant (and later Captain) of Company A under Colonel John P. Slough.

Among the officers was another well-known figure of early Colorado history—Jacob Downing, who became Captain of Company D. Downing was born in 1830 in New York, a child of Quakers. He was admitted to the bar in Illinois in 1858 and set out for Pike's Peak in 1859. He had prospected at Mountain City and Gregory's Point but did not stay in the mountains long and returned to Denver in 1860, where he became involved in local government. He and an associate, Nelson Sargent (former Division Agent for the Leavenworth and Pike's Peak stage company), were elected jointly as judges of the Court of Common Pleas. Downing said that "Two of us were chosen in order that every culprit might be assured of a fair trial."[6]

On August 10, 1861, Colonel Lewis Chivington, John's brother, was killed at the battle of Wilson's Creek in Missouri. In the same month, Governor Gilpin was trying to fill the position of Chaplain of the First Colorado Regiment. When he asked John Chivington to assume the post, Chivington, possibly influenced by grief or anger, declined, and instead insisted on taking an active military role in the organization. He was consequently appointed Major of the regiment and he applied himself enthusiastically to his new challenge. In his own words he "held quarterly meetings on Saturdays and Sundays, and then made recruiting speeches and drilled the battalion during the other five days and nights of the week." In November of 1861, Chivington, in full military uniform, was preaching "rousing patriotic sermons" at Methodist Sunday services. Shortly afterward he was allowed to retire gracefully from the ministry. Many years later Chivington's character was evaluated by a fellow Nebraska Methodist, Reverend David Marquette, who wrote: "John M. Chivington was one of those strong forceful characters who find it difficult to either control themselves or to subject themselves to the requirements of a church or to the rules of war, but are a law unto themselves; but for these defects he would have been a power for good, as he was a strong preacher and possessed many of the elements which constitute successful leadership."[7]

During the latter part of 1861 Colonel Edward Canby, who was in charge of the military force in New Mexico, was rapidly fortifying the defensive positions of that area because he anticipated a Confederate invasion from Texas by way of either the Pecos or the Canadian River. While increasing the manpower of Fort Union, he appealed to Governor Gilpin of Colorado for reinforcements, and subsequently two companies, A and B, of volunteer infantry from the Second Regiment of Colorado marched south to participate in the war between the states. At Valverde, New Mexico, south of Albuquerque, on the Rio Grande del Norte, Company A was involved in a battle between the forces of Colonel Canby and General H. H. Sibley. Canby was defeated and retired to Santa Fe, where he issued another appeal to Colorado for more assistance. Before the third of March, the entire First Regiment of Colorado marched south to defend the Territory.

By the twenty-fifth of March the Colorado forces were marching toward Santa Fe with Colonel John P. Slough commanding 1342 men and Major Chivington leading 418. The Coloradans camped at a ranch near the Pecos River, where they received information of the advance of 600 Texans north from Santa Fe. On the morning of March 26 a force of 210 infantry and about 180 cavalry under Major Chivington crossed La-Glorieta Pass and here, in an irregular defile called Apache Canyon, the miners from Colorado met Sibley's brigade. No one in the entire body of Colorado men had had any experience at warfare except the company which had been with Canby at Valverde. A member of this company, Ovando Hollister, described the battle at Apache Canyon as follows. When the encounter began, the infantry marching in front of the columns split and turned to the rear and up the canyon's sides in confusion. The officers lost control, everyone talking, no one listening, and above all was the sound of Confederate shells screaming and whistling over the heads of the terrified Pikes Peakers. As the Texans fell back to a better position, the Coloradans gained control as they followed cautiously. When a projecting point provided a safe place to regroup, Chivington positioned his infantry, then dismounted the cavalry and gave them orders to deploy in a flanking maneuver up the steep mountainside on either side, to the right under Captain Downing and to the left, led by Captain Wynkoop and Captain Scott J. Anthony of Company E. In the rear Chivington reserved one hundred mounted cavalry for later use.

"Major Chivington, with a pistol in each hand and one or two under his arms, chawed his lips with only less energy than he gave his orders," Hollister wrote, "He seemed burdened with new responsibility, the extent of which he had never before realized, and to have no thought of danger. Of commanding presence, dressed in full regimentals, he was a conspicuous mark for Texas sharp-shooters. One of their officers, taken prisoner, averred that he emptied his revolvers three times at the Major and then made his company fire a volley at him. As if possessed of a charmed life, [Chivington] galloped unhurt through the storm of bullets, and the Texans, discouraged, turned their attention to something else." The engagement lasted two or three hours, and accomplished a complete rout of the Texans who reportedly lost sixteen killed, thirty to forty wounded, and seventy-five prisoners. The Coloradans had five killed, thirteen wounded and three missing.

The First Regiment withdrew eastward over the pass to their former camp, where on the night of the twenty-sixth their numbers were increased by the arrival of three hundred infantry under Colonel Slough which had been in reserve at Vernal Springs. During the night and following day a bold plan was devised, probably by Major Chivington. On the morning of the twenty-eighth a force of seven companies would be detached under the command of Chivington and would be sent by a rough and untracked back route over the mountain to approach the camp of the Texans from the south. The balance of the command, under Colonel Slough, would proceed westward through the pass to engage the Texans from the front.

On March 28, in the middle of the pass at Pigeon's Ranch, the confrontation occurred sooner than expected. The fighting was fierce. Although the three hundred reserves had never seen battle before, and the balance of the force of Coloradans had only the previous day's battle for experience, they acquitted themselves with efficiency and bravery during the seven-hour battle, even though they were losing ground and were being driven back eastward. The battle was finally ended by an overnight truce for the purpose of burying the dead. The losses were heavy; in Downing's company alone forty-two of eighty men were killed.

After their departure from camp that morning, Chivington's command scrambled for sixteen miles through thickets of scrub piñon and cedar bushes over the mountain to a point that overlooked the camp of the Texans. The Confederate sentry was soon located and captured, but by that time it was afternoon. The officers of the detachment (including Captain Wynkoop) discussed their options for an hour or more. It was decided to attack the camp, and the men were commanded to lower themselves over the edge of the steep cliff. They were discovered and fired on, of course, but the camp of the Texans was poorly defended and the Coloradans virtually descended on them yelling and whooping. Chivington managed his attack well, sending Wynkoop with thirty men to capture one gun on a high hill, then dividing the remaining body of men into two columns, one to capture the main artillery and the other to surround the supply train. The guns and ammunition were destroyed, what was estimated to be seventy-three heavily loaded wagons were overturned and burned, and all of the animals corraled nearby were bayoneted.

Chivington's forces, with seventeen prisoners, then returned over the mountain by the way they had come to avoid meeting the Texans in the canyon. They arrived at Pigeon's Ranch at about ten o'clock, and when they saw campfires, they halted. "Whose camp do you think it is?" someone asked.

It is reported that Chivington replied, "I don't know whose it is, but if it an't ours we'll soon make it so. Fall in. . . fix bayonets!" The camp was that of the Coloradans, and it was not necessary to charge; but it was now evident that John Chivington had tasted blood and had worn the crown of glory.[8]

The battle was not resumed. Orders were given by Colonel Slough to return to Fort Union and the relieved Texans gladly stumbled back to Sante Fe.

Since William Bent had resigned from the Indian Agency, he lived part of the time at his freight station on the south bank of the Purgatory River, where the buildings were still in the process of being constructed. Here Bent lived with most of his family—his wife Yellow Woman, his oldest son Robert, and Julia, the youngest daughter. Some of the time the family spent in the two-story brick house in Westport which William bought or built before 1858. There are stories that the conventional women of Westport were amused or shocked by the independent habits of Yellow Woman, who could be seen riding horseback astride and was known to sleep in a tipi on the grounds of the Westport home.[9]

When the Civil War erupted William's son George was attending school at the academy in St. Louis. It had been ten years since he had seen his Cheyenne cousins on the upper Arkansas River, and it is quite conceivable that George Bent might never have returned to Colorado if he had not become involved in the emotional turmoil which was surging through the border state of Missouri. George now considered his home to be in Westport where he lived with his sister Mary and her husband, R. M. Moore, a Westport farmer. It was here that George went for summer vacation in 1861.

In St. Louis, Governor Claiborne Jackson professed to be in favor of neutrality for the state but was actually a sympathizer with the secessionists. The legislature vacillated, undecided between trade bonds with the north on one hand and blood bonds with the south on the other. Ostensibly for protection the Governor assembled a camp of militia called the State Guards just outside of St. Louis. General Nathaniel Lyon, the Commander of federal troops in Missouri, accompanied by Frank Blair, a friend of William Bent, led his troops against the camp of militia and dispersed it. Unfortunately, in the confusion the troops also fired into a civilian mob, which event aroused the sentiments of the hot-blooded young men of Missouri.

When George arrived at home in Westport for summer vacation, he found the young men flocking to join the State Guard and western Missouri arming for the South. At the age of eighteen, in Springfield, Missouri, George Bent joined Colonel Martin Green's cavalry regiment in the Confederate Army under General Sterling Price. Young Bent took part in the battle of Wilson's Creek in southern Missouri where the Confederates were victorious and the Union General, Nathaniel Lyon, was killed. It was at this battle also that Colonel Lewis Chivington, fighting on the Confederate side with George Bent, met his death. In the same year George fought in a battle at Lexington, Missouri, and, early in 1862, he fought in the battle of Pea Ridge in Arkansas during which the southerners were decisively defeated. With General Earl Van Dorn's troops, George withdrew into Arkansas and Mississippi, where, at the bloody battle of Corinth, in which more than three thousand Confederate soldiers were killed or wounded, George was captured during the retreat.

Among two hundred rebel prisoners who were marched north from Corinth through St. Louis on their way to a prison camp in northern Missouri was nineteen-year-old George Bent, bedraggled, thin and infinitely saddened. In the crowds who watched at curbside was a group of schoolmates of George's from the academy and the young men recognized George. The schoolmates were well acquainted with the Bent family so they went directly to Robert, who happened to be in St. Louis on a buying expedition for trade goods. Without delay Robert hastened to a family friend, Robert Campbell, George's guardian, who in turn contacted General John C. Fremont, a warm acquaintance of the Bents from the old days at the Fort on the Arkansas. Fremont immediately ordered George's parole, and he was released on the same day—under the condition that the young rebel would return to the Arkansas with his brother and would take no further part in the war.

In September of 1862, back at his father's ranch on the Purgatory River, George soon discovered that he was not to find a lasting peace; a despised rebel would not be tolerated easily in that area. He was tired of fighting, and only one course seemed to be open to the young but weary soldier—to go to live with his mother's people, the Cheyennes, which he did in April of 1863. George's younger brother Charley had already gone this route and was living among the Indians.[10]

Long before stagecoaches rattled along the South Platte Trail, in the 1830s, western Missouri was the frontier, and it was to the town of Weston that Benjamin Holladay migrated with his five brothers from a farm in Kentucky. Ben was a tall sandy-haired aggressive youngster, and the fact that he had little education seemed to be of no consequence whatever. He was about eighteen years old when he was known to have been working as an orderly for General A. W. Doniphan at the time of the Mormon conflicts in 1838. Ben traveled to Richmond, Missouri, in October of that year with Doniphan's troops under orders to intercept a Mormon retreat from the north. After the Mormon leaders surrendered and were imprisoned, Holladay was in a position to befriend and assist some of the Mormon women and children. He not only earned the gratitude of these ladies, but he was brought to the attention of Brigham Young, the Mormon leader. It was a fortuitous meeting.

By the age of nineteen Ben was working as a store clerk in Weston. A short time later, in May of 1839, he applied for and received a license to sell liquor, and within a year he was operating a saloon and hotel. With the help of the Hughes family, wealthy relatives of the Holladays, Ben purchased a drugstore and became the postmaster. In partnership with his brothers, he was also involved in a general store and a packing plant.

After about ten years of reasonable success, Holladay formed a partnership with Theodore F. Warner to initiate a freighting venture to be financed by Warner's credit and transported by Holladay's wagons and oxen. The partners launched a freighting train of fifty wagons and $70,000 worth of merchandise bound for Salt Lake City, where Holladay was warmly received by Brigham Young. This first train brought a large profit to the partners; the second train was twice as large. Holladay opened a store in Salt Lake City, and from here he made a contract to deliver a herd of Mormon cattle to California, where it was sold to a military base. In 1855, he brought out his partner, Warner, and there was plenty of money left over to start making loans to William Russell to underwrite the latter's flighty schemes. Ben Holladay had a great deal of time to study the stagecoach business before he became the owner.[11]

On March 21, 1862, the Central Overland and California and Pike's Peak Express Company was sold at public auction in front of the old Massasoit House in Atchinson. There was only one bidder; Ben Holladay bought the stage line for $100,000. He also paid nearly $500,000 worth of debts outstanding for grain, forage, provisions and wages. After Holladay bought the COC&PP, reorganization started immediately. Holladay retained his cousin, Bela Hughes, as financial advisor and legal representative, and though he continued to operate under the charter of the COC&PP, Holladay shortened the name of the company to the Overland Stage Line.[12]

On May 24, 1862, the *Rocky Mountain News* noted that Ben Holladay, accompanied by John Livingston and George K. Otis, had arrived in Denver by special coach. After that Byers remarked that for three days there were no stagecoach arrivals in Denver and that this had never happened before. On March 28 he was informed that Holladay had bought the line. The station agent in Denver told Byers that Holladay had offered to transport the mail free of charge to and from the mines.[13]

As Holladay set up his new organization it was headed by a General Superintendent, Isaac E. Eaton, whose authority extended from St. Joseph to Salt Lake City. George Kingman Otis succeeded him in September of 1863 until October of 1864, when William Reynolds was appointed to the position. The general superintendent would be required to make a trip over the entire line about four times a year.

David Street was in a class by himself as Paymaster of the Overland. He had been a bookkeeper for the freighting firm of Russell, Majors and Waddell, and he was working for them at Camp Floyd in Utah when he met Ben Holladay in the spring of 1862 in Salt Lake City. Holladay hired him without delay, and Street began in June to make the rounds of the stage stations on the Overland four times a year for the purpose of adjusting accounts. The certificate system was retained from the old COC&PP days but with a difference. Since the employees of the stage line had their board and shelter furnished, they seldom needed cash, but if cash had been issued to an individual during the three-month period, the stationkeeper made a notation on that employee's account certificate. When Paymaster Street arrived the balance of the employee's wages were paid in full and a new certificate was issued. Street also settled with the ranchers who boarded stock, and he paid them for their services and the forage which had been provided.

On the second level of command in Holladay's hierarchy were three Division Superintendents, limited geographically by the route from Atchison to Denver, from Denver to Salt Lake and then from Salt Lake City to Placerville, California. Under each Division Superintendent there were three Division Agents, one for each hundred miles. On the South Platte Trail the best known of these was Reuben S. Thomas, who was Division Agent from Julesburg to Denver from 1864 to April of 1865 during the devastating period of the Indian assault on the South Platte Road. The Division Agent was in charge of stock, buying grain, upkeep on the stations, and discharging unsatisfactory employees as well as hiring new ones.

Of those who traveled for the stage company, one of the most difficult jobs, but also the most exciting, was that of Express Messenger. He rode the coaches, day and night, for three weeks relieved by a layover of nine days once a month. His responsibility was the care of gold, large amounts of cash, or important papers which were transported by the Overland.

There were seventy-five drivers employed by the Overland Stage at one time, and each drove a run of fifty to sixty miles. They were well paid—$75 to $100 a month—during times of great danger, as much as $200. Various writers, including Mark Twain, have written extensively of the arrogance and eccentricity of stage drivers. Twain noted that a driver would not speak to underlings such as stock tenders and would not share the common towel with the stationkeeper and passengers. Eugene Ware wrote that the drivers of his acquaintance were "proud as brigadier-generals" and as tough, hardy and brave a lot of people as could be found anywhere. "As a rule," Ware wrote, "they were courteous to passengers and careful of their horses. . . . They gathered mail from the ranches and travelers along the road and saw that it reached its destination." The flamboyant, hard-drinking drivers were the ones most frequently remembered by the old-timers, but it was the steady veterans like William Trotter who drove most of the coaches. William Trotter drove for the Western Stage Company in Iowa in the 1850s, for the COC&PP during its period of existence, and then for Ben Holladay in different areas over almost the entire length of the line.[14]

While they were not actually employees, the Carlyle brothers, George Henry and Alexander, freighters from Kentucky, had a long association with Holladay before his purchase of the stage line. When Holladay discovered that the suppliers who had worked for the COC&PP were unsatisfactory, he formed a partnership in 1862 with the brothers, combining his own freight trains with theirs under the supervision of George Henry Carlyle as manager. The Carlyle brothers spent their full time and energy transporting grain and supplies to the stations of the Overland from their headquarters at Fort Kearny.[15]

Ben Holladay made a trip twice a year over the entire route of the Overland Stage Company. He traveled in his private coach, which was a legend. It had been custom built for him with spiral springs and luxurious appointments. It was unmistakably part of the romance of the stagecoach King as it announced his passage by the flag flying over the top—the flag which bore the large insignia "BH." Eugene Ware saw it pass Cottonwood Springs in 1864 and he described it as a "sort of Pullman conveyance," with a mattress on the floor of the coach for sleeping. Another writer said that the coach had a built-in writing desk. Behind the special coach was another which carried servants, a cook, and supplies. Each coach was drawn by six horses and traveled at exceptional speed. Holladay himself could be seen riding on top of the coach with the driver.[16]

The average person was so overwhelmed by an encounter with the famous coach and its romantic owner that it became a high point in that person's recollections. In later years at a dinner party, a minister told a story of his first meeting with Holladay at a remote station on the plains. The minister had been in the process of making a long journey, and when the stagecoach stopped to deposit mail and change teams the driver announced that Holladay's private coach with the flag flying was approaching from the opposite direction. Once out of his coach, Holladay greeted the stage passengers warmly and passed a box of cigars. He then noticed that the minister looked ill, and Holladay suggested that he had some good medicine in his coach and he invited the minister to join him. The minister claimed that at the time he had no idea what the "medicine" was, but since "it did him a great deal of good," he and Holladay continued to drink it. While the stagecoach and passengers waited, Holladay and the minister drank two bottles of the medicine and threw the empty bottles out the window to break them on the rocks.[17]

Besides shortening the name of the stage line, Holladay also attempted to change some of the more objectionable station names; Fremont's Slough became Cold Springs, and Julesburg was called Overland City. The old names were too firmly entrenched in history, however, and in spite of the thirst-quenching connotation for sweltering passengers in mid-summer, the new name of Cold Springs was disregarded, and the alternate name for Julesburg was stubbornly ignored.

Holladay also revised the printed schedule, adding a mile or two to some figures and subtracting a mile or two elsewhere, so that the distance between stations seemed to be more nearly equal. It looked better in print, and how many weary travelers could tell if the schedule had been doctored when the time of passage actually depended upon the weather and the terrain rather than the miles traversed?

Very soon after the Overland changed ownership, Indian trouble on the road to Fort Laramie provided an unexpected boost to the prosperity of the South Platte Road. On July 11, 1862, the Post Office Department ordered the Overland Stage Company to remove their stations on the Sweetwater portion of the route and relocate them on the South Platte. Holladay and Isaac Eaton made a rush trip to Salt Lake City to check the new route. It was ordered that beginning on the twenty-first of July the mail coaches would continue from Julesburg up the South Platte to the mouth of the Cache la Poudre where they would ford, or be ferried across, the river at Cherokee City and then continue north to La Porte, the Big Thompson, a station called Virginia Dale, Big Laramie and on through Bridger's Pass. This route from the South Platte northward was called the Cherokee Trail. Superintendent Eaton visited Denver and told the *News* that the mail would be delivered daily to Denver from the turn-off point at the Cache la Poudre. At this junction, originally called Cherokee City and later Latham, a new station was built, consisting of one house. The crossing at Latham was not a difficult one, the water usually ran only two or three feet deep, but augmented by spring rains it was sometimes deep enough to "swim a horse."[18]

The new route brought about a revitalization of Fremont's Orchard which had not been used by the coaches since the Western Stage had been terminated. Fort Lupton was also pressed into service as a station once again.

Russell and the COC&PP had provided almost enough home stations for boarding stage drivers and feeding passengers on the South Platte route, but there was a great need for the auxiliary stations, called swing stations or feed stations, where teams were kept and fed, held ready for changing. Holladay's organization addressed itself to the task of supplementing its number of stage stops. From Cottonwood Springs, the first of these to be built upriver was an entirely new station called Elkhorn, eleven miles from Fremont's Springs, and then twelve miles up from Alkali Lake was another called Sand Hill. Probably neither of them ever became more than a lonely sod house like Alkali Lake. Holladay seems to have instituted some sort of station at the Lower Crossing which was called Antelope. A feed station, usually called Moore and Kelly's, appeared between Valley Station and Beaver Creek, and a post named Eagle's Nest seems to have been located between Fremont's Orchard and the mouth of the Poudre. A location seventeen miles above Fort Lupton called Big Bend was noted, and another was fourteen miles from Denver at Pierson's. All of these so-called stations seem to have been not much more than names—with the exception of Moore and Kelly's which became well-known, perhaps because of the genial Irish stationkeeper.

At Antelope station the stage company owned the house, the barn and corral, but Holladay did not always own the dwelling house at these intermediate stations. At Dennison's, for instance, and also at Kelly's, the Overland owned the barn and corral but not the houses. A brief description of a typical house has survived, one located at Moore and Kelly's Station. The dwelling was a two-room structure of sod or adobe, the front room for the family and the back rented to travelers, or "pilgrims," as was the custom. The stage company barns were typically frame buildings about fifty by twenty-five feet in size. They were divided into a room for storing grain and provisions and another room which served as a bedroom for stock tenders. A space large enough for ten or twelve mules and horses faced the corral, which was probably constructed from sod blocks.

To the previously established stations some buildings and improvements were added. When Holladay acquired the Julesburg station, it consisted of two stables, one blacksmith shop, a wagon shop and a station. By 1864 there was a large boarding house, a large stable, a warehouse, a blacksmith shop, a telegraph station and a large sod corral. The warehouse and the station which had a frame front and large attached shed, were made of cedar logs. The other buildings were made of sod. Spring Hill Station was also improved. It was said to have been one of the best stations on the entire line, with excellent houses, barns and corrals.[19]

Changes were made in personnel as well under the administration of the Overland. Dennison's continued to function as before, but Fred

Lamb was no longer in the Bijou area; the stagecoaches were now serviced by a rancher named Murray at his post, seven miles below Junction. George Turner, a former stagecoach driver who had kept the station at Junction in 1861 with his wife and son, was now stationed at Beaver Creek in 1862. Beaver Creek ceased to be a home station and the passengers were now fed at Valley Station. Hester and Mahlon Brown, formerly at Beaver Creek, moved to Valley Station in July of 1862, and it is likely that William A. Kelly, formerly of Valley Station, was now moved to the feed station called Moore and Kelly's. He was joined there some time soon after by his wife. Albert Thorne, formerly of St. Vrain Creek, where he had been postmaster, was moved to Spring Hill to become stationkeeper of the home station.[20]

There is no explanation for the association between James A. Moore, the Pony Express rider, and Kelly's station, but there must have been a reason for the name "Moore and Kelly's" which was being used in May of 1863 by travelers. The double name persisted until after the spring of 1864. Whether James Moore worked for Ben Holladay at this location is not known for sure. James Moore's obituary stated that he had worked for the great Overland Stage Company and the Pony Express, but the reporter may have mistaken the name of the stage company, intending rather to mention the COC&PP. If Moore did work for Holladay, then it was probably for a year or so at Moore and Kelly's Station before resigning to start his own ranch, called the Washington ranch, at a location about three miles downriver from Valley station. William Breckenridge, a friend and employee of the Moore brothers, wrote that the Washington Ranch "was founded by Jim Moore after the Pony Express was abandoned." "After he started his ranch," Breckenridge said, "his brother Charles joined him . . .[21]

Post offices were established and postmasters were appointed on the upper South Platte, with Hiram J. Graham replacing Albert Thorne at St. Vrain on May 24, 1862; Thomas C. Moore postmaster at Cherokee City, on March 25, 1862; Arthur C. Lewis, postmaster at Lillian Springs, July 20, 1863; John D. Kinnear at Fremont's Orchard, August 25, 1863, and William A. Kelly at the American Ranch, February 9, 1863. This was the first appearance of the name "American Ranch" in this area. It may have been bestowed by the Post Office Department. A post office called Fleming's Ranch was situated on St. Vrain Creek on March 23, 1863, with George A. Fleming as postmaster. The Fort Lupton post office, tended by Henry Sprenger and George E. Blake in 1861, was turned over to Marcus P. Wells on January 16, 1863, and the post office which had been at Julesburg under William W. Letson since April 2, 1862, was moved to Clearwater under George B. Ackley on September 10, 1863. This was moved back to Julesburg in the care of Samuel D. Bancroft on January 20, 1864.[22]

Another ranch was founded in the vicinity of Valley Station in 1863 by another pair of the ubiquitous Irish immigrants throughout the South Platte Valley. John Coad and his brother Mark, who was ten years older, were both born in Wexford, Ireland, and with their parents and sister came to New York state in 1859. From there they progressed westward to Dubuque, Iowa, and after their father's death in 1859 the family moved to Nebraska City. It was probably here, the headquarters of the Russell, Majors and Waddell Freighting Company, that Mark and John found employment in the winter or spring of 1860. Judging from the census, John worked briefly as the stationkeeper for the Pony Express station at Julesburg, but by 1861 the brothers had formed a partnership for the purpose of shipping military supplies to posts in Colorado, Montana and Wyoming. The brothers soon assembled trains as extensive as twenty-five wagons, each pair drawn by twelve oxen.

After one or two trips west the two young men observed that prices in Denver were usually higher during January and February, when the number of freight trains which arrived was decreased due to the hardships of extreme cold weather. The Coads reasoned that if materials and supplies were freighted to a location near Denver in the summer, then stored until the harsh winter season, these supplies could be transported more easily to Denver and sold at much higher prices than the same freight would have brought in the summer. With this plan in mind the brothers began to build two freight warehouses, one at Julesburg and the other located about eight miles southwest of Valley Station. This location was called the Wisconsin Ranch.[23]

These new ranches were made of sod, with walls three feet thick, and corrals and fences five to seven feet high with portholes at intervals through which to see or shoot. Begun in 1862, the buildings at the Wisconsin Ranch were said to be of adobe. The largest building at this place was the main house, which had three bedrooms and a kitchen. The ranch manager and his wife had a separate house, and there was a cookhouse and a bunkhouse for the employees besides the warehouses for storing freight goods. One fanciful source reported that at the Wisconsin Ranch there were buffalo heads on the walls and every employee had his own washtub for bathing and laundry.

Perhaps it was the intractable stretch of sand and steep hills near Fremont's Orchard that brought about a revived interest in toll roads on the South Platte Trail. On August 14, 1862, a charter was granted by the Weld County Comissioners to Charles L. Hill and M.C. Keith (who was Holladay's Denver agent), representing the Fremont's Orchard Plank Road and Turnpike Company, to construct a toll road from Bijou Creek to Fremont's Orchard. On January 5, 1863, a sizeable contract was granted to the Platte Valley Wagon Road Company which, in consideration for the privilege "agreed to improve the road from Fremont Station to Gerry's Store." This latter commitment, however, proved to be too much of a challenge, and on September twenty-first the company reported that at a cost to them of one thousand dollars they had improved a portion of said road, but they had not cut down and improved the sand hills at Fremont's Orchard because the expense of doing so would be very heavy and they would not realize any return therefor. They desired to be released from the obligation to complete said improvement.

Holladay's resourceful people had devised their own method of dealing with the inhospitable stretch of road. This innovation was called the spike team, an arrangement of five tough, well-rested mules, two teams abreast and a leader harnessed alone at the front. These specialized teams were added at Junction Station, but even with their exceptional ability, they could not go much faster than a walk over the rugged trail.

There were other toll gates constructed on the South Platte Trail. Ben Holladay had a charter for the right to collect toll from the bridges at Beaver Creek and Cache la Poudre River, but the greater wagon roads were let to the Platte Valley Wagon Road Company, who maintained and collected toll on the road from nine miles west of Julesburg to the mouth of Bijou Creek, and the Julesburg and Fort Lupton Wagon Road Company, which located a toll road at some distance between those two places. The apparent overlapping of the two companies indicates that the operators must have been closely associated. The former company was headed by T. L. McRoy, Edwin Toole, A. J. Clarke, and I. A. Cook. The second was administered by H. J. Williams, M. C. Keith and Moses Halette. The fees varied from sixty-five cents to $1.50 for each vehicle drawn by one yoke of cattle or one span of horses, depending on whether the road was completed or not. Each additional span of animals brought in from ten cents to $1.50 when traveling west, half-price when returning empty. For loose head of stock the charge was three cents each, and for sheep or hogs, one or one and a half cents. A man on horseback was charged ten to twenty-five cents.[24]

An intimate glimpse of the dwellers of the plains was provided by one or two writers who took an interest in individuals. In May of 1863 Maurice O'Connor Morris stopped at Lillian Springs and met the rancher there, undoubtedly Arthur Lewis. "Lillian Springs, where the heaven was illuminated with lightning more fantastic than fireworks; but there was no rain. At this ranch I felt convinced, by a fence that I saw, that an Englishman or Irishman had been at work, so I went and found it tenanted by a North of Ireland man: he had left a good farm in Illinois on account of the war, which he disapproved of, and as he considered talking a thirsty process, he insisted in my joining him in some whiskey, modified by a cordial much approved of I believe, called the 'Good Samaritan.' I had my fears as to the results, but they proved groundless.''[25]

In September of that year a young woman named Harriet A. Smith kept a diary of her journey which provides an idea of these people who are otherwise only names in impersonal itineraries. Harriet was traveling with her uncle, Porter Hinman, his wife and their sons, one of whom was named Frank. Harriet remembers passing Spring Hill Station then stopping to make lunch near Lillian Springs, where she noted a very fine spring beside the house. During that afternoon, the family stopped to visit the Dennisons. Hinman had boarded with L. S. and Mary Dennison while with a haycutting crew in 1860, and now he wanted his family to meet his old friends. Harriet said that the Dennisons were a ''pretty nice family.''

She did not say where they camped that night but the following day, while they were creeping along just past Valley Station, young Frank fell from the wagon seat and was run over by the wheel. Miraculously, he survived, but the worried family hurried along as fast as they could for twelve miles to Godfrey's store. Harriet was impressed by the kindness of the Godfrey family. Holon Godfrey came to the wagon, lifted Frank down, carried him into the house and put him to bed. The Godfreys made the Hinman family welcome for supper and the night. Mr. Hinman slept on the floor while his wife sat up until one o'clock with her injured son. The other boys slept in the wagon, but Harriet lay down on the double bed against the wall behind Frank. The fleas were so annoying, however, that she could not sleep, so she got up and took her aunt's place at the bedside while Mrs. Hinman slept. Another day passed while Frank was still unable to travel. The older boys went hunting and shot a deer, and that night the fresh meat attracted a pack of large gray wolves, which must have interfered further with Harriet's sleep.

After that, Frank recovered rapidly, but before resuming their journey the Hinmans were invited to attend a dance at Kelly's on Saturday night. Everyone went to the party except Harriet and Frank, the ''old woman'' (Matilda Godfrey?) and the ''babies.'' (In the early 1860s two daughters, Carrie and Nettie were born to the Godfreys.) It is unfortunate that Harriet did not go to the party because her description would have been of great interest. The dance lasted until two o'clock in the morning, and the next day everyone slept late.

Sunday at Godfrey's might have been a typical sabbath on the plains. ''Frank is quite well,'' Harriet wrote. ''He thinks he is able to go and ride. He cannot walk but Aunt put on his pants and he can sit up. I got breakfast but no one felt like eating much after the dance. By the time I got breakfast ready I did not feel like eating for I took a pain in my stomach but I ate and got better. After breakfast and the dishes was washed I went into the wagon and slept about two hours and then I felt better. The folks have not been doing much of anything. Ate some bread and milk about three o'clock in the afternoon. Mr. Godfrey got supper about five so we have spent the day and now the evening shades begin to appear . . ."[26]

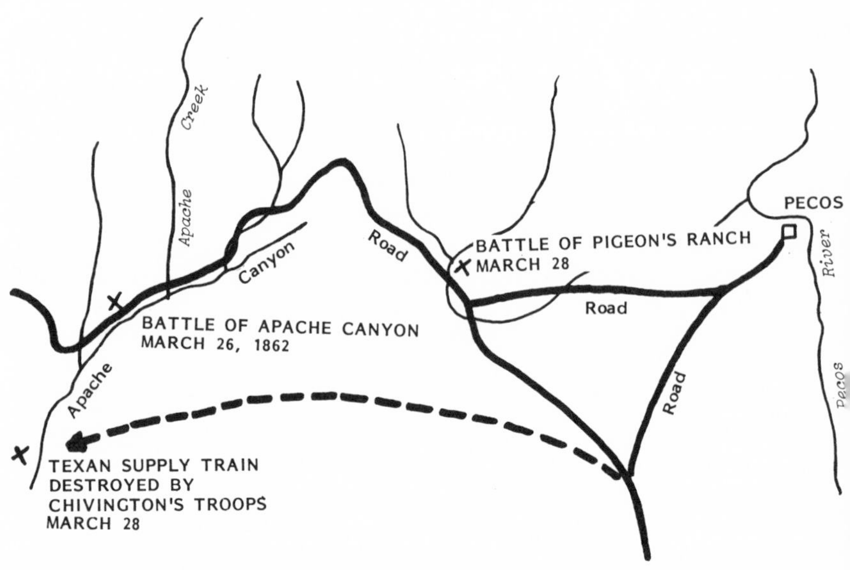

Battle of Glorieta Pass

1. William Bent, most prominent of the brothers who founded Bent's Fort on the Arkansas River (Denver Public Library, Western History Department.)

2. Mary Bent, eldest daughter of William Bent and sister of George. (Colorado Historical Society.)

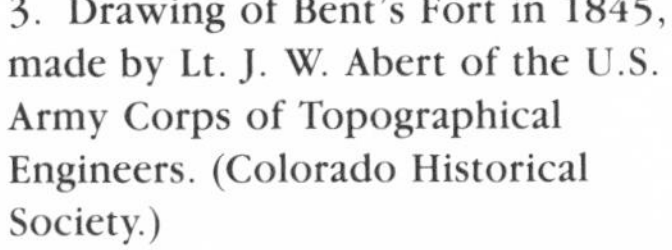

3. Drawing of Bent's Fort in 1845, made by Lt. J. W. Abert of the U.S. Army Corps of Topographical Engineers. (Colorado Historical Society.)

4

5

4. Bent's Fort has been carefully excavated, researched and reconstructed. This view, facing the southwest watch tower, shows the interior of the courtyard of the reconstructed fort.

5. In one of the storerooms of the reconstructed Bent's Fort, this bale of buffalo robes is exhibited.

6. In 1935 Fort Vasquez on the South Platte River was reconstructed by WPA workers. This reconstruction has now eroded to ruins. This view from the main gate faces toward the northwest corner of the courtyard. Originally, rooms lined the walls.

7. Typical buffalo-robe bed used by western travelers as shown in one of the rooms at reconstructed Bent's Fort.

6

7

8

9

8. Contemporary drawing of freight wagons drawn by oxen fording a river. (Denver Public Library, Western History Department.)

9. William Newton Byers, pioneer newspaperman of Colorado. (Denver Public Library, Western History Department.)

10. Edward Wanshear Wynkoop, the exuberant young pioneer, actor, sheriff, and soldier of the early years of Colorado's history. (Colorado Historical Society.)

11. Louisa Brown Wynkoop, the attractive actress who married Ned Wynkoop. (Colorado Historical Society.)

12. A decayed but complete Conestoga wagon which is preserved at Bent's Fort National Historical Site, LaJunta, Colorado.

0

11

12

13

14

13. Conestoga wagon with modern canvas cover is exhibited at the Scottsbluff National Monument on the old Oregon Trail.

14. View of Denver, near Larimer Street, taken from a wood engraving published by *Frank Leslie's Illustrated Newspaper* on August 20, 1859. (Colorado Historical Society.)

15. William Hepburn Russell, founder of the Leavenworth and Pike's Peak Express and the Central Overland California and Pike's Peak Express stage lines. (Colorado Historical Society.)

16. Painting by W. H. Jackson of wagons crossing the South Platte at Julesburg. (Colorado Historical Society.)

15

16

17

18

17. Jack Morrow, infamous trader located on the South Platte Trail near Cottonwood Springs. (Denver Public Library, Western History Department.)

18. John F. Coad, freighter and co-proprietor of Wisconsin Ranch on the South Platte Trail. (Nebraska State Historical Society.)

19

20

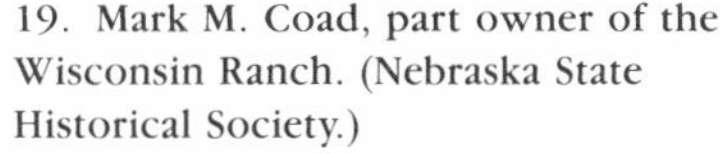

19. Mark M. Coad, part owner of the Wisconsin Ranch. (Nebraska State Historical Society.)

20. Crayon portrait of Elbridge Gerry, South Platte trader who was prominent in government–Indian relations preceding the Indian War of 1864–65. (Colorado Historical Society.)

21. Molds for making adobe bricks and finished brick (standing upright). (Denver Public Library, Western History Department.)

21

22

23 24

22. Very early sod house with vegetation on the roof. (Denver Public Library, Western History Department.)

23. Holon Godfrey, proprietor of Godfrey's Store on South Platte Trail. (Overland Trail Museum, Sterling, Colorado.)

24. Matilda Godfrey, wife of Holon Godfrey. (Overland Trail Museum.)

25. Godfrey's Store (called Fort Wicked by its owner) as shown in *Harper's Weekly* of October 13, 1866.

25

26

PIKE'S PEAK

27

ROCKY MTN NEWS OFFICE.
EXPRESS OFFICE
INDIAN VILLAGE BLAKE ST.

28

26. This wood engraving of the Pike's Peak gold rushers was published in Harper's Weekly Magazine of August 12, 1859. (Denver Public Library, Western History Department.)

27. Arapahoe village in Denver, 1859. From Albert Richardson, *Beyond the Mississippi*, published by American Publishing Co., Hartford, Conn., 1867. (Denver Public Library, Western History Department.)

28. Little Raven visits Albert Richardson. Also from Albert Richardson, *Beyond the Mississippi*. (Denver Public Library, Western History Department.)

29. Major John Milton Chivington of the First Regiment of Colorado Volunteers in the Civil War. (Colorado Historical Society.)

29

30

31

32

30. Mouth of Apache Canyon facing east. Photographed summer, 1955. (Colorado Historical Society.)

31. Main building and corral at Johnson's Ranch where Confederate encampment and wagon train were destroyed by Major Chivington's detachment. (Colorado Historical Society.)

32. Territorial Governor William Gilpin. (Colorado Historical Society.)

33. Ad for Ben Holliday's Overland Stage as it appeared regularly in the *Rocky Mountain News*. (Denver Public Library, Western History Department.)

34. Stagecoach which is believed to have been used at one time on the Overland Trail. (Denver Public Library, Western History Department.)

35. Ben Holliday. (Denver Public Library, Western History Department.)

TRANSPORTATION.

33

The Overland Stage Line,

BEN HOLLIDAY, Prop'r.

CARRYING THE GREAT THROUGH MAIL BETWEEN THE

Atlantic and Pacific States,

THIS LINE is now running its Daily Coaches to and from Atchison, Kansas, and Placerville, California, through the City of Denver.

Coaches for Salt Lake, Carson Valley, and California, leave every morning at eight o'clock.

Coaches for Atchison leave every morning at eight o'clock.

Quick time, and every convenience afforded to passengers.

A Treasure and Freight Express carried weekly between Denver and Atchison, in charge of the most competent and trustworthy messengers.

The Express leaves Denver every Tuesday morning, and secures to shipments certainty, security, and celerity.

This Line also runs Daily Coaches, carrying Passengers, Mails, and Express matter between Denver and the Gregory Gold Regions.

Coaches for Central City leave every morning at seven o'clock.

Returning, leave Central City every morning at the same hour.

Close connections made to and from all points East, West, and in the Mines.

☞ THE ONLY DIRECT ROUTE TO—

Chicago,	Cleveland,	Baltimore,
Toledo	Cincinnati,	Washington,
Detroit,	Louisville,	New York,
Buffalo,	Pittsburg,	Boston,

And all other principal cities in the United States and Canadas.

Through Tickets for sale at the office of the Overland Stage Line, Denver City, for all points east of the Missouri River.

Time to Atchison 6 days.

Time to Salt Lake City 5 days.

Time to Placerville 13 days.

Full particulars will be given at the office, under the Planter's House, in Denver, and at all other offices on the Line.

C. F. DAHLER, Agent.

may3dtf.

34

35

36

37

38

36. Indian Agent Samuel G. Colley, photographed in Washington with the Cheyenne and Arapahoe chiefs who made the trip to the nation's capitol in 1863. (British Museum.)

37. John Evans, Territorial Governor of Colorado. (Denver Public Library, Western History Department.)

38. Captain Jacob Downing. Reproduced from Wm. Clarke Whitford, *Colorado Volunteers in the Civil War,* published Denver: The State Historical and Natural History Society, 1906. (Colorado Historical Society.)

39. View of Battle Canyon facing southeast in the direction of Cedar Creek and the South Platte. This was the site of Downing's attack on the Indian camp May 3, 1864.

39

40

40. Bull Bear, prominent leader among the Cheyenne Dog Soldiers. (Smithsonian Institution, National Anthropological Archives.)

41. Engraving from photo of the Cheyenne and Arapahoe leaders who traveled with Wynkoop for the meeting with Governor Evans at Camp Weld, September 28, 1864. Reproduction from Louis Simonin, *The Rocky Mountain West in 1867*, translated by Wilson O. Clough, published by University of Nebraska Press, Lincoln, 1966. (Denver Public Library, Western History Department.)

41

42

43

42. Captain Nicholas O'Brien, 7th Ohio Cavalry, Commanding Officer at Camp Rankin. (Denver Public Library, Western History Department.)

43. Eugene Ware, 1866. As Lieutenant Ware of the 7th Ohio Cavalry, he was instrumental in establishing Camp Rankin near Julesburg. (Kansas State Historical Society, Topeka.)

44. Battleground at Sand Creek, facing northwest from site of tipis. Photo taken October, 1956. (Colorado Historical Society.)

45. Approach to Sand Creek battleground, facing southeast from site of tipis. Photo June 1931. (Colorado Historical Society.)

44

45

46

47

This is a drawing of the burning of Julesburg No. 1 made by an eye-witness of the scene, a soldier of the Colorado cavalry, Williams, February 2, 1865. This is the original Julesburg established as a trading post prior to 1859, probably in the thirties, by Jules Beni. The town was raided by the Indians who afterwards completed the affair by setting fire to the settlement. The town was then moved a few miles east; with the coming of the railroad, it was again moved north across the river to what is now Weir station, and again fove miles east to the present site.

46. Drawing from a sketchbook found at Summit Springs battleground in 1869. The camp which was captured at Summit Springs was that of a band of Cheyenne Dog Soldiers. This drawing seems to depict two soldiers being shot from their wagon. (Colorado Historical Society.)

47. Several drawings of the burning of Julesburg, February 2, 1865, were made by a soldier of the Colorado Cavalry named Williams. He was apparently with the wagon train at Burt's ranch since his viewpoint seems to be from the east. (Denver Public Library, Western History Department.)

48. Second view of destruction of Julesburg, also apparently sketched by Williams. Location of picture is unknown.

48

49. Photo of diorama of the final plan of Fort Morgan as reconstructed at the Fort Morgan Museum.

50. George Bent and his wife Magpie, niece of Black Kettle. Photo probably taken in 1867. (Colorado Historical Society.)

49

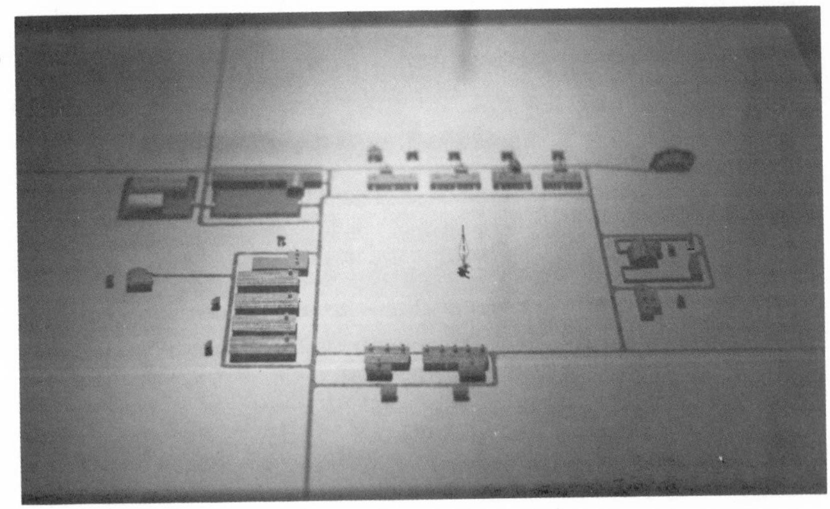

50

Chapter

7

Sowing the Seeds of Dissension

Perhaps if John Evans had been a lawyer rather than a medical doctor he would have been less impressed with the legality of the Treaties of Fort Laramie and Fort Wise. He actually believed that it was necessary for the Cheyennes and Arapahoes to relinquish their rights to the vast rectangle occupied by the High Plains, the South Platte Valley, and Denver City itself before the white man would be able to occupy the area rightfully. Furthermore, he confidently believed that he could persuade the Indians by one means or another to confine themselves to the Arkansas River reservation allotted to them.[1]

Appointed to the office of Governor of Colorado Territory, John Evans arrived with high spirits in Denver on May 16, 1862, by the Overland Stage. Evans was forty-eight years old. He was not hampered by the unrealistic expectations of youth, and neither was he motivated by the prospect of financial success; he was already a wealthy man. As a log-cabin child, the product of Quaker parents from a farm near Waynesville, Ohio, Evans was eventually educated at Cincinnati College, where he was graduated from the medical department in 1838. He served for a time as a staff doctor at Rush Medical College in Chicago, in which city he was able to accumulate a substantial fortune from real estate investments. In 1851, when Northwestern University was founded, Evans not only worked with the organization but contributed financially to its establishment. The town of Evanston, Illinois, was named for him.

As a supporter of Abraham Lincoln he earned the President's gratitude, and in appreciation Evans was offered the governorship of the

Territory of Washington, which he refused. When the President discovered that it would be necessary to replace Governor Gilpin in Colorado Territory, Evans was asked to succeed him.

If a man's motives are not apparent, history sometimes demands that they be examined; in John Evans's case, this has been done many times, and continues to be a challenge. He was an ardent supporter of the Methodist Episcopal Church, but he did not make a point of combining religion with politics. Since he was no longer driven by the need to make his fortune, avarice can be excluded. As an alternative, he has been condemned by some critics as an opportunist who intended to use the Colorado governor's chair as a rung of a ladder to the U. S. Senate, perhaps even the presidency. If this was his intention, the determined resistance of a handful of Cheyenne chieftains changed the course of his life.

In New Mexico, after the encounter with the Texans at Apache Canyon, John Chivington had been in command at Fort Craig on the Rio Grande for three months before he was relieved and allowed to return to Fort Union, where he left his troops and obtained a leave of absence to go to Washington. With victory still ringing in his ears, his greatest ambition at that time was to become involved in the greater activity of the Civil War. His reason for going to Washington ostensibly was to ask permission for the First Regiment to be transferred to a cavalry unit. He was granted the transfer to cavalry on November 1, 1862, but it was decided that the First Regiment of Colorado was needed more urgently in the Territory than in the South, especially since a second regiment was being recruited from Colorado Territory and the companies were being marched off to the States almost as soon as they were mustered in. By detachments, Chivington's men gradually were returned to Camp Weld near Denver in the late months of 1862, and after the first of the new year, Chivington found himself once again in Denver. He arrived with a flourish along streets lined with cheering spectators. A heroic Chivington, in company with Major Edward Wynkoop and other officers, led a procession down the streets of Denver City.[2]

The outfitting of the First Regiment with cavalry gear provided entertainment for the city for several weeks. When the Sharps rifles and sabers were distributed to the men there was such a dazzling display of flashing swords in the military camp that the citizens feared for the safety of their defenders. Befitting a beloved officer, Ned Wynkoop was presented with a magnificent sword by his subordinates, Captain J. R. Schaeffer and First Lieutenant H. H. Hines at a ceremonious dinner party in honor of the occasion. The sword's scabbard was chased with gold and engraved with the names of the donors.

The new mounts of the cavalry men were as resilient as their blades, and just as difficult to control. On the fifth of February, Colonel Chivington's horse became restless on the way to Camp Weld. It started to "leap violently" until it fell heavily on its side, catching the Colonel's foot in the stirrup to some extent before the strap broke. Ned Wynkoop provided even more of a show as he rode his handsome new black horse in a funeral procession. As the horses approached the Larimer Street bridge, his animal was unnerved by the sound of clattering hoofs on the wooden planks. The horse reared and charged back along the street until he finally raised himself so high that he fell backward with his full weight on the Major. Although Ned was temporarily injured, he managed to hold the frightened animal until help came.[3]

Governor Evans and John Chivington readily became friends. They were both deeply involved in the administration of the Methodist Episcopal church and necessarily they became closely associated. The two men were sufficiently well acquainted by November of 1862 that when Evans hired a private coach to bring his family from the States, the Governor invited the Denver pastor's wife and John Chivington to accompany the Evans family on the long trip from the Missouri River to Denver. In addition, similar political inclinations concerning statehood for the Territory brought them closer together. Their conversations must have been private, since there is almost no remaining correspondence between them from which to obtain an idea of the manner in which they may have influenced one another's opinions. However it may be concluded that they shared one view: they both regarded the Indians as an obstruction in the path of progress.[4]

Early in his administration the possibility of an Indian uprising troubled Evans, but the return of the First Regiment with Chivington in late 1862 gave the Governor a measure of security. He wrote in his report to the Commissioner of Indian Affairs, ". . . now that the War Department has ordered the Colorado troops home, and mounted one regiment, giving us ample military protection, we have little but danger to apprehend from Indian hostilities, for like that of other people the disposition of the Indian to go to war is greatly modified by the strength and preparation of his antagonist." Of the primary goals that faced Evans in January of 1863, two of them concerned the Indians: one was to stop the fighting between the Plains Indians and the Utes, and the other was to obtain the consent of the Arapahoes and Cheyennes to be removed to the Arkansas River reservation and remain there. These objectives represented a formidable undertaking.[5]

One of the conditions of the signing of the Fort Wise Treaty had been the promise that a number of Indian chiefs would be sent to Washington to meet the President. Believing that it might help his cause to impress a few influential chiefs with the power and force of the U. S.

Government, Evans encouraged the project, and arrangements were made for its accomplishment in early 1863. Indian Agent Samuel Colley of the Upper Arkansas Agency assembled representatives from the Arapahoes and Cheyennes, but except for Lean Bear, who was already a confirmed pacifist, they were not the real leaders of the tribes.

The Ute chiefs from the Rocky Mountains were treated with considerably more ceremony. With a military escort under Captain George Sanborn, they arrived in Denver on February 19, all of them painted in joyous colors. They were lined up at the photographers to have their picture taken and then installed at Camp Weld until their party was ready to leave for the States. Since they would be passing through enemy country, it would be necessary to provide an impressive escort for them in the country of the Cheyennes and the Pawnees, so on February 26 they began their journey, protected by Company H under Sanborn and Company D under Captain Bonesteel. In mid-April the chiefs were reported to be enjoying themselves hugely in Washington, being courted and feted like foreign ambassadors. Still colorful and festive, they returned like world travelers on July 2, accompanied by the same military escort.[6]

In March of 1863 a bold raiding party of Cheyennes paused on the way to the mountains long enough to rob some settlers at the mouth of the Cache la Poudre. The Indians casually forced entry into several houses and took as many provisions as they could carry, but they harmed no one. After the settlers complained, troops were sent out from Camp Weld under Captain Samuel Logan and Lieutenant G. W. Hawkins, who proceeded to the junction of the two rivers, the Poudre and the South Platte; from there Hawkins was sent down the South Platte with twenty men. Three days and seventy-five miles later, he found a village of twenty-one lodges of northern Cheyennes on Bijou Creek. Justifiably, the chief of the village protested the accusation of theft but suggested to Hawkins that other chiefs farther upstream might be guilty. Abandoning the fruitless search, Hawkins returned to camp with his tired men and hungry horses. After this incident Chivington sent troops to the area to prevent a recurrence and also to protect the stage line; one company of calvarymen went to Camp Collins and another to a point seventy miles from Denver on the South Platte.[7]

Major John Loree, the Indian Agent of the Upper Platte Agency, came into Denver in May bringing his suspicions that there would be an Indian War based on the grumbling and dissatisfaction of the northern tribes about the Treaty of Fort Wise. Loree reported that he believed negotiations were going on between the Arapahoes, Cheyennes and Sioux for possible warfare. Evans drafted a plan for a Council Committee composed of the Indian Agents and himself for the purpose of reconciling the Indians to the Treaty of Fort Wise and to make an effort to settle the tribes on the reservation. Evans sent Loree on April 10 to present the plan to Commissioner of Indian Affairs, William P. Dole, in person.

A large gathering of Arapahoes, probably including Friday and Left Hand, chiefs who were both staunchly cooperative, was camped near Fremont's Orchard. Directly after Loree's departure, Evans sent to this camp asking for a group of chiefs to visit with him in Denver. Several chiefs and headmen came and confirmed that there had been talks between the tribes regarding war and that another council was planned for the first of May on Horse Creek. Evans told the chiefs to circulate a threat that if the tribes went to war, it would result in a war of extermination for the Indians. On June 15, when Chivington and his escort passed along the Cache la Poudre they found Friday's Arapahoe camp peaceful as usual. Friday was a protegé of Thomas Fitzpatrick, who had sent the Arapahoe chief to St. Louis to be educated, and as a result the chief was strongly sympathetic with the whites. Chief Friday told the soldiers that the Sioux were planning to fight but that the Arapahoes had refused to join them.[8]

Loree returned in June with Commissioner Dole's permission to meet in council with the Indians. He had received a document naming himself, Samuel G. Colley of the Upper Arkansas Agency, and Governor Evans as special commissioners. The next step in the plan for the council was to inform and assemble the Indians, which was probably the most difficult part of the undertaking. Samuel Colley was instructed to accumulate the tribes who frequented the Arkansas Valley. A squawman, Antoine Janisse, was sent to the Yellowstone River country to summon far-wandering bands of Cheyennes. Loree returned to his agency and offered a new agreement to the local families of Indians for their signatures. This agreement stated that the Cheyennes and the Arapahoes of the triangle between the two branches of the Platte would abide by the Fort Wise Treaty and that they had been notified that another treaty was pending. The paper was signed (by mark, not by signature) by the compliant Friday and two other Arapahoes, Black Bear and Roman Nose. For the Cheyennes, two chiefs signed, Shield and Spotted Horse. No presents were given by the Indian Agent to obtain the signatures, except the regular dole of annuities usually distributed at this time.[9]

The two Cheyenne chiefs who signed for Agent Loree were not important leaders. Shield was never again noticed by history, but star-crossed Spotted Horse was caught up in a maze of conflicts from which he never escaped. He was actually a chief among the Cheyennes, although it was said he was part Sioux. He must have been a well-to-do chieftain as well, because he claimed that he had owned a hundred ponies before the trouble began. But Spotted Horse spoke English, which indicated that he had been exposed to trading posts more than most Indians, and his loyalties to white or red may have been mixed since childhood. He does not seem to have been an idealist, it is likely that he was simply confused by events which puzzled minds greater than his.[10]

Elbridge Gerry had been in Governor Evans' employ for some time as a spy on the Indians. Gerry was probably proficient in several Indian languages—Cheyenne and Sioux from his two wives, and Arapahoe from the local tribes who traded at his store. It was said that he was well liked by all. Governor Evans, wisely informed of the men who could help him the most, sent for Gerry in July and instructed him to find the main body of Cheyennes of the Republican River area and bring them to the place appointed for the conference.

On July 29, Gerry set out with a wagon full of provisions and presents drawn by a four-mule team with a driver named Edward Gansee. Gerry took one riding horse for scouting. It proved to be a very durable horse. From the best information he had been able to obtain, it seemed that the main body of the Cheyennes was near the headwaters of the Kansas River, but Gerry traveled up and down and back and forth for 600 miles before he found them, and then he could locate only 150 lodges near the head of the north fork of the Smoky Hill. Gerry was encouraged though, because these were the most independent bands of the Cheyennes, many of them members of the Dog Soldier Society, such as Long Chin, George Bent's uncle. Long Chin was also related to Gerry by marriage, since Long Chin was part Sioux and Gerry was married to one of Long Chin's Sioux nieces. Long Chin talked to Gerry and explained politely that the Cheyennes would be unable to meet the white chief from Denver because they were starting the fall hunt and the tribe was dispersing into small bands to fatten their ponies. In spite of the apparent dismissal, Gerry believed that he had persuaded at least some of the Cheyennes to meet with the Governor, so Gerry traveled north to meet the commission.

It was nearing the last of August when Agent Colley wrote Fort Lyon that the tribes in that area said they would not be able to attend the great conference because of adverse traveling conditions: thin horses, poor grass, inadequate water supply and so forth. In the north, Antoine Janisse was held up by illness and his mission was not completed. The small group who met Gerry at Julesburg was not impressive. Governor Evans was undoubtedly escorted by a body of soldiers, and there may have been a few random Indian headmen, but Agent Loree was accompanied by one lone chief—Spotted Horse. Friday, the Arapahoe, had promised to come but never arrived. Gerry guided the group to the junction of the Arickaree and Cherry Creek (South Fork of the Republican), where he met a family of four lodges of Cheyennes who assured him that a delegation from the main village was coming to the council grounds.

On the sixth of October Gerry was retracing his steps back and forth up Beaver Creek to the place where he had planned to meet the Cheyennes, but there was no one there. Finally he followed the Creek until he found the main camp, now numbering 240 lodges. Gerry soon discovered that the Cheyennes had no intention of attending the Treaty Commission's conference. Reluctantly the principal chiefs of this congregation gathered together to talk with Gerry. They had many speeches prepared for him. Of the chiefs and warriors who attended, Gerry noted Bull Bear, Crooked Neck, Little Robe, Tall Bull, White Horse, Long Chin, Two Wolfs, Sitting Bear and White Antelope. Black Kettle was in the village but was absent from the meeting. Long Chin was of the older generation of the Dog Soldier Society, but Bull Bear and Tall Bull were the emerging leaders.

This was an influential selection who met that day with Elbridge Gerry, and Gerry reported a number of reasons why the Cheyennes chose not to meet with the commission. They said thirty-five children in the village had recently died of whooping cough and diarrhea. In addition to their grief was the technical matter of the validity of the Treaty of Fort Wise: the men who had signed it had not known what they were signing. White Antelope and Black Kettle denied having signed it at all.

Someone of the group brought up a well-gnawed bone of contention concerning a drunken Cheyenne at Fort Larned who had been shot by a terrified sentry. The speaker said that the hands of the white man were dripping with blood—even though it had been agreed by the Cheyennes that the soldier's action was justified.

When Gerry threatened the loss of annuity presents and the danger of a railroad passing through the center of the hunting grounds, the Cheyennes replied defiantly that their food supply was assured. The buffalo would be plentiful for a hundred years more, and as far as the railroad was concerned, let them build it—but the Cheyennes would not allow settlements along the tracks.

Finally one of the more conciliatory chiefs assured Gerry that the Cheyennes would be glad to see the commissioners—sometime—and that they wished to remain friendly, but they would not sign a treaty until all of the clans had been consulted.[11]

During the conference, when Gerry was trying to explain the concept of a reservation to the circle of leaders, Bull Bear, an aggressive warrior, questioned the restrictions that might be imposed. What might this life be like, he wondered. Gerry explained about the farms, the houses and the schools.

"Do you mean they want us to live like white people?" Bull Bear asked.

Gerry answered with enthusiastic qualifications; "Yes, that's what [they] want and [they] will give you every assistance that you want, to make it comfortable. . . ."

Bull Bear shook his head and replied, "You can just go back to the governor and tell him we are not reduced quite that low yet."

Gerry then took another direction in the seduction of Bull Bear. He promised a very special horse as a reward if the chief would consent to go to the conference. Bull Bear succumbed and agreed to accompany Gerry to the council grounds, but a thunderclap of protest arose from the chieftains. Sheepishly, Bull Bear declined the invitation. Gerry had no choice. He returned to the Arickaree Fork alone.

Burning with frustration and disappointment, Evans and the commission turned the wagons, heavy with presents, and drove them back to Denver. Not quite sure what to do about the one faithful chieftain, Spotted Horse, Gerry allowed him to tag along. Spotted Horse told Gerry that the northern Cheyennes were very angry because Spotted Horse had signed Loree's agreement, and the word had gone out from Little Crow, a northern leader, that Spotted Horse would be punished. Even though it would mean that his pony herd must be sacrificed, Spotted Horse thought it best not to return to his people. Gerry allowed him to stay in the compound at Crow Creek.[12]

After the failure with the Cheyennes, Evans's chagrin was alleviated by a successful treaty concluded in October with over a thousand Tabequache Utes. Initiated by a Treaty Commission which consisted of Evans, Secretary Nicolay from Washington, Indian Agents Simeon Whiteley and Lafeyette Head, and Superintendent of Indian Affairs Mathew Steck of New Mexico, a reservation was set aside for the Utes in the upper part of the San Luis Valley and on the headwaters of the Rio Grande del Norte. In exchange for this the Utes relinquished the central part of the Rocky Mountains including the entire gold-mining area, a cession of land equal to one third of Colorado Territory. The Utes, however, declined to learn the practice of agriculture.

Near the first of November a party of Arapahoe Indians raided the ranch of Isaac P. Van Wormer of Box Elder Creek, about thirty miles east of Denver City. Van Wormer lived in the city, and the one hired man who lived at the ranch escaped. The house was ransacked, provisions taken and nineteen horses driven off. Another horse was taken from a nearby ranch, and several which belonged to a Mr. Sprague, a liveryman in Denver, also disappeared. Van Wormer and Sprague went in pursuit of the Arapahoes. Some of the horses were recovered with the help of a squawman named Robert North who lived among the Arapahoes. A cavalry detachment was requested and a fruitless search was made for the remaining animals.[13]

Governor Evans sent for the guilty Arapahoes, and their leaders obediently came into his office. He chastised them and told them they must give up the horses or make recompense. Robert North accompanied the Arapahoes on this visit and was brought to the attention of the Governor during the conversation. Apparently Evans indicated that he was interested in information and that he sometimes paid the informant.

Within days North sent word that he had information. Evans sent for him and North, who could not read or write, dictated a statement which provided an often-quoted document intended to prove the existence of war plans among most of the Indian tribes of the Plains. North said that he had recently been honored by a medicine dance because he had rescued an Arapahoe squaw from the Utes. The medicine dance took place on the Arkansas River below Fort Lyon and a number of principal chiefs attended. North said that he heard the chiefs discussing means of obtaining ammunition and making plans for attacking the settlements in the spring. North testified that he had heard that the "Comanches, Apaches, Kiowas, northern Arapahoes, all Cheyennes and the Sioux had pledged to go to war with the whites as soon as they can procure ammunition in the spring." Evans sent copies of the statement to the Commissioner of Indian Affairs and Secretary of War Stanton requesting military aid, authorization for militia aid, and more troops to protect the major roads.[14]

In the same month Governor Evans had a meeting with the South Platte Arapahoes, and during this council Roman Nose, the northern Arapaho who had signed Loree's agreement in August, told the Governor that the Arapahoes would never move to the Arkansas River reservation and they they would not attend another council unless a new and more suitable location for a reservation was found. Evans made a trip to Washington in December, asking for authorization to hold another treaty council for the purpose of assigning a different area of reservation for the Cheyennes and Arapahoes. Apparently nothing was accomplished by this request.[15]

It was a bad winter for the Indians; there had been a major drought, the Arkansas River was nearly dried up and there was no game. The government was feeding the Indians inadequately, and they had no other food supply. Spotted Horse collected his annuities with the Sioux that winter.[16]

The conflict was renewed the following year on April 5 when 175 oxen disappeared from Bijou Basin, a lush temperate haven for winter grazing. The cattle belonged to Irwin and Jackman, longtime freighters who hauled for the government, and the stock was pastured out for the inclement winter months to fatten them for the spring haul. The herders reported the missing animals and said that the Indians had taken them. According to Colonel Chivington's report, the Indians were trailed for fifteen miles, until they left Bijou Creek and turned eastward. Chafed by boredom, Chivington sent a company of artillery and a company of cavalry under Lieutenant George S. Eayre in pursuit with orders to either recover the stock or chastise the Indians if they refused to give the cattle up. Eayre proceeded east. He burned a Cheyenne village after the inmates had escaped and he located along the way a mere nineteen cattle which the herder identified as belonging to the Irwin-Jackman stock. Since Eayre's heavy wagons were causing him a great deal of vexation, he returned to Camp Weld. He intended to obtain better transportation and undertake another campaign, but smaller wagons were not readily available.[17]

Early in the spring of 1864 the northern Cheyennes sent a runner to the Dog Soldier camp on Beaver Creek informing them that during the previous summer the Crows had killed a noted Cheyenne named Brave Wolf, and now that the customary period of mourning had elapsed the Cheyennes were going out after the Crows to avenge the killing. Any southern Cheyennes who wished to join the war party were welcome.

Little Chief was still alive in 1906, and at George Bent's request dictated his story, somewhat clouded by the forty-two-year interval. From the Dog Soldier camp that spring, Little Chief, Bull-Telling-Tales, Mad Wolf, Wolf-Coming-Out, Bear Man and ten other young men started north. They were well armed; they had been collecting rifles, pistols and ammunition all winter. As they came near the South Platte they found four unattended mules, which they appropriated as strays. The Dog Soldiers went into camp on the river bank that night, where they were overtaken by a rancher named W. D. Ripley who claimed the mules and demanded their return. Not well known for their diplomacy, the Dog Soldiers defied him. Bull-Telling-Tales insisted that he receive pay for the return of the animals and that Ripley bring some suitable compensation.[18]

On January first a military camp had been set up seven miles above Fremont's Orchard by Captain George L. Sanborn of the First Colorado Cavalry. The post was called Camp Sanborn. Ripley rode directly to this camp and reported that the Indians had stolen stock from him. On the morning of the twelfth of April Sanborn sent Lieutenant Clark Dunn with forty men, Ripley serving as a guide, to follow the Indians. Since Gerry was on Beaver Creek trading with the Dog Soldiers, there was no one to interpret for Dunn except Spotted Horse, who was summoned and sent with the troops. Sanborn ordered Dunn "to recover the stock, also to take from them [the Indians] their firearms and bring the depredators to this camp"—an unreasonable task which proved to be said more easily than done.[19]

Dunn divided his command and sent half of them directly to Bijou Ranch with Ripley while Dunn and his cavalrymen searched the sand hills on the south side of the Platte. About two o'clock in the afternoon the two companies were reunited and about three o'clock discovered an Indian trail going northwesterly toward the river. As Dunn followed the trail the men noticed a smoke column on the right, and Dunn again divided the command and sent one company to investigate the smoke. As Dunn and his cavalrymen came out of the sand hills at about four o'clock, two parties of Indians could be seen near the river. Dunn reported that one party was driving a small herd of stock toward the hills on the opposite bank, while another party of about thirty Indians was still crossing the river.

There had been very little water in the hills, and Dunn's horses had traveled about seventy-miles, so he paused to let the men and animals drink while he sent Ripley and one soldier ahead to look at the stock which the Indians were driving. Ripley returned and claimed that not only was his stock in the herd but he also recognized the Indians as the thieves who had taken the animals. The soldier reported that the Indians were forming a line and were loading their rifles.

Dunn ordered a gallop to open ground, where he found a line of Indians waiting for him. Another group was still driving the horses and mules away into the hills. Dunn followed the stock, but when he saw that the waiting Indians likewise started riding in the same direction, Dunn wheeled to face them. Dunn sent four men and Ripley to follow the stock.

Unfortunately Dunn had no interpreter with him. Spotted Horse was with the detachment sent down the river to investigate the smoke. Dunn faced the Indians without even a basic vocabulary of sign language with which to communicate. Dunn wrote two versions of events which followed. In one story Dunn said that he dismounted and walked alone toward the line of Indians; in the other, he said he rode 150 yards ahead of his companions and requested that one or two of the Indians come to talk with him. In the first version Dunn said that he requested from their chief that the Indians return the stock but the chief replied with a scornful laugh. In the second account Dunn said that the Indians did not reply but continued to ride toward him with their bows strung and rifles in their hands. Dunn's men called out to him to come back, which he did, and discovered that his men had their pistols drawn. Dunn claimed that he ordered his men to return their pistols to their holsters. He told them that when the Indians were about six feet away, they were to dismount and take the weapons away from the Indians. When the men were dismounted the Indians began to fire on them, Dunn reported. Dunn ordered his men to remount and commence firing. They were armed with 36-caliber Whitney pistols, besides their calvary sabers.[20]

There is another report of the encounter told to Captain Sanborn by an eyewitness, which has a strong sense of credibility. The soldier said that, ". . .after a hard ride they [Dunn's company] came up with a party of some fifteen or twenty Indians who on seeing the soldiers approach, drew up in line of battle and made all preparations for a fight but sent forward one of their party to shake hands and at the same time began to drive the stock back into the bluffs. They soon all came up and wished to shake hands. Lt. Dunn then demanded the stock and commenced disarming the Indians when they turned and ran, turning and firing, wounding four of Lt. Dunn's party."[21]

As Little Chief remembered it, the Dog Soldier party saw fifteen or twenty soldiers galloping toward them. The Indians mounted their war horses and turned towards the soldiers with pistols and bows in their hands. Mad Wolf and Wolf-Coming-Out were still on the ground, not having mounted their horses yet, when the soldiers commenced firing at them. Little Chief had his rifle across his saddle in front of him, but he turned his horse around and started to run away. Mad Wolf called out that the Indians should stay and fight. The Indians faced the soldiers and began to fire at them with guns and arrows.

One of the soldiers, whom the Indians thought to be an officer, rode toward Bull-Telling-Tales, who was on foot in the rear of the party of Indians. Believing that the soldier intended to take his arms, Bull-Telling-Tales shot the soldier with an arrow, and the soldier fell off his horse at the Dog Soldier's feet. Bull-Telling-Tales, confident that the soldier was dead, removed his coat, his watch and field glasses. After this, the soldiers stampeded. Another soldier was shot and fell from his horse. The troops were now in retreat and Little Chief said that someone called out to stop.

The Cheyennes had three braves wounded; Bear Man who had been in the thick of the battle among the soldiers was wounded twice in the body, Mad Wolf was wounded in the hip, Wolf-Coming-Out was wounded in the leg. The Dog Soldiers retired from the field.[22]

Dunn wrote that the party of Indians facing him was originally about twenty-five strong and was reinforced soon after with about twenty. Shortly after, Dunn's company of fifteen men was joined from down river by the detachment of about twenty men. Ripley and the four soldiers abandoned the chase after the stock and returned also. With customary exaggeration, Dunn reported that the battle lasted from one-half to three-quarters of an hour, that eight or ten Indians were killed and twelve or fifteen wounded. Dunn said that his command followed the Indians for about sixteen miles but darkness and a storm made the pursuit impractical so the soldiers returned to camp.[23]

In an official capacity as Assistant Inspector General, Major Jacob Downing was at Camp Sanborn when Lieutenant Dunn came in after the engagement. Downing listened to Dunn's story then almost immediately left for Denver to confer with Chivington. It is apparent that Lieutenant Dunn was advised not to write his report of the encounter until he received further instructions. What happened at Fremont's Orchard must have been potentially damaging in a political way, or at least embarrassing, and when Downing and Chivington had talked over the matter they concocted an implausible story which was formally reported to Governor Evans on April 15. As Chivington described the crucial actions which fixed responsibility for the fight: ". . . Lt. Dunn dismounted and advanced about 200 yards and met the chief of the band of whom he demanded the stock, but the chief informed him he would fight him before he would give it up. The lieutenant told him that if they did not stop running it off he would have to disarm them. To do which the chief defied him and giving the signal, the Indians opened fire on the troops. The troops returned the fire. The fight lasted about one hour when the Indians began to give way. Lt. Dunn followed up and a running fight ensued for about fifteen miles when, owing to the tired condition of his horses, the lieutenant ceased the pursuit and returned to Camp Sanborn, now about ten or twelve miles distant."[24]

Having decided on their course of action, Chivington appointed Major Downing as Commanding Officer of Camp Sanborn on April 16. Downing arrived at the camp on the afternoon of the eighteenth. Also on the eighteenth, Lieutenant Dunn wrote his long-delayed report of the battle. It agreed substantially with the description written by Chivington.[25]

Little Chief said that after the fight at Fremont's Orchard the Dog Soldier party started back to the main village on Beaver Creek, but with three badly wounded warriors it must have been necessary to camp for a time in the neighborhood to provide time for partial healing. There were Indian raiders present on the South Platte for several days, and it was very likely that they were the idle Dog Soldiers.

Before the eighteenth of April Lieutenant Dunn had been well occupied chasing the Indians. On the morning of April 13, with Lieutenant George H. Chase and Gerry as a guide, Dunn and his men set out with four days rations to find Indians, but the weather turned for the worse, snowing and blowing so that the trail was obliterated. At sunset, after about sixty miles of travel, Dunn and Chase returned to camp.[26]

A surgeon for the wounded men was requested from Denver, and Dr. Lewis C. Tolles, Assistant Surgeon of the First Regiment, was sent to Camp Sanborn with medical stores for their care. Captain Sanborn reported that he had one soldier, named J. B. Brandly, with an arrowhead in his back; A. J. Baird had an arrowhead in the right shoulder. John Crosby had been wounded by a pistol ball in his arm which was broken between the shoulder and elbow. Brandly died on the morning of the fifteenth and Baird in the afternoon; the other two men recovered.[27]

It was important to the command at Camp Weld to establish without a doubt that the antagonists at Fremont's Orchard had been Cheyenne Indians. A report was requested from Elbridge Gerry in writing on the activities of local Indians. He said that two lodges of northern Cheyennes had come in from the North Platte and they knew nothing about Dunn's adversary. Three southern Cheyennes had come from the main village on Beaver Creek to trade with Gerry. They claimed that no war party had left the village. Ten lodges of Sioux were camped at the mouth of Beaver Creek and thirty lodges were near Valley Station.

Everyone in the area knew that the Indians involved in the Fremont's Orchard fight had been Cheyenne. The lances and arrows left on the battlefield were identified by local traders as being of Cheyenne design and the implements were sent by wagon to Chivington, who had them examined again. Chivington informed the Assistant Adjutant General at Fort Leavenworth that the weapons definitely belonged to Cheyennes.[28]

There was great confusion in Denver. Whether the Dog Soldiers had actually cut the telegraph wires before April 12 or whether they were down from natural causes is not certain, but the results were the same. Newspaper stories of the battle were widely diverse. One story reportedly came from a stage passenger, another from a messenger who came to summon Surgeon Tolles. The telegraph remained down until the fifteenth, when it was repaired by the Denver stage agent Matt France, but it was down again by the twentieth. Consequently the events of the week were often telescoped in the dispatches, making them difficult to separate.

On the fifteenth the *Black Hawk Mining Journal* printed a hysterical story. "Valley Station, April 13th. Four men were killed by a band of Sioux, twelve miles back of Beaver Creek Station yesterday P.M. A general rising of Indians anticipated—people leaving valley of the Platte with families and stock." There was no foundation for this story. The fighting occurred on the previous day in the afternoon, but the four wounded men were still alive on the thirteenth. It was true that the ranchers were terrified and there were angry Cheyenne warriors in the neighborhood thieving and killing.

Scouts of Captain Sanborn brought information that on the fourteenth or before, the Indian participants in the battle had returned, taken a herd of cattle from a ranch, killed two herders, and wounded the owner, Bradley, in the neck with an arrow. Sam Ashcraft of the Junction Ranch said that on the thirteenth the Indians had driven off some of his stock and killed one of his men, evidently a herder. The *Rocky Mountain News* reported that a man from a train going east had been killed upstream from Beaver Creek on the fourteenth.[29]

Captain Sanborn dispatched Lieutenants Dunn and Chase with thirty men of Companies C and H at 12:01 A.M. on the fifteenth to "cross over to the Cut-Off and take the trail" at daylight. When dawn broke, the troops were at Bijou Creek; here they paused until 2:30 P.M. Dunn said that they then went to Dry Creek and finally to Bijou Ranch, where the stock had been stolen. They had picked up Sam (or Granville?) Ashcraft as a guide, and from there they followed the Indian trail. About noon they reached the ranch on Beaver Creek where the herders were supposed to have been killed and Bradley wounded. They found no signs of bodies or a "struggle." There was no one present, however. In the late afternoon the troops found about forty head of cattle, secured them, and continued along the creek in a southeasterly direction to its headwaters. It was now four o'clock in the morning of the sixteenth, and Ashcraft determined that the Indians must have continued on toward the Arkansas. The pursuit was abandoned.[30]

While Major Downing was conferring with Chivington in Denver in the middle of April, Downing proposed and asked permission to lead an expedition against the Indians. After what Downing called "considerable persuasion," Chivington agreed. Consequently, Downing was put in charge of two hundred men stationed at Camp Sanborn. He had orders to "give direction in person to the movements against the Indians and see that they are appropriately chastised for their outlawry."[31]

As soon as Major Downing arrived at Camp Sanborn on the eighteenth, he sent for Gerry and organized a reconnoitering party to go to the Junction on the nineteenth. He wrote to Chivington, "It is very difficult to get the truth of anything here without talking with the men. . . ." Downing intended to attack someone, preferably Cheyennes, and he said "As soon as I can satisfy myself as to what band these Indians belong I will be after them as I talked. . . . Shall I go into these Cheyennes on the Platte?"

Conveniently, on the evening of the eighteenth, a man came upriver from Beaver Creek for assistance from the soldiers. He arrived at Camp Sanborn about one A.M. on the nineteenth. He said that "the ranches on the Platte had been attacked and at [his] ranch every person had been driven away and their lives threatened." He also said that a party of Cheyennes had taken possession of a ranch called Morrison's [upstream on Beaver Creek] and were "despoiling property, getting drunk and raising the mischief generally." The *Rocky Mountain News* on the nineteenth told of telegraphic dispatches to the effect that the Indians had robbed and plundered at several ranches between Valley Station and Julesburg on the eighteenth. On the strength of the warning from the man at Beaver Creek, the down-going coach returned to Beaver Creek, where it remained until morning before proceeding.

An hour later, at two A.M., Major Downing left Camp Sanborn with Lieutenant Dunn, and sixty men, heading for Morrison's Ranch. Downing reported that he arrived at this ranch (which he called "Indian Ranch") about 1:00 P.M. on the nineteenth, his horses "almost jaded out." Downing wrote that it was true that all of the inhabitants had been driven away and their lives threatened. In addition he said that "The Indians have taken all they wanted." Downing said he had learned that the Indians had crossed the river going north at a point about four miles below Beaver Creek. "Every person with whom I have talked concurs in my opinion that they are Cheyennes," he said, "I intend to take the trail tonight as they only started this morning and hope to catch some of them."[32]

Downing had asked Gerry to guide him on this trip, but whether he actually did is not confirmed. Downing does not mention him by name. Downing said that on the arrival at Morrison's of his guide and some soldiers who preceded the command, the guide was informed that an Indian had been seen on a hill on the north side of the South Platte about seven miles distant from the troops. As soon as he arrived, Downing sent the guide and escort to investigate. They returned, reported that "they found a fresh trail, evidently made by three or four Indians, and after following it several miles the guide returned and informed [Downing] that he believed that they [the Indians] were going to the Indian camp about thirty miles distant on Dry Creek as the trail led in that direction." The guide said that there was only one place on the creek where the Indians could camp, and he believed that a party could reach them by daylight next morning. Starting at eight P.M. Downing and his men marched to Dry Creek, reaching the camp grounds at daylight. It was a disappointment; there were no signs of recent occupation.

From Dry Creek, which must have been the southern branch of Pawnee Creek, Downing continued to march toward Cedar Bluffs in the direction of Lodgepole Creek, but found nothing. If he had been able to continue to Cedar Bluffs he would have found a small Cheyenne village, but instead he turned west until he was nearly north of Camp Sanborn. Here he might have camped, since his men had been marching all night, but he was not able to graze his horses because he lacked ropes for pickets. He continued to Camp Sanborn, where his command arrived in the afternoon after marching 140 miles.

According to plan, Downing then divided his men. Lieutenant Chase with twenty-five men was sent to Murray's Ranch (seven miles below the Junction) with orders to keep his soldiers concealed. Lieutenant Dunn was dispatched with thirty men to Moore and Kelly's Ranch (twenty-seven miles below the Junction). Both officers were cautioned to send scouts only at night and to keep themselves hidden at all times. Downing then stationed another detachment at the Junction, which he planned to use as temporary headquarters for his expedition against the Cheyennes. Before leaving Camp Sanborn on the new search, Downing learned that a few lodges of Dog Soldiers were camped at Gerry's. Downing instructed Captain Sanborn to tell Gerry to send the Cheyennes away immediately and warn them that Downing intended to punish any of them that he found on the river for depredations committed by members of their tribe.[33]

There was not sufficient forage at Murray's for twenty-five horses so Lieutenant Chase's company moved down to Moore and Kelly's to join Lieutenant Dunn. Chase had arrived at this ranch just in time to learn that the Indians had stolen 800 dollars worth of horses from there. Dunn and Chase immediately set off toward the southeast in pursuit. Nothing was mentioned in their reports about finding the horses, but the Lieutenants did find a Cheyenne village so recently abandoned that nothing had been salvaged by the owners. Dunn and Chase burned eleven lodges complete with cooking utensils and implements. Two lodges contained a large number of buffalo robes, both dressed and undressed, which were appropriated by the soldiers.[34]

A messenger had been sent upriver to Downing by Lieutenant Dunn, but the messenger had taken a different route and Downing did not know of this incident until he reached the Junction on April 25. The news pleased him. Downing remained at the Junction long enough to make an excursion to Cedar Bluffs, but still he did not discover the Cheyenne village. Three days later, on May 1, he joined Dunn and Chase at Moore and Kelly's.[35]

Since Elbridge Gerry had been ordered to warn the Cheyennes that they would be punished if found on the river, it may have been for the purpose of warning them that Spotted Horse was in vicinity of Kelly's station. He probably assumed that he need not fear for his safety because he had been camped at Gerry's on Crow Creek for six months, and he claimed to have been with the soldiers at Fremont's Orchard. As

Spotted Horse rode by the station, Downing sent a squad of men to bring him in. Downing professed, in a letter to Chivington, that his first impulse was to kill the captive, but since Sam Ashcraft and some of the soldiers recognized Spotted Horse, his life was spared.

Since the Indian could speak English, Downing questioned him persistently about the location of the Cheyenne camp, but Spotted Horse refused to divulge the desired information. Both Ashcraft and Downing later wrote of imprisoning Spotted Horse overnight with the threat that if he did not capitulate by morning, he would be burned alive. When morning came, Spotted Horse remained silent. Downing claimed that he ordered his men to lead the former chief to a stake and to lay a ring of kindling around his feet. A fire was lighted and, as the first pain reached the Cheyenne's consciousness, he relented and agreed to lead Downing and his troops to a campground at Cedar Canyon.[36]

Leaving ten men at the Junction and a like number at the American Ranch to present a show of force for the protection of the road, Downing, with Dunn's assistance, assembled a force of forty men from Companies C and H for a five-day march to the north and west. The troops started about two P.M. on May second, marched about fifteen miles, then rested until ten. Downing usually based his strategy on night marches as the only possible way of accomplishing a surprise attack against Indians. At ten o'clock the troops started again and marched until six A.M., when they reached the area of the camp at Cedar Canyon. Spotted Horse had come this far as a guide, but now, according to the legend, he was forced to accompany the troops into battle. It is said he asked for a weapon to defend himself, and it was given to him.[37]

The canyon at Cedar Bluffs originates high on a rock-encrusted plateau where the spring once flowed from below a rock shelf into a depression which stretches parallel to the valley below. This depression is nearly hidden from view by the zigzag course of the erosion which descends through the canyon. There were only five lodges in the camp, and they must have been erected on the plateau where there was level land. While the Indians could not be seen from the valley below, neither could they see more than through a small area at the opening of the canyon. The family camped here was that of the aged headman, Bull Rib; his son, Lame Shawnee, a friend of George Bent's; and a tall strong warrior named Big Wolf. They were on their way north and were apparently unaware of the several recent incidents which had taken place on the South Platte.

On the morning of May third, the pony herd of the village was grazing in the valley in plain sight of Downing's soldiers as they approached. His first move was to separate the herd from the village. The boy herder was killed and another captured. Ten men were detailed to guard the ponies. Major Downing dismounted his thirty men, divided them into four companies, and after delegating the first company to hold the cavalry horses, Downing and Dunn with twenty-five men advanced into the canyon.[38]

Any Indians who were visible immediately scurried for cover. The women and children abandoned the camp to the northwest to hide in the rocks; without ponies the camp was helpless. Downing said that the canyon was naturally fortified, and it was; the sides of the declivity were laced with bony fingers of fallen rock which furnished an abundance of hiding places.

Early in the fighting Lame Shawnee shot a soldier with an arrow, and when he fell from his horse, Lame Shawnee ran out in the open, mashed the soldier's skull with his war club, and picked up the soldier's carbine, running back to the protection of the rocks without being hit. This may have been the one soldier killed in the battle: Isner of Company C. After Lame Shawnee was again in hiding, he used the rifle to shoot another of Downing's men, Wilcox of Company C, off his horse.[39]

Downing attempted to draw the Indians out of the rocks by skirmishing, without success. Downing reported that he "then directed his men to confine their efforts to killing as many Indians as possible, as though they had not yet attempted to do so. The Major wrote that after three hours the troops had "scarcely been able to get a man." The ammunition was running low, so Downing decided to return to the American Ranch with the captured horses. In the evening of the same day, May 3, the troops arrived at Moore and Kelly's. In proper military tradition, Downing claimed to have killed about twenty-five Indians and wounded thirty or forty more, but the Indians claimed that only two squaws and two children—probably the boy herders—were killed. It is doubtful that there were more than twenty-five people in the village if there were only five lodges as the Indians claimed. Downing increased the number of lodges to fifteen large ones and several small ones in his report. The Indians generally agreed that about one hundred horses were captured and, surprisingly, this was the amount which Downing said he had divided among his soldiers.[40]

After the soldiers marched away the Cheyennes were finally convinced that they were in danger, so they prepared to leave the camp. Since they had no horses for transportation, they rolled up all of their possessions and hid the bundles under the rock ledges of the ravine. They started westward across the plains on foot.[41]

Downing had requested artillery on or near April 25, and Chivington wired that two howitzers were being sent out with Captain McClain and his artillery company, who were on their way to the East; but when that officer arrived at the American Ranch, McClain said that he knew nothing about it and moved on. After Downing returned to Moore and Kelly's on the third of May, he continued to wait for the arrival of the artillery. He intended to go back to Cedar Bluffs as soon as he had guns to penetrate the canyon. On the ninth day of May he decided to march without the artillery, and taking eighty men, he left the American Ranch at two P.M., marched to "Moore and Chesby's" (the Washington Ranch) where the troops rested until six o'clock. From here the command marched overnight up Cedar Creek, reaching Cedar Canyon at daylight.[42]

There were no Indians there, but Downing claimed that he destroyed fourteen lodges with equipment, 130 saddles and a quantity of dried meat. No doubt this was all dragged out from the hiding places in the rocks. On his return trip Downing met a large encampment of Sioux. The Sioux told Downing that they had been asked for assistance by the Cheyennes but had refused. The Sioux said that the main body of people from Cedar Canyon had gone toward the north, but that a war party of about twenty-five Cheyennes had turned toward the South Platte to steal horses.

After two hours rest, Downing set off for the river in an attempt to avert the horse-stealing raid. He reported that he reached the river about eight o'clock on the evening of the tenth and learned that Indians had been seen in the afternoon. He sent out patrols and returned to the American Ranch. Downing intended to send Lieutenant Chase with his company to Camp Sanborn and Lieutenant Murrell (a recent arrival) with his detachment to Junction Station as soon as the men were rested, but on receipt of a message sent by Chivington on May 7, instructing Downing to gradually withdraw his men from the South Platte, no orders were given. On May 11 all of Downing's men except the patrols were still at Moore and Kelly's.[43]

On that day the telegraph operator from Junction told the *Rocky Mountain News* that a man from a commissary train had been shot recently and two horses had been stolen from a stage station. Early on the twelfth the *News* thought the horses had been recaptured. Later in the day the operator sent a dispatch reporting that on the afternoon of May 11, one man from a government train had been killed near the Junction and two more men were killed out in the bluffs near Beaver Creek (nineteen miles below the Junction) while searching for lost cattle. One horse had been stolen from Valley Station on the twelfth and, furthermore, Indians had been "lurking in the bluffs between Junction and Beaver Creek all day on May eleventh," but by the following day they had disappeared. It would seem that the Cheyennes crossed the river on their way to the Arkansas while Downing and his soldiers rested at the American Ranch.[44]

His campaign apparently ended, Downing started for Denver on the morning of the twelfth of May to talk with Chivington. A disconsolate Spotted Horse accompanied him. The Cheyenne was supplied with an old army uniform and he rode silently and sadly to Camp Weld with the soldiers, where he remained. Perhaps troubled by conscience, Downing said that he became so uncomfortable in the presence of the tragic Indian that the Major gave him ten dollars and suggested that he should "seek other hunting grounds." Spotted Horse took the money and went back to Gerry's compound on Crow Creek.[45]

Chapter

8

The Ripening of Dragon's Teeth

Black Kettle was not a peaceful chieftain because he was a coward; on the contrary, he had been elected chief partly because he was a good warrior. Black Kettle was sixty-three years old when the war began with the whites in 1864. His days for fighting had passed long ago, but their memory was bright.

Before the summer of 1838, when the Cheyennes were at war with the southern tribes of Kiowas, Comanches and Apaches, Black Kettle had led several pony-stealing expeditions into the enemy country. In that year he led a party of scouts to find the camping place of the three tribes, and his discovery of their location was the determining factor of the Cheyenne victory at Wolf Creek. A tragic expedition against the Utes in 1849 may have been successful in other ways, but resulted in a great loss for Black Kettle. His handsome wife was thrown from her horse just ahead of the enemy in the Ute camp. She disappeared, never to be heard of again. Some time later Black Kettle married a woman from another tribal division called the Wotapio, a time-honored family of Sioux–Cheyenne intermarriages. According to custom, Black Kettle went to live with his wife's family, and when the chief of this band died in 1850, Black Kettle was elected chief. From this point his warrior days were over.

The traditional responsibility for the welfare of women, children and the aged, which the ruling chief automatically assumed, weighed heavily on Black Kettle's shoulders. He was henceforth committed to peace by tribal law, but his insistence on the pursuit of it was a personal dedication, supported by logical conclusions. His reputation was so well established that when he signed the Fort Wise Treaty in 1861, Albert Boone and the other officials placed too much emphasis on Black Kettle's influence on the corporate body of the Cheyenne nation. George Bent said that the Cheyennes were annoyed that such a small delegation as the six chiefs who signed this document could be thought to represent all of the Cheyenne people. At the time Black Kettle's prestige was not diminished, but as the rift widened between white and red man, the position of the "peace-chief" became more and more difficult to maintain.[1]

After his first raid, Lt. George Eayre had no intention of abandoning his pursuit of the Cheyennes when he returned to Denver for lighter transportation and supplies about April 23, 1864. With some difficulty he managed to outfit rapidly for another expedition. On the twenty-fifth he left Denver with eighty-four men, fifteen wagons and two howitzers. He marched deep into Cheyenne hunting grounds and wandered for almost three weeks, eventually coming to a point on the Smoky Hill fork where a large camp of Cheyennes had congregated.[2]

This camp had been assembling since news arrived of the recent conflicts with soldiers. About 100 lodges, including the Hill Band with which George Bent traveled, were there when the Dog Soldiers from Fremont's Orchard arrived. Crow Chief and Coon's families were both present, the victims of Eayre's first expedition. Most of their destroyed possessions had been replaced from the matter-of-fact generosity of the Cheyenne people for tribemen who had suffered adversity. Now, on the fifteenth day of May, the village had been further enlarged by worried bands of Cheyennes and Arapahoes from Ash Creek, near Fort Larned. Not far to the east from this camp was another large village of Brule Sioux on the Solomon River and for some time Lt. Eayre had been leading his men nonchalantly into and through the area between these powerful villages.

At dawn on the sixteenth George Eayre's disconnected column was discovered by Cheyenne hunters who were just leaving their camp. Eayre's command was marching casually; the cavalry was moving in front of four companies, the guarded artillery was in the center and the wagons brought up the rear without guards. A distance of one and a half miles separated the wagons and guns, while a mile's distance removed the cavalry from the guns.[4]

The Indian camp, having been warned by criers, came alive. Both Black Kettle and Lean Bear were in camp, but considering Lean Bear's past association with the whites it was accepted that he should do the talking with the white soldiers. Lean Bear had been to Washington in 1863, and besides the medal which President Lincoln had presented to him, he had papers to prove that he was a friendly Indian. Lean Bear and Black Kettle mounted their horses and, accompanied by an impressive number of warriors, rode out and waited on a nearby hill for the column to approach. Surprised, the soldiers drew up in line.

Little Chief, who had been at Fremont's Orchard, also took part in this fight, and he told George Bent that Lean Bear and his son Star rode toward the soldiers to shake hands. Ned Wynkoop (who was not present) said that he was told that a Sergeant named Fribley approached Lean Bear and conducted him back to the troops.[5]

From this point the stories conflict. The Cheyennes said that the soldiers opened fire. Lt. Eayre, Lt. A. W. Burton and Private Asbury Bird, all of whom may be quoted, claim that the Indians attacked first. Little Chief said that Eayre ordered the troops to fire when Lean Bear was twenty or thirty yards from the soldiers. In order to avoid making liars of everyone, one might expect that, considering the precipitate behavior of young impetuous Cheyennes and relative inexperience of the troopers, there may have been untimely shots and arrows from both sides. Little Chief said that his warriors were in a position to fire at the soldiers from their flank while the troops were still firing straight ahead. The Cheyennes did not reach this point by dawdling in their advance. Little Chief and his group shot two soldiers with arrows; the cavalrymen fell from their horses. At the first order to fire, Lean Bear and Star had been hit and slid to the ground. Little Chief said that the soldiers rode forward and shot the two Cheyennes while they lay helpless on the ground.[6]

The two howitzers were loaded and fired, and grape shot began to fall among the crowd of infuriated Indians, who were charging recklessly into the soldiers in small parties. Black Kettle rode up and started shouting to the Indians, ordering them to "Stop the fighting! Do not make war!" He was unable to make an impression at first, but when their blood began to cool the Cheyennes heard his cries and drew back, taking with them fifteen saddled and bridled cavalry horses. The soldiers left the field followed by a small group of determined warriors. Eayre withdrew his forces to Fort Larned.[7]

The report which Lt. Eayre sent by wire was brief. He said he had been attached by four hundred Cheyennes and, after a persistent fight of seven and one-half hours, succeeded in driving them from the field. The Indians lost three chiefs and twenty-five warriors killed, Eayre said. The wounded, Eayre admitted, he was unable to estimate. He reported his losses as four men killed and three wounded.[8]

From the Indians' viewpoint, three Indians were killed, including Lean Bear and Star, and some were wounded. Eayre did not mention losing the horses, but Wynkoop, who talked to Eayre later at Fort Lyon, reported that a number of horses were killed, wounded and stampeded during the fight. There was little discrepancy in the reports as to the number of Cheyennes in the battle. There were between four and five hundred present, both sides agreed. While Wynkoop was told that it was a "complete victory" for the whites, it was acknowledged among the Cheyennes that if Black Kettle had not stopped the fight, Eayre's command would have been hunted down to the last man. For the rest of the summer vengeful Cheyennes, raiding on the South Platte and the Santa Fe Trail, added imaginative butchery to their former practices of mischief, theft and killing.[9]

Black Kettle was at a loss to explain to his puzzled tribesmen why the soldiers had made the two attacks on their people in their home territory. He was as amazed as they were. He sent a runner to find William Bent.

The people of Denver were not interested in George Eayre's exploits on the plains. By the time the news reached Denver, the city was wringing out the mud and sand of the South Platte River and Cherry Creek, which had suddenly flooded on May 23. Buildings erected in the dry bed of Cherry Creek were demolished, including the city hall and the office of the *Rocky Mountain News.*

Major General Curtis, Commander of the Department of Kansas, which included all of the country traversed by the Overland Trail to South Pass, was no more concerned with the consequences of Eayre's skirmish than the people of Denver. Curtis was absorbed by the danger in which the Kansas frontier to the south was placed by the very real menace of Confederate General Sterling J. Price. Curtis created a new District of the Upper Arkansas and established two new forts, Fort Ellsworth on the western corner of the great bend of the Smoky Hill, and Fort Zarah on the northernmost bend of the Arkansas. In order to defend this line it was necessary to draw in troops from the north, and Colonel Chivington was instructed to concentrate all of his forces at Fort Lyon.

Chivington was delighted. He had watched the Second Regiment of Colorado Cavalry gathered together, trained and marched away to Missouri in 1863, and part of the First Regiment had gone to Kansas in the spring of '64 while Chivington and Downing were left to guard stagecoaches from infrequent Indian attacks. In spite of his political involvement in the Colorado statehood faction, this was not the way John Chivington wanted to sit out the war. He began to dream of a campaign into Texas against the Confederates there. Leaving behind two companies, Chivington arrived at Fort Lyon on June 11, 1864, and wrote to Curtis assuring him that the Colorado troops would be able to protect the upper Arkansas road from Indians and also make a campaign into Texas.[10]

The runner from Black Kettle found William Bent near Fort Lyon on his way to Westport. He had already talked with Eayre, whom he had met on the road as Eayre was traveling to Fort Lyon. Eayre had informed Bent about the fight and had claimed to have killed seventeen Cheyennes. Bent continued his journey until the messenger overtook him and asked him to meet with Black Kettle to explain the reason for the quarrelsome attitude of the whites. Bent postponed his journey and sent word that he would meet with Black Kettle on Coon Creek within a week. They met as planned, and Black Kettle protested that he did not want to fight. Could Bent help avoid further conflict? Bent asked him to keep his young men from committing depredations for twenty days to give Bent time to go to Fort Leavenworth and talk with General Curtis.

After leaving Coon Creek, Bent reflected and decided that rather than going to General Curtis, he would talk with Chivington at Fort Lyon. The following morning he met Chivington and told him of the conversation with Black Kettle. Chivington replied that "he was not authorized to make peace and that he was there on the warpath" (or words to that effect, Bent said).[11]

Before leaving Denver, Chivington had assured Governor Evans that he was confident that the Indians would not be troublesome on the South Platte. Evans was not so sure, he complained to Curtis, and suggested a bold plan. Since so many troops were concentrated on the Arkansas, Evans believed ". . . as the best protection to our settlement and the best economy to the government, that at least half of the regiment go up from the present place of rendezvous on the Arkansas River, which is not very far from the Indians' haunts on the Smoky Hill and Republican, and chastise them severly until they give up hostilities." One wonders how history might have been altered if Curtis had adopted this proposal.[12]

On June 7 at Moore and Kelly's American Ranch on the South Platte one hundred head of cattle and fifty horses were run off by raiders—Cheyennes and Sioux, reportedly. John Ford, the telegraph operator at Junction Station sent the message to the *Black Hawk Mining Journal.* Ford said that there was "no possible show to recover stock since troops have all been withdrawn from the road." He asked, "Where is Chivington and his bloodthirsty tigers?"[13]

On June 15 an indignant emigrant on his way from Kansas to California wrote to the District Commander of Colorado complaining about the lack of protection. Even [sic] Reynolds, the emigrant, told how his party of three families had been robbed on June ninth of all their stock, six horses and four mules, by Indians who came upon their camp at dusk and stampeded the animals. The party was left helpless on the prairie near Bijou Creek, sixty-five miles from Denver.[14]

On June 13 William Kelly of the American Ranch had been surprised by a party of Indians while hunting, and he felt the Governor should know about it. In words that were rhythmic with Irish lyricism, he wrote, "Dear Sir: Having finally become uneasy at the repeated presence of Indians near my place, I have thought it proper to inform you of the fact. I speak from personal observation as I have been disposed to think the principal part of the seeing of Indians, within three or four miles of here, the result of frightened imagination. So yesterday, I started off thinking to kill an antelope. When about three miles from home, suddenly saw about sixteen Indians riding furiously toward me. I immediately started for home, they pursuing and firing upon me repeatedly, but, having a good horse, I made my escape unharmed. . . ."[15]

Comparatively speaking, these incidents were insignificant; however, within the week, on June eleventh, not far from Denver an act of violence occurred—an event so grim that it demanded attention. Shortly after noon on Saturday, Nathan Hungate and a hired man named Miller were out looking for strayed stock which belonged to Isaac Van Wormer, their employer. As the pair approached a hill overlooking the valley of Box Elder Creek, they could see smoke rising from the ranch where they lived and where, just a few hours before, Hungate had taken leave of his wife, his four-year-old daughter and the baby. Hungate rode toward the house as fast as he could go while Miller headed for Denver to notify Van Wormer and obtain help.

When Van Wormer arrived at the ranch, the buildings were burned to the ground, there were bloodstains and signs of a struggle, but the Hungate family was not to be found. Van Wormer discovered that thirty of his horses and mules had been driven off and he no doubt went in pursuit. On the following day, with the help of neighbors, a search revealed the bodies of Mrs. Hungate and the children in the well. The throats of the children had been cut so savagely that the heads were nearly severed from the bodies. Mrs. Hungate had been brutally scalped and also raped. Johnson, a neighbor, helped Van Wormer extricate the bodies from the well and lay them in the wagon. A search was continued for Nathan Hungate.

In the meantime two freighters, J. S. Brown and Thomas Darrah, had been informed that forty or fifty of their mules, which had been grazing on Coal Creek, thirteen miles from Denver beside the Cut-Off Road, had been stampeded by Indians. In company with a hired man named Corbin, the freighters followed the trail in the direction of Box Elder Creek toward Van Wormer's ranch. As the freighters approached, they met Johnson who told them the gruesome story. Brown, Darrah and Corbin joined the search for Hungate. On the opposite side of the creek, they found him, his body "horribly mutilated and the scalp torn off." Van Wormer took the bodies into Denver and exhibited them in a shed on the edge of town.

Brown, Darrah and Corbin made a statement for Captain J. S. Maynard, Acting Adjutant General in Chivington's absence. In their statement the freighters identified the Indians as Cheyennes, but they did so totally without evidence. The culprits were later identified as northern Arapahoes. On June fifteenth Robert North made a statement in which he testified that he believed that the Arapahoe John Notnee, who had stolen Van Wormer's horses in November of 1863 and had been forced to return them, was the guilty party. North believed that this Indian had participated in the raid on the Hungates in retaliation against Van Wormer.[16]

Chivington sent Capt. Joseph C. Davidson with his company back to Denver and directed that Company C under Lt. Clark Dunn be ordered out from Denver to find the murderers. The officers were instructed not to "encumber your command with prisoner Indians," but none were found.[17]

The curious citizens of Denver who had strong stomachs went to view the bodies of the Hungate family; those who could not tolerate the sight listened to vivid descriptions and everyone talked about it emotionally. Fear and anger assumed panic proportions until the end of the week when a mob broke into the Army Ordnance storeroom to obtain arms. Lt. Charles Hawley, who was in charge of ordnance, was on the other side of the river, and the storeroom was being kept by a subordinate named Morgan. When Morgan refused to open the doors, the mob threatened to break the doors down. Captain John Wanless, the Provost Marshal, told Morgan to let the crowd in. Receipts were signed for some of the arms and ammunition but a large quantity simply disappeared.[18]

In the midst of the frenzy Governor Evans sent a telegram to Secretary of War E. M. Stanton, reporting the massacre and emphasizing the need for troops. "Should I call a regiment of 100-days men or muster in U. S. Service the militia?" he asked. When writing an urgent letter to General Curtis, Evans explained that the militia by itself was hampered by inadequate territorial laws for its subsistence or even for ordering its movements. To General Robert Mitchell, who was responsible for protecting the South Platte Trail, Evans sent the letter from William Kelly at the American Ranch which stated that the Indians were still in the area and greater protection was needed. Evans also sent statements from Robert North and another squawman both predicting that the worst was yet to come.[19]

Evans then issued a proclamation on June 27 to the Indians outlining a plan which he had formed for separating the friendly, amenable Indians from the hostiles. It read:

> "To the Friendly Indians of the Plains. Agents, interpreters and traders will inform the friendly Indians of the plains that some members of their tribe have gone to war with the white people. They steal stock and run it off, hoping to escape detection and punishment. In some instances, they have attacked and killed soldiers and murdered peaceable citizens. For this the great father is angry and will certainly hunt them out and punish them, but he does not want to injure those who remain friendly to the whites. He desires to protect and take care of them. For this purpose, I direct that all friendly Indians keep away from those who are at war and go to places of safety.
>
> Friendly Arapahoes and Cheyennes belonging to the Arkansas River will go to Major Colley, U. S. Indian Agent at Fort Lyon who will give them provisions and show them a place of safety.
>
> Friendly Kiowas and Comanches will go to Fort Larned where they will be cared for the same way.
>
> Friendly Sioux will go to their agent at Fort Laramie for direction.
>
> Friendly Arapahoes and Cheyennes of the Upper Platte will go to Camp Collins on the Cache la Poudre where they will be assigned a place of safety and provisions will be given them.
>
> The object of this is to prevent friendly Indians from being killed through mistake. None but those who intend to be friendly with the whites must come to these places. The families of those who have gone to war with the whites must be kept away from among the friendly Indians."[20]

When the proclamation was received by Agent Samuel Colley, he asked William Bent to find the tribes and interpret its meaning to them. Bent set out and found a concentration of the different tribes—Cheyennes, Arapahoes, Kiowas, Comanches and Apaches—near Fort Larned. Almost immediately after the talk with William Bent, when he explained the terms of Evans's proclamation, the Indians broke camp and moved northward. Black Kettle's band started north in late June or early July, and they soon met Sioux runners who told the Cheyennes about the raiding on the Platte. Eager war parties were formed from the Cheyennes at once, and they rode off to take part in the action. George Bent wrote, "I had just returned from my father's ranch on the Purgatory that summer. As I rode by each village I seen scalp dances in center of these villages. War parties came from all directions bringing in lots of plunder. . . . I seen all kinds of stuff they brought, fine silk, cloaks, bonnets, in fact everything in line of fine dry goods they took from trains that they plundered. Old Indians wore ladies' fine bonnets for hats.

Silks were made into squaw dresses and shirts for young men. I had half-dozen made of some silk."

"There was no particular leaders in these war parties. . . ." Bent explained, "Cheyennes and Sioux made raids on South Platte down to Little Blue River. . . Arapahoes made raids toward Denver."[21]

The raids on the South Platte began less than a month after the Hungate tragedy. The telegraph operators, John W. Ford at Junction and John Hines at Valley Station were kept busy tabulating the depredations and carnage. The least noteworthy of these events was an unsuccessful surprise attack on a party of emigrants near Fremont's Orchard. Fourteen miles upriver from Junction, about noon on the seventeenth of July, six Indians, called Cheyennes, attacked the camp of H. H. Wentworth and his partner, Battea, freighters from Topeka, Kansas. The horses of the train were picketed some distance from the wagons, and the raiders dashed between the herd and their owners, stampeding the animals, driving off eight horses.

Shortly, afterward, a mile or so down the road, the Indians circled around Bijou Ranch, trying to draw out the men who were inside. When the men refused to be fooled the Indians attacked a freight train belonging to Mr. Seavy of Golden City. The train, in charge of Mr. Hollingsworth, consisted of four wagons. The first wagon escaped, but the drivers of the two following—Wardman Jones, seventeen years old, of Golden, and Philip Rogers, also seventeen, of Iowa—were killed and subsequently scalped and mutilated. The driver of the fourth wagon was shot through the body with an arrow. Seven horses and mules were driven off from the train. A number of oxen were shot with arrows. The surviving freighters from both wagon trains took refuge in the corral of the ranch, keeping guard all night.

Farther down the river, at Junction Station, the war party drove off all the stock, both that of the stage company and the proprietor, seven head in all, five belonging to Ben Holladay. At Junction Ranch, operated by Reynolds and Ashcraft, fifty or sixty head of horses and mules were stolen. At Murray's Station, eight miles below the Junction, eight stage horses were taken, as well as two at Murray's. Twenty-one head of cattle belonging to Murray were shot with arrows.

Sometime during the day two unidentified emigrants were killed. Their bodies, cut nearly in two pieces and badly mutilated, were found by the eastbound coach on the afternoon of the eighteenth. At Beaver Creek Ranch one ox was shot, and at Beaver Creek Station one horse was taken. At Godfrey's one horse was stolen. For some reason the American Ranch, Wisconsin Ranch, and Valley Station were not molested, but at Moore's Washington Ranch twenty-eight horses were stolen. On the eighteenth it was quiet and the raid seemed to be ended. A party from Valley Station, headed by Reuben Thomas, the Division Agent for the stage company, went up the road to bury the dead at Beaver Creek. The strain had been too much for telegrapher John Ford at Junction, who reported wildly, "The women and children are all leaving for Denver. Dead cattle full of arrows are lying in all directions. A general Indian War is anticipated. . . . The excitement is intense!"[22]

When the emigrants at Fremont's Orchard had thwarted the Indian attack, they complained to Captain Sanborn, and twenty men were detailed to find the raiders. But before the troops could leave the base, a messenger arrived from Bijou Ranch reporting the attack there. Upon receiving this news Sanborn ordered Lt. George Chase to take twenty men and proceed to Bijou while Sanborn took the first detail out.

Lieutenant Chase rode down the river from ranch to ranch listening to the stories. At Junction Ranch he heard how Sam Ashcraft's Sioux mother-in-law had run for two miles through the cactus to Junction Station to warn the operator of the coming Indian attack, but she was too late, and the stage stock was driven off while the stationkeeper watched. She had warned Sam, too, that the marauders were coming, but his stock was grazing too far from the ranch to be driven in. Chase reached Murray's on the morning of the eighteenth; here he turned off toward the bluffs where he found a trail leading south. About twenty-five miles south of Beaver Creek he found five Indians eating breakfast. With them were 125 head of stolen stock. Chase opened fire, and he thought he wounded two of the Indians, but they ran off, relinquishing the animals which Chase and his men then drove back to Junction Ranch.

At Reynolds and Ashcraft's the owners were so delighted to get their horses back that a huge breakfast was prepared for the whole company of soldiers, and all of the horses were corralled and fed. The complacent troopers had just finished a hearty meal when they discovered that the Indians had followed them back as far as Murray's Ranch, where they had killed most of the cattle, and then had swept down on a government train and killed a driver.

In the meantime, Captain Sanborn had followed the Indians unsuccessfully on the seventeenth, then returned to Camp Sanborn and picked up four days rations and twenty more men. He traveled south to the headwaters of the Bijou, across to Beaver Creek and back to Junction without finding a trace of Indians. He returned to Junction Ranch, where he found Lieutenant Chase and his company. Sanborn rested his men and horses overnight. The following day he took forty men and scouted the area east of Beaver Creek with Granville Ashcraft as a guide. When it was apparent that the Indians had left the valley, Sanborn ended the search and returned to camp.[23]

On the night of July 18 a horse was stolen from Valley Station but all was quiet for another day until the stationkeeper at Murray's Ranch went out in the evening of the twentieth to hunt stock, was fired upon and narrowly escaped. On the morning of the twenty-first William Kelly reported to the *News* that three parties of Indians had been seen, "One numbering three, another four, and another seven."[24]

The news of the attack on the South Platte spread both ways, causing new apprehension in Denver and tying up traffic at Julesburg. A rumor had been passed along that General Mitchell was planning an inspection trip up the North Platte, and wagons heading in that direction pulled out to wait for military protection. In addition to this the order had been sent from Mitchell's headquarters that any trains headed for Denver could not proceed past Julesburg until they were in sufficient number to withstand attack. A drizzling rain on July 22 had soaked three miles of idle freighters thoroughly; discontent turned to anger. The friction and quarreling were epidemic when the General arrived. In the General's command was a young lieutenant named Eugene Ware. It was his first trip to Julesburg.

Eugene Ware had lived in Iowa since his school days, and in that state, at the age of twenty, he had enlisted three times in various branches of the service; he had been mustered out twice. In 1864 he was serving as a Second Lieutenant in Company F of the 7th Iowa Cavalry. His memories of service at Fort Cottonwood and Camp Rankin, near Julesburg, provided a considerable contribution to the history of the South Platte Trail.[25]

Things were not going well for William Bent at the ranch on the Purgatory. Yellow Woman was a very independent female, and she must have been a great deal younger than her husband. There may also have been household difficulties, since Mary Bent Moore and her husband had come from Westport with their civilized ways to live in William Bent's compound. Some time during the summer Yellow Woman fell in love with a young half-breed named Joe Barroldo. Without warning, in the first week of August, Yellow Woman and Joe Barroldo slipped away from Bent's ranch without farewells and headed into the buffalo country to join the Cheyennes. William Bent was furious. "I am not in a very good humor," he wrote to Agent Colley, "as my old squaw ran off a few days ago with Joe Barroldo, as she likes him better than she did me. If I ever get sight of that young man, it will go hard with him. . . .[26]

If Long Chin, the Dog Soldier, was George Bent's uncle, then he must have been Yellow Woman's brother, so Yellow Woman and Joe Barroldo went north to join her family. They arrived in the midst of the raiding bordering on the Platte River and Joe became involved immediately.

It seemed as though the Indians knew that the white man's most vulnerable time was early on Sunday morning. The carnage which occurred two miles east of Plum Creek Station on the Platte River on August 7, 1864, began at 7:00 A.M. Three-quarters of a mile away, at the Thomas Ranch, Lt. William R. Bowen of the Seventh Iowa Cavalry watched helplessly as the assailants—about one hundred Indians of an unidentified tribe—encircled and attacked a group of wagons camped beside the Platte. The men of the three trains involved were apparently armed with nothing more suitable than revolvers, and were soon overcome. The first of these trains—ten four-mile teams with wagons carrying dry goods, clothing and household goods—was owned by Thomas Morton of Sidney, Iowa. Morton was accompanied on this trip by his wife Nancy. The second train belonged to Michael Kelly of St. Joseph, Missouri, and his six wagons were loaded with corn and machinery.

Camped some distance from the first two was the third train. It has not been established who the owners were. From the names James and Baker found on some of the packages in the debris it was thought that Judge James and Sheriff Baker of Council Bluffs had been present and among those killed, but Lt. Charles F. Porter of the First Nebraska Cavalry wrote from Fort Kearny that these men were not involved. The *Rocky Mountain News* seemed to recognize the name, W. C. James, which was engraved on a cane found in the wreckage, and the *News* identified him as a former resident of Denver City. All the wagons were burned and about fifty mules stampeded. Of the freighters, Morton and Kelly were killed, besides six other men whose bodies were found. Porter said that Col. Samuel W. Summers and Lieutenant Comstock, of the Seventh Iowa Cavalry, found thirteen bodies, most stripped of clothing, several scalped and mutilated. Another soldier counted eleven graves at a later date. Porter attempted to name some of the men: Charles Iliff, Mable [sic] and boy, Smith and his partner, all of Council Bluffs, and William Fletcher of Colorado. There were probably only two survivors; "Mable's boy" (Daniel Marble, whom Porter had reported dead) and Nancy Morton, who were both taken as prisoners. A Mrs. Smith was reported captured also, but all of the women in the area named Smith seem to have been located subsequently.[27]

At eleven o'clock on the same morning, a short distance down the road, a band of sixteen warriors attacked the Fred Smith Ranch were they killed the hired man, burned the store and took all but five of the cattle. Fred Smith and his wife were not on the ranch, having set out for Fort Kearny a bare two hours previously.[28]

On the same day, on the other side of Fort Kearny down the Little Blue River on the Overland Route, the destruction and bloodshed was inflicted generally along a stretch of sixty-seven miles between the fort and Kiowa Station (in the west part of present Thayer County, Nebraska). At Kiowa Station the stationkeeper, Douglas, escaped with the stage teams, but the station was completely burned.

At Little Blue Station, eight miles upstream, the interior of the building was damaged and the furnishings destroyed. Another eight miles farther at Liberty Farm, Emery, the ranch owner, was able to escape with the Overland's horses, but the station and stable were burned. An equal distance farther at Pawnee Ranch, near Pawnee Station, a Mr. Burke was killed and scalped near the ranch house. Near Little Blue Station was camped a large train of about eighty wagons—several trains traveling together, all headed by wagonmaster George Constable of St. Joseph. Nine of these wagons belonged to George Tritch of Denver. The freighters of this train were hired to deliver a cargo of crockery and hardware said to be worth $22,000. A second train of twenty wagons carried liquor. All of the men escaped, but the wagons and their contents were destroyed.

In the middle of this road at Lone Tree Station, where the attack began on that Sunday morning, nine horses were lost, and stationkeepers from nearby stations rode so hard to escape the Indians that they killed five additional horses. At both Thirty-two Mile Creek Station and Summit Station the stationkeepers and their families escaped but the buildings and supplies were all destroyed; between the two stations six men were found dead.

David Street, the Overland paymaster, had been delayed by a late train at St. Joseph; consequently, the coach was running behind schedule when they reached Summit Station. They arrived immediately after the raids had occurred and they found the six dead men on the road. They could not find a stationkeeper on the whole route so the coach driver had no choice but to continue on to Fort Kearny.

John Coad, of the Wisconsin Ranch, also pulled his freight train into the fort to wait out the Indian scare. Terrified settlers, travelers and stage personnel poured into the fort—some on foot or on horseback, in all states of dress and undress; coatless, hatless and in nightgowns.

Ben Holladay was at the fort, interrupting a trip west. Since David Street had brought word of the desolation of the stage line to the south, Holladay stood over the telegraph operator, anxiously awaiting any news from outside the fort. On Sunday afternoon, George M. Lloyd, the Division Agent at Fort Kearny, went down to Thirty-two Mile Creek, where he found the six bodies. He returned to Fort Kearny after dark. The coach arrived from the east on the morning of August 8 with the report that there was "not a living soul on the road within fifty miles of Kearny and not a hoof of stock to be found." Those passengers who wished to take the risk were assigned to two coaches which left Fort Kearny going west on Monday.[29]

The most horrible event on Sunday, August 7, occurred near Oak Grove, a settlement situated just west of Kiowa Station. William Eubanks, his wife and family lived here. Daughters Hannah and Dora lived at home as well as two teen-aged sons, James and Henry. A married son with his wife Lucinda and there two children, Isabelle (aged four) and William (an infant), also lived on the family farm. An older son, Joe, lived west of Kiowa Station, and other sons and daughters lived in the area.

On the day of destruction, Joe Eubanks, his brother Fred, and his brother-in-law, John Palmer, were cutting hay across the river from William's farm.

Earlier on that Sunday, at a farm a mile and a half from the Eubanks place, golden-haired, sixteen-year-old Laura Roper, whose family was away, decided to spend the day visiting her friend, Lucinda Eubanks. She set out on foot, wearing a large hat to shade her fair skin from the August sun, but before she had gone far she was picked up by two young neighbors, Kelly and Butler, who were on their way to Kiowa Station to cut hay for the stage company. At the Eubanks farm, Laura jumped off the wagon and waved a cheerful farewell to her friends—for the last time.

Kelly and Butler drove on to the Comstock Ranch, six miles above Kiowa Station. Here a group of Indians had asked for food and were allowed to join the family for dinner. Since Kelly and Butler were in the neighborhood, the Comstocks invited them also. When dinner was finished, the Indians suddenly turned and fired on their white hosts, killing both Kelly and Butler.

The marauding Indians moved toward Kiowa Station. Joe and Fred Eubanks and John Palmer were widely separated from one another; they were attacked and killed. Two neighbors, a man named Kennedy and a youth named Ulig, were also killed, scalped and mutilated.

Most of the family were at home at the Eubanks farm, except for the mother and the daughter Hannah, who were away visiting relatives. Spending the day with his grandfather was seven-year-old Ambrose—who was probably the son of Joe Eubanks. Everyone was happy to see Laura's sunny smile.

About four o'clock when Laura felt she should start home, Lucinda and her husband offered to walk part way with her. Lucinda carried the baby and her husband led tiny, frail Isabelle by the hand. As they left the farmhouse, the elder William started in the opposite direction to take his grandson home; they had gone only a short distance when the attack came. William Sr., was killed, and Ambrose was taken prisoner.

The area through which Laura and her friends were walking was sandy, so Laura took off her slippers and was carrying them. William, who was barefoot, discovered that he had picked up a sliver in his foot and sat down to remove it, telling the others to continue on, that he would catch up with them. Laura took Isabelle's hand. They were passing through a wooded area when they heard the terrifying whoops of Indians coming from the farm. In a depression in a nearby field Lucinda, Laura and the children hastily found a hiding place. When Isabelle began to cry from fear, Lucinda stuffed her handkerchief into the child's mouth. William ran back to the house.

After a long time, when it seemed that they were safe Lucinda took the handkerchief out of her daughter's mouth and Isabelle made up for lost time with a loud wail. Within minutes the women and children were surrounded by seven Cheyenne warriors. The Cheyennes dragged their captives onto ponies and took them back to the house, where the horror of the scene put both young women into a state of dazed emotional shock. The Indians were so completely occupied with destroying the farm and mutilating bodies that they paid little attention to the two women and children. Oblivious to her surroundings, Lucinda wandered through the wreckage of her home, salvaging items of clothing. She found two little dresses for the baby and a sunbonnet for herself to protect her lovely red hair and sensitive freckled face. As though unaware of what was before her eyes, Laura was concerned about hiding a precious gold chain which she wore. She took it off and hid it in her underwear. Not far away, on the riverbank, William Jr. lay dead and scalped. Close by, the two boys were dead and bleeding. In the farmyard lay Dora, staked-out, naked, scalped and pinned to the earth with a stake driven through her body.

The nightmare was not over. Laura, Lucinda and the children were tied on horses and led off to witness further activities. Farther down the road a demented woman lived with her son. The woman, crazed with fear, scratched and bit the warriors who attempted to capture her. They killed and scalped her, and took the boy prisoner. As the Cheyennes who took the scalp passed Laura, he swung the long black hair against the girl, leaving a splash of blood reaching from her face down the front of her dress. It was now six o'clock in the evening. At last the day's work was done. The Indians turned south with their prizes and traveled all night.

The attacks on the Overland Route were not initiated only by Cheyennes, but the reports of various incidents did not identify the assailants. Laura Roper was certain that she was captured by Cheyennes. Soon after, Lucinda Eubanks was traded to the Sioux, and she went west with them. The baby was sent with her, but Isabelle remained with Laura because their captors believed that she was Laura's child.[30]

On Tuesday, August 9, the Indians struck the road again near Cottonwood Springs, where they killed a man named Gilette, his son and his partner. The men were building a ranch near Gilman's Ranch. At Gilman's no one was hurt; but seventeen horses were driven away from there, and a number of animals from Dan Smith's Ranch also. At noon, nine miles below Cottonwood Station, Robert Corriston was shot while mowing hay. Major Nicholas O'Brien was sent from Fort Cottonwood with a detachment of cavalry. Fifteen horses were recovered. Sol Riddle, the Division Agent at Julesburg, came down the road almost immediately after the attack. It was too late to help the victims even though they were still breathing. Riddle rode on to notify the military.[31]

Nearer to Fort Kearny the Indians attacked the Pawnee Ranch again on the afternoon of the ninth, but a number of settlers gathered there for protection were able to discourage the marauders. At Fort Kearny, the crowd behind the walls of the fort was impatient to know what damage had been done. George Henry Carlyle wired Holladay from Julesburg telling him that all of the stations in the Julesburg–Kearny Division were abandoned except for a few stationkeepers and the drivers. Holladay wired back to keep the line running, so Carlyle took over the management. Holladay arrived at Julesburg soon after and decided that the entire Overland Route to Julesburg would have to be reorganized. Superintendent George Kingman Otis ordered the road to be closed and all of the stock to be removed on the sixteenth of August. An order was given that no passengers were to be booked out of Denver going east. The last mail arrived from the east at Latham on August 15 and mail from the west continued to pile up until the little station was full and overflowing. Some coaches did go though, but at one crucial time nearly one hundred passengers were delayed here, and a rumor of Indian attack sent the stage stop into full panic.[32]

General Mitchell robbed the troops from the Laramie Road to fortify the South Platte Road, Company C of the Eleventh Ohio Cavalry under Captain Thomas D. Clark was stationed at Fremont's Orchard; another company was moved to Camp Collins. One company of the Iowa Cavalry was stationed at Julesburg, patrolling in both directions.[33]

There were raids on the South Platte in August, but they were lesser incidents. John Ford, the telegraph operator, reported from Junction on August 13 that the Indians had made a raid at Ashcraft's Junction Ranch, running off four horses and taking also an unspecified number of horses from a train camped nearby. Six cattle were killed and a number wounded. Ford said that the Indians were in sight of the station until 9:00 A.M., and twenty-six were counted at one time. Some men cutting hay came in and reported seeing thirty Indians. The ranchmen of the area decided to move their cattle west to the Cache la Poudre. A portion of Company C from Fremont's Orchard was sent in pursuit of the Indians.

On the lower South Platte Major O'Brien reported a skirmish with Indians near Fort Cottonwood on August 16, and the telegraph operator at Alkali Station was frightened away. The ranchers in that area were reported to be erecting a fort for defense. From Coberly's Ranch, the bodies of a rancher named John Zeckery and a boy named Edwin Garrett were brought into Denver on the seventeenth. South of Denver on Running Creek, several families were attacked and two girls were reported murdered on August 18. Governor Evans sent a frantic telegram to General Curtis in which he presented a disproportionate summary of Denver's difficulties. "It is impossible to exaggerate the danger," he said. "We are doing all we can for our defense."

In the previous week, on the tenth of August, the Governor had asked that a letter be published in the *News.* He began with an appeal for the organization of militia companies and announced that he was sending all standing militia companies to search for the Indians. He then requested that private citizens join the militia and promised that these citizens would be "entitled to all the property belonging to hostile Indians that they capture." Evans went on to say, ". . . any man who kills a hostile Indian is a patriot but there are Indians who are friendly and to kill one of them will involve us in greater difficulty." The letter suggested that the expenses of these citizens would probably be paid by the War Department. Another announcement followed on August 11, in which Evans defined hostile Indians as any who had not responded to his June proclamation and gathered at the points designated. This included almost all of the red men, except for Friday and his Arapahoes on the Cache la Poudre and Left Hand and his Arapahoes on the Arkansas. Evans again authorized citizens of Colorado, alone or in parties, to pursue hostile Indians and to appropriate any property acquired by such pursuit.[34]

The settlers below Denver became very agitated. Many families moved into Denver. Farmers were gathering together to build fortifications. Simeon Whiteley, the Indian Agent, told Governor Evans that the people were so frightened that they threatened to attack friendly Indians. Whiteley heard of a party of a hundred men who armed and started out to clean out Friday and his Arapahoes, but on their way had learned of some hostile Indians at Fort Lupton, so they changed direction, and the peaceful Arapahoes were spared.[35]

On August 11, after the raids on the Little Blue River and the Platte, the War Department finally capitulated and Evans was notified that he might authorize the raising of a regiment of infantry to serve for 100 days in order to protect the roads and the territory from the Indian menace.[36]

Owing to the relationship by marriage between Long Chin and Elbridge Gerry, Long Chin felt obligated to warn Gerry about rumors of attack that were circulating through the Indian villages. It was after dark on the evening of the nineteenth of August that Long Chin, the Dog Soldier, and another Cheyenne named Man-Shot-by-a-Ree slipped quietly into Elbridge Gerry's stockade. Long Chin said that he had a message for Gerry. The Dog Soldiers brought information that there was a large encampment at the Point of Rocks on Beaver Creek, a camp made up of eight hundred to one thousand Apaches, Comanches, Kiowas and Arapahoes; no Cheyennes were mentioned. Long Chin said the Indians planned to separate into war parties and strike the South Platte above Fort Lupton, at Latham and at the Junction. A party would go to the head of Cherry Creek and another to the Fontaine qui Bouille (Fountain Creek). The old warriors brought news of the prisoners taken on the Little Blue and in a recent attack at Fort Larned. Long Chin and his fellow Cheyennes warned Gerry as old friends to remove his stock from the river before the attack was launched.

Whether motivated by loyalty or promised compensation, Gerry and Spotted Horse—both still in the employ of Governor Evans as informers—set off the following morning on the sixty-seven mile ride to Denver to notify the Governor. They arrived at Denver at 11:00 P.M. on the twentieth. Evans at once notified the Military Headquarters, and all militia companies, as well as those 100-day infantry as had been recruited, were sent to the points of danger.

Gerry was oddly unconcerned about the possible attack. Considering that he had been warned by Long Chin to secure his stock, it seemed strange that he did not return immediately to Crow Creek. As the Governor later explained it, Gerry's return was delayed "in taking care of a friendly chief who had accompanied him." What sort of care was required by Spotted Horse was not specified, but is was sufficiently serious to keep Gerry in Denver until the twenty-second. In the meantime, on the twenty-first, a party of Indians actually did come to Gerry's ranch and ran off 150 horses belonging to Gerry and a neighbor named Antoine Raynal. Gerry may have been surprised when he returned home on the following day. He discovered that the raiders had come from the north, not Beaver Creek, and they had returned to the north with the stock. Gerry thought that they would probably cross the river at the Junction and go south, so he raised a party of men and followed the trail on the twenty-fourth of August, only to discover that the Indians had crossed the river about two miles below Fremont's Orchard and would now be swallowed by the vast plains beyond the river.

A week later, when Indian Agent Simeon Whiteley stopped at Gerry's store, he discovered that Gerry and Spotted Horse were planning a trip to the camp of the Dog Soldiers to attempt to talk the Indians into returning the stolen stock. Whiteley said that he wrote a "passport" for Spotted Horse in order that he might accompany Gerry. Whether the passport was intended to protect the unfortunate Indian from white or red man, Whiteley did not say. Gerry never recovered his horses, but George Bent said that just before the Sand Creek massacre the Indians were talking of taking Gerry's horses back to him. The shock of the horrible affair at Sand Creek ended all such intent.[37]

In accord with their orders, a company of militia under Capt. S. E. Browne ranged up and down the Cache la Poudre from the Big Thompson and back. On the twenty-fifth Browne followed vague reports of sightings and one of a burning house, but after marching back and forth around Latham he concluded that there were no Indians in that country. Similar results were achieved at the other rumored points of attack.

The summer's warfare was far from ended. The Santa Fe Road and the Platte Road were attacked repeatedly; the South Platte suffered less. The telegraph lines were now being cut frequently, a new harassment recently discovered by the hostile Indians. On the twenty-fourth and twenty-fifth of August the line was cut three times between Valley Station and Cottonwood Springs, and then on the twenty-fifth, cut beyond Cottonwood. On September first, Mr. Cornforth of Blake Street, Denver, reported that his eastbound train had been attacked at O'Fallon's Bluffs on the twenty-ninth of August. The driver was wounded and ten oxen were stolen.

On August 21 the American Ranch was burned. The *Rocky Mountain News* had an affectionate regard for the genial Irishman William Kelly of the American Ranch, and it was with great sympathy that the newspaper noted his misfortune. "All of the household property and everything else was destroyed," the report said, "the storeroom only being saved." No one knew what caused the fire. Indians were not mentioned. With great regret, William Kelly and his wife abandoned the ranch and moved to Denver.[38]

Chapter

9

An Uneasy Autumn

The big scare had abated for the time being, and on September 16, 1864, the *Rocky Mountain News* reported that, after a month's stay in the city, William Kelly and his wife had departed from Denver with high spirits and firm intentions to rebuild the American Ranch on the South Platte. Judging from subsequent events, it would seem that the couple took one look at the wreckage and their resolution shriveled. They moved on, no one knows where.[1]

The situation was not hopeless, however, since newcomers were still arriving along the South Platte Trail. The story of the American Ranch was not finished; new life would be forthcoming. The second generation of pioneers who crossed the Missouri River seemed to be strung together with a tougher fiber than most. Whether it was because they were genetically equipped for survival or were already toughened by the rigors of frontier life is debatable; probably both factors were important. One of these children cradled in a covered wagon and well equipped for hardship was Sarah J. Iames.

Sarah J. and her twin sister Lydia were born in Pennsylvania in 1838 to Rezin and Eleanor Iames. Rezin Iames was a land-clearing, cabin-building type of westerner, and his wife was sturdy and durable. Six years before the twins were born Rezin had taken up land in Niles Township of what would become Delaware County, Indiana, but the family did not move there until 1844. Even then, the necessities of life were hard to come by. In 1849 Rezin went to California with the gold rushers, leaving Eleanor on the primitive farm in Indiana with six children—the youngest not more than a year old.

Rezin did not stay long in California, but when he returned with stories of his adventures, Sarah and Lydia were old enough to listen carefully. Sarah may have been well prepared for the frontier when she married William Morris in March of 1860. She was not surprised when her new husband began to talk of going west.[2]

The migration of Sarah and William Morris was delayed until 1864. In the meantime their son Charley was born, and another older child, Joseph, was adopted by the couple. Whatever their original plan had been, it was altered when they reached Kansas. After the terrors of August of 1864, a considerable number of stationkeepers like the Kellys had resigned from the Overland Stage Company and the stage officials were hiring new personnel. When William Morris applied for employment, he was asked if the Morrises would be interested in operating a burned-out swing station on the South Platte River called the American Ranch.

With admirable courage Sarah agreed, and the family arrived at their new home sometime in September. How discouraging it must have been—a two-room adobe shell filled with the rank odor of burning, the bricks blackened with smoke, the roof beams charred and the sod roof crumbling with black grizzled roots. The challenge was met. The stage company provided four hired men to help with rebuilding the house and stable, and the Holon Godfrey family, who lived only two miles away, offered encouragement and neighborly friendship to the young couple. The Morrises settled in.

When Governor Evans received the long-sought authorization in August for a 100-days volunteer regiment to be raised for protection from the Indians, recruiting offices were set up in almost every town in Colorado Territory. During August, 800 to 900 men enlisted, and by mid-September the maximum allowed— 1200 men —was nearly reached. By August 31 four companies had assembled from Denver, while one from Boulder, one from Central City, one from El Paso and Pueblo counties combined, and five others from other parts of the territory were in training. Supplies of ordnance and horse equipment arrived very slowly, so the men were held at Camp Evans, established above Denver, until they were outfitted.

The first companies sent out to protect the main arteries of travel were neither well trained nor well equipped. On August 30 Colonel Chivington sent one company of cavalry to Fort Lupton, one to Valley Station, and one to the Arkansas River; one company of infantry went to Junction Station. Thomas Clark and his company of Eleventh Ohio was still at Fremont's Orchard.[3]

Filling in the gap of the South Platte Road was a remarkable company of militia called the Tyler Rangers. This body of men, ninety in all including officers, was recruited by Clinton M. Tyler, who was commissioned as a Captain by Governor Evans. All except three of the men came from the mountain town and area of Black Hawk, and they were enrolled on August 15.

With a lively esprit de corps they marched forty miles to Denver the following day. They spent two days in Denver being outfitted, and on the nineteenth they began a persistant march along the river road. Scouting parties were detailed constantly to travel in parallel lines on the flanks of the main company, scouring the country for signs of Indian activity. They reached Julesburg on the twenty-eighth and by the sixth of September had arrived at Cottonwood Springs with only one minor incident, in which Indians attempted at night to stampede the horses but were unsuccessful. The greatest problem of the march was the continual worry about the safety of the scouting parties.

From Cottonwood Springs a strong party of Rangers was sent out to the Republican River, and a day or two later the entire command followed them until the twelfth of September, when they met General Mitchell. From this point the General seems to have kept the impulsive Rangers out of trouble. When a scouting party was besieged by Pawnees, Mitchell came to the rescue; when a trail of about fifty Indians was discovered near O'Fallon's Bluffs, Mitchell restrained the Rangers from following it. When information was received that the Sioux were crossing the river at Beauvais Ranch and the Rangers set out in pursuit, Mitchell sent orders to them to return to the road. After reaching Julesburg their adventure seemed to be ended, so they marched back to Black Hawk, where they were relieved from service on October 14. Oddly, the log of their travels never mentioned camping closer to Junction Station than four miles distant, but for some reason the name was kept alive in the area, and "Camp Tyler" was believed to be the site of the subsequent military post called first Camp Wardwell and later Fort Morgan.[4]

Realizing the need for a fortified post on the South Platte Trail, and aware that Julesburg occupied a crucial location at the fork of the north and south roads, General Mitchell decided to build a fort here and set up his headquarters. At the time the decision was made, Company F of the Seventh Iowa Cavalry was serving as an escort for the General, and in this company were two bright young men who would be deeply involved in the project: Capt. Nicholas O'Brien and Second Lt. Eugene Ware.

Company F arrived at Julesburg on September 4 and the men put up pup tents near the river by Julesburg Station. They found quite a collection of frightened people there who had dug rifle pits and appointed watches against Indian attack. Patrols were operating on the Colorado side of Julesburg by Colorado soldiers from Valley Station, and from the east by the Seventh Iowa Cavalry originating from Alkali Lake. The traffic was light—it was too late in the summer for large numbers of freighters—so the escort details were chiefly occupied with horse or mule wagons and occasional stagecoaches. Since Company F would be stationed through the winter at Julesburg, they dug pits under their pup tents and filled in the ends with sod, fervently hoping that something better could be erected before winter came.[5]

Mitchell turned his attention to getting the regular mails started again. An order was given by the Overland Stage Company that the stock be returned to the stations on September 9. An encouraging wire was received by the *Rocky Mountain News* on the twelfth promising a daily coach in "a week or so," and on the morning of the twenty-ninth a mail coach finally arrived; but it had been nine days in transit.[6]

Mitchell directed that two or more stagecoaches travel together with escorts, and all of them were crowded. It had become a practice since the tragedies of Plum Creek and Oak Grove to take the names and addresses of the passengers. Julesburg was designated as a check point for this inventory. Escorted, the coaches were not molested, and regular travel was soon resumed; but no coach or wagon was allowed to go over the road without military protection.

On the twenty-ninth of September Col. Robert R. Livingston of the First Nebraska Cavalry, a young man with an iron will, was ordered to take command of the Eastern Subdistrict of Nebraska which extended from the Missouri River to and including Julesburg. When he visited the South Platte portion of the command, he found Capt. John Wilcox of the Seventh Iowa Cavalry, a seasoned veteran, at O'Fallon's Bluffs with seventy-nine men. They were occupying the deserted Bob Williams Ranch and they had purchased another set of buildings, so they had a good stable and a defensible stockyard. At Alkali Station, Captain E.B. Murphy of the Seventh Iowa Cavalry (whom Eugene Ware described as "active, industrious and enduring") was stationed with seventy-three men. The original sod house and stable had been enlarged and sod buildings erected to house 100 men and provide stabling for forty horses. Lt. Miles S. Tuttle of the First Nebraska Cavalry had only twenty-five men at Beauvais Ranch. The company was housed in the outbuildings of the trader's ranch.[7]

At Julesburg, Captain Nicholas O'Brien was in charge of sixty-seven men, supported by a white-haired, ineffective First Lieutenant named John S. Brewer. But O'Brien was also assisted by the energetic capable Second Lt. Eugene Ware. A good combination, O'Brien and Ware were nearly the same age and were usually involved equally in any plans which were undertaken for the intended military base. When the officers received a wire to start building fortifications, they directed an appraising eye toward a nearby ranch.

Samuel D. Bancroft, the Julesburg postmaster, had built his ranch a mile west of Julesburg Station opposite the mouth of Lodgepole Creek. He had built an adobe house, a storeroom, and part of a sod corral. The place had two fine wells. Captain O'Brien and Lt. Ware thought it might form the nucleus for a good military camp. O'Brien wired for and received permission to buy the completed buildings. Bancroft was agreeable to the terms, and by September 15 Company F was cutting sod, mixing mortar and laying up walls. Under escort, post wagons from Cottonwood Springs brought poles for rafters. Inside the corral all of the buildings were erected: stables, barracks, headquarters and quartermaster's depot. The high sod walls had rectangular lookout towers at the southeast and northwest corners.

After Colonel Livingston's arrival the men moved on the twenty-sixth of October from the sod-lined pits into the luxury of roof and walls, and by mid-November, they had doors and glass windows. The fort was named Camp Rankin, but it was seldom called a name other than Julesburg by the soldiers.[8]

While the panic of late August was running wild among the ranchers on the north side of the South Platte, the town of Boulder was so alarmed that ditches for defense were dug in the streets of the town and the settlers who lived along Boulder Creek erected an adobe fort called Fort Chambers. This was the headquarters of the 100-days volunteers in that area. The response was so great to the call for enlistment that Ellen Coffin, who lived in the neighborhood with her brothers, wrote that "there were not enough men left on the creek to care for the crops, or to have protected our homes if Indians came."[9]

The officer commissioned to recruit Company D from Boulder was Capt. David Nichols, who at thirty-eight years of age was a veteran of the Mexican War, a former lumberman, a former Baptist Minister and a California forty-niner. Nichols was tough enough to demand respect (he was one of a few California veterans who had returned east across the Isthmus of Panama, through the jungle) and he was a charming, easy-going and popular leader.

Among the men of Company D was Ellen Coffin's younger brother, Morse, an Illinois farm boy through and through. Morse had come west with his brother George among the first tide of gold seekers and the boys had stayed on Boulder Creek to farm and build a fine log cabin. It was a matter a honor to Morse that he must join the 100-days volunteers to protect the farm from Indians.

By late September Colonel Chivington had units of the Third Colorado Regiment—the formal title for the 100-days volunteers—who were better supplied and better trained. On September 23 he sent two companies, Company D under Capt. David Nichols and Company F under Lt. Fry, to replace the former troops at Valley Station and Junction. Both Companies D and F were under the command of Major Samuel Logan. Now that the traffic on the South Platte Road was defended, there was not an Indian in sight. The men of Company D at Valley Station were detailed in groups of four to six men to escort each coach or guard small companies of travelers. For a change, a detail of forty men with fourteen wagons would be sent to Cedar Bluffs to cut and bring back firewood.

The men of Company D had traveled this road before, and some had friends along the way. Porter and Platt Hinman visited the Dennisons and Holon Godfrey, at whose home the family had stayed when young Frank had been run over by the wagon. The Hinmans were sorry to learn that the Kellys were no longer at the American Ranch, but they made friends with William and Sarah Morris. The young couple were well liked by all of the soldiers. Morse Coffin spoke of them warmly.[10]

After the August raids, when Laura Roper was taken prisoner at Oak Grove, the first thing her captor did was to take her hat and place it on his own head. Her shoes were lost. When the raiding party was finally ready to turn away from their trail of destruction, her hands were tied and she was placed on a pony behind a warrior, since there were no extra horses. The children, Ambrose and Isabelle, and Lucinda and the baby were in the charge of the other warriors of the group of seven Cheyennes which had attacked the Eubanks family.

As they rode through the night, one of the Cheyennes rode up beside Laura in the dark. "Are you scared?" he asked in English. Laura was surprised. She admitted that she was certainly frightened.

"Is it because you think they are going to kill you?" the Indian asked.

"No," Laura shuddered, remembering the horror of Dora Eubank's death. "I think if they were going to kill me, they would have done it back there."

"I think you'll be all right," he agreed. "It may take a while but I think they'll give you up. What's your name?"

She told him. "What's yours?" she asked.

"Joe Barroldo," he answered.

Without resting, the party of Indians with their captives traveled all day. In the afternoon five more Cheyennes joined the party with extra horses, and Laura was mounted on a pony by herself. Since she had no hat her delicate skin was badly sunburned. The flies swarmed around the blood on her dress and she was unable to brush them away. As the day wore on, things became worse. At night her pony stumbled, and Laura fell off. The frightened animal kicked her, breaking her nose. After this, the Cheyenne warrior whose captive she was took her on his horse behind him again.

When the Indians finally stopped to rest, Laura's nose was badly swollen and she could scarcely see. Her captor spread a buffalo robe for her and painted her face with a red-colored unguent. Laura said that the swelling went down overnight.

When the party reached the main village, Laura had barely dismounted when she was attacked by a group of Indian women who pulled her hair, pinched and pummeled her until she thought this would be her final hour. But after a few minutes they stopped, and one of the squaws led her away to a bed of buffalo robes and she was finally allowed to sleep undisturbed.

Laura was separated from the other prisoners from that point. Lucinda and her baby had gone west with the Sioux some time ago. Laura never saw Nancy Morton, who was taken away by the Sioux but Isabelle Eubanks, Danny Marble and Ambrose Eubanks were in the same village as Laura. Laura believed that she was living with Black Kettle's band. After the first few days the Indian women of the village accepted Laura. They gave her moccasins to wear and allowed her to wash her dress, which was now crawling with maggots, and they took turns combing her hair. She was installed in a lodge where unmarried girls lived. She was welcomed into the activities of making moccasins and doing beadwork which occupied the other girls of her age.

Laura Roper was much too Victorian to write about sexual abuse or the absence of it. It is possible that she was not molested. However, she did tell that her original Cheyenne captor traded her to Neva, the Arapaho chief for five ponies. Neva and his brother, No-ta-nee, could speak English, and they were very kind to her. They told her that she should not have been captured and they would try to send her back to her people soon. After a week, however, the Arapahoes sold her back to the Cheyennes, and four days later the Cheyennes traded her again to the Arapahoes.

She seldom saw the children, but one day she found Isabelle, Danny and Ambrose among the Indian children. She asked them if they were getting enough to eat.

"Well, Danny does," Ambrose answered.

"How does he get it then?" Laura asked suspiciously.

"You see," Ambrose explained, "when the little Indians come around with something to eat, Danny stands on his head and turns his eyes inside out. They drop whatever they have in their hands and run, and then he picks it up and eats it."

Later on there was another captive in the village, but Laura never saw her alive. Her name was Mrs. Snyder, and she had been captured on the

Arkansas River Road. Mrs. Snyder attempted to escape and managed to go several miles from camp before she was recaptured. That night she tore her skirt into strips and twisted them into a rope with which she hanged herself from the crossing of the tipi poles. The women took Laura to see the corpse before she was cut down.[11]

The main camp of Cheyennes on the head of the Solomon River included Black Kettle's people, and among these were George Bent and Edmond Guerrier, who had not been with the Cheyennes for more than a few weeks. While the Cheyennes camped here the chiefs received a letter from William Bent urging them to hold a council concerning peace with the whites. A council of these chiefs in the camp was held, and Bent and Guerrier were asked to write letters to Fort Lyon suggesting peaceful overtures.

In the two letters, which were alike, "Black Kettle and Other Chiefs" promised to contact other tribes about a peace conference, and they offered to surrender the white prisoners from the Little Blue in exchange for Indian prisoners they believed to be in Denver. The chiefs claimed that only three Cheyenne and two Arapahoe war parties were still out but would soon rejoin the main village. One copy of the letter was to be sent to Major Colley and the other to the Commanding Officer at Fort Lyon.[12]

The letters were to be delivered by One Eye—who openly did spy work for the officers at Fort Lyon—his wife, and another Indian named Mah-ne-mick, or Eagle Head. Before the delegation reached the fort on September 4, they were picked up by some soldiers who delivered them to Major Wynkoop, who was now commanding Fort Lyon. The onlookers were inclined to be hostile. Major Wynkoop spoke harshly to the messengers and told them to get off their horses. Dexter Colley, son of the Indian Agent, who was present and recognized the Indians, assured Wynkoop that they were friendly. Wynkoop then asked the Indians to come to his office, where he read the letter and listened to their story.[13]

Ned Wynkoop was a romantic, and he was not lacking in self-confidence. Proper military procedure did not concern him in the least; as he saw it, the release of the prisoners was the most compelling part of the situation. After confining the Indians in the guardhouse, Wynkoop called a conference of his officers, Capt. Silas S. Soule, Lt. G.H. Hardin, Lt. Joseph A. Cramer and Lt. Charles E. Phillips. They concurred that even though they might be walking into a trap, recovering the prisoners was of prime importance. Within forty-eight hours Wynkoop set out with his officers, John Smith the interpreter, 120 men, and one section of artillery. As hostages Wynkoop brought One Eye, his wife, Eagle Head, and a Cheyenne known as the Fool, who lived at Fort Lyon. The expedition traveled four days to the northeast, where on the south branch of the Smoky Hill at Hackberry Creek they met the Indians' camp on September 10.[14]

Not as peaceful as represented, 600 warriors, Cheyennes and Sioux, were drawn up in line with bows and arrows ready. The Dog Soldiers were itching for a fight. Wynkoop proceeded cautiously, sending One Eye to talk with the belligerent Indians, to assure them that he had come for a consultation only, that he had no wish to fight but would do so if it was required of him. One Eye also pleaded with his people that he had guaranteed the safety of the soldiers. Black Kettle intervened and the army of warriors dispersed. Black Kettle advised Wynkoop to remove his men farther away from the Indian village and Wynkoop did so.[15]

The soldiers formed a wary camp with a string of nervous sentinels surrounding it. Captain Soule said that "after we were in camp [the Indians] closed around us as though they meant to gobble us up." They were again sent away by their chiefs.

On the morning of September 10 the Indian village had moved some distance away, so Wynkoop moved his camp to the place where the village had been. From here he sent word to the chiefs that he was ready for a council. Between nine and eleven A.M. about sixty Cheyennes and Arapahoes arrived, including most of the chiefs and headmen of the village, and they brought George Bent as an interpreter.

At the very beginning of the talk Wynkoop told the chiefs that he was not authorized to make peace, but that in exchange for the prisoners he would take a delegation of chiefs to Denver for the purpose of making a peace agreement.[16]

A litany of complaints followed from the resentful chiefs concerning their grievances against the whites and the ways in which they had been persecuted. Bull Bear, representing the Dog Soldier Society, remonstrated bitterly about the killing of his brother, Lean Bear, who had been a peaceful and friendly chief, by Lt. George Eayre's soldiers.

Each of the chiefs took a turn. Even One Eye, who ranked as little more than a headman, made an impassioned speech reminding his brothers of their honor and their promises to the Major. He said he was ashamed to hear the chiefs talk in this accusing way, especially about something as unimportant as stolen horses. He offered to divide his own horses with any of the offended chiefs if they would be quiet. Everyone fell silent except Bull Bear, who could not resist the offer and selected two of One Eye's finest horses before he stopped talking.

Finally Black Kettle spoke. He said he believed that the whites had started the war, but that bad men, both white and red, had caused the trouble. He said he had always been opposed to fighting and he was willing to surrender the prisoners for the good of his people, but that the other chiefs felt that there should be an assurance of peace before relinquishing the white captives.

Wynkoop repeated that he was not in a position to talk about peace but believed that if the chiefs would discuss it, they would see the advantage of his proposition. He said he would wait for their answer.[17]

The council ended about two P.M., and later that afternoon, the Arapahoe Left Hand brought Laura Roper to Wynkoop's camp. He told the Major that Black Kettle would bring the other prisoners on the following day. Laura wrote that she was so overjoyed when she saw the soldiers, ". . . that all I could do was cry, and when I was turned over to the officers, could not so much as speak, but I was careful to keep close to them on the trip back to the fort."[18]

The Cheyennes brought the children to the soldiers' camp the following day. Ned Wynkoop rode out in advance of his escort to meet Danny Marble.

"Well, my boy," he smiled, "How are you?"

"My name's Dan," the boy replied, "and I have been a prisoner with the Indians. Are you the soldier man who has come to get me?"

"I am."

"Well, bully for you!" he said.

"Are you glad to get away from the Indians?" Wynkoop asked.

"You bet, but say, will they let me keep this pony?"

"No," the Major replied, "but you shall have a better one."

Wynkoop's attention was distracted by a squaw with a blanket-wrapped bundle. Among the folds, Ned could see yellow ringlets of hair. As the Major approached, the little girl emerged from the blanket and stretched her arms toward him. Taking the child from the arms of the Indian woman, Ned held her close to him on the front part of his saddle. Isabelle put her arms around him and began to sob, "I want my mama." Major Wynkoop galloped some distance away from the Indians and his own men to gain time to control his emotions.

Dan Marble and Ambrose Eubanks were taken in charge by Lieutenant Cramer. As the boys reluctantly gave up their Indian ponies, Danny was heard to remark glumly that he "would just as leave have stayed with the Indians as not."[19]

Having promised at the council on Hackberry Creek that he would take a representative group of chiefs to Denver to talk with Governor Evans, Major Wynkoop led an entourage of about fifty Indians back to Fort Lyon. The chiefs who accompanied him were Black Kettle, White Antelope and Bull Bear for the Cheyennes. Left Hand did not go, but in his stead there were four Arapaho chiefs, all close relatives of Left Hand—Bosse, Heaps of Buffalo, Neva and No-ta-nee. At Fort Lyon, Colley distributed some annuity goods and Wynkoop issued some military stores which the chiefs sent back to Hackberry Creek with reassurances.

After a few days' preparation, Wynkoop left for Denver with the prisoners and Captain Soule. They traveled about two days ahead of the Indian chiefs, who were escorted by Lieutenant Cramer, with John Smith the interpreter and a detachment of cavalry. Wynkoop hoped to be able to prepare the Governor in advance for the proposed conference.[20]

When Wynkoop arrived at the Governor's house he was informed that the Governor was sick in bed and could not see him. However, the next morning Governor Evans went to Wynkoop's hotel to talk to him. In the lobby parlor Evans found Dexter Colley, who remained during the entire interview. Major Wynkoop had sent a report in advance, but now he repeated the events of Hackberry Creek and told the Governor that the chiefs would be arriving in a few days for an interview.

Governor Evans was not pleased. He said that he was sorry that Wynkoop had taken this action because the Governor wanted nothing to do with the Indians, since he believed the Cheyennes and Arapahoes had declared war against the United States and therefore were the responsibility of the military authorities. Also, the Governor did not think the Indians had been sufficiently punished.

The Major reminded Evans that as a military officer he had promised the Indians an interview with the Governor, and the Major respectfully asked that Evans honor the commitment.

Evans replied "querulously" that he intended to start the following day to visit the Ute Agency. Wynkoop became even more persuasive as he pursued his argument. Several times during the interchange the Governor brought up the subject of the one-hundred-days men who had been recruited specifically to fight Indians. What would Washington think if their time expired without firing a shot? The government would question Evans's adminstration after needless expense of feeding and equipping these men. Finally Governor Evans asked Wynkoop, "What shall I do with the Third Regiment if I make peace?"[21]

Colonel Chivington, too, wondered what to do with the short-term volunteers if peace was made at this time. Even before Wynkoop arrived in Denver, Chivington had wired Major General Samuel Curtis, Commander of the District of Kansas, on September 26 tersely suggesting a course of action to his superior. He told Curtis that Wynkoop was bringing the chiefs who, Chivington stated, wanted peace because winter was approaching and they were afraid to fight the Third Regiment, which was now fully recruited. The Colonel said, "I hope the Major General will direct that they make full restitution and then go to their reserve and stay there." The reply from Curtis did not arrive in Denver until after the conference had been completed.[22]

The Camp Weld conference was held on September 28, 1864. Governor Evans presided, and the military was represented by Colonel Chivington, Col. George Shoup, Commander of the Third Regiment, Major Wynkoop, Captain Soule and Lieutenant Cramer. A few Camp Weld officers and some local Denver officials were present. John Smith acted as interpreter, assisted by Sam Ashcraft. The proceedings were painstakingly recorded by the Indian Agent, Simeon Whiteley.[23]

As the conference began, the Indians shook hands with everyone in the room, then lighted a pipe which was passed around. The Governor asked to hear what the chiefs had to say. With great dignity Black Kettle responded with an eloquent and poetic oration. His people had been living under a cloud, Black Kettle said, and he and his brothers had come to hear the words of the Governor that would dispel those clouds and let the light of peace shine on them again.

Black Kettle admitted his doubts. He said that such were his fears for the safety of the chieftains that it was like passing through a flame, but he had closed his eyes and passed through the fire and was now here to know if the great father would make peace with him and his people.

He said he had been trying to get his people together since William Bent had brought the Governor's Proclamation of June 27. Black Kettle said he had been doing everything in his power since then to keep peace with the whites. He spoke in detail about the return of the prisoners, and he made no complaints or recriminations against the whites.[24]

Governor Evans was not so poetic, but he made his points systematically. First he praised the work of the Indian Commission on the reservation. He then went on to point out that he had gone to great lengths to hold a peace conference in July of 1863. "I had presents and would make you a feast, but you sent word to me that you did not want anything to do with me. . . Bull Bear would come in to see me at the head of the Republican but his people held a council and would not let him come." Black Kettle admitted that this was true. Evans accused the Indians of smoking the war pipe with the Sioux. The Chiefs denied this but acknowledged that their actions might give that impression.

Evans did not believe that the Indians could form an enduring treaty. "I understand that these men who have come to see me now have been opposed to the war all the time, but their people have defied them, and they could not help themselves. Is this so?"

The Chiefs admitted that this was so.

Evans shook his head. "The fact that they have not been able to prevent their people from going to war in the past spring when there was plenty of grass and game makes me believe that they will not be able to make peace which will last longer than until the winter is past.''

He then went on to explain how the situation had altered since the previous year. ''So far as making a treaty now is concerned, we are in no condition to do it, your young men are on the war path, my soldiers are preparing for a fight. . . . The time you make war best is in the summer time, the time when I make war best is in the winter. . . . The war is begun, and the power to make a treaty of peace has passed from me to the great war chief. . . .'' This point, at least, was clear.

Unfortunately the message was interspersed with lines like: ''My proposition to the friendly Indians has gone out. I shall be glad to have them all come under it''; and ''My advice to you is to turn on the side of the government. . . .''

When the Indians inquired what was meant by ''being on the side of the government,'' there was some difficulty explaining it. Suggestions came so fast and from so many people that Whiteley did not get it all transcribed. During the subsequent investigation, he had only a vague recollection. He thought the officers had suggested that the Indians ''render such assistance as they could, by giving information, acting as scouts etc.''

It was understandable that the conference disintegrated. Interpretation was required for every comment, and Whiteley frequently interrupted for clarification as he was copying all testimony in longhand. Much time and patience produced only a small amount of text.

In a desultory fashion, the conference wore down into a question and answer session of little consequence and less information. White Antelope answered too many questions in a manner suggesting early senility. Black Kettle wisely said nothing. Bull Bear answered one question about the origin and activities of the Sioux on the Platte, and then offered to fight the enemies of the whites to prove his peaceful intentions. The Arapahoes were forced to answer questions about depredations near Denver, but were accused of lying by Whiteley, who was in a position to know the facts.

Colonel Chivington made one statement. ''I am not a big war chief,'' he said, ''but all the soldiers in the country are at my command. My rule of fighting white men or Indians is to fight them until they lay down their arms and submit to military authority. You are nearer to Major Wynkoop than anyone else, and you can go to him when you are ready to do that.''

Why did the Chiefs consider this to be a successful meeting? John Smith said, ''The Indians appeared perfectly satisfied, presuming that they would eventually be all right as soon as the authorities could be heard from, and expressed themselves so. Black Kettle embraced the

Governor and Wynkoop and shook hands with all the other officials present, perfectly contented, deeming that the matter was settled.''[25]

General Curtis had been thinking of a winter campaign against the Indians himself, but his plans were barely formed and still secret. His supportive wire reached Chivington on September 28 but after the Camp Weld meeting had adjourned. ''I shall require the bad Indians delivered up,'' Curtis began, ''restoration of equal numbers of stock, also hostages to secure. I want no peace till the Indians suffer more...No peace must be made without my directions.'' Immediately after the council, Governor Evans contacted Colonel Shoup and, admitting that he was in no position to advise, he offered an ''extra-official suggestion'' to be passed on to Major Wynkoop that he treat the Indians as surrendered prisoners of war for the time being.[26]

The problem of feeding Indians while under the protection of the military had been evident for a long time. In June of this year, Charles E. Mix, who had succeeded Dole as Commissioner of Indian Affairs, had written to Governor Evans telling him to ''contract no debts for feeding Indians on reservations.'' On September 29 Evans wrote Agent Colley at Fort Lyon telling him that no peace had been made and informing him that since the Arapahoes and Cheyennes were considered to be at war with the United States, ''...this arrangement relieves the Indian Bureau of their care until peace is declared...''[27]

When the liberated prisoners had arrived in Denver with Major Wynkoop they were turned over to a warm-hearted military wife named Mollie Sanford. She was a Nebraska girl who had lived in the Little Blue country. Laura and the children stayed with her for several days. ''The tales of their captivity were harrowing,'' Mollie wrote. ''Miss Roper was subjected to all the indignities usually given white captives and the children were brutally treated by the squaws.... (Isabelle) was scarred all over with prints of arrow points that the squaws tortured her with.''[28]

Clothing and money were collected for Laura to return to Nebraska and she was finally sent on her way with a train of wagons in mid-October. But misfortune continued to plague her. All of her meager possessions, clothing and money, were lost before she reached Cottonwood Springs. There she was obliged to accept another collection made for her relief.[29]

Mollie Sanford kept little Isabelle, intending to adopt her, but the child was so mentally disturbed that Mollie could not stand it. ''She saw her father butchered...can and does recount the whole tragedy.... She would wake from a sound sleep and sit up in bed with staring eyes and go in detail over the whole thing.'' Mollie turned the child over to Dr. Caleb Birdsall, the Post Surgeon, who in turn put her in the charge of a Dr. Thomas. She was living with a Mr. Davenport when she died in February of 1865.[30]

Ambrose Eubanks also died in Denver in 1865; but no one seems to have recorded the fate of the indomitable Danny Marble.

The season had not ended for the war parties preying on the Platte Road. On or about September 11 a freight train was attacked about thirty miles below Julesburg. Baker's ranch in the same vicinity was also raided, and several men were killed. During the same week the Platte Route was struck also at Cottonwood, and two soldiers were surprised near Plum Creek; one of them was killed. Major O'Brien and General Mitchell moved out from Julesburg in pursuit, but accomplished nothing. On September 19, four dead and mutilated bodies were brought into Fort Cottonwood, but the details of this attack were not published in Denver because the telegraph line went dead at a critical moment.[31]

On September 30 Colonel Chivington and Samuel Elbert, the Territorial Secretary, met Ben Holladay at Latham. Chivington's purpose was to convince Holladay that the stage line could be defended more easily if it ran on the old Cut-Off Route from Junction to Denver. Chivington's men of the Third Regiment were at that time escorting trains and coaches to Latham, and then either to Denver or to Camp Collins. They were also escorting private travel on the Cut-Off Road. Chivington had other plans for these soldiers.

"Too expensive," Holladay objected.

"Not if I order you to do it," Chivington countered.

The change of route suddenly became more attractive. If the stage company was following military orders, the U.S. Government could be charged for the expense. Chivington wrote a letter to Holladay ordering the change.

> Benjamin Holladay Esq. Sir: I am directed to furnish your line complete protection against hostile Indians which I can only do by its removal from the Platte to the Cut-Off Route. As it now runs I am compelled to protect two lines as well as one. You will, therefore, remove your stock to the Cut-Off Route, which will enable me to use troops retained for an active campaign against these disturbers of public safety. [Signed] Chivington.[32]

Reuben Thomas, Division Agent for the stage line between Julesburg and Denver, said that it was necessary for him to "tear down and move Fourteen Mile Station barn forty miles, Big Bend Station, consisting of a house, barn and corral, sixty miles, and Eagle's Nest Station with its barn, house and corral twenty-four miles, with the hay and grain and all other property pertaining to the said station." William Reynolds, the General Superintendent of the line, said that over a fifteen-month period, twelve new stations were built on a new road, 150 miles long. It took a long time to get the money, but Holladay billed the government $50,000 for these changes.[33]

The *Rocky Mountain News* was delighted. The road from Denver to Julesburg was shortened by thirty to forty miles, the delay of transfer of passengers and express at Latham would be eliminated and now the overland traffic would pass through Denver.[34]

As a raw recruit, Morse Coffin from Boulder Creek was assigned escort duty at Valley Station, and he found soldier life to be a paralyzing bore. Major Samuel Logan alternated between Junction and Valley Station to drill the companies stationed there; but the boys of Company D did not enjoy military training, and when they eventually received a compliment from the Major, Morse was certain they didn't deserve it.

Colonel George Shoup, who had become Regiment Commander on September 21, visited the camps after his appointment. It was the first time many of the boys had seen him. Colonel Shoup was a personable man and readily achieved popularity. From Valley Station Colonel Shoup and his company escorted a train to Julesburg. Eugene Ware met him there, and later called him a "rollicking gentlemen."[35]

After sixteen days the boys of Company D were almost convinced that there were no Indians in Colorado Territory. Then on October 9, a Sunday evening, a messenger came into Valley Station from the Wisconsin Ranch. The messenger asked for Captain Nichols, and told him that an Indian wearing full war paint and battle dress had been seen about sundown in the bluffs near the Wisconsin.

As a few of the boys overheard the news, the camp of bored soldiers made a dash for their horses and saddles. The herders, out with the grazing horses, saw the excitement at camp and soon had the herd rounded up and driven to camp. Within minutes the entire company was ready to follow the trail of the lone Indian. Nichols and Lieutenant Dickson selected about thirty-five of the men and gave strict orders for the rest to stay in camp.

Nichols and the lieutenant rode with the detachment to the Wisconsin Ranch, but it was now too late to find the trail of the Indian. A sergeant with ten men was left at the Wisconsin as a guard while Nichols and the troops returned to Valley Station.

Sam Ashcraft was detained at Valley nursing a rattlesnake bite, so Captain Nichols asked him for advice. Ashcraft said there might be a camp of Indians at the springs about twelve miles to the southeast of the Wisconsin. Nichols decided to take a chance that this was the case.

Coffin was directed to notify twenty-nine men to be ready to march at 2:30 A.M. Ashcraft, cursing with frustration, was not well enough to guide the expedition, but he suggested that Nichols ask Ashcraft's brother, Granville, to meet the troops at the Wisconsin.

The company moved out from Valley at a walk, making no noise. At the Wisconsin Ranch they were joined by the eleven soldiers, along with Mark Coad, Granville Ashcraft and Duncan Kerr, a scout for the First Regiment who just happened to be in the neighborhood. The first light of morning appeared as the company left the ranch, the guides some distance in advance. The troops moved silently until they came up a slope toward a bluff. As the guides could see over the crest of the bluff, they made motions to indicate that the quarry was there. Every fourth man was detailed to hold the horses while the remainder advanced to the edge of the cliff.

Big Wolf should have known better than to camp so near to Valley Station where there was a company of soldiers. He had been at Cedar Canyon, and although his family had all survived Downing's raid, they had lost their horses, lodges and equipment. Now they were on the South Platte again, on their way south for the winter. The habit of camping at the White Butte was so strong that Big Wolf had no doubts about the safety of his family.

There were only two lodges in the valley and there was no movement in the camp. Morse Coffin did not recall any orders being given but one shot rang out in the early dawn. This was followed by a volley of firing, and the Indians ran out of the lodges in terror, the women and children scrambling to find hiding places in the rushes beyond a protecting ridge.

One old warrior, carrying his weapons, started a dance-like performance, making strange motions, moving back and fourth in a sidling manner drawing attention to himself. Since this was probably his intention, it is very likely that he was not surprised when the inevitable occured. Captain Nichols shot him and his dance ended.

The ponies were grazing a short distance away in a hollow, and some of the men were ordered to secure them. Other soldiers were sent down the valley to prevent escape in that direction. With the camp surrounded, the soldiers closed in.

Two wounded warriors, lying at the edge of a pool of water, were finished off. The soldiers began to search for others hidden in the brush. As they came closer to the hiding places, another gallant attempt was made by a warrior whom Morse thought might be the headman of this small band. After making his presence known, the Indian ran slowly in a stooping position, zigzagging back and forth but not too far out of range for the soldiers' guns. Of course he distracted many of the soldiers who fired at him. Morse said he fired "his first and only shot at him."

As the soldiers came closer the warrior managed to shoot back at them once, but the second time his defective gun exploded and splintered in his hands. Morse did not say who killed him.

When the slaughter of the women and children began, Morse shouted in protest. He was joined by a few others who refused to be a part of it, but the killing continued: four women, two babies and an adolescent boy who almost escaped. He was four hundred yards or more from camp when he was shot. One of the women stood in a pool of water, bent over her child, making a last desperate attempt to protect it. The mother fell and the child stood wide-eyed looking at the soldiers.

"Boys, don't kill it," Morse pleaded. The soldiers didn't, but one of the guides calmly shot the child.

Duncan Kerr removed most of the scalps from the Indians. It took quite a long time. The soldiers went through the lodges and discovered a great deal of loot from wagon trains: bills of lading for Denver firms, fancy women's clothing and other incriminating items including a pair of worn lady's shoes covered with dried blood. They also found a certificate of good character issued to a Cheyenne named Big Wolf.

The soldiers selected some trophies and then burned the lodges and their contents. When the troops returned to Wisconsin Ranch there was much cheering and drinking, and Duncan Kerr performed a scalp dance. Some of the soldiers celebrated far into the night. Morse took no part in festivities.[36]

Colonel Chivington was jubilant. "Our boys are awake," he crowed in a wire to Ben Holladay. Impatient to start after Indians himself, he resented the delays in outfitting the Third Regiment. On October 16 he wrote to Major Wynkoop at Fort Lyon. "Major, I have the best of evidence that there are a large number of Indians on the Republican and design to go after them. Revolvers have not come. The rascal who started them left them at Atchison and took on some mining machinery. This leaves us with nothing but our muskets for the Third. Send as quick as possible those Star carbines. I have moved the Third out sixty miles and will be after the Indians as soon as we can get those carbines. . . ."[37]

By the middle of October Company D at Valley Station, not only short of efficient weapons and suitable horses, was also running short of supplies. Beef could be bought from the Moore brothers and was. But other food was not available. Trains of wagons loaded with groceries passed every day, and quite often the freighters camped nearby. These freighters could easily be drawn into a game of poker, and the soldiers had done little but practice the game for several weeks. Some of the men devised a plan. Captain Nichols and Lieutenant Dickson could not openly countenance this method of replenishing the larder so when the next train camped nearby the officers rode off on a conveniently timed hunting trip. A sergeant and a squad of men spent a profitable noonday with the freighters and returned with a sack of dried apples, a sack of sugar, ten sacks of flour and even a supply of salt.

During the month of October Company D had been divided into squads of men which had been distributed, six to ten men at a place, at each of the stage stations from Valley Station to Julesburg. Very early in November orders came from Company D to collect itself together to be transferred, and two less well equipped companies were sent out to replace all of the Third Regiment which had been stationed on the South Platte. On November 5, in extreme cold, Captain Nichols marched his company to Bijou Basin, east of Denver. On the way Company D paused at the American Ranch to say goodbye to William and Sarah Morris.[38]

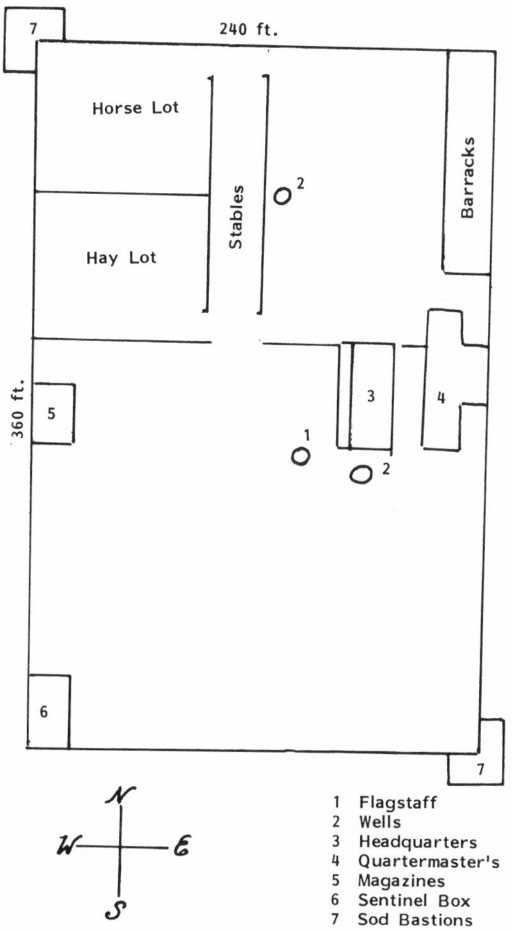

Plan of Camp Rankin, after a sketch by Eugene Ware

Chapter

10

Bloodshed on Sand and Snow

When Major Wynkoop returned to Fort Lyon with the peace chiefs, he followed Governor Evans's suggestion, which coincided conveniently with his own inclinations. He told the chiefs to bring all of the people in closer to the fort, and for ten days Wynkoop had prisoners' rations distributed to 500 Indians. In addition to feeding the Indians, however, Ned Wynkoop made promises.

Immediately after his arrival at Fort Lyon, Wynkoop had sent Lt. W.W. Dennison to headquarters at Leavenworth to ask permission to make peace with the surrendered Indians. Wynkoop talked with the chiefs, telling them they would be protected until the messenger from General Curtis returned and that, even if Curtis did not approve of peace, the Indians would be notified so they could remove themselves to a safe place before any fighting should begin.[1]

General Curtis not only disapproved of making peace with the Indians, at this point he also disapproved of Wynkoop. Orders were sent to Major B.S. Henning at Fort Riley, who was temporarily in command of the District of the Upper Arkansas, to relieve Wynkoop of his post and replace him with someone less friendly to the Indians. In consequence, Maj. Scott Anthony was transferred from Fort Larned to take command of Fort Lyon on October 17. Arriving on the second of November, he talked to Agent Samuel Colley. "It is different from what I expected here," Anthony confessed. "I supposed these Indians were riding in here and making demands and you were obliged to give in to them. I cannot fight them."[2]

Anthony agreed with Wynkoop that there was only one course to follow: to continue the prisoners' rations. The two officers held another council with the chiefs, and Anthony repeated the pledge of protection; but Anthony later denied that he had promised to give the chiefs notice in case the soldiers intended to attack them. Through the month conditions worsened. Anthony insisted that the Indians make retributions of stock and give up their arms as Curtis has demanded. The Indians gave up a few poor arms and worn horses. Then Anthony decided that he was no longer able to feed the Indians. He returned their arms and told them to leave the fort and hunt buffalo. Some Indians came in to the fort, and it is reported that Anthony fired on them. Alarmed by this turn of events, Little Raven took his band of Arapahoes south, but Left Hand and his family joined the Cheyennes who were camped on Sand Creek.[3]

On November 16, Governor Evans left on the coach to begin a journey to Washington. He carried papers and messages encompassing a wide scope of government business. A part of this was confidential matter delegated to him by General Curtis, who hoped that Evans might influence the War Department to grant additional men and support to Curtis for a campaign against the Indians. This was still a secret as far as Curtis was concerned, but it is evident that he had not been informed of Colonel Chivington's plans, and it is likely that Governor Evans had not been apprised of them either.[4]

To examine John Chivington's motives is a pursuit which should be undertaken with a great deal of gravity and caution because there are only hints to reinforce any viewpoint taken. Chivington knew in mid-November that, except for the bands of Indians at Fort Lyon, the main body of Cheyennes was wintering on the Smoky Hill River. Scouts had ascertained its location. Logically, one must believe that this was Chivington's target.[5]

Due to the unusual snowstorms of early November, the 125 miles of prairie to the east between Bijou Basin and the Smoky Hill were blizzard-whipped, and snow was drifted two or three feet deep in places. The troops marched south instead of east from Camp Elbert. On November 26 Ned Wynkoop left Fort Lyon, heading for the States, lucky to be removed from the developing situation. On the same day Colonel Chivington and about 500 men arrived at Bent's Old Fort on the Arkansas, guided there by some force other than luck. Colonel Chivington kept his approach a complete secret by detaining travelers, arresting traders and ranchers known to have Indian relatives, and by sending a lieutenant with a squad of men to put a guard on Bent's Ranch on the Purgatory. George Bent had been visiting there but had left one or two days previously to join the Cheyennes on Sand Creek. As soon as the body of soldiers arrived at Fort Lyon the fort was surrounded, and no one was allowed to leave.

Although Colonel Chivington and Major Anthony seemed to be in complete agreement about an attack on the village at Sand Creek, Anthony vacillated between the promises he had made to the chiefs in conjunction with Wynkoop on the one hand and the domination of Colonel Chivington on the other. Anthony was also worried that an attack on the village would bring the hordes from the Smoky Hill down on Fort Lyon, an onslaught which the soldiers would not be able to withstand. In later testimony Anthony claimed that he believed that Chivington intended to surround the Indian village, select the bad Indians for punishment and retrieve stolen stock—allowing all peaceful and friendly Indians to remain unmolested. In support of this testimony, Anthony claimed that he issued twenty-three days rations to his men, enough for a three-week campaign.[6]

The attitude of the other officers at Fort Lyons was emphatically opposed to the expedition. Captain Silas Soule and Lieutenant Joseph Cramer had been with Wynkoop during the whole sequence; the Hackberry Creek Council, the Camp Weld Conference and several meetings with the chiefs at Fort Lyon. Lieutenant Baldwin also disapproved. Captain Soule tried to reason with Major Anthony, who reassured the Captain that "pledged Indians" and white men in the camp would not be killed; and he also said that Colonel Chivington intended to go on to the Smoky Hill after the Sand Creek village.[7]

Cramer also argued with Anthony and was given the same replies, Lieutenant Cramer then tackled Colonel Chivington with a careful description of Wynkoop's pledges. Chivington brushed him aside, saying that "such men as Major Wynkoop and [Cramer] had better get out of the United States service."[8]

Colonel Chivington issued an order to march at 8:00 P.M. Some officers of the New Mexico volunteers, Agent Colley and some Fort Lyons residents made a final appeal to Chivington to reconsider. Exploding with anger, Chivington shouted, "Damn any man who is in sympathy with an Indian!"[9]

The military force which marched from Fort Lyon at eight o'clock on the twenty-eighth was headed by Colonel Chivington and Colonel Shoup in charge of about 450 men of the Third Regiment. Chivington was accompanied by Major Jacob Downing and Capt. A.J. Gill, who was a volunteer aide from the militia. The scouts were Duncan Kerr from the South Platte, Jim Beckwourth from Denver, and Robert Bent, who had been forced at gunpoint to join this treacherous expedition as a guide. William Breakenridge of Company B was appointed as a courier for Colonel Chivington.

From Camp Weld, Lt. Luther Wilson was in charge of 100–125 men of the First Regiment of Colorado Cavalry, and Major Scott Anthony commanded 125 men of the First Regiment from Fort Lyon. The entire force was divided into five battalions—one under Lt. Col. Leavitt Bowen of the Third Regiment with two howitzers, another battalion under Major Hal Sayre of the Third. A battalion under Capt. Theodore Cree of the Third included Company D, headed by Captain Nichols. The fourth battalion of the First Regiment under Lieutenant Wilson had two pieces of artillery, the battalion under Major Anthony included companies headed by Captain Soule and Lieutenant Cramer. Company G of the Third Regiment, which included Irving Howbert, was also attached to Anthony's battalion.

It was a clear night with no moon, and the course was set by the north star. The companies were arranged in ranks of four abreast, kept at a sharp pace by a sequence of walk, trot, gallop, dismount and lead. It was about forty miles to the big bend of Sand Creek, and once during the night the guide led the troops through a lake. Some thought Robert Bent was responsible and was trying to get the ammunition wet.

Irving Howbert, riding with Company G, said that he would willingly have risked being scalped by the Indians for a half-hour's sleep. Morse Coffin in Captain Cree's battalion said some of the boys managed to fall asleep in their saddles or, when a halt was called, would fall to the ground and sleep for the few minutes they were allowed to pause.

At the first break of dawn the troops were still a mile away from the Indian camp, so the pace was hastened to double-quick and the artillery made so much noise that it could be heard for miles. Someone in Company D remarked that this was a queer way to surprise the Indians.[10]

At that time Sand Creek flowed from the north and stubbornly resisted being diverted to the east by the slope of the land, resulting in a deep channel about 200 yards wide which was furrowed into the sand with high undercut banks, from six to twelve feet high. Farther along, after the curve to the east was accomplished, the channel leveled, and before it turned gently again to the south it provided sloping banks, a favorite place for camping Indians. On this day, along the north side of the west–east segment were from 80 to 100 lodges of Cheyennes and Arapahoes. Farthest west was the clan of War Bonnet; then, ranging back from the stream behind the largest concentration of tipis was that of White Antelope and the family of Lone Bear. Black Kettle's band stretched from the banks of the stream toward the sand hills. More to the east were the five or six Arapaho lodges of Left Hand. Somewhat apart, on the southerly bend, another family was camped under Chief Sand Hill.

In the camp were a few whites and half-breeds. John Smith had been sent out a few days previously with trade goods by Major Anthony, who wished to know what the temper of the Indians might be. With

Smith had come a soldier, David Lauderback, and a driver from Fort Lyon named Watson Clark. John Smith's Sioux wife was with him, and also John Smith's adult half-breed son, who was in camp on a separate trading mission. In the lodges of the Hill People, White Antelope's band, were George Bent and Edmond Guerrier. Edmond was related to White Antelope's family. It is not certain with which band Charley Bent traveled, but he was in camp also.

When the women of the camp heard the approaching soldiers they ran to John Smith's lodge, imploring him to go out and talk to the soldiers to assure them that the camp was peaceful. Others of the Indian women, who had more faith in flight than in negotiation, headed for the ponies picketed on the north side of the camp and began moving as many of the women and children as possible away from the camp to the north. Edmond Guerrier was asleep when he heard the excited women outside his lodge debating about whether the approaching sounds were buffalo or soldiers. He dashed out and headed for John Smith's tent. Smith was ahead, and Lauderback suggested that he and Guerrier go out to meet the troops also. Before the interpreter reached the perimeter of the camp Guerrier could see soldiers dismounting; he was confident that the troops were going to begin shelling the lodges. When the soldiers opened fire with rifles and pistols, Guerrier struck out to the north where he came across his cousin, White Antelope's daughter, who was driving a herd of ponies. Edmond joined her and they moved hastily in the direction of the Smoky Hill River.[11]

As Chivington's forces approached the Indian camp, their first objective was to capture the ponies, about 500 of which ranged both to the left and right of the troops. Chivington dispatched Major Anthony's battalion to capture and secure the horses on the left. Irving Howbert was in this command, and he remembered that they started immediately on the run to get between the herd and the Indian camp. They had not proceeded far when they saw six or more mounted Indians riding over the ridge from the village toward the herd. After seeing the number of soldiers facing them, the Indians turned around and rode back to camp. The ponies were surrounded and driven off by a detachment of Company G which was detailed to guard them. Major Anthony moved his battalion rapidly over the ridge down to the south bank of the dry creek and waited for the Third Regiment to come up.[12]

In the meantime, Lieutenant Wilson with his battalion was sent across the creek to the right to capture the pony herd grazing there. This done, Wilson's men took a position on the northeast side of the village and began firing into the lodges.

In the ranks of the Third Regiment behind Chivington and Shoup, Morse Coffin was not more than forty feet behind the leaders. The men were directed to shed their overcoats, canteens and encumbrances and to dismount. It was here that Chivington exhorted his men to remember the women and children who had been killed by Indians on the Platte. Morse said he thought the Colonel's lip quivered as he said, "Boys, I am not going to tell you who to kill, but remember our slaughtered women and children." Jim Beckwourth, who had a more extravagant taste for rhetoric, was beside Chivington, and Beckwourth quoted him as saying, "I don't tell you to kill all ages and sex but look back on the plains of the Platte where your mothers, fathers, brothers and sisters have been slain and their blood saturating the sands on the Platte." Chivington must have repeated the admonition, because as the soldiers charged past him Robert Bent heard him say, "Remember our wives and children, murdered on the Platte and Arkansas!"[13]

Major Anthony's men formed a line along the creek bed at just about the same time as the first wave of men from the Third crowded behind from the southeast. As they started firing, the bullets whistled over and between Captain Soule's men. Soule reported the fact to Anthony, and was ordered to take his company up the south and west bank. Soule waited until there was general firing from both banks. Since he was strongly opposed to the whole military action, he decided it was unsafe to remain there. He led his men up the left bank, skirting the area of fighting. Soule's company managed to avoid the battle entirely.

Cramer's company was positioned farther down the creek to the right of Anthony's body of men. When the howitzers were brought up behind him, someone called out to him to get out of the way, so he moved his company across the creek to the north bank on the edge of the village. From here he moved north up the creek.

George Bent slept through the early alarm in the camp, and by the time he was awakened by the shouting and activity the troops were advancing at a rapid trot. He ran out of his lodge and found people dashing about in confusion, women screaming, men shouting to one another, everyone only partially dressed. Some of the men, already armed, started out with lassoes and bridles hoping to catch some of the ponies before the troops reached them. Bent went back to his lodge for his weapons, and when he came out, fell in with a group of four middle-aged warriors who intended to run to the west into the sand hills. Before they reached the first rise, they were in such danger of being overtaken by the soldiers that they took a desperate chance. Bent's party made a dash back to the creek bed and the relative safety of the deep channel of the creek. Here they ran up the sandy path, passing dead and dying men, women and children before they gained the protection of the high banks where other warriors had dug in and were attempting to defend themselves. The place where they were was too exposed and when the soldiers approached one of Bent's group, calling out for the others to follow, Bent made another sprint for a place farther up the stream, where women and children had dug deep pits and thrown up breastworks of sand on their exposed side. Just before he reached the pits George was struck by a bullet in his hip, and he crawled the last few feet to shelter.[14]

A young Cheyenne named Little Bear was in the camp. He had just become a warrior. His war bonnet was new, and his weapons had never been used. Little Bear had risen early that morning and gone out to bring his family's ponies in, but before he crossed the ridge he met another warrior who was running back to camp with the news that the soldiers had captured the pony herd. By this time Little Bear could see the advancing column so he ran back to the village. He passed Black Kettle's lodge where a group of people were huddled in fear around a flagpole.

Little Bear ran to his lodge to get his weapons, and while he was fastening his war bonnet in place the bullets began to hit the outside of his lodge like hailstones. Slipping around the backs of the lodges, Little Bear reached the creek bank and joined five other warriors. The people of the village were running north as fast as they could in the sand of the creek bed, and the warriors were too, until the soldiers rode up on both banks beside them. The five warriors made a choice and struck out for the sand hills to the west, while Little Bear continued up the creek. The five warriors were soon overtaken and killed but Little Bear reached the breastworks. He had lost most of his feathers from his war bonnet and there were bullet holes in his shield but he was safe.[15]

With Major Anthony's battalion advancing up the southwest side of the creek and Lieutenant Wilson's cavalry moving along the edge of the village on the east and north, it is not surprising that when the Third Regiment reached the camp Morse Coffin noted that the village was almost deserted. They proceeded through the village with the two colonels a little in advance of the troops. Jim Beckwourth was considerably behind Colonel Chivington, since his horse was slower, and Robert Bent, the reluctant guide, was probably close to Beckwourth. The courier, William Breckenridge, was nearby, as was Duncan Kerr, the South Platte scout.

Robert Bent and many others saw Black Kettle and the close group of Indians with the large U.S. flag, but Chivington later denied seeing either the leader or the flag on the lodgepole.

Beckwourth recalled seeing White Antelope, who dashed among the lodges toward the officers shouting "Stop! Stop!" White Antelope must have been closer to Beckwourth and therefore behind Chivington and Shoup as he ran toward them. There was much noise and confusion, the soldiers were excited and out of control, the officers were trying to settle the men. No one paid any attention to the old chief except Duncan Kerr—who shot him.[16]

Left Hand, the Arapaho chief whose band was camped where they would have been encountered by the soldiers very early in the assault, may have been one of the first to die. It is said that he stood before his lodge with his arms folded, refusing to fight the whites to the very last.[17]

It is puzzling to determine how Black Kettle, after abandoning the flag, crossed the village with his followers and fled up the creek bed ahead of the Third Regiment while the firing was so intense from the banks. Most of them were killed here. Black Kettle's wife was struck down and was left behind among the dead. Black Kettle reached the dug-out caves safely.[18]

The whites and half-breeds in the Indian camp had gathered together in one lodge; John Smith, his wife, his son Jack, Charley Bent, David Lauderback and the teamster Clark. When John Smith had made his first attempt to talk to the soldiers, he had been fired on, and was forced to return to the lodge. Clark rigged up a pole with a tanned buffalo skin for an improvised flag of truce and Lauderback sat down on a wagon tongue to wait. The firing from the soldiers of the Third was so insistent that Lauderback went back into the lodge to wait for Chivington to come up. As he did so Lauderback called out and Chivington recognized him, telling him to join the troops. Lauderback said that there were other white men in the lodge, and Chivington told him to have them join the ranks also. John Smith ran out of the lodge and was fired on again. A soldier in Cramer's company named Pierce rode forward, supposedly to save John Smith. Pierce was fired on by an indiscriminate soldier and was killed. Colonel Chivington recognized the interpreter and called to him, "Run here, Uncle John, you are all right." Lieutenant Baldwin's company with the two howitzers was just coming along, and the lieutenant looked around for a horse for the old man but there were none, Baldwin advised Smith to hold onto the gun carriage and keep up with the column. Lauderback eventually found a horse for John Smith and one for himself. Clark and Charley Bent fell in with the ranks.[19]

The flood of Volunteers moved up the creek bed. One company would move up, dismount and fire until the Indians were out of range, then remount and move to the sides while another company charged ahead, dismounted and fired—not necessarily in an orderly manner. These were untrained and undisciplined men, and they were in constant danger of being shot by fellow troopers. The devastation continued. There were still a few Indians escaping into the sand hills and a number of soldiers wandered off in separate pursuits. Smith thought there were only about two hundred soldiers in the body which converged on the strip of creek where the pits were located. The howitzers were brought up, and shot was peppered into the creek bed between the high banks. Some of the inexperienced men of the Third ran too close to the banks and were struck by arrows. The soldiers concentrated their fire on the people in the pits, who fought back as well as they could with bows and arrows and only a few guns. The troops did not charge the pits but were content to wait for opportune shots from the bank. If most of the warriors in a particular pit had been killed, the soldiers rushed in when the fighting diminished, and killed the wounded and helpless.

Morse Coffin asked permission to go with a detachment to follow a small group of Indians believed to be escaping to the right, and Irving Howbert now became involved in an engagement between some soldiers trading rifle fire with Indians hidden behind a pile of driftwood. Howbert had barely reached the place of this engagement when a man from Company D was hit, and Howbert took the responsibility for caring for the wounded man and finding Captain Nichols. Isolated duels and small battles between individual warriors and one or two soldiers took place in the brush and gullies bordering the open area. One Indian, burrowed into the sand under a buffalo robe, was almost undetected. Before his death he killed one of the soldiers of Company D. Other Indians buried themselves in the sand, and perhaps some of these did escape detection. Of the nine dead soldiers and thirty-seven wounded, these one-to-one encounters were responsible for most of the fatalities.[20]

The soldiers began straggling back to the Indian village after noon, although the main fighting did not really cease until the ammunition ran low about 2:00 P.M. After the last of the soldiers returned to camp about five, the Indians began to leave the protection of the pits and slip away to the north. Lieutenant Dickson of Company D could see fifteen or twenty of the Indians moving away and called it to the attention of Colonel Shoup, but the men were too tired and hungry to follow.[21]

Charley Bent had been able to remain unnoticed all day; but with his pronounced Indian features, he was in considerable danger of being shot by someone who did not know him. Apparently he had gone into hiding with a squaw. When he was discovered, it was fortunate that he was rescued by Charles Autobee, a good friend and neighbor of William Bent. Autobee took both Charley and the squaw to Jim Beckwourth, who said that Charley begged him to save both their lives. Beckwourth put them in an ambulance with a wounded man and took them to the hospital area where they would be safe for the time being. Later, when

Beckwourth returned, Charley had gone off, but the squaw was smuggled into camp in another ambulance. Beckwourth left her in John Smith's lodge with Smith's wife, who had never left the village.[22]

About three o'clock Major Anthony was making preparations to ride to Fort Lyon to escort the supply train back to Sand Creek. Captain Soule's command was ordered to accompany him. Robert Bent would be returning with the Fort Lyon soldiers. It was thought best to get Charley Bent out of camp, but Captain Soule was reluctant to do so without the consent of his superior. After weighing the influence which William Bent still wielded against the fact that Robert Bent would probably not like having his brother returned to Fort Lyon, Colonel Chivington shrugged and gave his permission for Silas Soule to take Charley Bent with him to Fort Lyon.[23]

The prisoners were gathered into John Smith's lodge: Smith's wife and child, the squaw found with Charley Bent; another squaw, the wife of the sutler at Fort Lyon, with her two children; and an old Arapahoe woman and her grandson, who had been found hiding in a ravine. There were two or three other children who survived but were not put under guard. The enlisted men fed them and cared for them indifferently while they were in camp.

Another survivor, who was not technically a prisoner but who—because of his relationship to John Smith—was quartered with the other prisoners, was Smith's son, Jack. It is reported that the day after the battle, when the guard was removed from the prisoners, Lt. Clark Dunn was responsible for a seemingly pointless act of violence in which Jack Smith was shot and his body dragged around the camp ground.[24]

The murder was the culmination rather than the beginning of the orgy of savagery which took place at Sand Creek. It began with the taking of scalps; probably every man who killed an Indian took the scalp of his conquest. A scalp was worth ten dollars in Denver, and even Morse Coffin took one; he knew a merchant who had promised him a pair of boots in exchange for it. But there were not enough scalps to go around, and after the fighting was over the gruesome mutilation began; scalping of women and children, the slicing of ears, noses and genitals. Fingers were chopped off; bodies were cut open and organs removed—hearts, entrails, and vaginal canals. Heads were smashed, and when survivors were discovered, pleading women and small children were shot with callous indifference. The body of White Antelope was virtually dissected and carried away piece by piece. The bestiality revealed at Sand Creek proved once and for all that barbarity is not the exclusive prerogative of the nominally uncivilized.

John Smith and Lt. Col. Bowen made a count of the dead, and Smith attempted to identify the mangled bodies of the headmen. He mistook another man for Black Kettle, but he found One Eye, whom Chivington did not mention. Before the count was made, Chivington claimed a great victory, between 400 and 500 Indians dead, including Chiefs Black Kettle, White Antelope, "Knock Knee" (Notanee) and Little Robe.[25]

There was so much variation in the number of dead counted by various persons that analysis is impractical. In many cases exaggeration to a higher figure or a lower number was calculated for effect in many testimonies. Morse Coffin went over the field, and he guessed that there must have been somewhat in excess of 125 killed—males, females and children together. John Smith thought there may have been seventy or eighty, twenty-five or thirty of them warriors. Much later George Bent did not estimate a number but said most of Black Kettle's clan was killed and over half of Yellow Wolf's band, including Yellow Wolf, an old chief. Half of War Bonnet's band was killed and almost all of White Antelope's people. Sand Hill's band, which was camped farther down the creek, escaped. Only four of the fifteen lodges of Arapahoes under Left Hand survived.[26]

The plundered village was burned on November 30, and on December 1, Chivington and his men marched toward the Arkansas River, ostensibly in pursuit of Little Raven's Arapahoes. At the mouth of Sand Creek, Company G was detailed to take the dead and wounded to Fort Lyon. With them went three squaws and three children. Several days later, when Chivington abandoned his campaign and returned his forces to Fort Lyon, it was discovered that Charley Bent had been released and disappeared. The Indian women and children were sent to William Bent's ranch on the Purgatory. In the afternoon Major Anthony sent Lieutenant Cramer with twelve men to William Bent's ranch to offer protection for the family. Cramer found the prisoners stranded on the river bank by shifting ice, and the party had to wait until nightfall, when the river froze again, to cross and proceed to Bent's ranch. The enlisted men took a young Arapahoe boy, two girls and an infant, but the baby was abandoned at the mouth of Sand Creek.

The three surviving children were exhibited in a sideshow as prisoners of Sand Creek until several years later the government responded to complaints from the Indians and some officers were appointed to kidnap the children from the man who was exhibiting them. They managed to abduct the boy, but the girls were hidden and never recovered. The Arapahoe boy was returned to his people.[27]

By the time the soldiers left the field, many of the people in the dugout shelters in the bed of Sand Creek were wounded. George Bent wrote, "Soon as they left us, we, all that was left of us, started up Sand

Creek. About half of us in the party were wounded. I myself was badly wounded in the hip; as there were no bones broke I was able to walk.''[28]

Slowly and painfully the tragic group of survivors moved slowly, dragging themselves along. The Cheyennes walked a long time before they were cautiously approached by a group of fugitives who had ponies—some of the fortunate ones like Edmond Guerrier and White Antelope's daughter, who had escaped at the earliest signs of attack. One of George Bent's cousins had an extra pony so he could ride, but the ponies were scarce and the group was forced to move so slowly with wounded and the unmounted that it proved necessary to camp in a ravine for the night after only a few miles.

As soon as it was completely dark, Black Kettle went back for his wife's body and was amazed to find that she was still alive, even though she had been wounded in nine separate places.

It was extremely cold. There was no wood for fires, no buffalo robes, not even extra clothing. Those who were able collected armsful of grass and brush to make feeble fires. Piles of grass over the bodies of the wounded also served as a meager defense against the freezing winter night.

At dawn the fugitives made a tedious and painful progress toward the camp on the Smoky Hill, where they were met by crowds of wailing and keening mourners.

Grieving gave way to anger and anger to craving for vengeance during the month following, while Bent's wound was healing. Runners were being sent out to the Sioux with a war pipe, and George Bent and Edmond Guerrier obtained horses and rode to the Sioux camps with the Cheyenne council party. At their camp on Solomon Fork, the Sioux smoked the war pipe.

Following this council Guerrier and Bent rode south to the Arkansas River. Chivington's men had taken eight of George's horses—all he had in camp—but he had left a few animals at his father's ranch on the Purgatory, and it was George's purpose to pick up his horses. As they approached Fort Lyon, Guerrier became uneasy. He reasoned that if he gave himself up at the fort his chances for survival would be better than if he was captured and taken forcibly. Guerrier went into Fort Lyon while Bent went on to his father's ranch. Guerrier was relieved to learn that the military had no quarrel with him personally, and he was released. He does not seem to have joined the Indians again that winter.

George found his father camped about twenty-five miles upstream from the ranch as a precaution against a return of Chivington's unpredictable soldiers. After rounding up his horses and resting a few days, George set out again to the Cheyenne camp. With him went a young

Cheyenne named Howling Wolf, who lived at the ranch, and the two of them escorted the three women and three children prisoners that had survived Sand Creek.[29]

The party traveled for four days before overtaking the village which was now camped on Cherry Creek, a branch of the Republican River. The village had swollen while Bent had been away; two bands of Brule Sioux under Spotted Tail and Pawnee Killer had joined the Cheyenne camp. Eighty lodges of northern Arapahoes had been wintering with the Sioux in preference to going into the dangerous area of the Arkansas River as they had planned. They too smoked the pipe.

What the village needed most was food, and the Sioux knew where to find it: in the huge warehouse at Julesburg. About the first of January an important council was held and the decision was made to attack the stage station on the South Platte. A thousand warriors were ready and eager to march, and women and ponies were recruited to bring back the plunder. George and his brother Charley, who had gravitated back to the village after Sand Creek, both planned to join this great Indian army.

Black Kettle chose not to join the great northern movement. The Cheyennes had been angry with him at first after Sand Creek, holding him responsible for their having had faith in the promises of white men, but George Bent said they "soon got out of that notion in a few days." Nevertheless, Black Kettle mourned the loss of so many of his family. There were few men left—only women. Black Kettle decided to go south of the Arkansas to join the Kiowas and Comanches. George went to each lodge to say goodbye to close friends who intended to accompany Black Kettle. It would be neccessary for many of the band to walk since they had few horses. Their lodges were gone, but they did have buffalo robes, and they would be able to find plenty of food since the buffalo were plentiful farther south. When the destitute band reached the camps of the southern Indian tribes, they received many presents, as it was customary to give elaborate gifts of ponies, saddles, bridles and lodges to visiting tribes.[30]

On about the fifth of January, 1865, the columns marched, in exceptional order because of the determination of the experienced older fighters—members of the warrior societies—who knew that if younger men were allowed to wander off their mischief could cause the failure of the entire attack. This was no longer summer adventure; this was serious business. There were new names marching with the Cheyennes, among them the Dog Soldiers, who for the most part had held themselves aloof from contact with the whites for so long. The leaders of this movement were not the Cheyennes, however. The Sioux had smoked the pipe first, the Sioux had planned the raid, and in company with other chiefs it was the Sioux who led the column. It is evident that a camp was made between Cherry Creek and Julesburg, probably someplace on Whiteman's Fork on the Republican.[31]

The term of service for the Third Regiment had expired on December 23, and they were mustered out. Colonel Chivington's term in the First Regiment had actually expired sometime previously, but he resigned his commission on January fourth. He was replaced immediately by Colonel Thomas Moonlight of the Eleventh Kansas Volunteer Cavalry. Moonlight arrived in Denver on the day of Chivington's resignation in foreboding weather, so chilly and damp that the cartridges loaded in the guns for the welcoming salute "went off with a sort of wet whisper, a good deal of smoke but no sound." Major Samuel Logan, who led the men of the First Regiment to meet and escort Colonel Moonlight, called for hearty cheers from the men to welcome the new commander, but the soldiers refused to respond.[32]

Colorado was not well defended and the South Platte Trail was left without defense when the 100-day men were drawn away from Junction and Valley Station. Viewing the situation as desperate, Moonlight asked the current legislative assembly of the Territory to amend the militia law to provide pay, bounties and compensation for the use of horses, and a bill to this effect was introduced into the assembly. But as haggling over it continued for two weeks Moonlight declared martial law, demanding volunteers. In the meantime the intense gravity of the situation became apparent to everyone.[33]

The vulnerable South Platte Trail brought to Denver its vitally necessary contact with the East. Besides the stagecoaches and the travelers, there was only that slender thread of communication, the telegraph wire. Three newspapers— the *Rocky Mountain News,* the *Black Hawk Mining Journal* and the *Denver Republican and Commonwealth*— depended on news passed on to them from both John Ford at Junction Station and John Hines at Valley Station, but the switch operators at Julesburg were a constant source of annoyance. The editors did not speak kindly of the telegraph operators. The *News* referred contemptuously to Samuel Bancroft, the first operator, as "Julesburg." Another newspaper bitterly concluded that " 'Julesburg' is drunk again!" By the time Philo Holcomb and S.R. Smith had assumed the duties at the Julesburg switch, they were faced with undisguised rancor from the Denver press. In November of 1864, after one particularly frustrating attempt to publish an important story about an Indian attack on a stagecoach and a train at Plum Creek, the *Rocky Mountain News* wrote, "Today our accomodating operators endeavored to wake up the Julesburg operator in order to learn more of the particulars but in vain. By appearances the great business of the latter office is sleeping until ten and spending the rest of the time among the Nebraska officers stationed there. In order to get any news from the east of Denver, it is necessary that the Julesburg chap be always on hand so as to 'switch off' the same towards Colorado. Otherwise, he being out of his office, the news runs into the ground as far as we are concerned, there being no one to 'adjust' the machine. Wish we were on the main line!''[34]

Now in January, without soldiers, the telegraph operators were faced with keeping the line in working order with only the protection they could get from the ranchers. Apparently the Indians had not realized that there were no soldiers in the neighborhood, because the line had not been cut recently. Frequent parties of Indians were seen during December, but they confined their activities to raiding. For instance, a party of fifteen warriors was seen near Valley Station on December 5, and a party of ranchers went out after them. On the sixth, five more Indians drove off ten head of cattle from Bijou Ranch. Scouts discovered that the party had gone in a southeasterly direction, but they were not overtaken.[35]

In January of 1865 Camp Rankin, at Julesburg, was in what was called the Eastern Subdistrict of Kansas and the Territories. The post was commanded by Col. Robert R. Livingston, who had his headquarters at Fort Kearny since General Mitchell no longer maintained headquarters at Julesburg. Camp Rankin was still in the charge of Major Nicholas O'Brien and his lieutentants, and the officers were supported by one company of the Seventh Iowa Cavalry. In this month, Colonel Samuel W. Summers, O'Brien's superior officer, was visiting at Camp Rankin. He had evidently been escorted to the post by Capt. Edward Murphy with a detachment of Company A from Alkali Lake Station.

The stage station at Julesburg was a banquet spread on the plains, inviting the hungry to partake. Located about a mile east of Camp Rankin, it consisted of a prosperous-looking row of buildings facing the telegraph line, the telegraph office and adjoining living quarters. On the opposite side of the street stood the Overland Stage Company's buildings side by side, a large boarding house, a large stable, a great warehouse and a blacksmith shop—all built of cedar logs. There were other storerooms and a granary made of sod. The rear of the buildings was all enclosed by a large sod corral. Beside the stage company's property, the trader G.W. Thompson continued to operate a privately owned store, crammed with a rich assortment of goods.[36]

The vengeful Indian army was on the move from Cherry Creek. The warriors and women with travois and ponies arrived at White Butte Creek, where Big Wolf's family had been slaughtered the previous October, and from here they moved to a camp in the sand hills south of Julesburg on January 6. The soldier societies posted a guard around the camp—not to intercept intruders but to prevent any hot-blooded impatient warriors from slipping out. The Sioux were well acquainted with the area. They knew that the fort and the stage station lay in the center of a broad treeless plain with only a sparse growth of brush growing on the islands of the sprawling river. The only defensible natural irregularity was a ravine called the Devil's Dive, which extended from the sandhill bluffs down to the river bank, running southwest to northeast, about three miles east of the station. The ravine was deep enough to provide cover for a decoy group of warriors to approach the station without attracting attention.

The Indian camp was alive long before daylight. George Bent and his brother Charley dressed themselves as warriors, George allegedly for the first time against the whites. Any of the young men who owned one of the impressive feathered war bonnets characteristic of the Cheyenne tied it on his head. Other warriors applied paint to match their shield design, and assembled their weapons. The women prepared the pack ponies to move into the settlement as soon as resistance had ceased.[37]

The war chiefs knew that the sight of the entire force of Indians would freeze the soldiers inside the fort. George Bent believed that it was the intention of the leaders to send a well-chosen group of warriors down to the fort to draw the soldiers into a chase which would lead them into the sand hills, where the main body of hidden warriors would surround them and finish them off. In accordance with this plan, Big Crow, leader of the Crooked Lance Society, was chosen to guide this decoy party. Big Crow took ten picked warriors with him, and they worked their way down the ravine just as day was breaking. Suddenly, they were aware of the stagecoach approaching from the east. The opportunity for attack was too much to resist. As the coach plummeted down one side of the steep arroyo, William Baker, the driver, was going as fast as the animals could run in order to have enough momentum to ascend the other side. This speed may have saved him and his one passenger, William Hudnut, the express messenger, because even though the party of Indians shot their arrows and three of them struck the coach, the men were not hit.

Without slackening his pace, Baker ran the coach directly to Bulen's Ranch, about one mile east of the station. The small band of Indians followed, but after the coach was in the corral, Big Crow returned with his men to the arroyo. When it seemed safe, Baker took the coach out and proceeded to the station, where the horses were changed and he and the messenger drove on to Camp Rankin to ask for an escort along the South Platte to the next home station. Captain O'Brien was roused, but regretted that if there were Indians in the neighborhood he could not spare men for an escort. Baker and Hudnut returned to the stage station, stabling the horses but leaving the coach standing in front of the station with the treasure boxes filled with greenbacks still in the front boot under the driver's seat.[38]

Not far from Bulen's Ranch two Denver-bound wagon trains were camped; Clark's and Cook and Keith's. Abandoning the chase after the stagecoach Big Crow directed his group toward the wagon trains, which they circled, whooping and pitching arrows into the circled wagons. The men had no time to retreat to Bulen's corral and were forced to defend themselves from behind the wagons.[39]

This attracted the attention of the garrison, a bugle was sounded, and in half an hour's time O'Brien ordered out thirty-eight men to aid the wagon trains. Colonel Summers wished to go also, as well as Captain Murphy with his troops of Company A. A few civilians, including the trader Jack Morrow, were said to have joined the soldiers. It was 9:30 A.M. by now and Smith, the telegraph operator, signalled an excited wire to the *Rocky Mountain News* that the attack had begun, that troops were starting off, and that he, Smith, intended to accompany them. Holcomb took over the key and sent a wire to the *Black Hawk Mining Journal* that 100 soldiers had gone in pursuit and that the Indians were retreating to the bluffs.[40]

This was the opportunity which Big Crow had anticipated. The soldiers were following; he would draw them into the hidden horde of armed Indians above the arroyo. George Bent, still with the main body of warriors, said they could hear shooting and the bugle blowing. The Indians charged down out of the hills.

The teamsters from the besieged wagon trains made a frantic retreat to Bulen's Ranch, carrying four wounded and leaving two dead behind. It would seem that two of the wounded died before the day was over. As the terrifying throng of Indians poured out of the hills, it did not take long to see that the soldiers were overmatched. Colonel Summers ordered a retreat, shouting to Captain O'Brien to take a portion of his men back to the post to man the artillery while he, Captain Murphy and Lieutenant Brewer covered his withdrawal. The officers and one platoon fell back toward Bulen's Ranch. Some of the men were on foot, as their horses had been killed. Fourteen men were killed and several wounded. It was necessary to leave the dead on the field while the rest of the troops barely reached safety.[41]

As O'Brien and his detachment passed the stage station, the employees all ran out in fright, and O'Brien shouted to them to save themselves, to go to the fort immediately. Hudnut snatched the most easily accessible packet of money but was obliged to leave the heavy treasure chest and express packages behind. Holcomb gathered up all of the necessary telegraph apparatus, and the stage employees made a frantic dash over the mile between Julesburg and Camp Rankin.[42]

George Bent, riding by, saw the dead bugler among the dying soldiers, and he could see the people from the stage station running toward the fort. With the soldiers out of the way, the pillage began. The bodies of the dead soldiers and teamsters were systematically mutilated, probably by those who had been deprived of participation in the fighting. The majority of the Indians moved on to the main purpose of the attack: packing up as many supplies as could be carried. The young braves took an obvious delight in the business of destruction—breaking windows, destroying furniture, tumbling bolts of cloth from Thompson's store and unrolling them in glorious banners behind their horses onto the prairie. The defenseless stagecoach was stripped, the mailsacks were riddled and the letters scattered to the wind. The treasure chest was yanked out and forced open. The green paper was a disappointment—the Indians had hoped for coins—so the bundles of paper money were chopped into bits and allowed to flutter away in a greenish flurry. Bent went directly into the large building which he called the sutler's store. He discovered that the breakfast set out for the stage passengers and personnel was still on the table and still hot. He called out to his comrades, who sat down to a generous meal. Bent said it was the first time he had seen butter in many years, and he ate his share of it.

The soldiers at the fort began to fire the howitzer at the Indians. When Bent saw how the shots were falling he deduced that the soldiers did not want to hit the buildings, so he advised the Indians to stay behind the shelter of the walls. Bent wrote that the soldiers only fired the gun three or four times. Later, when a band of Indians crossed the river to round up a herd of cattle, the guns were fired again, but the Indians were out of range.

The women with ponies had loaded them at once, pulling whole hogs-heads of molasses behind them on pole drags, and had taken the booty to the hills. They returned and loaded them again. Finishing late in the day, the Indians wanted to fire the buildings as they departed but the chiefs deterred them with the reminder that it might be necessary to come back again after the warehouses were restocked. The destruction was therefore limited to broken windows, furniture and other items which could be replaced.[13]

After the Indians had withdrawn, O'Brien and his men and some civilians went out to Bulen's Ranch to increase the numbers of the platoon and officers still besieged there. The Indians must certainly have paused here to ransack the undefended trains and drive away the stock.

If there were still a few straggling warriors at Bulen's they soon drifted away, and the troops, teamsters and Bulen the rancher, as well, returned to the post.[44]

Official reports numbered the attacking Indians between 500 and 1500 and claimed that thirty to fifty-six of them were killed, including the commanding chief. Captain O'Brien at first reported fifteen soldiers killed, but later changed the number to fourteen—which was the accurate number, because one of the fifteen men had not yet been mustered in and was still technically a civilian. On January 9, William Hudnut wired from Julesburg that they had buried twenty men on that day: fifteen soldiers, four teamsters and one man for which there is no account. George Bent said that not one single Indian was killed.[45]

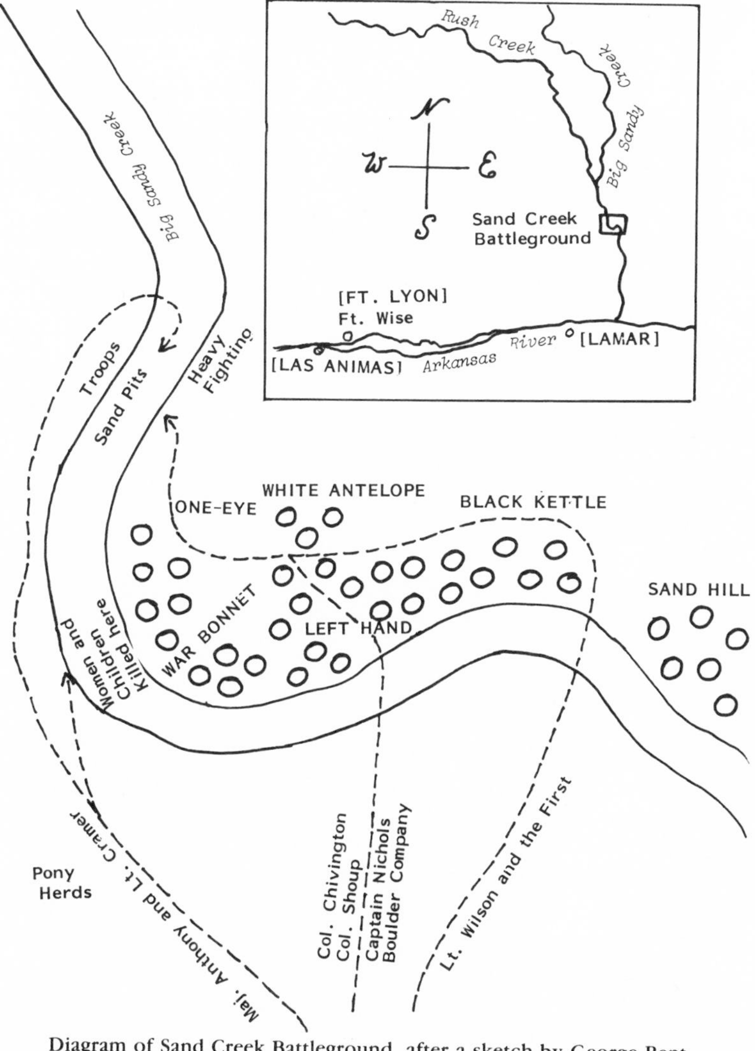

Diagram of Sand Creek Battleground, after a sketch by George Bent

Chapter

11

Vengeance, Fire and Ice

Not all of the huge army of Indians went from Whiteman's Fork to Julesburg on the sixth of January. A party of them remained behind and planned their own raid. At dawn on the seventh they struck the South Platte Road near Dennison's Ranch. John Hines, the operator at Valley Station, wired the *News* at 9:30 A.M. (almost concurrently with Holcomb's wire about the Julesburg attack). Hines reported that about seventy-five Indians, who came from the south, had attacked a train which was camped for the winter at Dennison's. There had been twelve men killed, and all of the wagons burned. Frightened travelers fleeing into the station corral thought that some emigrants also had been attacked downriver from the train. Hines announced his intention of leaving the station almost immediately for Moore's Ranch, which was more extensively fortified than Valley Station. However, he was still at his telegraph key at ten o'clock when he sent another wire to the *Black Hawk Mining Journal* saying that a man had just come in reporting the fight at the wagon train. A short time later Hines added that Dennison's Ranch was on fire; the burning haystack and buildings could be seen clearly. Taking his instruments under his arm, Hines and other refugees made rapid progress three miles downriver to Moore's.

At Moore's Washington Ranch Hines found Reuben Thomas, the Division Agent of the stage line, who informed him that the destroyed wagon train had belonged to a man named Payne and that there had been fifty wagons. He repeated that twelve teamsters had been killed and that a family of emigrants, of uncertain number, must certainly have been killed also. There were about fifty Indians in sight from

Moore's Ranch. Later in the day news was brought from upriver that the Indians had made a raid on the American Ranch the previous night and had run off the stage stock. Reuben Thomas wired Dahler, the Denver stage agent, to hold all passengers but to send a coach with guns and ammunition.[1]

The interior of the deserted Valley Station was nearly demolished. About $2000 worth of provisions were taken, kerosene oil was poured out, and probably the only thing which prevented firing the remainder was a carboy of sulphuric acid, which, when broken on the floor, made further activity in the building extremely uncomfortable for the feet of the marauders.[2]

A coach had already departed from Denver, but wires dispatched from Dahler to John Ford at Junction stopped the vehicle there, much to the dismay of the passengers, including Mr. and Mrs. G. W. Clayton of Denver. After a few hours wait Mr. Clayton wired Denver that they considered the danger over and would proceed as soon as Reuben Thomas would allow it. Thomas did not allow it. The coach did proceed to Valley Station, where it was detained for several days before being sent back to Denver.[3]

On Sunday, the eighth of January, a party of twelve men, including Reuben Thomas and John Hines, went down to the site of the ruins of the wagon trains to bury the dead or assist the wounded. Sorting out the facts took some time. There had actually been two wagon trains involved in the first attack on Saturday, but nothing like the fifty wagons which had been reported. Payne's train had three men killed, seven were missing and four wagons were burned. Marsh's train had one man killed and two or four wounded, his wagons burned and his stock killed. Along with the ashes of the other two there seemed to be the remains of another train from which all the men were missing. There was evidence of desperate struggle, and "goods of every kind were lying around." Reuben Thomas remembered helping to bury four men here beside the trail near Dennison's Ranch. The missing men were found later to be safe at various ranches in the vicinity.[4]

On the other side of Valley Station a four-mule wagon owned by a Mr. Post, and driven by a Mr. Cross, was carrying six passengers who were casually enjoying the scenery, all with unloaded weapons. About halfway between the American Ranch and Valley Station the presence of Indians was announced when an arrow grazed Mr. Cross's cheek. The Indian struck at the mule in the leading team, intending to make it change its course and turn off the road. The passengers huddled down into the body of the wagon while arrows pricked the canvas cover above them. Cross whipped up the teams, now that he was aware that he was being pursued by a large number of shooting Indians. His first assailant, who seemed to be a white man, kept pace beside him and finally shot him in the arm, shattering the bone. Cross could no longer control the team; the wagon swerved and turned toward the river. The Indians now abreast shot the wheel animals and the wagon jerked to a stop. The passengers jumped out and dashed for the river, using their guns as clubs as their only defense. They were all wounded, some many times. One of them, a young man named Andrews did not escape. While the Indians were occupied with scalping and mutilating him, the other passengers contrived to hide themselves until the Indians drifted off; then the wounded men made painful progress to Valley Station, carrying one of their number since he had a fractured skull.

Shortly after the occupants of the Post wagon had staggered into Valley Station, another party reached the station. They also had been attacked not far from Wisconsin Ranch, and they were all wounded. These men had a team of mules, one of which dropped dead from its arrow wound as soon as it reached the station.[5]

Still later in the morning a one-horse wagon came down the road to Valley with two discharged soldiers: Lieutenant Cushman of the First Regiment and John Booth of the Third. They had been at Sand Creek and were openly boastful about the scalps they had taken and other Indian relics which they displayed to the men at Valley Station. The two soldiers went on alone fearlessly. It was some time before news of them was heard again.

The Military Surgeon J. E. Hamilton coincidentally arrived at Valley Station on Sunday or Monday and was hard-pressed to care for all the wounded in the wrecked station and at Dennison's. It was necessary to amputate Cross's arm, and Hamilton had almost no medical supplies. When he had done as much as he could, he rode farther down the road, almost to Spring Hill, but did not find any more wounded, so he returned to Valley Station.

George Bent did not hear many of the details of this raid on the center of the South Platte Trail, but he was told by his friends, Little Bear and Touching Cloud, what happened to the two soldiers from Sand Creek. They had passed only a mile and a half down the road from Moore's Ranch when they were overtaken and killed. One of them was shot with a ball in the hip and many arrows in his breast. They were both stripped and the heart was cut out of the breast of the other man. Only one was scalped, but both throats were cut. One man had his nose cut off, and deep cuts were inflicted on his body. In their belongings, the Sand Creek relics and the two Indian scalps were found and indentified—one as that of a warrior, Little Wolf, who always wore a certain little shell in his hair; the other, who had unusually light-colored hair was known as White Leaf. When George Bent was in the area again his party located the bodies of the soldiers. Bent saw them and agreed that the Indians had "cut them all up."[6]

The main body of the Indian army went back to the great camp on Cherry Creek, the ponies so heavily loaded it took three days to reach their destination. After days of feasting, dancing and drumming, the chiefs held a council and decided to move north of the Platte to the Black Hills and Powder River country. They sent runners to notify the northern tribes of their coming and to ask them to join the Cheyennes and Sioux in warfare.[7]

Many of the Indians did not return to Cherry Creek. James Beckwourth met 130 or 140 lodges of Indians between January 9 and 11 on Whiteman's Fork. He said there were Cheyennes, Kiowas, Comanches, and some half-breed Cheyennes in the party, but mostly Cheyennes. One of these half-breeds may have been the "white man" who shot Cross in the arm. Beckwourth named the Cheyenne leaders in this camp as Leg-in-the-Water and Little Robe, the son of a chief of the same name believed to have been killed at Sand Creek. Beckwourth said the Indians were traveling north.[8]

The day after the raid at Julesburg, Captain O'Brien sent out Joe Jewett and another scout with fifty men to follow the trail of the Indians. They returned on Monday the ninth, telling O'Brien that the body of Indians who had been at Julesburg had reached Whiteman's Fork, sixty miles south, and that there was another village ten or fifteen miles south of the fork.

General Mitchell began to collect a large force at Fort Cottonwood, intending to march to the Republican. He was confident now that all of the hostile Indians were concentrated in an area where an open battle could be fought. O'Brien was ordered to take all of his men to Cottonwood, leaving Camp Rankin in the hands of the wounded and civilians. All trains were to be stopped there and the teamsters conscripted as provisional soldiers. Only fifteen dismounted soldiers remained at Fort Rankin. Mitchell marched 500 troops south to scour the valleys of the branches of the Republican River. He arrived at the recently deserted campground of the main body of Indians on January 19.[9]

The stage stock was withdrawn from the South Platte road on the eleventh, and no more stages were allowed to pass until military protection could be provided. On January 7, immediately after news of the raid at Julesburg, Colonel Moonlight sent all of the available troops, about seventy men, under Lieutenant Judson J. Kennedy of the First Colorado Cavalry, to march to Valley Station to provide scouting parties from that place.

Determined not be cut off from the main artery connecting Denver to the States as had happened the previous autumn, wagon train operators began to advertise for participants for one huge invincible train to travel in a body from Denver to Julesburg with military protection. When assembled, it was called "The Big Train" and it included 105 wagons and 300 men. It was led by Capt. John Wanless, and was escorted by Lt. Albert Walter of the First Colorado Cavalry with a company of forty raw recruits of the hastily mustered Second Colorado Cavalry and several pieces of artillery. The Big Train left Denver on January 14.[10]

Reconstructing the events of January 15 on the South Platte Trail is like trying to piece together the bits from a discarded pile of broken crockery. Rumors and exaggerations complicate the problem. Northeastern Colorado is usually frozen almost solid with a crisp shell of snow in the middle of January, and 1865 was no exception. At first light on Sunday the fifteenth, the sky seemed to be clear and cloudless. A war party had been traveling from Whiteman's Fork for some hours toward the South Platte. Among the Cheyennes in the party was one Sioux, a Minneconjou Chief named White White. He was past the age to be out in the bitter cold with a raiding party, but he had a daughter who was married to a white man, and he had reason to believe that she was living somewhere in the area which this band intended to strike. He hoped to save her if it was possible. When the sun rose the warriors were still an hour or more distant from the river.[11]

Surgeon Hamilton had left Valley Station several days previously. He had traveled downriver thirty miles to Julesburg, then returned, proceeding on toward Denver. He passed Godfrey's Ranch on the morning of the fifteenth. All was quiet. Lt. J. J. Kennedy passed Godfrey's, headed for Valley Station, in midmorning. The soldiers passed the American Ranch and Wisconsin Ranch. All was quiet here too.

Kennedy was unsaddling his horse at Valley when he discovered his rear guard, trailing at some distance was being attacked by a "considerable body of Indians." Kennedy issued a hasty order to some of his men to throw up a barricade with the only available material, sacks of shelled corn and a few unused adobe brick. Kennedy then took twelve men and went to the aid of his rear guard. By now it was apparent that both the American and the Wisconsin Ranches were in flames.

As the reinforcing soldiers approached from Valley Station, the Indians abandoned the attack on the rear guard and withdrew to Wisconsin Ranch, where fighting was still going on. Mark Coad was at the ranch with his sister, his brother-in-law, Ben Danielson, and their two infant children. The other occupants were an old man and a young boy. Mark Coad always claimed that he killed twenty-two Indians in that fight, and he probably did wound one of two before Kennedy's soldiers arrived. (Colonel Livingston reported that three Indians were killed here.) The battle with the Indians must have consumed some time at the Wisconsin Ranch, because it was nearly dark before Lieutenant Kennedy escorted the family to Valley Station for safety.[12]

At the American Ranch were William and Sarah Morris, their two little boys and five hired men. In late morning two employees named Gus Hall and "Big Steve" hitched an ox team to a wagon to make a trip to Cedar Canyon for a wood supply. They had just crossed the river on the frozen ice when the ranch was attacked. The two men were still in sight, and a handful of warriors pursued them, wounding both of them and then leaving them for dead. The Indians returned to the ranch. The haystack, which was perilously close to the house, had been fired, and smoke was pouring into the two-room building where the five adults and two children were huddled. The men fought and they did kill two Indians, but it was not long before the door burst into flames and fire began to spread into the room. Forced into the open, the desperate men ran toward the river. William decided that his only hope was to follow them. His last advice to Sarah was to make for the river, but if she did not reach it, to give herself up—women were sometimes taken as prisoners. Within seconds, Sarah was surrounded so closely by Indians that she could not see when the three hired men were killed; and although William Morris reached the river bank, he too was overtaken and killed.

Several crazed Cheyennes attacked Sarah simultaneously, stabbing her with knives and arrows, and striking her about the head with a whip. White White, the Sioux, thinking of his daughter perhaps, threw himself into the savage attack, warding off blows, telling the Cheyennes to stop, and offering a U.S. Army horse to anyone who would stop the killing. The first Cheyenne to catch this message pulled the others away and accepted White White's offer of a horse in exchange for the fainting female, bleeding rivulets of crimson onto the snow.

The children were not harmed. They were taken onto ponies with warriors, and Sarah, too weak to hold herself up, was cradled in the arms of the kind-hearted Sioux on his pony as the group of raiders rode off to return to their camp. It is likely that they were hurried in their departure by the uneasy apprehension of soldiers, since there was evidently no thought given to scalping and mutilating Gus Hall and Big Steve across the river.

Gus and Big Steve were still alive. Gus's leg was fractured and useless, but the two men dragged themselves toward the Wisconsin Ranch, where they crawled into the shelter of the burned-out buildings, burrowing into the warmth of the graying ashes.[13]

At Godfrey's Ranch, the two buildings—the house and stable—overlapped with a connecting door, so that it was possible to go from one building to the other without going out doors. The sod corral stretching behind the buildings, was built with high walls. The haystack was situated a distance from the buildings. There were five men present: Godfrey, Si Perkins, Wes Mullen and two unidentified hired men. Matilda was there with Margaret Perkins, wife of Si, and Celia Godfrey, a teen-age girl. There were three small Godfrey children. The Godfreys were warned by the smoke at the American Ranch, two miles away, and they were armed and had assumed battle stations on all sides of the enclosure by the time the Indians attacked. Godfrey had plenty of weapons, and the women reloaded the guns as soon as they had been fired. When a fire arrow flamed into the haystack, Godfrey had pails of water ready to extinguish the fire. The Indians circled and made rapid sallies to fire into the enclosure. The test of nerves continued until nightfall, when the Indians withdrew.

After dark, Si Perkins muffled the feet of his horse with sacks and stole silently in the darkness up the river to Junction Station. He arrived at the telegraph office about eleven o'clock, asking for assistance for the besieged ranch.

John Ford fired off a panic-stricken wire to Denver. "The American Ranch is burned to the ground by Indians . . . The inmates are all destroyed. Valley Station is burned and the Wisconsin Ranch probably destroyed. A messenger just got here after help. The Indians attacked Godfrey's Ranch . . . and are fighting there now. The messenger got away and is here for help. That is probably why the line is down. I have my horse at the door and will start immediately and get the line O.K. as soon as possible. All people in the ranches attacked were killed."[14]

Within an hour a group of citizens were summoned and with John Ford and Si Perkins set out for Godfrey's. They arrived at daylight Monday morning, but there were no Indians in sight. The ranchers rested here and no doubt had breakfast. John Ford went on alone, riding along the telegraph line to find where it had been cut.

Ford paused at the American Ranch and imagined seven burned bodies in the ruins (actually all of the dead were out doors except one Indian). At Wisconsin Ranch the telegraph line was cut, but Ford could not repair it alone. While poking around in the buildings of the Wisconsin, Ford found Gus Hall and Big Steve either asleep or unconscious, but breathing. Ford rode on to Valley Station and reported the two wounded men.

Lieutenant Kennedy had not ventured out of the corral at Valley Station overnight. "The Indians camped on the river Sunday night, killing all the cattle they could find," Kennedy said in a wire to Moonlight to be sent later. "Their signal fires could be seen in all directions." Kennedy had other problems. Several of his men broke out with measles on

Monday morning. A party with a wagon was sent to Wisconsin Ranch to see if the men there could be saved. When the rescuers came into the building, it has been reported that one of them said, "Here is a dead man." Gus Hall is supposed to have answered weakly, "I'm not dead yet but I think I will be before long."[15]

On Sunday night Kennedy had sent ten men to Dennison's to check on the wounded. Then on the morning of the sixteenth, it was necessary to send more soldiers to encourage the return of the first group. The wood supply was low, so part of his men were sent to the canyons for firewood. Late on the sixteenth Kennedy wrote to Colonel Moonlight saying that a surgeon was needed desperately, not only for the teamsters at Dennison's but also for Gus Hall, whose leg was shattered below the knee. John Hines wanted to go to the Wisconsin to repair the telegraph line. Kennedy gave him an escort of twenty men, but they were driven back by Indians. Kennedy composed another wire to Moonlight telling him that a large body of Indians were plainly to be seen on the north side of the river, moving downstream. After dark John Ford went out and repaired the telegraph line. The wire was kept hot all night with backed-up messages.[16]

By this time, George Bent wrote, the large body of Cheyennes and their allies had moved west and were camped on White Butte Creek, which seems to coincide with what Lieutenant Kennedy called Buffalo Springs. On the seventeenth Kennedy wrote that the campfires had been seen at Buffalo Springs since the day before. A party of men sent downriver by Kennedy were driven back by what was estimated to be 300 Indians. The estimate could very well have been correct. George Bent said that war parties of Cheyennes, Arapahoes and Sioux were raiding up and down the river from The White Butte camp. On Wednesday the eighteenth a large body of Indians appeared at Valley Station almost seeming to taunt the small number of soldiers; but after creating great concern among the men at the post, the Indians withdrew.

Sometime during the time that the telegraph line was down, Beaver Creek Station was burned. The occupants were either absent or defended themselves. At Murray's Ranch, the corn and hay of the stage company was burned. It was said that some of the buildings were burned but no one was killed. Bijou Ranch lost its corn and hay, and even Box Elder Station had hay burned.

In the middle of the week there was a slackening of tension, and Reuben Thomas and a party went up to the American Ranch to dig three graves in the rock-hard earth. When they finished, they erected a low paling around the graves. The January sun set early, and the sky blazed fire-red, amber light transforming the hills of snow into glowing embers.[17]

On January 17, at Camp Rankin, S. R. Smith and Philo Holcomb, assisted by the Post Surgeon, erected a memorial pole inside the stockade of Camp Rankin. At the foot of the pole they buried at note of dedication; "This pole is erected by Philo Holcomb and S. R. Smith, operators, Pacific Telegraph line, and J. F. Wisely, Surgeon, USA, six [sic] days after the bloody conflict of January seventh, 1865, between 500 Cheyenne warriors and forty brave men of the Seventh Iowa Cavalry, under command of N. J. O'Brien. On this occasion, the telegraph office and hospital at the mail station were totally destroyed and both institutions reestablished at the post. The lives of fifteen soldiers and five citizens were lost during this terrible raid and their remains are interred nearby. While this pole stands the wires will whisper a mournful requiem over the graves of the gallant dead . . ."

The idle teamsters and ranchers who stood by watching this ceremony thought the pole was a little short for a flagpole. "That's not for a flag," one of the operators frowned, "that's a telegraph pole!"[18]

The Big Train passed. On the eighteenth of January they had reached the Junction; the night of the following day they camped near Godfrey's Ranch. On the twentieth, Captain Wanless wired the *News* from Valley Station. On the twenty-second they arrived at Julesburg. They had been harassed by Indians attempting to stampede their stock at almost every camp, but without success; the trip had been entirely without event. When the Big Train arrived at Valley and Dennison's, it seems that they made room for the wounded men, and Gus Hall was taken to Omaha where his leg was amputated. On the twenty-third the train was fifty miles east of Julesburg and not an Indian in sight. On January twenty-second, two stage coaches with mail were allowed to go through to Denver under escort.[19]

Lt. Albert Walter, with his forty men, had accompanied the Big Train from Denver to Julesburg, and now, relieved from that duty, was ordered to escort another train from Julesburg to Denver. On the twenty-fourth, when he reached Gilette's, nine miles west of Julesburg, he discovered that all of the oxen from the train had been run off by Indians. Lieutenant Walter sent a party of eight soldiers with a guide to attempt to recover the animals. Five soldiers with twenty-two cattle returned, but three soldiers were missing. On the following day Walter sent out another party to search for the missing men, but they had disappeared. The recovered oxen were not sufficient for the entire train, so Lieutenant Walter left the helpless wagons behind and marched upstream, watched by Indians on both sides of the river until he arrived at Valley Station on the twenty-seventh.

At this time defense was still poor on the South Platte Trail. On or about January 23, forty more volunteer militia recruits were sent to Junction Station. Kennedy was at Valley Station, but Julesburg and eastern posts were almost defenseless, since General Mitchell was still marching on the Republican with most of the soldiers in western Nebraska in his command.[20]

When the northern movement of the Indians began, the war parties went out from White Butte Creek a day in advance of the women and children. The main body of the camp moved north on January 29, and by the time they reached the river, the country had been cleared for their passage across. The war parties struck the South Platte Road on the twenty-eighth, and spread themselves from Valley Station to Julesburg.[21]

Bypassing Morrison's, Godfrey's and the American Ranch, George Bent and a party of a hundred struck the Washington Ranch, where, after a brief exchange of firing between the ranchmen and the raiders, and setting fire to 100 tons of government hay, Bent and the warriors crossed the river to where the Moores had moved their cattle. The cattle were scattered all along the north bank. In order to cross the Indians dismounted and led their unshod ponies across the frozen surface of the river. Here they rounded up what Bent estimated to be a thousand cattle, but after going some distance north they sorted out the poorer animals and left them behind, proceeding with about 500 head toward the bluffs.

Lieutenant Kennedy reported that after the raid on the Washington Ranch he sent eighteen men in pursuit, who followed the Indians for fifteen miles before engaging in a fight that lasted three hours, killing ten Indians and seven ponies. Livingston, making a second-hand evaluation, reported that the soldiers were surrounded and forced to retreat but that thirteen Indians were killed. George Bent commented rather vaguely that they had a fight with some soldiers and captured a lot of mules. The Indians continued with the cattle toward the bluffs, where they camped for the night.[22]

Early on the morning of the twenty-eighth, Lieutenant Walter had marched from Valley Station toward Denver. He had not proceeded more than twelve miles when he was overtaken by a messenger from Lieutenant Kennedy asking him to return at once. Lieutenant Kennedy believed that the Indians were coming his way in large forces, and he expected to be attacked at any time.

In the meantime, in the middle of this doomed section of road, two stagecoaches with thirty passengers and a train of eleven wagons left Lillian Springs going west. When they saw the band of a hundred Indians coming from Washington Ranch, they turned around and went back to spend the night. Dennison's Ranch was burned again sometime during the day or night of the twenty-eighth, but it may have been abandoned, since there is no record of dead or missing occupants. The telegraph line east from Valley Station went dead the night of the twenty-eighth; but the train and coaches at Lillian Springs made a dash for Valley Station, and reached there on the morning of the twenty-ninth. John Hines wired the *News* that large fires could be seen down the road; he supposed them to be Lillian Springs and Spring Hill Station. Lillian Springs must have been attacked soon after the train departed. Three men at Lillian Springs fought their assailants off from the main building all day. Just before dark, the Indians left, burning the hay and running off four horses and eight head of cattle. After dark the three men escaped. Traveling only at night and hiding during the day, they managed to reach Camp Rankin two days later—a day before the ranch was burned. Harlow's Ranch, Buffalo Springs Ranch and Antelope Station were also burned, probably on the twenty-eighth.[23]

On the afternoon of the twenty-eighth, Lieutenant Kennedy with twelve men and Lieutenant Walter with another dozen troopers went down the river with the hope of recapturing at least some of the stolen stock. They were not eager to overtake the 100 Indians. At 10:00 P.M. they found some of the animals which the Indians had left behind. Here the troops camped until daybreak. They then marched at sunrise and discovered the camp of the Indians at Cedar Bluffs. There were some shots fired. Walter said his command killed nine Indians; Kennedy wrote that there were twenty killed. Three of Lieutenant Walter's men were wounded. Lieutenant Kennedy claimed to have recovered 400 of the stolen cattle. The three versions of this skirmish provided an interesting comparison. According to Lieutenant Kennedy, "Some of the red devils followed us twenty miles back." Lieutenant Walter wrote; "After I reached the level ground, the Indians retired to the bluffs, looking very distressfully after us . . ." George Bent said, "Early in morning soldiers came up on bluffs and fired a few shots at our war camp. We jumped on our horses and chased them over the hill. He then insisted, "In this fight no one was killed. Officer is mistaken."[24]

The general opinion of writers has been that the main body of Indians crossed the river on the ice near Harlow's Ranch, which Livingston said was twenty-two miles west of Camp Rankin. On the north side of the river a vast camp of Indians was stretched for several miles along the river bank. The Indians felt perfectly safe; they knew there were not enough soldiers in the area to threaten them. Here George Bent's party brought their herd of cattle. The fattest cattle were killed first, and the feasting was general. After the feasting were scalp dances. The drums could be heard for many miles along the valley. Bent said he had been out with war parties at night, and they would stop at intervals to listen for the drums to determine their direction and the distance which still remained between the party and the camp.[25]

The warriors who made the first assault on Julesburg made an effective sweep to remove all of the cattle from the area. The stock from Bulen and Conley's ranches, about 150 head, was driven off, and a few animals from the quartermaster at Camp Rankin and forty more from J. R. Burt's Ranch were acquired. Then, in a final drive, nearly 260 head belonging to parked wagon trains and ranches were rounded up at Gilette's Ranch. It was estimated that the Indians drove away about 400 cattle that day.

After the destruction of all the ranches from Dennison's to Antelope Station, the next objective was that of Gilette's Ranch. This ranch was a prize. There were two or three large wagon trains parked here, one loaded with government stores headed for Denver, another with at least one wagon loaded with liquor, and a less interesting train belonging to Bridgeman and Chandler consisting only of a cargo of mining machinery. Bridgeman and Chandler had gone to Camp Rankin with some of their animals and wagons to haul wood for the post, but there were eighteen teamsters in the ranch house. It was about eight o'clock in the morning on January 29 when a horde of feathered and painted warriors charged on Gilette's. They burned the hay and the stables, but the teamsters defended the ranch house so well that the Indians were not able to get close to the building. The wagons were much more interesting, however. Provisions were hauled out and scattered. Lightweight parts of wagons were ripped off and added to a glorious bonfire. When the bottled liquor was discovered, the raid ended and the celebration began. The anxious men in the ranch house were grateful for the respite, as they were nearly out of ammunition. By sunset the Indians had forgotten the trapped teamsters, who then squeezed through a small window in the rear of the house and disappeared over the ice into the willow-grown islands of the river. All eighteen of them reached camp Rankin about 9:00 P.M.[26]

A similar scenario was played at George Ackley's Nebraska Ranch, only five miles from Julesburg. A train owned by a man named Foster was parked here. When the Indians attacked Ackley the teamsters fought the Indians off until they lost interest and withdrew and the men were able to escape to the fort, sacrificing a train of seventeen wagons.[27]

On the thirtieth of January, the Indians had very little unfinished business to occupy them. The buildings at the deserted Nebraska Ranch and Gilette's were burned, but there was a challenge yet to be met—Moore's Washington Ranch.

On the morning of the thirtieth Lieutenant Walter left Valley Station with the remainder of his troops, marching toward Denver. With him traveled two families who had lost their homes. When he reached Godfrey's the buildings were still standing but the family had had enough. The Godfreys also accompanied Lieutenant Walter to Junction Station, which was now well protected since the forty recruits had arrived.[28]

The inhabitants at the Washington Ranch had finally decided that the time had come for them to seek safer country. On the morning of the thirtieth they were packing to leave. At one o'clock in the afternoon Jim Moore was hitching horses to a wagon when about 200 Indians swarmed down out of the sand hills. Jim Moore was shot in the neck with a minnie ball. There were twelve men at the ranch, and they were well stocked with arms. Jim Moore was helped into the house and positions taken for defense. The assault lasted for nearly two hours and after three (or five) Indians were killed, the attackers withdrew, taking 100 head of cattle with them. At Valley Station Lieutenant Kennedy saw twenty Indians coming down the opposite side of the river and sent out fifteen men to meet them. They skirmished and the soldiers returned to the station, claiming to have killed one Indian.[29]

The war party moved down the river with the cattle. As they passed along, they cut the telegraph wire in pieces and dragged it with them for miles. They built fires around the base of telegraph poles and burned them off at ground level or simply hacked off the more slender poles, with their tomahawks and made huge bonfires to warm themselves. Raiding parties continued to roam along both sides of the river, hoping to find an unwary traveler, loose cattle or something more to burn.

On Monday the thirtieth Lieutenant Brewer returned to Camp Rankin with Captain O'Brien's men, but O'Brien and Lieutenant Ware were delayed and planned to come along later. Including all the fugitive teamsters and ranchers—about sixty-five men—there was now a rather substantial force to defend the fort.

On special assignment from officials of the Overland Stage Company, Andrew Hughes, son of Bela M. Hughes, was traveling in a stagecoach with an assistant superintendent identified only as Mr. Clift. On the morning of January 30 the stagecoach was parked at Alkali Station, under the protection of Captain Murphy's troops, waiting for an opportunity to go to Julesburg to evaluate the situation. On that morning Captain Nicholas O'Brien and Lt. Eugene Ware came along with a piece of artillery and ten men. One man was ill and was left behind at Alkali, but Captain Murphy furnished an escort of ten additional men for O'Brien's passage to Julesburg. Grateful for the military escort, Hughes and Clift, with their two drivers, asked to accompany the soldiers.

On January 31, O'Brien and his entourage passed Beauvais Ranch, and since it was so poorly defended, left six soldiers here. In the meantime a large force of Sioux surrounded the military compound at Alkali

Station but withdrew without doing any damage. Their scouts may have warned the attackers that Colonel Livingston was not far away, moving toward Alkali with "all of the spare men he had in his subdistrict."[30]

O'Brien's diminishing troops reached Dick Van Cleve's Ranch, which was also nearly defenseless. Captain O'Brien left four soldiers there and the rest took Mrs. Van Cleve in the stagecoach—supposedly away from danger. A train of nineteen wagons overtaken along the way was joined with the reduced military force. The party reached the Devil's Drive about 2:00 P.M. on February 2. The smoke was already billowing into the sky above Julesburg.[31]

C. B. Hadley had started from Nebraska City in late January with a load of apples in a light wagon drawn by a span of young fast mules. He fell in with a small train carrying groceries to Denver, and the caravan reached Julesburg on February first. They were ordered to stop, so they picketed their animals near the fort for the night. In the morning, with the hay supply desperately low, it was agreed that a party would go to the Bulen and Conley's ranches, so close to the fort that they had not yet been burned. Conley was in Nebraska City, but Bulen was at the fort and agreed to sell the hay for a bargain rate. Twenty men went out with a wagon and two teams of oxen each man riding his own horse or mule. With all haste the men bound the hay in bundles and tossed them on the wagon, but before the wagon was loaded Bulen lost his nerve and rode back to the post. Sensing that something was wrong, the other men mounted their animals and followed. Hadley was the last to leave, but since his mule was fast he reached the post before some of the others. They did not have a minute to spare.[32]

It had been so quiet at the fort that morning that Lieutenant Brewer sent a detachment of twenty-nine men to Gilette's to see if the Indians had broken camp. They had not. There was still a large number of angry warriors destroying everything that would burn, and when they saw the soldiers, they chased them back to the fort. About noon the main body of warriors descended on the fort. It was thought that there were 800 to 1000. George Bent took part in this; he wrote: "This time six or seven Indians with good horses went behind the stockade to try to get the soldiers to follow them out but the soldiers would not follow them. . . Soldiers were peeping over the stockade at us but would not come outside. . . They shot at the Indians several times. The Indians then all rode out from behind the hills. When they seen the soldiers would not come out, we all made for the store and warehouse to plunder. This was at noon. . . I went with party below and drove off lot of fat cattle."[33]

The stage station had been completely deserted by all of the personnel. The Indians plundered at their leisure, and then, one by one, they set the buildings afire. The smoke hung over Julesburg in a mournful pall.

The story of a dramatic entrance into Julesburg with guns blazing and horses galloping madly through a crowd of dazed Indians was told so often by both O'Brien and Ware that the principals began to believe it, and it has become a legend. Unfortunately, another exciting tale of the West must be reduced to fact by the testimony of witnesses. When Captain O'Brien and his command saw the smoke from the burning stage station, the nineteen wagons made a circle for defense at a safe distance from the scene of pillage. When the Indians finally retired over the river to the north, Lieutenant Brewer sent out a detachment of men and a piece of artillery, shelling the river bank. Now that it was completely safe, the soldiers and the stagecoach pulled into the fort.[34]

Except for a few badly smoked bags of shelled corn and the wagonload of hay still at Bulen's Ranch, the destruction was complete. C. B. Hadley still had his wagon, his apples and his mules, and he went back to Bulen's to pick up the hay he had bought. Others were not so fortunate. When Hadley passed Foster's wagons at the Nebraska Ranch on February 6, all that remained of Foster's seventeen wagons of groceries was a pile of fish that had been frozen but had fallen out when the barrel in which they were packed had burned away. The train of mining machinery was largely intact. A frustrated half-breed, unsuccessful in an attempt to burn it, had picked up a charred stick and written "Go to Hell!" on the wide rim of the flywheel.[35]

In abandoning the telegraph office at Julesburg Station this time, the operators had not been able to take the instruments with them. Camp Rankin was unable to communicate either east or west. Lieutenant Ware sent men to repair the line to the east and soon it was humming, but there seemed to be no way to receive messages which must be crowding the line. Ware had not reckoned with the resourcefulness of Philo Holcomb. Holcomb "chopped an axe in the ground" and taking a wire in his hand, he touch the end to the grounded metal poll of the axe, transmitting what he believed to be code signals to the east. In order to receive, he put the end of the wire into his mouth and received a message by the impulses against his wet tongue. The message he reported was ". . . Am coming, Livingston." Ware was skeptical.[36]

But Livingston came the following day after dark. With him were about 300 cavalry men, half from the Seventh Iowa Cavalry and half from the First Nebraska Volunteer Cavalry. Captain Murphy with Company A accompanied him from Alkali Lake. Livingston brought four pieces of artillery and fort-six wagons of supplies, but perhaps more important, he brought telegraph instruments.

The first message east was to Cottonwood Springs asking for many wagons loaded with light poles, and that they be sent as fast as the animals could bring them. Since there were no Indians left to fight, Livingston set his men to the arduous labor of digging post holes in the frozen earth in order to rebuild the telegraph line.

On February 5, Captain Murphy, with a hundred men, was sent upriver to ascertain the extent of the damage; Philo Holcomb accompanied him with instruments. Murphy went to within twelve miles of Valley Station and counted 130 missing poles. From this point Holcomb communicated with Hines at Valley Station and discovered that all but a handful of soldiers had been recalled to Denver from there. Holcomb wired Denver, only to learn that Denver was in a state of panic, not knowing what was happening on the South Platte beyond Valley. Holcomb reassured them that the main body of Indians seemed to have moved north.

Captain Murphy and Holcomb returned to Rankin on February 6, and the same day a huge train of vehicles, including stagecoaches, came into Camp Rankin from the east. Captain O'Brien was detailed to escort the train through to Denver.

On February 3 a small but courageous train, assembled and moved down the river from Denver, and sent word of their safe arrival at Valley Station on the seventh. Hallie Riley was one of the passengers in a wagon in this train. She said it was early evening when they reached Valley Station and the soldiers advised them not to continue. But the drivers bought some whiskey and, warmed and encouraged by the lively beverage, pushed on at a run.

At Washington Ranch Hallie met Jim Moore, who had been unable to move since the Indian attack on January 31. The minnie-ball was still lodged in his neck, dangerously close to his jugular vein. The swelling reached almost to his shoulders. Hallie and another woman from the train did what they could to make Moore more comfortable. Meanwhile the wagons of the small train circled, and the occupants were badly frightened when they saw a dark line moving toward them from the horizon to the north. It proved to be the large train from Julesburg led by Captain O'Brien. It also camped at Washington Ranch. The security of numbers made everyone sleep better. The following morning the small military escort which had been with Hallie Riley's train returned to Denver with the large one while Captain O'Brien and his troops rode back to Julesburg, accompanying Hallie's group.[37]

Chapter

12

The Prairie Claims Its Own

Colonel Thomas Moonlight had declared martial law in Colorado Territory on February 6 to provide necessary troops for the defense of the roads. Faced with being drafted, men flooded in to volunteer. Where six companies had been planned, Acting Governor Elbert asked for seven. As early as January 25 the First Regiment had been reorganized into six companies. It was for this reason that Lt. Judson J. Kennedy was withdrawn from Valley Station at a crucial time. Now it was necessary to arrange the distribution again to incorporate the new recruits.

On a higher level, General Grenville M. Dodge had been placed in command in January of the Department of the Missouri, which now included the District of Colorado. Moonlight, deterred by the handicap of erratic mail service and constant trouble with the telegraph lines, tried to acquaint Dodge with the problems in Denver, about most of which Moonlight had only a superficial understanding. Petulantly, he whined to Dodge that he had been expected to protect the route to Julesburg with only 200 total troops in the territory; and then he objected to having his district limited. Julesburg was in the Territory of Colorado, he reasoned, therefore Julesburg should be in his district. He complained that he had not "cooperation with troops whose duty it was to do the work."[1]

When the telegraph poles reached Camp Rankin on February 11, Captain Murphy, Lieutenant Ware and forty-six men with two pieces of artillery were detailed to build a new telegraph line to Valley Station.

They started at midnight in full moonlight. The men were divided into squads with various duties; two squads would use picks, another shovels, and the fourth would hold horses. They moved forward with almost no rest, the wagons with the telegraph poles trailing along. It was soon discovered that it was easier to pull the old stump out of the ground and use the excavated hole for the new pole. In sequence, the stumps were pulled, new poles were brought up, inserted and tamped down. The telegraph wire was uncoiled as the train moved along and insulators passed out. A squad or two followed to mount the line and draw it tight with mule teams. By working all night and all the next day, the line was brought to the vicinity of Harlow's Ranch, where a camp was made. On the following day the detachment proceeded to Valley Station, moving more rapidly since fewer repairs were required on this part of the line.

At Valley Station there was a report of Indians in the hills, and a citizen train from Denver was corralled there. When Murphy and Ware, with their troops, teamsters, and guns, appeared at Valley after 3:00 P.M., twenty-five Indians could be seen in the hills. Valley Station did not have a broad expanse of valley surrounding it as did Fort Rankin. From the corral barricade at Valley, the river was on one side and a long low hill lay parallel to the river on the other side of the stage road. Ware and Murphy realized that the maximum height their howitzers could reach was not high enough for a shell to clear the top of the hill. But there was a large supply of sacked shelled corn in the stage station warehouse, which was used to erect a barricade out on the prairie, with embrasures left for the guns. The defense proved to be needless however, because the Indians went away at sunset. Camp was made that night, February 13, at Valley Station. The soldiers and officers were exhausted; but the telegraph line was operating again. Their rest was well deserved.

The men started the trip back to Camp Rankin the following morning. Ware reported that by the time their train reached Harlow's, they were overtaken by a detachment of cavalry from the west with a number of stagecoaches. The stagecoaches went on to Julesburg with the escort of Murphy and Ware while the detachment stayed to make a permanent camp at the burned-out ranch.[2]

Meanwhile this strange event was explained by telegrams which must have crossed one another on February 13. General Curtis, in command of the Department of Kansas, ordered General Mitchell to establish a post at Valley Station. Mitchell ordered Colonel Livingston to garrison Valley Station. Moonlight wired Livingston that he had only about a hundred recruits to date and could not go past Junction Station with his defense. On the fourteenth Livingston sent a wire to Moonlight that he was sending fifty men to Harlow's Ranch and more men to Valley Station on the following day. On the sixteenth Livingston informed Moonlight that he had been directed not to send men to Harlow's because that was in Moonlight's district. That was too much for Moonlight to comprehend; Livingston was sending men to Valley Station but not to Harlow's. (Harlow's was the deserted ranch halfway between Valley Station and Julesburg.) "Where is Harlow's?" Moonlight wanted to know.

"Harlow's Ranch, twenty-seven miles east of Valley, twenty-three west of Julesburg, at point where Indians crossed South Platte," Livingston telegraphed. Moonlight then dispatched a detachment of men to make camp at Harlow's. It was fortunate that the Indians had left the South Platte River.[3]

The soldiers who were charged with the defense of the South Platte Trail were undisciplined and indifferent militia. On January 31, when Lieutenant Walter arrived at Junction Station, he reported that the detachment which had been stationed at Junction in his absence had not acted "soldier-like." One of the Ashcraft brothers reported to Walter that the Junction soldiers had not put out a guard for two nights in a row. On March 8 things had not improved. A traveler arrived at Junction Station to spend the night only to find that it was filled with a drunken rabble of soldiers; the traveler and his companions bribed the driver to go on. One passenger in a stagecoach was amazed to find that their escort from Junction Station to Valley was to be teen-age boys—new recruits into the militia. One of the drivers chuckled. "Seems like they ought to send out an extra escort to protect these boys."[4]

Rebuilding the stations and ranches along the South Platte Trail was a slow process in the spring of 1865. At first, work was hampered by extreme cold. The ground was frozen, of course, and sod could not be cut to erect new buildings. In early March it was so cold that, as one traveler wrote, a layer of ice would form in the cup when water was taken from the river. Wood was so scarce at Valley Station that travelers were charged five cents a pound for firewood in order to keep warm. On March 8 the temperature fell to twenty degrees below zero.[5]

Washington Ranch continued to flourish and Jim Moore recovered, although he carried the minnie ball in his neck for the rest of his life. It seems that the Moore brothers took over the operation of Valley Station as a stage stop. Some sort of stage stop was set up at the American Ranch, and James Shirland, formerly of Bob Williams's Ranch on the lower South Platte, was hired to run it. The post office at the American Ranch, which had been discontinued in December of 1864, was reestablished in the following May. Like Harlow's, Dennison's Ranch continued to be mentioned by name for several years, but whether the

Dennisons actually lived there is not known. Arthur Lewis clung tenaciously to Lillian Springs Ranch, and he probably operated the reopened station at Spring Hill. The Overland Stage Company did not rebuild the line to its former state. Since a railroad was certain to be built in the near future, the remaining days of the stagecoach on the South Platte Route were limited.[6]

Holon Godfrey added more sod and adobe to build higher and stronger walls. He dug tunnels and excavated an underground hiding place for his family. He delighted in telling the story of the fight at his ranch on January 15, and he lettered a sign "Fort Wicked" which he nailed over the front door. Why he chose this name has never been satisfactorily explained, and when he was asked for a reason, he mumbled something like "The Cheyennes and the Sioux know well enough, I guess."[7]

When the boys of the Colorado militia were mustered out in April the days of the "Galvanized Yankees" began. The Third Regiment of U. S. Volunteers was composed of Confederate prisoners who had been given a choice: either go out on the plains to fight Indians or languish in prison camps. The choice was clear, and they exchanged their gray uniforms for blue. On March 28, 1865, the District of the Plains was formed and Brigadier General Patrick Connor was named Commander. On April 9, General Connor received word in Denver that the rebel soldiers—wearing blue coats—had arrived at Kearny. Connor's Assistant Adjutant issued orders for two companies each to be sent to Kearny, Cottonwood, Julesburg and Laramie. The two companies at Julesburg were divided and stationed at nearby stage stations. Two companies—Company G under Capt. S. W. Matthews and Company H under Capt. Thomas Kenny of the Third U. S. Volunteers—were sent to Junction, where they were divided, and some were sent to a new post set up at Wisconsin Ranch. Evidently the Coad brothers had decided not to rebuild this ranch as a supply station since they had moved their headquarters to a location they owned near Julesburg. Twelve men of Company G went to the Wisconsin where a number of veterans of Company A from the First Colorado Regiment were also posted.[8]

On May 11 General Connor moved his headquarters to Julesburg and Col. Christopher McNally was named commander of the southern soldiers and also given command of Fort Rankin, which was rebuilt and enlarged during the summer and the name of the post changed to Fort Sedgwick in September of 1865.

Although the military post at Junction may have been informally called Camp Tyler, the name was never used by the military there in 1865. In the earliest post records it was called Post Junction. This indefinite name persisted even though it was renamed Fort Wardwell in

June, 1865. A general order in July ordered that it be known as Camp Wardwell instead. An old freighter remembered that at that time there were three commissary buildings, six officers' quarters and ten small structures which were used as barracks. These were arranged along the sides of a quadrangle enclosed by a five-foot sod embankment.

Colonel McNally designated Forts Rankin and Wardwell as checkpoints where wagons were detained until a sufficient number had been gathered together to travel safely through the dangerous country between the two posts. Going either up or downstream from these two forts, it was required that there be not less than fifty wagons in a train. In addition to this police action, Wardwell functioned as a counting station, recording the number of vehicles passing along the trail.[9]

When the Moore brothers found themselves in the company of forts all along the line (including Fort Wicked), Jim and Charley Moore, not to be outdone, built a toll road between Valley Station and the Washington Ranch and rechristened the ranch "Fort Moore."[10]

As the spring advanced, bodies were found that had been missing since January. The bodies of the two soldiers with the trophies from Sand Creek were found on April 29. On April 19 the body of William Morris from the American Ranch was found on a willow island in the river. The usual "horrible mutilations" were not mentioned by the *Rocky Mountain News* but Morris's body had been pierced seventeen times with arrows."[11]

The two dead Indians at the American Ranch suffered even more grisly treatment. One had been burned nearly to extinction, but the other was mangled with all of the odious indignities that hatred could devise. Several days after January 15 someone had found it and dragged it into the foreyard, probably for the scalp. Soon after a traveler with some sense of decency put the stiff frozen body inside the enclosure where the graves were. Sam Ashcraft and a group of hardened locals came by and, angered by the idea of a dead Indian sharing the graves of white men, took the body and threw it into the road. Almost every day travelers left their mark on it. By February 20, when Frank Root came by, the still frozen Indian was found standing against the wall of the burned station and another body was now leaning against the paling of the graves. Both had been scalped. Slices of skin, a nose, one eye, fingers and two arms from the elbow down had been hacked away. In April the body of one Indian was still lying in the road, "staring at the sky." Both legs and one arm were missing.[12]

Of the live prisoners taken by the Indians in 1864 and January of 1865 on the Platte and South Platte Rivers, there were three women who survived—all captives of the Sioux. Nancy Morton was ransomed by the government in exchange for $1600 worth of supplies. She was brought in to Fort Laramie in February of 1865 and left it on the 26, accompanied by the sutler's wife and a company of militia returning to Omaha. She returned to her home in Sidney, Iowa, where she later remarried.[13]

When Sarah Morris was carried away from the American Ranch by the Sioux chief, White White, she was bleeding profusely from five arrow wounds and six stabbings with knives. As she remembered it, the chief attended to her personally. At the campground, the Indians remained four or five days, celebrating and holding scalp dances. An Indian who spoke English talked with Sarah and told her that if she showed her wounds to the Cheyennes, she might receive better treatment. White White said it had been necessary for him to pay another horse to a vindictive brave in order to save her life. After only four days of rest, Sarah was required to ride day after day to the north, camping only a few days at a time. They crossed the Platte River, where White White and his charges joined other Sioux tribesmen. Sarah's two children had been carried along with their mother up to this point but now Joseph, the adopted child, was taken away with another band and Sarah never saw him again. She was allowed to keep Charley, her baby, with her.

Sarah was well treated. She shared the lodge of White White in company with his squaws, and she was well fed. She was required to care for her pony and carry water for the animal, but was not expected to perform any other duties. At one of the camps, where two bands of Sioux met temporarily, Sarah found Lucinda Eubanks, and was allowed to talk to her for an hour. She asked to see her again but was not allowed to do so.

Sarah's captivity by White White might have been bearable except for the tragedy of little Charley. The baby was afraid of the old chief, and cried at his approach. This angered the Indian until finally, losing his temper irrationally, White White picked up the child by the neck, threw him down and stamped on him. The child lingered in a deathlike coma for three weeks; when he finally died, the squaws put him in a coffee sack and laid the little body in a hole in a ravine. Sarah begged to be allowed to dig a proper grave, but the Indians would not wait for her to perform this simple rite of grief. She was forced to move on.

Eventually, while the tribe wandered in Dakota Territory, an enterprising officer of the First U. S. Volunteer Infantry Regiment at Fort Rice, Colonel Charles Dimon, heard about the woman prisoner and began negotiations for her release. White White was not reluctant to trade his prisoner for a sufficient amount of coffee, sugar and two American horses. He brought her into Fort Rice on June 21, 1865. The post ladies provided her with clothing, and the military arranged passage for her on a river boat. Rezin Iames met her at the dock on July 14. Her physical wounds were not yet quite healed, and her emotional wounds would take even more time. Rezin Iames wrote to Holon Godfrey, telling Sarah's story, and said she was in "as good health as could be expected after all the hardship she has undergone. . ." Sarah Morris returned to Granville, Indiana, where she lived with her parents. She was still there with her mother in 1870, but her father was apparently dead. By 1880 the whole family except for a brother had moved away, died or disappeared.[14]

Shortly after Lucinda Eubanks was captured by the Cheyennes at Eubanks farm on August 7, 1864, she and her infant son, William, were separated from the other prisoners. She remembered crossing the Republican to camp on a creek to the south. The Cheyenne, whose property she seemed to be, raped her and then generously shared her with his tribesmen—how many she could not remember. After a time she was traded to the Sioux where she became the property of the chief, Two Face. Although Two Face had a reputation among the whites as a good and friendly Indian, Lucinda thought otherwise; Two Face beat her terribly and treated her as a slave. Before long Lucinda was traded to another Sioux, Blackfoot, who also beat her constantly. When she resisted the sexual advances of her master, his squaws abused her. However, the Sioux gave her more to eat than the Cheyennes had and they allowed her to keep her baby with her.

When the word went around in October of 1864 that Black Kettle wanted to ransom the prisoners taken at Plum Creek and Oak Grove, Two Face heard about it and bought Lucinda back from Blackfoot. But when the Cheyennes came to ransom her and the child, Two Face changed his mind and would not let them take her. He told Lucinda that the Cheyennes intended to burn her. Another white woman, Fanny Kelly, who had been taken on the North Platte, was being held among the Sioux in the Yellowstone country. Mrs. Kelly's husband made it known that he would pay many horses for her return. Two Face picked up this information and, believing that any white woman would do, decided to bring Lucinda Eubanks into Fort Laramie for the reward.

According to Colonel Moonlight, who was now commanding Fort Laramie, Two Face and his band camped on the opposite of the North Platte. A local resident who handled many negotiations between the military and the Sioux went with a party of Indians across the river and brought Two Face, Lucinda and the child to the fort. Other members of the band were also brought in. Moonlight was angered by Lucinda's pathetic conditions, and the stories of abuse and cruelty which she told him did nothing to assuage his anger. Lucinda told him where Blackfoot was camped, some 100 miles northeast. Moonlight sent out a party of soldiers to bring Blackfoot in, "dead or alive," and when the Sioux was brought in he was lodged in the guardhouse with Two Face and his companions. Moonlight's choice of words in his description of the execution provide an interesting study. "Both of the chiefs openly boasted that they had killed white men and they would do so again," he reported, ". . . so I concluded to tie them up by the neck with a trace chain suspended from a beam of wood and leave them there without any foothold."[15]

Lucinda and her baby son were taken to Julesburg. She was still wearing filthy cast-off Indian garb when she arrived, her long beautiful red hair greasy, uncombed and matted. She was left with Mrs. Noble Wade, the laundress at Fort Rankin, who attempted to make the young woman presentable. According to Mrs. Wade, Lucinda told the whole bitter story and then, in a final burst of resentment and rage, confided that she was pregnant.

While she was still at Fort Laramie, an inquiry was made in the Denver paper about the location of Lucinda's daughter, Isabelle. A Mr. Davenport, the last person with whom Isabelle had lived before she died, came to Julesburg to see Mrs. Eubanks, and brought her the ragged garments which Little Belle had worn. On June 22 Lucinda made a formal statement about her captivity to a captain at Fort Rankin, and when she was finished she boarded the stagecoach for the east. It was said that she married again and lived in Atchison, Kansas.[16]

Of the many tragedies and events of the January raid on the South Platte, there is yet one more story to tell. Gus Hall, who lost the lower part of one leg at the American Ranch on January 15, was tougher than average. In Omaha he was fitted with a cork leg and soon returned to the South Platte country to live and work. Sam Ashcraft, who was fond of happy endings for his long-winded tales, said that eventually Gus went back to Indiana and married Sarah Morris. However, another valley resident, W. S. Coburn, as inventive as Ashcraft, said that Gus was killed by Indians at Ceder Bluffs. Judging by logic and the absence of hard cold evidence, neither story seems probable.[17]

The story of the South Platte Trail ends on the day the railroad reached Cheyenne: November 13, 1867. After the final raid on Julesburg in February of 1865 there were still almost two years of life for the road, even though these were declining days.

The Indians came back in the spring of 1865, of course, but they were more wary, and they stayed mostly on the north bank of the South Platte and Platte Rivers. Groups of warriors crossed occasionally, cutting telegraph wire at every opportunity, but avoiding the posts where soldiers were stationed. It was believed that there was a large camp during the summer far up Cedar Canyon and on the central portion of Lodgepole Creek. A large war party was seen on the South Platte Road between Junction and Valley Station in the week before the twentieth of June. They cut the telegraph wires before they disappeared.[18]

Much farther down on the Platte, a party of twenty or thirty Indians struck Dan Smith's Ranch, seventy-five miles west of Fort Kearney, where they attempted to drive off stock. The ranch was defended for half a day. The Indians also attacked a post wagon downriver from Fort Cottonwood, and two men were wounded. Fearing that a massive attack, like that on Julesburg might be made on Fort Cottonwood, Major O'Brien at Julesburg sent out all the mounted men at Fort Rankin to Cottonwood Springs for assistance.[19]

Maintaining the telegraph line became a continuing struggle. The telegraph operator at Junction rode toward Valley Station looking for the damaged line on June 20 and from this time on, all though the summer, Drake—the new operator at Julesburg replacing Holcomb and Smith—and J.D. Turner at Valley Station—replacing John Hines—were kept busy with mending chores. In June Drake reported from Julesburg that it was not only the Indians who were destroying the line, but emigrants, who cut down the poles for firewood. With lines extending both towards Denver and Fort Laramie, Drake said that he had men out almost every day replacing poles.

Six miles of line were carried away at Valley Station on July 29. On the thirty-first the operator at Julesburg attempted to repair the line near that station but was forced by Indians to make a hasty retreat to the fort. On August 22, the *Black Hawk Mining Journal* said, "The telegraph line has been broken upon the plains for nearly two months with one or two exceptions, when it remained repaired for only a few hours."[20]

A new station called Fairview Station was installed opposite the mouth of Lewis Creek in the vicinity of Dennison's Ranch sometime in 1865, and this station provided a much needed connecting link in the telegraph line between Valley Station and Julesburg. The name of this station was later changed to Riverside.

Although the telegraph operators lived precarious lives during these last years, all of them on the South Platte survived except one. In the autumn of 1867 an unidentified young telegraph lineman, who was riding his horse along with a stagecoach, offered to trade places for a portion of the trip with a guard riding the box on the coach. Suddenly the Indians rode down out of the sand hills and attacked the coach. The telegraph operator was the only one killed. His head was cut off and his body left by the roadside with forty-two arrows in it. It was taken into Fort Morgan (formerly Camp Wardwell) and buried in a coffin made of cracker boxes.[21]

The South Platte military forts were late bloomers, and their greatest period of development occurred after the major Indian raids had ceased. The first companies from the Fifth Regiment of U. S. Volunteers, also converted rebels, had been ordered west to replace the Third Regiment—H, I, and K—to be stationed at Fort Rankin, now renamed Fort Sedgwick, the men divided between that fort and Harlow's and the Wisconsin Ranch. Company H under Lt. Charles H. Hoyt was destined for Wardwell, but since they were unmounted and stationed at an out-of-the-way post, they were late in arriving at Fort Kearny and did not march with the other companies. At Fort Kearny there were seventeen desertions from the company before they marched again. At Wardwell on October 21 there were not enough men to do patrol duty. In the meantime a detachment of the Thirteenth Missouri Cavalry under Lt. J. W. Thornton, having arrived in December of 1865, did guard duty from Valley Station. The southerners of Company H arrived at Wardwell near the end of the year, only to be transferred again in the spring. The Thirteenth Missouri were ordered east to be mustered out in January of 1866. The constant change of personnel at Camp Wardwell is bewildering.[22]

In April of 1866 Wardwell was garrisoned by the Twenty-first New York Cavalry under Capt. W. G. McNulty. On the occasion of a visit from their superior officer, Maj. Charles Otis, in May the boys at Camp Wardwell erected a magnificent flagpole on the twelfth. The Major was given the honor of designing the pole, and the post carpenters and doctor, Dr. Yates, erected it. One of the soldiers wrote that he was confident that it was the finest pole in the territory. "Rigged like the mizzenmast of a Clipper ship . . . it seemed emblematic of the progress of civilization which will . . . cause the ship of commerce to float through this sandy desert . . . ."

When the pole was erected the command was paraded, the cannons manned and thirty-seven guns fired as the flag ascended the pole. The ceremony over, Dr. Yates pulled the plug of a beer barrel and the event was celebrated with an evening of "whiskey poker." A man of obvious conviviality, Captain McNulty was found lacking in other ways. Later in the month he was sent under arrest to Fort Collins. His offense is not recorded.[23]

The following month, on June 23, the fort was rechristened Fort Morgan in honor of Col. Christopher A. Morgan, Additional Aide de Camp of the U. S. Volunteers.

Some of the men stationed at Camp Wardwell gained such notoriety that they gave this little fort an unsavory name as a nest of outlaws and deserters. Desertion was a monthly problem; even officers never made an appearance at the camp. In January of 1866 two men of Company F of the Thirteenth Missouri Cavalry murdered two men at Junction Station. The two soldiers, heavily manacled, were brought into Denver by Lieutenant Hoyt and placed in the guardhouse at Camp Weld for trial.

On January 14, 1867, Denver was unexpectedly alerted by news that thirty-one soldiers at Fort Morgan had deserted in a body and were on their way to Denver to rob the banks. The sheriff and mayor of Denver assembled the citizens at the city hall, telling them to arm themselves well, and patrols were sent out to watch the approaches to the city. Most of the night was spent by the civilians warming themselves in the saloons. The following morning word was received that the deserters had eaten breakfast at Kiowa Station on the Cut-Off Road. One of these deserters had been badly frozen during the night while drunk on the open prairie. The deserters were reported to have followed Kiowa Creek upstream. The sheriff and mayor and a posse followed them without results. It seemed that the deserters were headed for Mexico.

Four days later, four of the deserters appeared in Denver and gave themselves up, asking to be returned to Fort Morgan. They said the desertion had been planned by a sergeant and the night guards on duty. They took seven unwilling men with them as hostages. After the party had reached the Smoky Hill Road, the seven men were relieved of their horses and guns and were abandoned on the road. Four of them reached Denver after several miserable days in the cold. They believed that the other three hostages were also safe and would come in soon. A message was received from Pueblo that the main body of the deserters had had their horses shod at that place and were heading south.[24]

In the waning days of the South Platte Trail, Company G of the Fourth U. S. Infantry under Capt. William Powell was assigned to Fort Morgan. The men were unmounted and were brought to Julesburg in a supply train. From Julesburg 115 men marched to Fort Morgan in five days, arriving in September of 1867. The fort was now the size of a city block; there were some log buildings as well as sod. It had earlier been discovered that the mud from alkalied ponds would dry to a surprising whiteness and the inside walls of the adobe barracks at Wardwell had been plastered with this mud, providing a measure of refinement for the roughly constructed buildings. There was a heavy stockade around the whole surrounded by a deep trench. One cannon was installed in the southwest corner and one at the northeast corner of the parade grounds, and another was at the base of the flagpole.

Down near the river at Junction Ranch, recently vacated by Sam Ashcraft, Martin Boughton kept a store and post office as well as a supply of whiskey and beer, depending mostly on the soldiers and travelers for his livelihood. A special order issued in May of 1865 instructed Captain King, commanding officer of the fort, to arrest any ranchers who were known to be selling liquor to soldiers, to bring them to the post and destroy their supply of liquor. "In accordance with orders" Captain King went out and arrested ranchers named Stevens and Holon Godfrey and brought them to the post. A hurried telegram from King's superior officer brought Godfrey and Stevens release after signing an agreement not to sell intoxicating beverages to the soldiers. A letter of instruction was distributed to all the ranchers from Camp Junction to Washington Ranch. Martin Boughton, however, was a constant offender, and after several warnings his stores of liquor were destroyed.

In 1867, after the coaches stopped and there was nothing for the soldiers to do, they spent a very cold winter in the fort playing poker. The post doctor had a thermometer and recorded that on several nights the temperature went to thirty-three degrees below. When the stage route was discontinued in September of 1867, the telegraph offices were closed along the South Platte Trail except at Fort Morgan, where messages continued to be received from Denver.

On May 18, 1868, Fort Morgan was discontinued and dismantled; everything movable was sold at auction. Ox teams came to haul the salvage away. A witness described the closing ceremony. "Company G formed a line and presented arms. The flag was lowered and the cannon fired a salute. At this, the forty-two dogs in camp also gave one loud long salute to the flag." One hundred wagons with military supplies and the troops of Company G passed through Denver on May 20 on their way to Fort Laramie.[25]

During the summer of 1865 the Indians camped in Lodgepole Valley harassed the central part of the South Platte Route through the month of July. First sighted on July 5, the body of Indians appeared near the Wisconsin Ranch. There was a rumor that a traveler was lost, supposed to be either killed or captured. On July 28 at Fremont's Orchard thirty Indians crossed the Platte and drove off six beef cattle, six mules and two horses. The owners rode to Camp Wardwell and complained. The Captain then in command set out with seventeen Colorado soldiers on the usual fruitless pursuit. On July 29 a large body of Indians attacked a train in which two civilians were killed and scalped near Dennison's Ranch. A team of army horses and a wagon loaded with supplies was captured; the rest escaped. On the same day twenty soldiers who were camped on Cedar Creek were surprised by a large body of Indians. The soldiers lost all of their stock and barely escaped to Valley Station, three or four of them wounded. Later that night, about 11:00 P.M., a party of Indians surprised another fifteen soldiers thirty miles up into the Cedar Bluffs. The Indians captured four yoke of work cattle, one mule, one horse and two wagons. The soldiers escaped on foot and although they were pursued, they arrived unhurt at Valley Station at seven o'clock the next morning. On August 8, four men were out near the Wisconsin

Ranch cutting hay. A body of Indians appeared on the north bank of the river but the soldiers did not cross to attack. After this the Indians seemed to have moved away and were not seen again for some time.[26]

On July 30, Brigadier General Connor marched out from Fort Laramie to occupy his place in a great encircling maneuver called the Powder River Campaign. With General Conner were Capt. Frank North and his Pawnee Scouts. The Pawnee Scouts were true Pawnee Indians, recruited by North to fight other Indians, and they were brutally effective. On August 15 Connor constructed a post called Camp Connor at the junction of the Bozeman Trail and Powder River. The following day Captain North and his Pawnees, while scouting, discovered the trail of a war party of Cheyennes returning from a raiding excursion to the North Platte. After following the trail for a day the Pawnees overtook the plunder-laden Cheyennes and attacked, taking them by surprise. The military report claimed that twenty-five Cheyenne scalps were taken by the Pawnees, one of them belonging to a female.[27]

According to George Bent, Yellow Woman was with the raiding party. The Cheyennes were not aware of the presence of the Pawnee Scouts in Connor's camp and they suspected nothing when a few Pawnees rode over the crest of a hill and made signals with their blankets that they were friends and indicated that they wished to talk with the Cheyennes. Five members of the raiding party turned and rode toward the Pawnees. The entire company of Pawnees and other soldiers suddenly charged over the hill and attacked. The main body of Cheyennes escaped, but Yellow Woman was one of the five who perished. Whether or not Joe Barroldo was with the group is not known.

Romantic fiction would demand a satisfactory ending to the story of this love affair between William Bent's wife and the half-breed with whom she ran away from the security of Bent's ranch, but history does not allow invention and has not provided sufficient facts for a conclusion. Laura Roper met Barroldo after her capture at Oak Grove. He was with the Cheyennes at the time; one might assume that Yellow Woman was also. Laura Roper believed that Barroldo was executed at Fort Lyon as a spy, she did not say when. This seems to be an unlikely story since there were many known informants in the camps of the southern Cheyennes. At Fort Lyon they were allowed to come and go at will in 1864. If Barroldo was killed, it was for another reason. The event does not seem to have been recorded. For the sake of avoiding loose ends, one might imagine that Barroldo went north with the Cheyennes and died with Yellow Woman in the Pawnee raid.[28]

By autumn the southern Cheyennes were homesick, and in October of 1865 they decided to return home. George Bent returned with them. As they reached the South Platte about October 20, some raids were made as they crossed the river. On the night of the nineteenth of October a small party made a quick dash on a government train and a civilian train some place below Dennison's and made off with four horses and killed one. At Harlow's Ranch the next evening about 150 Indians attacked a train (perhaps the same one attacked the day before), killing the assistant wagonmaster and wounding another. They cut the telegraph line and withdrew. At daybreak the following morning a party of about 200 Indians struck again at the same place and attempted to stampede the stock of the government train of sixty wagons. Some animals had strayed from a nearby ox train during the night, and two of the men had gone out to find them when they were discovered by the war party. One man was killed and the other ran into the corral with three arrows piercing his skin. A messenger was sent all the way to Camp Wardwell, where Lieutenant Thornton set out with thirty men of the Thirteenth Missouri Cavalry to aid the teamsters. The Indians cut the telegraph wires again and appeared to withdraw.

The train hitched up and moved about four miles up the road, where about 100 of the Indians swarmed down on it again. After circling and shooting at the barricaded teamsters, some of the warriors dismounted and climbed onto the wagons, attempting to set them on fire. The teamsters held out until the Indians drew back again. Doggedly, the train moved on toward Lillian Springs. Again the Indians attacked. Riding at double-quick time, Lieutenant Thornton arrived and the raiding party drew back. About two-thirds of them disappeared in the hills, but a determined group switched their attack to the civilian train coming up from below. They cut off two wagons and were about to plunder them when they were surprised by a detachment of Sixth Virginia Cavalry coming upriver at a propitious time. The Indians retired from the field.[29]

This was not the only attack. Since the telegraph lines were cut so frequently, much of what happened was not reported in Denver. On October 14 a government train was attacked at O'Fallon's Bluffs where one man, the leader of the train, was killed and three or four wounded. On Sunday, October 22, at 10:00 A.M., sixty to seventy-five warriors attacked a train east of Alkali Station. They cut off eight or nine wagons, hamstrung the oxen and left them hitched to the wagons after setting the wagons on fire. Four men were killed, including the owner of the train and his son. The other wagons of the train escaped. The telegraph operator at Alkali reported the attack to the west, saying that a squad of soldiers had ridden out but were soon driven back and hounded all the way to the station. Three soldiers were killed and one wounded. The Indians cut the telegraph wire in two places above Alkali, took 100 cattle and some mules and apparently went south.

On Monday, twenty soldiers were sent toward Alkali from Fort Sedgwick, leaving only twenty-five men at the post. Lieutenant Colonel Brown, who was in charge, was training and arming civilians to defend the fort. The Julesburg telegraph operator, Bloomfield, went out to mend the line.[30]

On the twenty-sixth of October a soldier who had gone to the river for a pail of water was assaulted and killed by Indians hiding in the rushes. More Indians crossed east of Julesburg on November 5 and cut the telegraph wire in three places. They also tore down the Laramie wires and destroyed the northbound mail. On the night of November third, a train was attacked near Spring Hill Station, all the stock was run off, and one man was wounded. On October 31 the *Rocky Mountain News* remarked acidly, "It has definitely been ascertained that the numerous bodies of Indians who have recently crossed the Platte and gone south, and have amused themselves to a reasonable extent with killing a few whites, burning trains, and running off stock, were not hostile, but a few Cheyennes and Arapahoes . . . who were enroute to General Sanborn's Council to lay in a supply of provisions and blankets for the winter."[31]

It was true that the Cheyennes and Arapahoes were once again at peace with the whites. On October 14, a treaty had been signed by Black Kettle and his peaceful brothers at a council held far away from the South Platte Trail on the Little Arkansas River in central Kansas. Eventually Ned Wynkoop managed to get some of the Dog Soldier bands to agree to the treaty, but it was never ratified by Congress.

George Bent returned to the southern Cheyenne bands, and in the spring of 1866 married Magpie, Black Kettle's niece; from that time he was a member of the old peace chief's family and lived in Black Kettle's lodge. Bent went to work for David Butterfield, later the founder of the Butterfield Overland Despatch freight and stage company. Bent worked as a trader and visited the Cheyenne camps, including the Dog Soldiers, frequently.

The war did not cease with the Treaty of the Little Arkansas but moved to central Kansas along the Smoky Hill River and to the Yellowstone country. Campaigns against the Dog Soldiers continued. The Cheyennes and the Sioux continued to strike the Platte Road from time to time, but their attacks, except for isolated incidents, were chiefly confined to the division of the road east of Julesburg.

On August 30, 1866, a body of Indians, believed to be Sioux, crossed the river from the north and drove off twelve head of stock, seven coach horses from Fremont's Springs Station and the remainder from nearby ranches. Soldiers, as usual, went in pursuit. On October 23, the 150 work cattle from a train owned by a Denver man were run off at

Elbow Station, eighteen miles west of Julesburg. The night herders were killed and several other men seriously wounded. A ranch was attacked five miles distant. Henry Carlyle's train of supplies for the Overland Stage Company lost a hundred head of mules. Two companies of cavalry chased the Indians and claimed to have killed five of them. The Indians left behind their lodges and ponies. Two soldiers were killed; one half of the stolen stock was recovered.[32]

On the central South Platte Trail marauding bands stole cattle from Jim and Charley Moore from time to time. On January 25, 1867, a train was attacked at Riverside Station, where three men were killed and a large number of stock run off. For three or four days, Indians were sighted frequently at Valley Station.

In June of 1867, as the railroad unrolled toward Julesburg, the Indians harassed the area around Fort Sedgwick incessantly. The stagecoaches traveled no fewer than three in a caravan. On June first a coach was attacked at Bijou Station; the driver fell with five bullet wounds and a passenger was hit in the thigh. The next day another coach was attacked. On June fourth a stage driver named Ed Kilburn and a stage employee named John Williams were killed near the American Ranch. The only passenger, a minister, escaped through the tall grass by the river bank. On June fifth a coach was attacked near Moore's Ranch, a stage employee killed and one passenger mortally wounded. The same day a ranch near O'Fallon's Bluffs was attacked and two employees were killed. On June seventh the war party attacked Fort Wicked, which was now at last a stage stop, and here they chased Holon Godfrey into his stronghold. The warriors made off with about seventeen head of horses, part of them owned by the stage company.[33]

In early 1866 E. L. Berthoud and W. G. Wilder surveyed a new townsite for Julesburg on the east boundary of the Fort Sedgwick reserve. By March they had erected two houses and were constructing a large (60 by 20 feet) store. They had plans for two more dwellings waiting for carpenters and materials to build them. By June 8 they claimed to have several business houses, a blacksmith and a bakery. This settlement was the short-lived town called Julesburg No. 2, which yielded the following year to the railroad town on the north side of the river called "End of Track" and later Weir's Siding.[34]

The railroad reached Julesburg on June 23, 1867, and the town of North Platte moved buildings and all to the end of track at Julesburg No. 3 directly north of Fort Sedgwick across the river. On July 10, 1867, the *Omaha Daily Herald* printed an item describing the railroad town. "Julesburg—where two weeks ago was a desolate prairie, now are four squares of houses, 150 scattered houses and about the same number of tents. It has every trade and occupation represented. Has got

120 grog shops, several gambling halls, and a few dens of vice. Its population is about three thousand. The principal amusements are getting tight, fighting and occasionally shooting each other down for pastime. For the past few days, the first of its existence, the city was ruled by extempore vigilantes, who amused themselves by the exercise of cowhide, leather and revolver. The mayor N. P. Cook is only a five days' resident of the city, and some of the city council have been there over ten days."[35]

Meanwhile another stage line in competition with Ben Holladay was developing. David Butterfield had been conducting freighting operations on the Platte River Route to Denver for some time before he switched his line of fast freight delivery to the old Smoky Hill Trail used sometimes in the gold rush. He built stations of a sensible design, with dugouts so low there was no more than a space for a narrow window under the roof on each side so that the outpost could be defended against Indian attacks. George Bent said that even the stables were dug in underground tunnels, connected with one another by passages, so that it was not necessary to go outdoors in times of danger. Butterfield's first trains traveled this route on June 24, 1865. The line did well during that summer and started carrying express and passengers in September. He called his company the Butterfield Overland Despatch. His success was greatly diminished when the Cheyennes returned from the north in October. The Indians resented the intrusion into the country they considered their own, and attacks on the trains, coaches and stations were unceasing. Butterfield had other problems; the economy of Denver in the winter of 1865–66 became depressed so rapidly that many of his bills could not be collected after the freight was delivered. In March of 1866 Ben Holladay bought the Butterfield company. Perhaps Holladay was thinking ahead because he knew that the new U. S. mail contract with his company would specify that the mail be carried over the Smoky Hill Route, perhaps in delayed reaction to the difficulties of protecting the coaches on the Platte Road. On May 4, 1866, a "magnificent new coach" brought the first mail to Denver by the Smoky Hill Route.

Changing the mail delivery to the Smoky Hill Route from the Platte Route caused much irregularity in the delivery. It was sometimes two or three days behind schedule. It was rumored that there were not enough horses to stock the route, which was probably the case because Holladay had all but sold the Overland Stage Company to Wells Fargo Company. The sale was concluded to Wells Fargo on November 1, 1866. It was rumored that Holladay received from one to one and a half million dollars cash and $500,000 in stock in the transaction.[36]

Wells Fargo and Company had stage lines along the Pacific Coast.

They had purchased all of the American United States Express Company's lines west of the Missouri River. And so now, with the acquisition of Holladay's western stage lines to Salt Lake City, Montana and Idaho—as well as the Overland Stage Company between Salt Lake City, and Virginia City, Nevada, and the Pioneer Stage Company from Virginia City to Sacramento—Wells Fargo had a virtual monopoly on all the stagecoach business in the western territories. The change of name and administration took place in Denver on December 10, 1866.[37]

The railroad rolled westward. On November 21, 1866, work for the winter stopped at Brady's Island (down the Platte from Fort Cottonwood), where the Wells Fargo coaches from Denver connected with the railroad. After the engines reached Julesburg in June of 1867, the ties were laid and the rails spiked down in constant motion to Sidney Barracks in Nebraska, where the portable end-of-track settlement was set down on a sunny slope between a high treeless bluff and the bank of Lodgepole Creek. Sidney Barracks was an outpost of Fort Sedgwick set up primarily to protect the railroad workers. Here Charley Moore came in late 1867 and opened a general store. Jim Moore stayed on at the ranch on the South Platte, but as the railroad moved on he went to Cheyenne and opened a feed corral and stable. The Washington Ranch was left standing; for a decade or more the brothers continued to use it as a hay camp, and later as a base for cowboys. The post office at Fort Moore was discontinued in 1868.

On November 13, 1867, the railroad was laid to Cheyenne and a terminal was established. A week before, on November 8, Wells Fargo began to remove stock from the South Platte Route, still maintaining service to Julesburg until the transfer was made to the new stage route from Cheyenne to Denver. Mail service was discontinued to Living Springs and Fort Morgan, with military mail to the post being supplied from Julesburg by ambulance. On November fifteenth the coaches stopped running on the South Platte Road.[38]

The American Ranch was finally abandoned in September of 1867. The post office there was moved two miles to Godfrey's Fort Wicked. On November fourth Holon Godfrey pulled away from Ft. Wicked with the last wagonload of salvaged materials. He and his family moved to the mouth of Big Thompson River on the new stage route. Mail service was formally discontinued to the area of the American Ranch on November 25, 1867.[39]

It is said that when the soldiers, relieved from duty at last, left the Wisconsin Ranch on November 24, they set fire to the barn and haystacks in a defiant celebration of freedom.[40]

Perhaps the best epitaph for the South Platte Trail is one taken from a contemporary source, the *Rocky Mountain News*. On November 5,

1867, the editor wrote, "It is evident that the glory of the Platte Ranches is fast departing. The railroad already wrought its changes and soon the numerous 'dobies' will be deserted and the hardy and brave. . . ranchers will have departed to other scenes of activity and travel. Success always to the brave frontier men!"[41]

The ruts left by the wagon wheels provided beds for tender shoots of weeds and grass, and in less time than one would imagine the South Platte Trail survived only in memory.

Epilogue

William Bent died quietly of pneumonia at his ranch on the Purgatory in 1869. His son Charley Bent, who had roamed the Smoky Hill and Arkansas River roads with the most savage and renegade bands of marauding Indians, preceded William in death. Charley had been wounded in a fight with the Pawnees, contracted malaria and died in November of 1867. Having become mentally deranged to a dangerous degree, he was mourned by no one, except perhaps by his sister Mary. Julia Bent married Edmond Guerrier and they both lived into the new century.

In a little town not far from his Crow Creek Ranch, Elbridge Gerry lived until 1875. He did at age fifty-seven. Young Seth Ward married Gerry's daughter Lizzie in 1866, and they lived near the old pioneer until after his death.

Spotted Horse died in 1864 or '65. Sam Ashcraft and Jacob Downing said he was killed as a traitor by his northern Cheyenne tribesmen. Possibly this was true, but it is more likely that he died of exposure due to alcoholism. His old adversary, Sam Ashcraft, left his ranch near the Junction in 1865 when he moved to Evans, Colorado. In 1874 he left Colorado to move to Webb City, Missouri. He returned to Denver often, and usually managed to give an interview to one newspaper or another about the old days. He was sixty-two years old at the time of one of his last visits in 1900.

Holon Godfrey also moved to the country near Evans. After 1869 he was active in organizing an irrigation ditch. He visited Denver occasionally, and at the *Rocky Mountain News* office, basked in his past glory. Matilda died in 1879; Holon died in 1899. Celia Godfrey married the hired man, Wes Mullens. The ruins of Fort Wicked were torn down in the early twentieth century and the sod was used to fill a low place on the land of the owner.

One of the more famous persons to affect the history of the South Platte Trail, John Evans remained in Colorado and became influential in the operation of railroads. In 1868 he was made president of the Denver Pacific Railway and Telegraph Company, and in 1872 he and others organized the Denver, South Park and Pacific Railroad Company of which Evans was the first president. John Evans died at his house in Denver at the age of eighty-three.

In 1866 Jacob Downing became the owner of two thousand acres of choice real estate adjacent to the growing city of Denver. Here he farmed irrigated sugar beets and alfalfa, which he developed from seeds brought from New Mexico in 1862. He also raised livestock, including prize-winning Arabian stallions and Hereford cattle. Later he laid out two subdivisions of Denver on his acreage and instituted legislation for the City Park. He died in December of 1907.

John Chivington maintained a respected reputation in Colorado, but he was usually unsuccessful in every endeavor he undertook after Sand Creek, the memory of which defeated him when he tried fruitlessly for election in the Ohio legislature. He lived his last years in Denver until his death in 1894.

Ned Wynkoop's subsequent life was a series of appointments and change. He was exonerated from blame for arranging the Camp Weld Conference without military sanction. He became a Lieutenant Colonel in the Cavalry in 1865, but resigned his commission the following year, when he was appointed Indian Agent of the Cheyenne and Arapahoe tribes. In 1868 he resigned this frustrating chore and returned to Pennsylvania and went into the ironmaking business. In 1874 he was back in the Black Hills, where he did some Indian fighting. After serving an appointment as timber agent for the state of Colorado, in 1882 he was appointed warden of the Territorial Penitentiary of New Mexico. He died in September of 1891 at the age of fifty-five. He is buried in the National Cemetery at Santa Fe, New Mexico, (the town which erected a monument in the city square to the First Colorado Regiment and the victory at Apache Canyon).

Few of the Indian chiefs survived for long. Black Kettle and his wife were killed at Custer's Battle of the Washita in 1868, and Tall Bull at the Battle of Summit Springs in 1869. But Stan Hoig, in *The Peace Chiefs of the Cheyennes,* says that Bull Bear grew to be a gray-haired toothless patriarch at the Darlington Agency in Indian Territory.

From among the cattle ranchers of the South Platte the Coad brothers moved to the Nebraska panhandle, where they raised Texas cattle. John married a girl from eastern Nebraska, and the couple had thirteen children. Mark Coad married in 1885. In 1884 the brothers sold the ranch and livestock and moved to eastern Nebraska. It is said that Mark Coad was killed by a drink-crazed cowboy about 1910.

Jim and Charley Moore both married women named Mary after relocating in Sidney. The four young people operated a hotel, a billiard room, a sample room, lunch stand, livery stable and later a dry goods store until after 1870, when James and his wife moved back to Cheyenne. James Moore became a well-known cattle rancher, operating headquarters ranches near the mouth of Lodgepole Creek and on the North Platte. His life was cut short after he fell from a haywagon behind a runaway team. He lingered for three months, dying in December of 1873. Charley Moore lived on in Sidney the rest of his life until he died of natural causes in 1915 at the age of 80. He had long lived in the shadow of his older, more outstanding brother, and by the time of his death Charley's sons believed that he was the one who had founded the American Ranch and ridden the Pony Express. Perhaps the most significant indication of his memory of the days on the South Platte Trail was the fact that he named his second son Washington, after the Washington Ranch.

George Bent and Magpie, who traveled with Black Kettle, escaped death at the Battle of the Washita because they were visiting George's family on the Purgatory at the time. When the Indian Agency was opened at Darlington, Brinton Darlington, the Agent of the Cheyennes and Arapahoes, hired Bent as an interpreter. George Bird Grinnell visited him many times to obtain information about the Cheyenne Indians, and Bent wrote many letters to George Hyde during the period between 1905 and 1914. He died in Indian Territory in 1918.

Notes

1. The Tangled Threads of Destiny

1. John R. Bell, "Journal" *Far West and the Rockies Series*, ed. LeRoy R. Hafen, vol. 6, p. 134.
2. C. M. Clark, *A Trip to Pike's Peak and Notes by the Way*, pp. 49–50.
3. Bell, "Journal," *op. cit*, p. 141. According to legend, Fremont said that a grove of gnarled cottonwoods in this area reminded him of an eastern apple orchard. If he actually said this, he did not record it in his published journal or in his memoirs as they were written by his wife, Jessie Benton Fremont.
4. Donald J. Berthrong, *The Southern Cheyennes*, p. 20; Edwin James, *Account of an Expedition from Pittsburgh to the Rocky Mountains*, p. 53.
5. James Mooney, *The Cheyenne Indians*, p. 368.
6. John Charles Fremont, *Memoirs of My Life*, vol. 1, pp. 98–99; Donald Jackson and Mary Lee Spence, *The Expedition of John Charles Fremont*, p. 200.
7. Richard I. Dodge, *The Plains of the Great West*, pp. 357–8; Berthrong, *The Southern Cheyennes*, p. 32.
8. George B. Grinnell, *Bent's Old Fort*, pp. 1–2; George Hyde, *Life of George Bent*, p. 59.
9. George Bent to George Hyde, 6/24/1914, in Bent–Hyde Letters, Beineke Rare Books Library, New Haven, Conn.; Allen Bent, *Bent Family in America*, p. 125. George Bent said that he was told by his stepmother, Yellow Woman, that William married Owl Woman at one of his forts—he did not know which one. Allen Bent said that Bent "went to the Upper Platte for a wife, a Cheyenne maid, daughter of a chief of great influence."
10. Bent–Hyde letters, 3/19/1905, 4/12/1906; George Bent, "Forty Years with

the Cheyennes," ed. George Hyde, in *The Frontier, a Magazine of the West*, 4–9 (Oct. 1905 to Mar. 1906): 3–4. Bent family genealogists seem to have contrived to make William Bent's situation conform to the conventions of another time and place. Consequently the dates of birth of Charley and Julia are confused and obscured. Even George Bent was uncertain about the dates, but this is not surprising—George was uncertain about most dates. He did state positively that Julia was his full sister, that his mother died in 1846, and that Charley was the son of Yellow Woman. Charley's age is the questionable point. It may be inferred from the statement made by George Bent (paraphrased by George Hyde) that he (George) and Charley joined the Confederate Army "when the war broke out." George Bent did not disagree with this statement when it was printed in the article edited by Hyde. If Charley was born after the marriage of Yellow Woman and William Bent, he could not have been born earlier than late 1846 or early 1847. In 1861, when the Civil War began, Charley would not have been more than fourteen years old. Even with an under-age enlistment, that age would not be credible.

11. Carl Ubbelohde, *A Colorado History*, p. 42.
12. Rev. Moses Merrill, "Diary," *Nebraska State Historical Society Transactions and Reports* 4:181; Bent–Hyde letters, 7/25/1911.
13. LeRoy R. Hafen, "Fort Vasquez," *Colorado Magazine* 41, no. 3: 204–211; James Beckwourth, *The Life and Adventures of James P. Beckwourth*, ed. Thomas D. Bonner, p. 433.
14. LeRoy R. Hafen, "Old Fort Lupton and Its Founder," *Colorado Magazine* 6, no. 6: 222–24; Frank Root and William E. Connelley, *The Overland Trail to California*, p. 225.
15. Howard L. Conard, ed., *Encyclopedia of the History of Missouri* vol. VI, p. 372.
16. LeRoy R. Hafen, "Fort St. Vrain," *Colorado Magazine* 29, no. 4: 247.
17. George Bent to F.W. Cragin, 5 Oct., 1905, manuscript in Western History Department, Denver Public Library. Bent wrote in a disconnected style. In order to make this material more cohesive, I have altered the sequence of his sentences and have added parenthetical words for clarity. For important information about the fur-trader forts, see Guy L. Peterson, *Four Forts on the South Platte*, which came out after this manuscript was completed.
18. Hafen, "Fort St. Vrain," p. 247; Hafen, "Fort Vasquez," p. 208; Hafen, "Old Fort Lupton and its Founder," pp. 223–34.
19. Hafen, "Fort St. Vrain," p. 244.
20. Hafen, "Fort St. Vrain," p. 251; Grinnell, *Bent's Old Fort*, p. 57; Bent–Hyde letters 4/14/1917.
21. C. G. Coutant, ed., *History of Wyoming*, p. 686; Merrill J. Mattes, "The Mountain Men and the Fur Trade," *The Far West and the Rockies Series*, vol. 3, p. 360.
22. Bent–Hyde letters, 2/26/1906, 2/19/1913; Berthrong, p. 114. Authors, including George Bent, differ about the year in which the fort was destroyed.
23. Bent–Hyde letters, 2/26/1906. Bent family biographers talk about school-

ing for the older Bent children—Robert, Mary, George and Charley—in St. Louis, where they supposedly lived with William Bent's sister, Dorcas Carr. After reading the Bent–Hyde letters, I see no reason to believe this.

24. George B. Grinnell, *The Fighting Cheyennes*, p. 99.
25. Berthrong, pp. 106, 109.
26. C. J. Kappler, *Indian Affairs, Laws and Treaties* 2: 595.
27. Grinnell, *The Fighting Cheyennes,* pp. 111–12, 113–16.
28. Berthrong, p. 137.
29. R. M. Peck, "Recollections of Early Times in Kansas Territory," *Kansas State Society Historical Collections* 8: 485–87.
30. Percival Lowe, *Five Years a Dragoon*, pp. 185–198.
31. Peck, p. 486, 493.
32. Lowe, p. 199.
33. Peck, p. 494.
34. Berthrong, p. 137.
35. Grinnell, *The Fighting Cheyennes*, p. 120; Bent–Hyde letters, 1/19/1905, 2/11/1916.
36. Peck, pp. 496–97.

2. Gold—The Elusive Seductress

1. Republished in the *Denver Post,* 31 Dec., 1903, Sec. 10, p. 4.
2. Jerome C. Smiley, *Semi-Centennial History of the State of Colorado* 1: 69, 198.
3. Ubbelohde, p. 59.
4. William Parsons, "Report of the Gold Mines of Colorado, 1858," *Colorado Magazine* 13, no. 6: 552–60; William Parsons, "Pike's Peak, Fourteen Years Ago," *Kansas Magazine* 1, no. 6: 560.
5. Libeus Barney, *Early Days in Auraria, 1859–60*, p. 18. I don't know why these prospectors put their gold dust in turkey quills. The only reason I can determine is that, once the gold was in the quill, the end could be cut off and the dust blown out from one end or the other. The dust was not as likely to adhere to the inside of the quill as it would to cloth, but it seems that paper would have been a better choice.
6. Smiley, pp. 223–27.
7. Smiley, p. 223; Albert Richardson, *Beyond the Mississippi*, p. 121.
8. Ubbelohde, p. 62.
9. Edward E. Wynkoop, "Edward Wanshear Wynkoop," *Kansas State Historical Society Collections* 13: 71.
10. Edward W. Wynkoop, *Unfinished Colorado History,* Manuscript no. II-20, p. 6, Colorado Historical Society Library, Denver.
11. Frank M. Cobb, "The Lawrence Party of Pikes Peakers in 1858 and the Founding of St. Charles," *Colorado Magazine* 10, no. 5: 196.
12. Edward W. Wynkoop, p. 14.
13. *Missouri Democrat,* 1 Feb., 1859. (Copied from the *Atchison Champion*, 22 Jan., 1859.)
14. Edward W. Wynkoop, p. 72. History does not provide an important detail here. When George Wynkoop arrived in Denver, he sued the Denver

Town Company. He claimed that when Ned arrived in Leavenworth the charter for St. Charles was already in the hands of the legislature and that Ned offered him shares in the town company if George would use his influence to have the St. Charles charter rejected and the Denver City application approved. The St. Charles charter was passed and the Denver City charter was not. George said that he spent considerable time and money in the affair and believed that he was entitled to the town shares. He won his case. The question is, how did the Denver City Company finally prevail?

15. Willard K. Burnap, *What Happened During One Man's Lifetime*, p. 153.
16. Richardson, *Beyond the Mississippi*, p. 53; William H. H. Larimer, *Reminiscences*, p. 63.
17. George S. Ball, *Go West Young Man*, p. 80.
18. Alice Polk Hill, *Tales of the Colorado Pioneers*, p. 53; Bayard Taylor, *Colorado, a Summer Trip*, p. 165; Richardson, *Beyond the Mississippi*, p. 289.
19. Eugene Ware, *The Indian War of 1864*, p. 101.
20. Marita Hayes, "D. C. Oakes, Early Colorado Booster," *Colorado Magazine* 31, no. 3: 216.
21. D. C. Oakes, "The Man Who Wrote the Guide Book," *The Trail* 2, no. 7: 9.
22. Levette J. Davidson, "The Early Diaries of William N. Byers," *Colorado Magazine* 22, no. 4: 152; *Portrait and Biographical Record of the State of Colorado*, p. 45.
23. Burnap, p. 156; Richardson, *Beyond the Mississippi*, p. 202. The best explanation I have read of "seeing the elephant" in is Merrill J. Mattes, *The Great Platte River Road*, pp. 61–62.
24. Everett Dick, *Tales of the Frontier*, p. 219.
25. "Reminiscences of W. N. Byers," *Rocky Mountain News*, 22 Apr., 1934. (Apparently written c. 1896.)
26. *Rocky Mountain News*, 18 June, 1859.
27. Lillian De La Torre, "The Haydee Star Company," *Colorado Magazine* 38, no. 3: 207–8; Edward E. Wynkoop, pp. 71–79; *Missouri Republican*, 23 Mar., 1859.
28. C. R. Husted, manuscript in Bancroft Collection, Western Collection, Colorado University Library, Boulder; *Greeley Tribune*, 15 September, 1875.
29. Floyd Edgar Bresee, "Overland Freighting in the Platte Valley." Master's thesis, University of Nebraska, 1937; Everett Dick, *Vanguards of the Frontier*, pp. 342–46; D. P. Rolfe, "Overland Freighting from Nebraska City," *Nebraska Historical Society Proceedings and Collections* 2nd ser., vol. 5: 281.
30. Dick, *Vanguards of the Frontier*, p. 346; Ware, p. 102. Rolfe, p. 281.
31. William Chandless, *A Visit to Salt Lake*, p. 19; Rolfe, p. 281.
32. Ware, p. 201; Dick, *Vanguards of the Frontier*, pp. 345–46; Rolfe, p. 281.

3. The Cradle on Wheels

1. John L. Dailey, Diary, Western History Department, Denver Public Library; W. N. Byers, in *Rocky Mountain News*, 13 Feb. 1860; Raymond and Mary

Settle, *Empire on Wheels*, p. 40; *Rocky Mountain News*, 14 May 1859.

2. For biographical material on Wm. H. Russell, see Settle, *Empire on Wheels*.
3. *Rocky Mountain News*, 14 May 1859.
4. *Rocky Mountain News*, 14 May 1859; Settle, *Empire on Wheels*, pp. 37, 42.
5. Settle, *Empire on Wheels*, pp. 71–72.
6. David Lavender, *The Big Divide*, p. 49; Settle, *Empire on Wheels*, p. 72; George A. Root and Russell H. Hickman, "The Pike's Peak Express Company," *Kansas Historical Society Quarterly* 13, no. 3: 486.
7. Root and Hickman, p. 490; Alexander Majors, *Seventy Years on the Frontier*, p. 164.
8. William Byers, in *Rocky Mountain News*, 22 Apr. 1934; Henry Villard, *The Past and Present of the Pike's Peak Gold Regions, 1860*, p. 16, footnote by LeRoy R. Hafen.
9. Root and Hickman, p. 486.
10. Majors, p. 165.
11. Settle, *Empire on Wheels*, p. 43; *Rocky Mountain News*, 11 June 1859.
12. Root and Hickman, pp. 491–93.
13. *Rocky Mountain News*, 13 Aug. 1859.
14. Root and Hickman, p. 495. (Emphasis added.)
15. *Rocky Mountain News*, 3 Sept. 1859, 9 Sept. 1859.
16. J. J. Thomas, "Days of the Overland Trail," *The Trail*, vol. 2, no. 6, pp. 5, 10, no. 12, p. 5; and vol. 10, no. 1, p. 20. Alkali Station was said to be about twenty miles up the South Platte from Cottonwood Springs, and Lillian Springs has been located four or five miles downstream from the present town of Proctor, Colorado (on the south side of the river). The actual location is believed to be in the southeast quarter of Section 25, Township 10N, Range 50W.
17. This mileage table was published in the *Rocky Mountain News*, 27 Aug. 1859. It is identical to a handbook published by Samuel Adams Drake, *Hints and Information for the Use of Emigrants to Pike's Peak.* The handbook was published in its entirety in the *Leavenworth Daily Times*, 14 Feb. 1860, and in the *Missouri Democrat*, 12 Dec. 1859.
18. *Rocky Mountain News*, 7 Mar. 1859.
19. *Rocky Mountain News*, 13 June 1860.
20. Charles Collins, *Collins Emigrant Guide*, 2nd ed., p. 62.
21. "On the Overland Trail," chap. 3, manuscript in Western History Department, Colorado University Library; C. M. Clark, p. 61; *Rocky Mountain News*, 16 May 1860. I am puzzled by the "humbug letter." I am not sure which station was called "Junction" on the Cut-Off Route at that time. This may have been an error caused by the many duplications of names, or there may have been an unnamed station on the route which was called Junction. It may even have been Living Springs.
22. H. O. Brayer, ed., *Reminiscences of W. H. Hedges, Pike's Peak or Busted*, pp. 20–21.
23. C. M. Clark, p. 61.

24. Harry E. Pratt, ed., "Edward J. Lewis, Diary of a Pike's Peak Gold Seeker in 1860," *Colorado Magazine* 14, no. 6: 201, 209–11; A. T. Claine, ed., "Journal of Jonah Girard Cisne, Across the Plains and in Nevada City," *Colorado Magazine* 27, no. 1: 49–50; C. M. Clark, p. 61. Throughout the remainder of this chapter these journalists are quoted without additional footnotes; they are credited in the text.
25. Francis Young, *Across the Plains in '65*; Root and Connelley, p. 211.
26. Mrs. Thomas Tootle, "Journey to Denver," ed. Roy E. Coy, *The Museum Graphic* 13, no. 2: 9.
27. Harriet Smith, "Day Book, To Pike's Peak by Ox-Wagon," p. 136 (formerly in *Annals of Iowa* [Fall 1959]), now detached at Denver Public Library Western History Department; Collins, p. 62; *Rocky Mountain News*, July 1860.
28. *Rocky Mountain News*, 10 June 1861; Ware, p. 255.
29. Root and Connelley, p. 262.
30. Root and Connelley, pp. 212–13. Frank Root made the trip in 1863 and again in 1865. When he mentions horses, one must remember that in the earlier days—1860–61—the stage company used only mules.
31. Ware, p. 179; Raymond and Mary Settle, *Saddle and Spurs*, p. 114; William E. Lass, *From the Missouri to the Great Salt Lake.* Lass suggests that Beni may have been a contraction of Benoit.
32. Collins, p. 63.
33. Ware, p. 179.
34. The mountains are not visible from the river valley at this point, but the clouds and bluffs sometimes combine to cause a deceptive illusion. The travelers were eager for the first glimpse of the Rockies. Geo. W. Kassler, manuscript no. 353 in Research Collection, Colorado Historical Society Library, Denver.
    Valley Station has been located in the Southwest quarter of Section 13, Township 8N, Range 52W of the 6th P.M. Peter Winne, "Sketches of the Indian War in 1864," *The Trail* 4, no. 11: 5.
35. Perhaps Clark expected Beaver Creek Station to be near the banks of the creek. It was actually two miles downriver at the ranch of Stephens and Moore.
36. A. H. Allen, "Pioneer Life in Old Burlington," *Colorado Magazine* 14, no. 4: 152.
37. Susan Riley Ashley, "Reminiscences of Colorado in the Early Sixties," *Colorado Magazine* 13, no. 6, 223–24; Mark Twain, *Roughing It*, p. 40.
38. Ware, p. 68; Ashley, p. 223.
39. Smith, p. 140.
40. Augustus Wildman, "The Wildman Letters and Other Documents," *The Far West and the Rockies Series* vol. 13, p. 262.

4. The People of the Platte

1. Ware, p. 44.
2. U. S. Census for 1860, Shorter County, Nebraska Territory, Residences 33,

34, 23; Ware, p. 46.

3. 1860 Census, Shorter County, Residences 26 to 32; Claine, p. 52; C. M. Clark, p. 47.
4. Richard F. Burton, *City of the Saints and Across the Mountains to California*, pp. 56. 59.
5. Ware, p. 245; 1860 Census, Shorter County, Residence 20.
6. Ware, pp. 71–72; 1860 Census, Shorter County, Residences 16, 17.
7. Collins, p. 62; C. M. Clark, p. 48; 1860 Census, Shorter County, Residences 10–15. Musetta Gilman writes this about William Bischopf: "Across the ravine east of Boyer's [Izador] William Bischopf and two French partners [located]. . .but in the spring of 1860, Bischopf traded his house for one owned by Jack Morrow, some 24 miles east of Cottonwood Springs. Here he went into business trading both with Indians and pilgrims. His partners were back in Iowa. This new ranch also became a Western Stage Station. . . ." (Musetta Gilman, *Pump on the Prairie*, p. 56).
8. Burton, pp. 59–60.
9. 1860 Census, Shorter County, Residences 2–5; Burton, p. 60.
10. Burton, pp. 61, 67.
11. 1860 Census, Platte River Settlement, Nebraska Territory, Residences 496 and 508.
12. LeRoy R. Hafen, "Elbridge Gerry, Colorado Pioneer," *Colorado Magazine* 29, no. 2: 137, 142, 146; W. G. Binneweiss (quoting Walter Ennes), CWA Writers Project, Pamphlet 343, Garfield and Weld Counties Document 12, pp. 1–44; Research Collection no. 264, Colorado Historical Society Library, Denver.
13. Osborn Russell, *Journal of a Trapper*, p. 96; Research Collection, no. 264, op. cit.
14. In 1880 Maria Gerry Kempton told the census-taker that her mother, Kate Smith, was born in Missouri. I think this was a misunderstanding on the part of the census-taker. I believe that Maria said "on the Missouri," meaning on the northern Missouri River where the northern Cheyennes roamed.
15. Research Collection no. 264, op. cit.
16. 1860 Census, Platte River Settlement, Residence 520; *Omaha Nebraskian*, 21 July 1860.
17. 1860 Census, Platte River Settlement, Residence 576; Ware, p. 360.
18. 1860 Census, Platte River Settlement, Residences 574, 575, 573, 567, 562, 565. It is possible that John "Code" of New York, age 21, and John Coad of New York (though born in Ireland), age 18, are not the same person. But subsequent events make it seem likely that John Coad was employed in this area in 1860.
19. 1860 Census, Platte River Settlement, Residences 564, 563, 566, 571.
20. 1860 Census, Platte River Settlement, Residence 566; 1860 Census, Shorter County, Residence 14.
21. 1860 Census, Platte River Settlement, Residences 561, 559, 560, 558, 553. The residence of William A. Kelly and E. E. Gordon at Valley Station in 1860 is providentially established by a want-ad in the *Rocky Mountain*

News of 12 September 1860, which reads as follows: "Horses taken up. Two at Valley Station, two at Julesburg. Kelly and Gordon, Valley Station, and Chrisman and Thompson, Julesburg."

22. 1860 Census, Platte River Settlement, Residences 556, 577, 553–556; Residences 552, 550, 546, 541, 533, 532.
23. Root and Hickman, pp. 72–74; *Rocky Mountain News* 15 Aug. 1860, 22 Aug. 1860.
24. *Rocky Mountain News*, 19 Sept. 1860, 14 Sept. 1860, 30 Sept. 1860, 12 Nov. 1860.
25. Collins, p. 63; Donald F. Danker and Paul D. Riley, "The Journal of Amos S. Billingsley," *Colorado Magazine* 40, no. 4: 244.
26. Collins, p. 63.
27. Quotation from Eugene Williams, WPA file of interviews, Colorado Historical Society Library, Denver.
28. A. R. Godfrey (grandson of Holon Godfrey) to Otto Unfug, 30 June 1969, Overland Trail Museum, Sterling, Colorado.
29. Maurice O'Connor Morris, *Rambles in the Rocky Mountains*, pp 47–49; Eugene Williams, WPA interview; Root and Connelley, p. 186.
30. Settle, *Saddle and Spurs*, p. 46.
31. Arthur Chapman, *The Pony Express*, p. 219; *Rocky Mountain News*, 22 Apr. 1934, sec. A, p. 4.
32. *Rocky Mountain News*, 6 Nov. 1860. The envelope for the Pony Express letter has been preserved, and a photograph of it can be seen on the cover of the *Denver Westerners Monthly Roundup* 16, no. 3 (Mar. 1960). It was addressed to "Alexander Benham, Julesburg, for the *Rocky Mountain News*, Election News, Lincoln elected."
33. Helen Cody Wetmore and Zane Grey, *Last of the Great Scouts*, pp. 74–77; Don Russell, *The Lives and Legends of Buffalo Bill*, pp. 47–52.
34. Thomas, p. 5; Settle, *Saddles and Spurs*, p. 43.
35. Obituary of James A. Moore, *Cheyenne Daily Leader*, 16 Dec. 1873, p. 4, c. 1; William Vischer, *The Pony Express*, p. 39; Dick, *Vanguards of the Frontier*, p. 289; obituary of Theodore Rand, *Denver Republican*, 28 Dec. 1902.
36. Settle, *Saddles and Spurs*, pp. 150–51.
37. There are several accounts of Jim Moore's record ride, and they are all different (except in those instances where one writer bases his story on that of another writer—in which case they usually agree). My information came from a Cheyenne, Wyoming, correspondent, calling himself "L," who wrote to the *Rocky Mountain News* of 17 December, 1867. I believe that this is most likely to be accurate because Jim Moore was living in Cheyenne in 1867 and the correspondent said, "Indisputable proof of the above facts can be had." I feel confident that the figures and dates used were obtained directly from Jim Moore at or near the time when the letter was written.
38. Dick, *Vanguards of the Frontier*, pp. 301–2.
39. *Rocky Mountain News*, 21 Aug. 1861.
40. Settle, *Empire on Wheels*, pp. 123–24.

41. Settle, *Empire on Wheels*, pp. 124, 188; *Rocky Mountain News*, 30 May 1861.
42. George Henry Carlyle testimony, 17 Dec, 1879, *Testimony as to the Claim of Ben Holladay*, 46th Cong., 2nd sess., Senate Doc. 19, p. 35. (Hereafter referred to in these notes as Sen. Doc. 19.) According to Carlyle's testimony, this was a system used by Ben Holladay, but it seems very likely that it was initiated by the COC&PP because of the latter's financial difficulties.
43. Obituary of George F. Turner, *The Trail* 8, no. 6: 27; Hester Brown, "Autobiography of Hester A. Rogers Brown," *Bits and Pieces* 5, no. 10 (1969): 2.
44. Binneweiss, pp. 1–44; Mark Gill, CWA Project, Pamphlet 351/1–110, Morgan and Sedgwick Counties, p. 57.

5. Descent From Innocence

1. John Dryden, *The Conquest of Granada* (1669–1670), pt.1, act 1, sc. 1; J. J. Rousseau, *Discourses on Inequality,* pt. 2.
2. James, vol. 2, pp. 176–78, 180–81.
3. Fremont, vol. 1, pp. 99–100; Mooney, p. 411.
4. Fremont, vol. 1, pp. 99–100.
5. James, vol. 2, p. 197; Bent–Hyde letters, 8/31/1910. George Bent told a story about two Cheyennes who had their first encounter with black men: ". . . they told us, 'white men were coming and two of them had their faces painted black, must have killed somebody'—as it was custom in those days when Indians killed anyone in battle they all blackened their faces."
6. Fremont, vol. 1, p. 98.
7. Grinnell, *The Cheyenne Indians and Ways of Life,* pp. 240, 336–337.
8. Hyde, pp. 335–339; Grinnell, *The Cheyenne Indians and Ways of Life,* pp. 238, 240.
9. James, vol. 2, p. 177.
10. Hyde, pp. 335–339.
11. *Annual Report of the Commissioner of Indian Affairs,* 1859, p. 507.
12. LeRoy R. Hafen, ed., "William Bent, Relations with the Indians of the Plains," *Far West and the Rockies Series,* vol. 9, pp. 183, 186. This was rewritten by someone before submitting it to the Commissioner. Bent's spelling and grammar left much to be desired. The letter was actually dated St. Louis, 5 October 1859. I have taken liberties with the time of writing.
13. Richardson, *Beyond the Mississippi,* p. 300 (describing camp in Denver) and pp. 172–73 (describing camp at Station Sixteen, Republican River Route of the L&PP).
14. *Rocky Mountain News,* 14 May 1859. Some of these stories may have been written by John Dailey rather than William Byers, but since I have no way to tell their writings apart, I have credited all newspaper stories to William Byers. John L. Dailey bought the interest of the original partner, Thomas Gibson, in August of 1859.

15. *Leavenworth Times,* 4 June 1859; *Missouri Democrat,* 25 May 1859.
16. Dailey, Diary; *Rocky Mountain News,* 14 May 1859.
17. It seems appropriate to quote an excellent paragraph from Richard Irving Dodge, *The Plains of the Great West and Their Inhabitants,* p. 265. (Written before 1876.):

> It may not be out of place here to remark upon the peculiar and unnatural style of speechmaking which obtains whenever whites and Indians meet in council, and in which there is always much twaddle about the Great Spirit, Great Father, etc. It is not a natural way of speaking for the white man, and from careful inquiry, I am convinced that it is equally foreign to the Indian. It is not fairly accounted for by the paucity of words in Indian languages, and must have originated with our 'Pilgrim,' 'Pennsylvania,' and other 'Fathers,' in whom a strong desire to convert the savage was constantly struggling with a painful lack of knowledge of his language, which would, of course, force them to recur over and over again to the same set of words. This peculiarity being accepted by the Indian as the white man's manner of speaking, he (being an imitative animal) adopted; and so we go on, year after year, making and listening to speeches which are as absurd to the Indians as ourselves.

18. C. M. Clark, p. 67.
19. Irving Howbert, *Memories of a Lifetime in the Pike's Peak Region,* pp. 17–18.
20. I. W. Stanton, Research Collection, no. 600, Colorado Historical Society Library, Denver.
21. A. D. Richardson, "Letters to the Lawrence Republican," ed. Louise Barry, *Kansas Historical Quarterly* (Feb. 1943), pp. 30–31.
22. Letter from James Beckwourth, *Rocky Mountain News,* 18 Apr. 1860. Recent writers have tried to establish that it was an Arapahoe camp where this assault occurred and that Beckwourth was mistaken about Cheyennes and Apaches. It is very unlikely that he made an error, he knew the Indians. He invited them to Denver, he traded with them, he listened to their complaint, and he made plans to visit them in a month's time. Beckwourth would know the difference between an Arapahoe and an Apache, and he was not misquoted. Evidence of this was brought out in the town meetings which were held after the incident. An attempt was made at these meetings to collect money for restitution, but the results were not published conclusively. John Poiselle (Poisel, Pyzel, etc.) identified Big Phil (Charles Gardiner) as one of the assailants.
23. C. M. Clark, p. 53; *Rocky Mountain News,* 22 Aug. 1860, 21 Oct. 1860.
24. Richardson, *Beyond the Mississippi,* p. 173; C. M. Clark, pp. 49–50.
25. Otis B. Spencer, "A Sketch of the Boone–Bent Family," (William A. Goff,) annotated by *Westport Historical Quarterly* 8, no. 4; Research Collection, no. 372, CHS Library, Denver; Berthrong, p. 146.
26. Stan Hoig, *The Sand Creek Massacre,* pp. 8–9.
27. Hoig, pp. 10–13; Berthrong, pp. 148–9.
28. Grinnell, *The Fighting Cheyennes,* p. 126 (quoting source as: "Report, Secretary of the Interior (1865–66), p. 703"); Bent–Hyde letters, 4/17/1906, 5/26/1906; Kappler, vol. 2, pp. 807–811. The description in the Treaty of Fort Wise of the reservation was as follows: "Beginning at the mouth of

Sandy Fork of the Arkansas and extending westwardly along the said river to the mouth of the Purgatory River to the northern boundary of the Territory of New Mexico, thence west along said boundary to a point where a line drawn due south from a point on the Arkansas River, five miles east of the mouth of the Huerfano River would intersect said northern boundary of New Mexico, thence due north from that point on said boundary of the Sandy Fork to the place of beginning."

29. Berthrong, p. 155 (quoting source as: "Boone to Dole, October 26, November 2, 1861, Upper Arkansas Agency, Letters Received.") (National Archives.)
30. Berthrong, pp. 155–56 (quoting sources as "Colley to Gilpin, December 19, 1861. 'Census Returns of the different tribes of Indians in the Upper Arkansas Agency up to the first of November 1861'; 'Boone to Dole, November 16, 1861, Upper Arkansas Agency, Letters Received." [National Archives]).
31. Berthrong, p. 157 (quoting source as "Colley to Gilpin, December 19, 1861, Upper Arkansas Agency, Letters Received." [National Archives]).

6. The Distant Sound Of Cannon

1. Danker and Riley, p. 241.
2. *Black Hawk Mining Journal,* 23 Aug. 1864.
3. Kenneth E. Metcalf, *The Beginnings of Methodism,* p. 75; John M. Chivington, *The Footprints of Methodist Itinerants in Colorado,* 26 Sept. 1889 (quoted by Metcalf); Eliphus Rogers, Letter, manuscript in Western History Department, Denver Public Library.
4. William Clark Whitford, *Colorado Volunteers in the Civil War,* p. 39.
5. Danker and Riley, p. 245.
6. Whitford, pp. 39–52, 48; *Denver Post,* 31 Dec. 1903, sec. 10, p. 3.
7. Chivington (quoted by Metcalf); Ashley, p. 225; Rev. David Marquette, *History of Nebraska Methodism, First Half Century 1854 to 1904,* pp. 57–58.
8. Whitford, pp. 39, 43–44, 52, 48, 75–127; Raymond G. Carey, "The Tragic Trustee," *University of Denver Magazine,* June 1965, pp. 9–10.
9. Merrill J. Mattes, "Seth E. Ward," *The Far West and the Rockies Series,* vol. 3, p. 380.
10. Bent–Hyde letters, 3/9/1905, 2/26/1906, 4/2/1906, 4/25/1918; see Edward A. Polland, *A Southern History of the War* for description of battles.
11. J. V. Frederick, *Ben Holladay, the Stagecoach King,* pp. 21–29; Root and Connelley, pp. 439–448.
12. Settle, *Saddles and Spurs,* p. 190; Root and Connelley, p. 466; Root and Hickman, p. 90.
13. *Rocky Mountain News,* 24 Mar. 1862, 27 Mar. 1862, 28 Mar. 1862.
14. Dick, *Vanguards of the Frontier,* p. 315; Frederick, p. 71; *Doc. 19,* p. 34; Ware, pp. 69, 472.
15. Root and Connelley, pp. 312, 358.
16. Ware, p. 307; *Denver Times,* 6 Dec. 1915, p. 5. In the *Denver Republican* of 9 April 1912, Hugh R. Steele, Secretary of the Colorado Pioneer Society,

wrote a short item: "Former employees [of The Overland Stage Company] were amused at the idea of 'fancy uniforms' and hitherto unheard of wonder coach fitted with bed, writing table and all of the comforts of home." Eugene Ware saw the coach but may have accepted the legend of its interior without actually looking inside. He did see the second coach with servants however. In the *Cheyenne Daily Leader* of January 20, 1878, an anecdote is related—supposedly told by Holladay himself—in which he mentions that his wife was ill and was lying on the floor of the stagecoach on buffalo robes.

17. *Rocky Mountain News,* 28 Oct. 1883, p. 11, col. 5. The newspaper reporter claimed that this story was told to him by Holladay personally.
18. *Rocky Mountain News,* 15 July 1862, 18 July 1862, 24 July 1862, 30 July 1862; Root and Connelley, p. 94; Frederick, p. 96.
19. "Testimony of Sarah Moore," *Frontier Scout,* 22 June 1865; Tootle, p. 10; Ware p. 180; Forbes Parkhill, "Decline and Fall of the Stagecoach Empire," *Westerners Brand Book* 7: 81; Sen. Doc. 19, pp. 87–88, (Bela Hughes testimony).
20. Turner obituary, *The Trail* 8, no. 6: 26; Hester Brown, pp. 1–10.
21. William Breakenridge, *Helldorado,* p. 39.
22. Official Record of Postmasters, State of Colorado.
23. J. Sterling Morton, *Illustrated History of Nebraska* 1: 620–21; John Coad interview, *Frontier Times,* June–July 1966; interview with Mark Coad, *Denver News,* 31 Oct. 1905 (in Dawson Scrapbooks, 70–501).
24. Clifford Clinton Hill, "Wagon Roads in Colorado," unpublished Master's thesis, Appendix, p. 139, Research Collection, no. 663, Weld County. CHS Library, Denver.
25. Morris, p. 67.
26. Smith, pp. 140–143.

7. Sowing the Seeds of Dissension

1. The law which troubled Evans most was called the Organic Act. Berthrong quotes this law in note 17 on p. 160:

> "...That nothing in this act contained shall be construed to impair the rights of person or property now pertaining to the Indians in said Territory, so long as such rights shall remain unextinguished by treaty between the United States and such Indians, or to include any territory which, by treaty with any Indian tribe, is not, without the consent of said tribe, to be included within the territorial limits of jurisdiction of any State or Territory; but all such territory shall be excepted out of the boundaries and constitute no party of the Territory of Colorado until said tribe shall signify their assent to the President of the United States to be included within said Territory, or to affect the authority of the Government of the United States to make any regulations respecting such Indians, their lands, property, or other rights, by treaty, law or otherwise, which it would have been competent for the Government to make if this act had never passed."

2. *Denver Weekly Commonwealth and Republican,* 15 Jan. 1863. In the spring of 1862 Chivington was promoted to colonel of the regiment, and

Edward W. Wynkoop was promoted to major. In November, Captain Jacob Downing was also promoted to major.

3. *Denver Weekly Commonwealth and Republican,* 15 Jan. 1863, 5 Feb. 1863.
4. Edgar McMechen, *Life of Governor Evans,* p. 104; *Denver Weekly Commonwealth and Republican,* 13 Nov. 1862.
5. *Report of the Commissioner of Indian Affairs,* 1862, pp. 373–76.
6. Hoig, p. 25 (Quote from *Washington Intelligencer.*); *Denver Weekly Commonwealth and Republican,* 19 Feb.1863, 26 Feb. 1863, 16 Apr. 1863, 2 July 1863.
7. *Report of the Commissioner of Indian Affairs,* 1863 (Evans to Dole), p. 122; *War of the Rebellion* (Official Record of the Civil War), ser. 1, vol. 22, pt. 2, p. 302.
8. *Report of the Commissioner of Indian Affairs,* 1863, pp. 122–23, 136.
9. Grinnell, *The Fighting Cheyennes,* p. 131; *Report of the Commissioner of Indian Affairs,* 1863, pp. 124, 131. There were two (or more) well-known Indians in the middle 1860s named Roman Nose. The Arapahoe chief Roman Nose, who signed Loree's agreement, was not the same as the nearly invincible Cheyenne warrior Roman Nose, who was killed at Beecher Island. The Cheyenne Roman Nose was not a chief.
10. *Condition of the Indian Tribes,* 39th Cong., 2nd sess., Senate Report 156 (hereafter referred to as Sen. Report 156), p. 72 (Bouser testimony).
11. *Massacre of the Cheyenne Indians,* 38th Cong., 2nd sess., Senate Report 142 (hereafter referred to as Sen. Report 142); pp. 129–30 (Elbridge Gerry report); *Report of the Commissioner of Indian Affairs,* 1863 (Evans to Dole), p. 124. There are three Beaver Creeks between the 39th and 40th parallels, near the 102° Meridian. The junction of the Arickaree Fork and what was known as the Cherry Fork must have been near the present town of Benkelman, Nebraska.
12. John Evans Manuscripts, PI-23, pp. 10-11, Bancroft Library, Berkeley, California; Sen. Report 156, p. 72 (Bouser testimony).
13. *Denver Weekly Commonwealth and Republican,* 22 Oct. 1863.
14. *Report of the Secretary of War,* 39th Cong., 2nd sess., Senate Executive Document 26 (hereafter referred to as Sen. Doc. 26.) (Evan's testimony); *War of the Rebellion,* ser. 1, vol. 34, pt. 4, p. 100.
15. Berthrong, p. 173.
16. *War of the Rebellion, loc. cit.,* pt. 3, p. 407.
17. *Ibid.,* pp. 113, 218.
18. *War of the Rebellion, loc. cit.,* pt. 1, pp. 880–82; Bent–Hyde letters, 3/26/1906.
19. *War of the Rebellion,* ser. 1, vol. 38, pt. 2, p. 152, and vol. 34, pt. 1, p. 883; Grinnell, *The Fighting Cheyennes,* p. 153; Sen. Doc. 26, p. 181.
20. *War of the Rebellion,* ser. 1, vol. 34, pt. 1, p. 884; Sen. Doc. 26, p. 181; Sen. Report 156, pp. 72–73.
21. *War of the Rebellion, loc. cit.,* p. 883.
22. Bent–Hyde letters, 3/26/1906, 3/5/1913, 9/17/1914.
23. *War of the Rebellion, loc. cit.* p. 884; Sen. Doc. 26, p. 181.

24. *War of the Rebellion, loc. cit.,* pt. 1, p. 883, and pt. 3, p. 166.
25. *Ibid.*pt. 3, p. 189, and pt. 1, p. 884.
26. *Ibid.* pt. 1, p. 884, and pt. 3, p. 167.
27. *Ibid.,* pt. 3, pp. 167, 189.
28. *Ibid.,* pp. 242, 303.
29. *Black Hawk Mining Journal,* 14 Apr. 1864; *Rocky Mountain News,* 15 Apr. 1864, 20 Apr. 1864.
30. *War of the Rebellion, loc. cit.,* pt. 1, pp. 887–88.
31. *Denver Post,* 31 Dec. 1903; *War of the Rebellion, loc. cit.,* pt. 3, p. 189.
32. *War of the Rebellion, loc. cit.,* p. 218; *Rocky Mountain News,* 19 Apr. 1864; *War of the Rebellion, loc. cit.,* p. 242. This letter, though dated April 20, was actually written on the nineteenth. The name "Indian Ranch" was not in common usage at the time. Downing identified the ranch as Morrison's on April 21, 1864.
33. *War of the Rebellion, loc. cit.,* p. 250.
34. *Ibid.,* p. 146 (the letter date of April 12, 1864, is a printing error; the date should be April 25, 1864), and p. 314.
35. *Ibid.,* pp. 314, 407.
36. There are two versions of the story of the capture of Spotted Horse. One was told to a reporter for the *Denver Post* by Jacob Downing when he was seventy-four, and the other was related by Sam Ashcraft to a writer for the *Denver Field and Farm* in 1891. Ashcraft was in his fifties at the time. When old-timers told stories in those times of journalistic laxity, it was almost mandatory that they make a good story better. It is ironic that while judiciously sorting out the embellishments one often passes over a valuable item of truth as another invention. This is regrettable but necessary. The original fanciful versions of this story may be read in the *Denver Post,* 31 Dec. 1903, sec. 10, p. 3, and the *Denver Field and Farm,* 19 Dec. 1891.

    The story does not appear in the Official Records (*War of the Rebellion*), in spite of the quotation which Hyde falsely credits to George Bent (*Life of George Bent,* p. 129): ". . . so the major had him tied up and 'toasted his shins over a small blaze' until he changed his mind. (These quotations are in Major Downing's own words and *are taken from the official record.*)" [Emphasis added.] This phrase is not in the official records (i.e. *War of the Rebellion*). When Grinnell (*The Fighting Cheyennes,* p. 137) used this quotation from George Hyde, he amended it to read: "A few years ago in the *Denver News,* Major Downing referred to securing information about the position of the hostile camp from an Indian he had captured by 'toasting his shins' over a small blaze." The *Denver Post* story referred to (December 31, 1903) does not use this particular phrase, and I have no other source. Evidently there is yet a third version of this charming little tale.
37. Bent–Hyde letters, 3/15/1915; *War of the Rebellion, loc. cit.,* pt. 3, p. 407 and pt. 1, pp. 907–08; *Denver Post,* 31 Dec. 1903, sec. 10, p. 3.
38. George Bent, "Forty Years with the Cheyennes," p. 4; Hyde, p. 122; Sen. Doc. 26, p. 32 (Cramer testimony).
39. Bent–Hyde letters, 3/15/1915.

40. *War of the Rebellion, loc. cit.,* pt. 1, pp. 907–08; Sen. Report 156, pp. 68–69 (Downing testimony).
41. Sen. Doc. 26, p. 32 (Cramer testimony); *War of the Rebellion, loc. cit.,* pt. 1, p. 916 (Downing to Chivington). In this letter Downing said that the Sioux told him that the Cheyennes had gone to the "Powder River." I believe that this was misprinted from "Poudre River."
42. *War of the Rebellion, loc. cit.* So far, no one knows who Chesby was; he may have been an employee at the Washington Ranch. Downing was frequently careless about the headings of his reports.
43. *Ibid.*
44. *Rocky Mountain News,* 12 May 1864.
45. *Denver Post,* 31 Dec. 1903, sec. 10, p. 3.

8. The Ripening of Dragon's Teeth

1. Bent–Hyde letters, 4/17/1906, 5/29/1906, 8/1/1913, 1/12/1914.
2. War Dept. Official Records *War of the Rebellion,* ser. 1, vol. 34, pt. 4, pp. 402–04 (report of Major James T. L. McKenney quoting a witness, Lt. Augustus W. Burton.)
3. Bent–Hyde letters, 3/26/1906.
4. *War of the Rebellion, loc. cit.* (report of McKenney.)
5. Bent–Hyde letters, 3/26/1906; Sen. Report 156, p. 75 (Wynkoop testimony); *War of the Rebellion, loc. cit.,* pt. 1, pp. 934–35 (Wynkoop to Maynard).
6. Bent–Hyde letters, 3/26/1906; *War of the Rebellion, loc. cit.,* pt. 4, pp. 402–04 (report of McKenney, quoting Burton.); Sen. Report 156, p. 72 (Asbury Bird testimony).
7. Bent–Hyde letters, 3/26/1906.
8. *War of the Rebellion, loc. cit.,* pt. 1, p. 935.
9. Bent–Hyde letters, 3/26/1906; *War of the Rebellion, loc. cit.,* pt. 1, p. 934 (Wynkoop to Maynard).
10. *War of the Rebellion, loc. cit.,* pt. 4, pp. 318–19 (Chivington to Charlot).
11. Sen. Report 156, p. 93 (William Bent testimony).
12. *War of the Rebellion, loc. cit.,* pt. 4, pp. 97–99 (Evans to Curtis).
13. *Black Hawk Mining Journal,* 7 June 1864.
14. *War of the Rebellion, loc. cit.,* pt. 4, p. 405.
15. *Ibid.,* pp. 513–14.
16. *Ibid.,* pp. 354–55 (Brown, Darrah and Corbin letters); *Report of the Commissioner of Indian Affairs,* 1864, p. 228 (North letter).
17. *War of the Rebellion, loc. cit.,* pt. 4, p. 320.
18. *Ibid.,* p. 449 (Hawley to Chivington).
19. *Ibid.,* p. 381 (telegram to Stanton) and pp. 421–23 (letter to Curtis); *Report of the Commissioner of Indian Affairs,* 1864, pp. 227–28 (letters from McGaa and Robert North, letter to Mitchell).
20. *Report of the Commissioner of Indian Affairs,* 1864, pp. 218–19.
21. Sen. Report 156, p. 93 (William Bent's testimony); Bent–Hyde letters, 2/28/1906.

22. *Black Hawk Mining Journal,* 18 July 1864; *Rocky Mountain News,* 18 July 1864, 19 July 1864, 23 July 1864; *Rocky Mountain News Weekly,* 20 July 1864.
23. *War of the Rebellion,* ser. 1, vol. 41, pt. 1, p. 73 (Sanborn to Chivington, 28 July 1864) and pt. 2, p. 323 (Sanborn to Maynard, 21 July 1864); Gill, Pamphlet 351/1-110, p. 99 (letter written to *Fort Morgan Times,* 13 Sept. 1889, by M. H. Slater, formerly of the First Colorado Cavalry.); Bent–Hyde letter 2/28/1906. In this letter, Bent recalled an incident of conflict between Arapahoes and soldiers on the South Platte in the summer of 1864 in which an Arapaho warrior, Spotted Wolf, was wounded in the heart. Since the exchange between the five Indians and Lieutenant Chase is the only contact soldiers had with Indians in this area during the summer, this must be the event of which Bent wrote.
24. *Rocky Mountain News,* 23 July 1864.
25. Ware, p. 181.
26. *War of the Rebellion,* ser. 1, vol. 41, pt. 2, p. 735.
27. *Ibid.,* p. 615 (Kuhl to Chivington) and p. 244; James Green, "Incidents of the Indian Outbreak of 1864," *Nebraska Historical Society Publications* 19, no. 5–6: 240–41 (pertinent material furnished by editors in the footnote); Mrs. Lulu Purinton, "Native Sons and Daughters of Nebraska Contest," *Nebraska History Magazine* 18, No. 2 (Apr.–June 1937): 146; *War of the Rebellion,* ser. 1, vol. 41, pt. 2, p. 612; *Rocky Mountain News,* 9 Aug. 1864. There were two Mrs. Smiths known to be in the area (both natives of Denver). They were found safe at Plum Creek Station later.
28. Green, pp. 240–41 (footnote by editors).
29. Sen. Doc. 19, p. 18 (Jerome affidavit).
30. John G. Ellenbecker, "Oak Grove Massacre, Indian Raids on the Little Blue River in 1864," *Marysville Advocate Democrat,* Marysville, Kansas (date not available); H. E. Palmer, "History of the Powder River Indian Expedition of 1865," *Nebraska Historical Society Publications* 2: 197; *Report of the Commissioner of Indian Affairs,* 1864, p. 254 (George K. Otis to Dole).
31. *Rocky Mountain News,* 10 Aug. 1864; Sen. Doc. 19, p. 14 (Sol Riddle testimony).
32. Green, pp. 240–41; Sen. Doc. 19, p. 35, (George H. Carlyle testimony); *Montana Post,* 27 Aug. 1864; Root and Connelley, p. 156.
33. *War of the Rebellion,* ser. 1, vol. 41, pt. 2, p. 734 (Mitchell to Curtis).
34. *Rocky Mountain News,* 13 Aug. 1864, 18 Aug. 1864, 18 Aug. 1864 (Extra edition); *War of the Rebellion, loc. cit.,* p. 694; *Rocky Mountain News Weekly,* 11 Aug. 1864.
35. *Report of the Commissioner of Indian Affairs,* 1864, p. 237 (Whiteley to Evans).
36. *Rocky Mountain News,* 13 Aug. 1864.
37. Bent–Hyde letters, 4/30/1906, 9/26/1905; *Report of the Commissioner of Indian Affairs,* 1864, p. 219 (Evans statement) and (Gerry statement); p. 232. Sen. Report 142, pp. 39–40 (Evans testimony); *War of the Rebellion,*

loc. cit., p. 843 (Gerry to Evans), and p. 864 (Browne to Evans); *Report of the Commissioner of Indian Affairs,* 1864, p. 237 (Whiteley to Evans) Bent–Hyde letters 9/26/1905.

38. *War of the Rebellion, loc. cit.,* p. 844 (Browne to Evans); *Rocky Mountain News,* 21 Aug. 1864, 23 Aug. 1864, 26 Aug. 1864, 1 Sept. 1864; Bent–Hyde letters, 2/28/1906. Bent said the Indians had not cut the telegraph lines before this summer because they had not understood the purpose of the wires.

9. An Uneasy Autumn

1. *Rocky Mountain News,* 16 Sept. 1864.
2. G. W. H. Kemper, ed., *A Twentieth Century History of Delaware County, Indiana,* pp. 113–14; U.S. Census,1850, Niles Township, Indiana, p. 848; Indiana State Library Marriage Records Index, Delaware County.
3. *Rocky Mountain News,* 13 Aug. 1864; Howbert, p. 117; Lonnie J. White, *Hostiles and Horse Soldiers,* p. 21; *War of the Rebellion,* ser. 1, vol. 41, pt. 2, p. 936.
4. James F. Willard, "The Tyler Rangers, the Black Hawk Company and the Indian Rising of '64," *Colorado Magazine* 7, No. 4 (July, 1930): 147.
5. Ware, pp. 216, 228, 230; *War of the Rebellion, loc. cit.,* pt. 1, p. 825.
6. *Rocky Mountain News,* 10 Sept. 1864, 12 Sept. 1864, 29 Sept. 1864; Ware, p. 246.
7. *War of the Rebellion, loc. cit.,* p. 825; Ware, p. 385.
8. Ware, pp. 272–73, 235.
9. William E. Davis, "Hell on Harmony," *Colorado Magazine* 41, no. 1 (Winter 1964): 43; Ellen Pennock, "Incidents in My Life as a Pioneer," *Colorado Magazine* 30, No. 2 (Apr. 1953): 130.
10. Morse Coffin, *The Battle of Sand Creek,* pp. 5–12; Sen. Doc. 26, p. 175 (Shoup testimony).
11. Ellenbecker (quoting Laura Roper); Mrs. Julia Lambert, "Plain Tales of the Plains," *The Trail* 8, No. 12: p. 6. Mrs. Lambert, wife of the station agent at Fort Lyon, met Laura Roper after her release. She quoted the story told her by Laura, but with some apparent embellishments—for instance, that Laura was forced to "submit" to Black Kettle, which seems unlikely when contrasted to Laura's story.
12. Grinnell, *The Fighting Cheyennes,* p. 158; Bent–Hyde letters, 3/15/1905; *Report of the Commissioner of Indian Affairs,* 1864, p. 233. Major Wynkoop testified (Sen. Doc. 26, p. 84) that the letter he received was actually addressed to William Bent; Bent–Hyde letters, 5/7/1906, 9/17/1914. Bent said that the letters were addressed to Major Colley and the commanding officer.
13. Sen. Report 142, p. 114, (Dexter Colley testimony). Reference to One-Eye as a spy is from Sen. Report 142, p. 8 (John Smith testimony).
14. Sen. Doc. 26, p. 84 (Wynkoop testimony).
15. Bent–Hyde letters, 3/15/1905.

16. Sen. Doc. 26, p. 50 (Silas Soule testimony); *Report of the Commissioner of Indian Affairs,* 1865 (Letter found here is identical with one signed "Old Tom" printed in the *Rocky Mountain News,* 24 Sept. 1864.)
17. Sen. Doc. 26, pp. 30–31 (Cramer testimony).
18. Lambert, p. 7.
19. Edward W. Wynkoop, p. 34; Sen. Doc. 26, p. 44 (Cramer testimony). It is logical to assume that when Cramer was talking about the "oldest" boy as having made this remark, he was referring to Dan Marble. Wynkoop described Dan as larger and seeming to be older than Ambrose.
20. Sen. Doc. 26, pp. 86, 89 (Wynkoop testimony); Sen. Report 156, p. 77. (Wynkoop testimony).
21. Sen. Report 156, p.77 (Wynkoop testimony).
22. *War of the Rebellion,* ser. 1, vol. 41, pt. 3, p. 399.
23. Sen. Doc. 26, pp. 213–218.
24. *Ibid.,* and pp. 39–40 (Amos Steck testimony).
25. Sen. Doc. 26, pp. 213–218; Sen. Report 156, p. 51 (John Smith testimony).
26. Sen. Report 156, p. 48 (John Evans testimony).
27. Berthrong, p. 192; *Report of the Commissioner of Indian Affairs,* 1864, p. 230; *War of the Rebellion, loc. cit.,* p. 495.
28. Mollie Sanford, *Mollie, the Journal of Mollie Dorsey Sanford in Nebraska and Colorado Territories, 1857–1866,* p. 189.
29. *Rocky Mountain News,* 16 Nov. 1864.
30. Sanford, pp. 189–90; *Rocky Mountain News,* 13 Sept. 1865 (statement of Lucinda Eubanks).
31. *Rocky Mountain News,* 19 Sept. 1864.
32. Sen. Doc. 19, p. 19. Why this order was dated December 2, 1864 is difficult to determine because the removal of the stage line began in November of 1864.
33. *Sen. Doc. 19,* pp 20, 21, 23.
34. *Rocky Mountain News,* 3 Oct. 1864.
35. Coffin, p. 12; Ware, p. 245.
36. Coffin, pp. 5–8; Bent–Hyde letters, 2/22/1917. On October eleventh Nichols reported to Chivington that there were six men, three women, one boy and two children, but Nichols claimed that he never saw the children. On October tenth Chivington wired Curtis that ten Indians had been killed. Chivington told Ben Holladay on October fourteenth that twelve Indians had been killed. Morse Coffin stayed on the battlefield and made a count of the dead after Nichols left. Coffin made three pages of notes written "a day or so after the affair." Coffin said there were four men (one rather young), four women, and two young babies, a total of ten." Another witness, Sergeant Henry Blake, was reported in the *Boulder Camera,* 2 Aug. 1941, as saying that there were five men, three women and two children. Evidently one of the wounded Indians, shot while lying by the pool of water, was thought to be a woman by Coffin and a man by Blake.
37. *War of the Rebellion, loc. cit.,* p. 877, and pt. 4, p. 23.
38. Coffin, pp. 9, 12.

10. Bloodshed on Sand and Snow

1. Sen. Doc. 26, pp. 19, 20, 28 (Silas Soule testimony).
2. Grinnell, *The Fighting Cheyennes,* pp. 165–66; Sen. Report 156, p. 27 (Colley testimony).
3. Sen. Report 142, p. 20 (Scott Anthony testimony).
4. *Rocky Mountain News,* 16 Nov. 1864; *War of the Rebellion,* ser. 1, vol 41, pt. 4, p. 709.
5. Carey, p. 10.
6. Amos Bixby, *History of Clear Creek and Boulder Valleys,* p. 399; Sen. Doc. 26, pp. 47, 51 (Joseph Cramer testimony), Sen. Report 142, p. 29 (Scott Anthony testimony); Bent–Hyde letters, 3/15/1905. Anthony's testimony about the twenty-three days of rations conflicts with that of Lieutenant Cramer (Sen. Doc. 26, p. 46), who said that Anthony told him "to report with every available man in my command with three days cooked rations in their saddlebags. . ."
7. Sen. Doc. 26, p. 25 (Silas Soule testimony).
8. *Ibid.,* pp. 46–47 (Joseph Cramer testimony).
9. *Ibid.,* p. 147 (Lt. W. P. Minton testimony) and p. 153 (Lt. Chauncey Cossitt testimony); Sen. Report 156, pp. 34, 62 (Samuel Colley testimony) and p. 54 (Lt. W. P. Minton testimony).
10. Howbert, pp. 122, 124; Coffin, p. 18; *Rocky Mountain News,* 17 Dec. 1864.
11. Grinnell, *The Fighting Cheyennes,* p. 171; Sen. Report 156, p. 65 (Edmond Guerrier testimony).
12. Howbert, pp. 122, 124; Sen. Doc 26, p. 48 (Joseph Cramer testimony).
13. Coffin, p. 19; Sen. Doc. 26, p. 68 (James Beckwourth testimony); Sen. Report 156, p. 95 (Robert Bent testimony).
14. Bent–Hyde letters, 3/15/1905, 4/30/1913.
15. Bent–Hyde letters, 4/14/1906.
16. Coffin, p.19; Sen. Report 156, p. 95 (Robert Bent testimony); Sen. Doc. 26, p. 70 (James Beckwourth testimony); Breakenridge, p. 34.
17. Sen. Report 156, p. 73 (Joseph Cramer testimony).
18. Hyde, p. 154; Grinnell, *The Fighting Cheyennes,* p. 178.
19. Grinnell, *The Fighting Cheyennes,* pp. 171–72; Coffin, p. 19; Sen. Report 156, p. 73 (Joseph Cramer testimony); Report 142, p. 5 (John Smith testimony); Sen. Doc. 26, p. 135 (Lauderback testimony).
20. Sen. Report 142, p. 6 (John Smith testimony).
21. Coffin, pp. 21, 26; Howbert, p. 125.
22. Sen. Doc. 26, p. 71 (James Beckwourth testimony); Bent–Hyde letters, 3/9/1905.
23. Sen. Doc. 26, pp. 22, 50 (Silas Soule testimony); Sen. Doc. 26, p. 51 (Joseph Cramer testimony).
24. Sen. Doc. 26, p. 51 (Joseph Cramer testimony) and p. 71 (James Beckwourth testimony); Hal Sayr, "Early Central City Theatricals and Other Reminiscences," *Colorado Magazine* 6, No. 2 (Mar. 1929): 53.
25. *War of the Rebellion,* ser. 1, vol. 41, pt. 1, p. 948.

26. Coffin, p. 34; Sen. Report 156, p. 42 (John Smith testimony); Bent–Hyde letters, 10/23/1914, 3/15/1905.
27. Sen. Doc. 26, p. 51 (Joseph Cramer testimony); Bent–Hyde letters, 6/5/1906.
28. Bent–Hyde letters, 12/12/1905.
29. Bent–Hyde letters, 3/15/1905, 12/21/1905, 3/20/1913. George Hyde caused confusion when he quoted George Bent as saying: "We took with us my step-mother and two women who had been captured at Sand Creek and turned over by the soldiers to my father." (*Life of George Bent,* p. 164). This is not what Bent said; he made no mention of his step-mother. He said, "I took these three women and three children back with me to the village." There is no indication that Yellow Woman was either in the camp at Sand Creek or at the ranch on the Purgatory.
30. Bent–Hyde letters, 1/12/1906.
31. Grinnell, *The Fighting Cheyennes,* pp. 179, 181. This Cherry Creek is in the extreme northeastern corner of present Kansas. Grinnell decided that the intermediary camp was on Whiteman's Fork, and since this is the location where Beckwourth found the camp of Cheyennes on January ninth to fifteenth, I believe that Grinnell is correct. Sen. Doc. 26, p. 72 (James Beckwourth testimony).
32. *Black Hawk Mining Journal,* 6 Jan. 1865.
33. Smiley, p. 428.
34. *Denver Republican and Commonwealth,* 16 Dec. 1863; *Rocky Mountain News,* 28 Nov. 1864.
35. *Rocky Mountain News,* 7 Dec. 1864.
36. Ware, p. 180.
37. Hyde, p. 170; Bent–Hyde letters, 5/10/1906. Bent had taken part in raids against the Pawnees previously.
38. Sen. Doc. 19, p. 25 (Hudnut testimony); *Rocky Mountain News,* 7 Jan. 1865.
39. Sen. Doc. 19, p. 25 (Hudnut testimony); *Rocky Mountain News,* 9 Jan. 1865.
40. *Rocky Mountain News,* 7 Jan. 1865; *Black Hawk Mining Journal,* 7 Jan. 1865.
41. *Black Hawk Mining Journal,* 7 Jan. 1865; *Rocky Mountain News,* 9 Jan. 1865; *Leavenworth Times,* 9 Jan. 1865 (Captain O'Brien report)
42. *Rocky Mountain News,* 9 Jan. 1865.
43. Bent–Hyde letters, 4/24/1905, 5/3/1905, 5/3/1906, 5/10,1906, 10/27/1914.
44. *Rocky Mountain News,* 10 Jan. 1865.
45. *Rocky Mountain News,* 11 Jan. 1865 (Livingston report); *Leavenworth Times,* 9 Jan. 1865 (Captain O'Brien report); Camp Rankin Post Records (O'Brien's report).

11. Vengeance, Fire and Ice

1. *Rocky Mountain News,* 7 Jan. 1865, 14 Jan. 1865; *Black Hawk Mining Journal,* 7 Jan. 1865.

2. *Miner's Register,* 14 Jan. 1865.
3. *Rocky Mountain News,* 9 Jan. 1865; *Miner's Register,* 14 Jan. 1865.
4. *Rocky Mountain News,* 9 Jan. 1865; *Black Hawk Mining Journal,* 9 Jan. 1865; Sen. Doc. 19, p. 19 (Reuben Thomas affidavit).
5. *Rocky Mountain News,* 9 Jan. 1865, 14 Jan. 1865, 16 Jan. 1865; *Black Hawk Mining Journal,* 9 Jan. 1865.
6. *Rocky Mountain News,* 29 Apr. 1865; Bent–Hyde letters, 5/3/1906, Hyde, p. 180. Some of this may have been Hyde's invention, particularly the means of identifying the scalps. Bent said no more in his letters than the names of the Indians who had been scalped.
7. Bent–Hyde letters, 5/14/1913.
8. Sen. Doc. 26, p. 72 (James Beckwourth testimony).
9. *Rocky Mountain News,* 9 Jan. 1865; Ware, p. 326; Camp Rankin Post Records (O'Brien report); Grinnell, *The Fighting Cheyennes,* p. 188; *War of the Rebellion,* ser. 1, vol. 38, pt. 1, p. 511.
10. *Rocky Mountain News,* 11 Jan. 1865; *War of the Rebellion, loc. cit.,* p. 43.
11. *Rocky Mountain News,* 20 Jan. 1865; *War of the Rebellion, loc. cit.,* p. 43; *St. Joseph Herald,* 25 Aug. 1865 (reprinted in *Black Hawk Mining Journal,* 2 Sept. 1865).
12. *Rocky Mountain News,* 16 Jan. 1865, 17 Jan. 1865; *War of the Rebellion, loc. cit.,* p. 40; Ralph Coad, "Transcript of a Speech," *Nebraska History Magazine* 19, No. 1 (Jan.–Mar. 1938): 39.
13. *Rocky Mountain News,* 20 Jan. 1865; *St. Joseph Herald,* 25 Aug. 1865; *Frontier Scout,* 22 June 1865 (Sarah Morris statement taken at Fort Rice); *Rocky Mountain News,* 31 July1865 (letter from Rezin Iames to Holon Godfrey).
14. Winne, p. 21; *Rocky Mountain News,* 16 Jan. 1865, 17 Jan. 1865. There are many accounts of the defense of Godfrey's Ranch—most of them fictionalized with details arranged to suit the writer's fancy. Of them all, even though he made errors, Peter Winne's is most credible.
15. *War of the Rebellion,* ser. 1, vol. 48, pt. 1, p. 40; Luella Shaw, *True History of Some of the Pioneers,* p. 28, quoting W. S. Coburn. Coburn was not above inventing details to make a story more interesting. The best can be expected from him is a slender thread of truth.
16. *Rocky Mountain News,* 17 Jan. 1865; *War of the Rebellion, loc. cit.,* p. 40.
17. *War of the Rebellion, loc. cit.,* p. 40 (Kennedy's report); *Rocky Mountain News,* 18 Jan. 1865; Bent–Hyde letters, 4/24/1905, 5/3/1906; *War of the Rebellion, loc. cit.,* p. 40 (Livingston report); Sen. Doc. 19, p. 19 (Reuben Thomas affidavit).
18. *The Telegrapher,* 27 Feb. 1865. This was a magazine printed for, or by, telegraph operators. A page is exhibited at the Julesburg Museum. Much of the information in this article is badly garbled, and details are invented. The pole might possibly have been intended for a flagpole, even though it was short.
19. *War of the Rebellion, loc. cit.,* p. 43; *Rocky Mountain News,* 20 Jan. 1865, 21 Jan. 1865, 22 Jan. 1865, 23 Jan. 1865.

20. *Rocky Mountain News,* 23 Jan. 1865; *War of the Rebellion, loc. cit.,* p. 842.
21. Bent–Hyde letters, 5/3/1906, 5/31/1913.
22. *War of the Rebellion, loc. cit.,* p. 40 (Livingston report). Livingston was mistaken about most of the dates in his report of February 5, 1865; adjustments were necessary in my text. *Omaha Weekly Republican,* 17 Feb. 1865. The reporter for this item was also mistaken about the date.

    There is great confusion about the attack on Harlow's Ranch. George Grinnell gives a detailed description of the ranch at Harlow's, the killing of two men and the taking of a woman prisoner by a Sioux named Cut Belly. I have not found verification for this story, but the correspondence between Grinnell and George Bent has not been preserved. In his letters to George Hyde, Bent wrote about it twice. In the first he wrote: "Just as the village crossed the South Platte, they attacked a ranch and a Sioux named Dog Belly captured a woman and her child here." In the second letter, May 3, 1906, he said: "That evening [February second]. . . This party I was with attacked ranch and killed three men and captured white woman." He mentions Dog Belly again. Both stories are culminated with the mistaken idea that this was Lucinda Eubanks, and Bent writes an uninformed story of the fate of the woman, confused with the story of Lucinda. It seems that if George Bent took part in the raid on Harlow's, the date is uncertain. On the twenty-eighth of January he was camped on Cedar Bluffs with the cattle from Moore's Ranch. Harlow's was attacked before February second. The woman and child from Harlow's Ranch were never mentioned again in any publication I have read.
24. *War of the Rebellion, loc. cit.,* pp. 42–43; Bent–Hyde letters, 6/6/1913.
25. Bent–Hyde letters, 5/3/1906, 5/31/1913.
26. *Omaha Weekly Republican,* 27 Feb. 1865.
27. James R. Harvey, "Interview with Elizabeth J. Tallman, Pioneer Experiences in Colorado," *Colorado Magazine* 13, No 4 (July 1936): 145; C. B. Hadley, "The Plains War in 1865," *Nebraska Historical Society Proceedings and Collections,* 2nd ser., 5: 275.
28. *War of the Rebellion, loc. cit.,* p. 44; *Rocky Mountain News,* 23 Jan. 1865.
29. *Rocky Mountain News,* 31 Jan. 1865; *Miner's Register,* 30 Jan. 1865; Mrs. Hallie Riley Hodder, "Crossing the Plains in War Time" *Colorado Magazine* 10, No. 4 (July 1933): 132.
30. Ware, p. 360; *Leavenworth Times,* 4 Feb. 1865.
31. *Omaha Weekly Republican,* 17 Feb. 1865; Sen. Doc. 19, p. 28 (Andrew Hughes affidavit). Information in the *Omaha Weekly Republican* was obtained from Lt. Charles F. Porter of the First Battalion of Nebraska Cavalry, who, with his troops, came to Julesburg with Livingston. He had previously been stationed at Gilman's Ranch, east of Fort Kearny, where he had reported less accurately on the Plum Creek massacre.
32. Hadley, p. 275.
33. Bent–Hyde letters, 5/3/1906, 10/23/1914. Bent wrote about the second attack on Julesburg in two letters. I have taken the liberty of combining

the two accounts so that the events could be told in consecutive order.

34. *Omaha Weekly Republican,* 17 Feb. 1865; Sen. Doc. 19, p. 28 (Andrew Hughes affidavit, Lt. J. S. Brewer testimony).
35. Hadley, p. 275; Ware, p. 377.
36. Ware, pp. 375–76.
37. Ware, pp. 380, 382; *Omaha Weekly Republican,* 17 Feb. 1865; *War of the Rebellion, loc. cit.,* p. 793 (Livingston report); John I. Dailey, Diary; Hodder, p. 132.

12. The Prairie Claims Its Own

1. *War of the Rebellion,* ser. 1, vol. 48, pt. 1 pp. 837–39; Smiley, p. 428.
2. Ware, pp. 386–90.
3. *War of the Rebellion, loc. cit.,* pp. 736, 853, 845, 924. On page 853, Livingston omitted the destination of the troops he was sending, but the meaning is clear from the context of the previous letters.
4. *Ibid;* pp. 43–44; Nathaniel Hill, "Nathaniel P. Hill makes Second Visit to Colorado, 1865," *Colorado Magazine* 34, no. 2 (Apr. 1957): 129–30; Root and Connelley, p. 384.
5. Nathaniel Hill, p. 130.
6. U.S. Record of Postmasters, National Archives.
7. Young, p. 198; J. F. Meline, *Two Thousand Miles on Horseback,* p. 45.
8. *Rocky Mountain News,* 8 Aug. 1865; Fort Morgan Post Returns and Post Records.
9. Gill, Pamphlet 351/1-110.
10. Emma B. Conklin, *A Brief History of Logan County,* p. 74.
11. *Rocky Mountain News,* 19 Apr. 1865, 29 Apr. 1865.
12. Interview with Sam Ashcraft from unknown newspaper dated 9 May 1900, in George F. Turner Scrapbook, Manuscript Collection of Western History Collection, Denver Public Library; Root and Connelley, p. 379; Young, p. 197.
13. Purinton, p. 146.
14. *Frontier Scout,* 22 June 1865; *Rocky Mountain News,* 31 July 1865; U.S. Census, Delaware County, Indiana, 1870 and 1880.
15. Mrs. Noble Wade, "New Lights on Mrs. Lucinda Eubanks," *The Trail* 13, No. 2 (July 1920): 20–24; *Rocky Mountain News,* 13 Sept. 1865 (formal statement of Lucinda Eubanks); *War of the Rebellion, loc. cit.,* pp. 276–77.
16. *Rocky Mountain News,* 17 May 1865, 13 Sept. 1865; Root and Connelley, p. 353.
17. Ashcraft interview, George F. Turner Scrapbook; Shaw, p. 191.
18. *Black Hawk Mining Journal,* 20 June 1865.
19. *War of the Rebellion, loc. cit.,* p. 270.
20. *Black Hawk Mining Journal,* 20 June 1865, 29 June 1865; 22 Aug. 1865; *Rocky Mountain News,* 29 July 1865, 31 July 1865.
21. Gill, Pamphlet 351/1-110, p. 136 (quoting G. W. Farrington, Sergeant of Company G, Fourth U.S. Infantry, who was stationed at Fort Morgan, September 1867 to May 1868.); Evelyn Bradley (quoting Mrs. Charles A. Find-

ing), "The Story of a Colorado Pioneer," *Colorado Magazine* 2, No. 1 (Jan. 1925): 54.

22. Gill, Pamphlet 351/1-110, p. 145; Dee Brown, *Galvanized Yankees;* R. O. Woodward, "With the Troops in Colorado," *Colorado Magazine* 3, No. 2 (May 1926).
23. *Rocky Mountain News,* 17 May 1866.
24. *Rocky Mountain News,* 14, 15, 16, 19, 23 Jan. 1867; *Black Hawk Mining Journal,* 1 Feb. 1866.
25. Gill, Pamphlet 351/1-110, pp. 135–6; U.S. Record of Postmasters; *Rocky Mountain News,* 20 May 1868.
26. *Rocky Mountain News,* 7, 29, 31 July 1865, 8 Aug. 1865.
27. *War of the Rebellion, loc. cit.,* p. 358.
28 Bent–Hyde letters, 1906, 7/19/1908, 9/23/1913; Ellenberger (quoting Laura Roper).
29. *Black Hawk Mining Journal,* 20 Oct. 1865; *Rocky Mountain News,* 21, 23 Oct. 1865.
30. *Black Hawk Mining Journal,* 14, 24 Oct. 1865, 3, 7 Nov. 1865; *Rocky Mountain News,* 23 Oct. 1865.
31. *Rocky Mountain News,* 28, 31 Oct. 1865; *Black Hawk Mining Journal,* 7 Nov. 1865; H. T. Clark. "Freighting to Denver and Black Hills," *Nebraska Historical Society Proceedings and Collections,* 2nd ser., 5: 299–312.
32. *Rocky Mountain News,* 23 Oct. 1866; Bent–Hyde letters, December (no date) 1913.
33. Root and Connelley, pp. 80, 362; *Rocky Mountain News,* 25, 29 Jan. 1867.
34. Henry M. Stanley, *My Early Travels in America and Asia* 2:119; Major Henry C. Parry, "Letters," *Annals of Wyoming* 30, No. 2 (Oct. 1958); *Rocky Mountain News,* 13 Mar. 1866; *Black Hawk Mining Journal,* 8 June 1866.
35. Omaha Daily Herald, 10 July 1867.
36. Leslie Linville, *The Smoky Hill Valley and Butterfield Trail;* Ella A. Butterfield, "Butterfield's Overland Despatch," *The Trail* 18, No. 7 (Dec. 1925): 3–9; *Black Hawk Mining Journal,* 4 May 1866; *Rocky Mountain News,* 8 Oct. 1866, 2 Nov. 1866; Bent–Hyde letters, 12/18/1906.
37. *Rocky Mountain News,* 30 Nov. 1866; *Pony Express* 2 (July 1944): 3. On February 5, 1866, the name of Holladay's stage line was changed at last to the Holladay Overland Mail and Express Company (Frederick, p. 68).
38. *Rocky Mountain News,* 8, 11, 25 Nov. 1867; U.S. Record of Postmasters.
39. *Rocky Mountain News,* 3, 5 Nov. 1867; U.S. Record of Postmasters.
40. *Rocky Mountain News,* 25 Nov. 1867.
41. *Rocky Mountain News,* 5 Nov. 1867.

Bibliography

Books

Baker, James B., and LeRoy R. Hafen, eds. *History of Colorado*. Vol. 1. Denver: Linderman Company Inc., 1927.

Ball, George S. *Go West Young Man*. Greeley, Col.: Greeley Tribune Republican Publishing Co., 1969.

Barney, Libeus. *Early Days in Auraria, 1859–60*. San Jose, Cal.: The Talisman Press, 1959.

Beckwourth, James P. *Life and Adventures of James P. Beckwourth*. Edited by T. D. Bonner. New York: MacMillan, 1892.

Bell, Captain John R. *The Journal of Captain John R. Bell, Official Journalist for the Stephen H. Long Expedition in the Rocky Mountains, 1820*. Vol. 6 of The Far West and the Rockies Historical Series, edited, with introductions, by Harlin N. Fuller and LeRoy R. Hafen. Glendale: Arthur H. Clark Co., 1966.

Bent, Allen. *The Bent Family in America*. Boston: David Clapp and Sons (printers), 1900.

Berthrong, Donald J. *The Southern Cheyennes*. Norman: University of Oklahoma Press, 1963.

Bixby, Amos. *History of Clear Creek and Boulder Valleys*. Chicago: O. L. Baskin Co., 1880.

Breakenridge, William. *Helldorado, Bringing the Law to the Mesquite*. Boston and New York: Houghton Mifflin Co., 1928.

Brown, Dee. *The Galvanized Yankees*. New York: Curtis Books, 1972.

Burnap, Willard K. *What Happened During One Man's Lifetime.* Fergus Falls, Minn., 1923.

Burton, Richard F. *City of the Saints and Across the Mountains to California.* London: Longman, Green, Longman and Roberts, 1861.

Chandless, William. *A Visit to Salt Lake.* London: Smith and Elder, 1857.

Chapman, Arthur. *The Pony Express.* New York: G. P. Putnam and Sons, 1932.

Clark, Charles M. *A Trip to Pike's Peak and Notes by the Way.* Chicago: S. P. Rounds Steam Book and Job Printing House, 1861.

Coffin, Morse H. *The Battle of Sand Creek.* Edited by Alan Farley. Waco, Tex.: W. M. Morrison, 1965.

Collins, Charles. *Collins Emigrant Guide. The Rocky Mountain Gold Regions.* 2nd ed. Denver: S. W. Burt and E. L. Berthoud, 1861.

Conard, Howard L., ed. *Encyclopedia of the History of Missouri.* New York, Louisville, St. Louis. The Southern History Company, Haldeman, Conard and Co., 1901.

Conklin, Emma Burke. *A Brief History of Logan County.* Daughters of the American Revolution. Denver: Welch Haffner Printing Co., 1928.

Coutant, C. G. *History of Wyoming.* Laramie, 1899.

Craig, Reginald S. *The Fighting Parson, The Biography of Colonel John M. Chivington.* Los Angeles: Westernlore Press, 1959.

Dick, Everett. *Vanguards of the Frontier.* Lincoln: University of Nebraska Press, 1941.

———. *Tales of the Frontier.* Lincoln: University of Nebraska Press, 1963.

Dodge, Richard Irving. *The Plains of the Great West and Their Inhabitants.* New York: Archer House, Inc., 1877.

Frederick, J. V. *Ben Holladay, the Stagecoach King.* Glendale: Arthur H. Clark Co., 1940.

Fremont, John Charles. *Memoirs of My Life.* Chicago and New York: Belford Clark Co., 1887.

Gilman, Musetta. *Pump on the Prairie.* Detroit: Harlo Press, 1975.

Grinnell, George B. *The Fighting Cheyennes.* New York: Charles Scribner's Sons, 1915.

———. *Bent's Old Fort and Its Builders.* New York, 1923.

———. *The Cheyenne Indians and Ways of Life.* Vol. 1. New York and London: Yale University Press and Oxford University Press, 1923.

Hafen, LeRoy R., ed. *Colorado Gold Rush. Contemporary Letters and Reports 1858–1859.* Glendale: Arthur H. Clark Co., 1941.

Hedges, W. H. *Reminiscences of W. H. Hedges, Pike's Peak or Busted.*

Edited by H. O. Brayer. Branding Iron Press, 1954.
Hill, Alice Polk. *Tales of the Colorado Pioneers.* Denver, 1867.
Hoig, Stan. *The Sand Creek Massacre.* Norman: University of Oklahoma Press, 1961.
Hollister, Ovando J. *Boldly They Rode.* Lakewood, Col.: The Golden Press, 1949.
Howbert, Irving. *Memories of a Lifetime in the Pike's Peak Region.* New York and London: J. P. Putnam's Sons, 1925.
Hyde, George. *Life of George Bent.* Edited by Savoie Lottinville. Norman: University of Oklahoma Press, 1968.
Jackson, Donald, and Mary Lee Spence. *The Expedition of John Charles Fremont, Travels from 1838 to 1844.* Urbana: University of Illinois Press, 1970.
James, Edwin. *Account of an Expedition from Pittsburgh to the Rocky Mountains, Performed in the Years 1819 and '20.* Philadelphia: H. C. Carey and J. Lea, 1823.
Kemper, G. W. H., ed. *A Twentieth Century History of Delaware County, Indiana.* 1908.
Larimer, William Henry Harrison. *Reminiscences of General William Larimer and His Son William H. H. Larimer, Two of the founders of Denver City.* Lancaster, Pa.: Press of the New Era, 1918.
Lavender, David. *The Big Divide.* Garden City, N.Y.: Doubleday and Co., 1949.
Linville, Leslie. *The Smoky Hill Valley and Butterfield Trail.* Colby, Kansas: LeRoy's Print, 1974.
_______. *Bent's Fort.* Garden City, N.Y.: Doubleday and Co., 1954.
Lowe, Percival. *Five Years a Dragoon.* Norman: University of Oklahoma Press, 1965.
McMechen, Edgar Carlisle. *Life of Governor Evans.* Denver: Walgren Publishing Co., 1924.
Majors, Alexander. *Seventy Years on the Frontier.* Rand McNally, 1893.
Marquette, Rev. David. *History of Nebraska Methodism. The First Half-Century, 1854–1904.* Cincinnati: The Western Methodist Book Concern Press, 1904.
Mattes, Merrill J. *The Great Platte River Road.* Lincoln: Nebraska Historical Society, 1969.
Meline, J. F. *Two Thousand Miles on Horseback.* New York: Hurd and Houghton, 1867.
Metcalf, Kenneth E. *The Beginnings of Methodism.* Denver: Iliff School of Theology, 1948.
Mooney, James. *The Cheyenne Indians, Memoirs of the American Anthropological Association,* Vol. 1. Lancaster, Pa.: American Anthropological Association, 1905–07.

Morris, Maurice O'Connor. *Rambles in the Rocky Mountains.* London: Smith, Elder and Co., 1964.

Morton, J. Sterling. *Illustrated History of Nebraska,* Vol. 1. Lincoln, Neb.: J. North and Co., 1905.

Polland, Edward A. *A Southern History of the War.* New York: The Blue and Gray Press, 1879.

Portrait and Biographical Record of the State of Colorado. Chapman Publishing Co., 1899.

Richardson, Albert D. *Beyond the Mississippi.* Hartford, Conn.: American Publishing Co., 1867.

Root, Frank and William Connelley. *The Overland Stage to California.* Topeka, 1901.

Russell, Don. *The Lives and Legends of Buffalo Bill.* Norman: University of Oklahoma Press, 1960.

Russell, Osborn. *Journal of a Trapper.* Boise, Idaho, 1921.

Sanford, Mollie. *The Journal of Mollie Dorsey Sanford in Nebraska and Colorado Territories 1857–1866.* Lincoln: University of Nebraska Press, 1959.

Settle, Raymond, and Mary Settle. *Empire on Wheels.* Stanford, Calif.: Stanford University Press, 1949.

———. *Saddle and Spurs.* Harrisburg, Pa.: The Stackpole Co., 1955.

Shaw, Luella. *True History of Some of the Pioneers of Colorado.* Hotchkins, Col.: W. S. Coburn, John Patterson and A. K. Shaw, 1909.

Smiley, Jerome. *Semi-Centennial History of the State of Colorado.* Chicago and New York: Lewis Publishing Co., 1913.

Stanley, Henry. *My Early Travels in America and Asia.* Lincoln: University of Nebraska Press, 1982.

Taylor, Bayard. *A Summer Trip.* New York: G. P. Putnam and Son, 1867.

Twain, Mark. *Roughing It.* Hartford, Conn.: American Publishing Co., 1872.

Ubbelohde, Carl. *A Colorado History.* Boulder: Pruett Press Inc., 1965.

Vischer, William. *The Pony Express.* Chicago: Rand McNally, 1908.

Ware, Eugene. *The Indian Wars of 1864.* With introduction and notes by Clyde C. Walton. Lincoln: University of Nebraska Press, 1960.

Wetmore, Helen Cody and Zane Grey. *Last of the Great Scouts.* New York: Grossett and Dunlap, 1918.

White, Lonnie. *Hostiles and Horse Soldiers.* Boulder: Pruett Press Inc., 1972.

Whitford, William Clark. *Colorado Volunteers in the Civil War, The New Mexico Campaign in 1862.* Denver: The State Historical and Natural History Society, 1906.

Young, Francis C. *Across the Plains in '65.* Denver: Lanning Bros., 1905.

Articles

Allen, Alonzo H. "Pioneer Life in Old Burlington," *Colorado Magazine* 14, No. 4 (July 1937).

Ashley, Susan Riley. "Reminiscences of Colorado in the Early Sixties," *Colorado Magazine* 13, No. 6 (November 1936).

Bent, George. "Forty Years with the Cheyennes," edited by George Hyde, *The Frontier, a Magazine of the West* 4–9 (October 1905–March 1906).

Bishop, C. W. "Stormy Times in Nebraska," *Nebraska Historical Society Publications* Vol. IV.

Bradley, Evelyn. "The Story of a Colorado Pioneer," *Colorado Magazine* 2, No. 1 (January 1925).

Brown, Hester. "Biography of Hester A. Rogers Brown," *Bits and Pieces* 5, No. 10 (1969).

Carey, Raymond. "The Tragic Trustee," *University of Denver Magazine* (June 1965).

Claine, A. T., ed. "Journal of Jonah Girard Cisne, Across the Plains and in Nevada City," *Colorado Magazine* 27, No. 1 (January 1950).

Clark, H. T. "Freighting to Denver and Black Hills," *Nebraska Historical Society Proceedings and Collections* 2nd ser., vol. V.

Coad, Ralph. "Transcript of a Speech," *Nebraska History Magazine* 14, No. 1 (January–March 1938).

Cobb, Frank M. "The Lawrence Party of Pike's Peakers in 1858 and the Founding of St. Charles," *Colorado Magazine* 10, No. 5 (September 1933).

Danker, Donald F., and Paul D. Riley. "The Journal of Amos S. Billingsley," *Colorado Magazine* 40, No. 4 (October 1963).

Davidson, Levette J. "The Early Diaries of William N. Byers," *Colorado Magazine* 31, No. 4 (July 1945).

Davis, William E. "Hell on Harmony," *Colorado Magazine* 41, No. 4 (Winter 1964).

De la Torre, Lillian. "The Haydee Star Company," *Colorado Magazine* 38 No. 3 (July 1961).

Ellenbecker, John G. "Oak Grove Massacre, Indian Raids on the Little Blue River in 1864," *Marysville Advocate Democrat,* Marysville, Kansas (no date). (Reprinted in the *Beatrice Daily Sun,* 12–21 August 1937.)

Green, James. "Incidents of the Indian Outbreak of 1864," *Nebraska Historical Society Publications* 19, Nos. 5–6. (Pertinent information provided by anonymous editors.)

Hadley, C.B. "The Plains War in '65," *Nebraska Historical Society Proceedings and Collections* 2nd ser., vol. v.

Hafen, LeRoy R. "Elbridge Gerry, Colorado Pioneer," *Colorado Magazine* 29, No. 2 (April 1952).

_______. "Ft. St. Vrain," *Colorado Magazine* 24, No. 4 (1952).

_______. "Fort Vasquez," *Colorado Magazine* 41, No. 3 (Summer 1964).

_______. "Old Ft. Lupton and Its Founder," *Colorado Magazine* 6, No. 6 (November 1929).

Harvey, James R. "Interview with Elizabeth J. Tallman, Pioneer Experiences in Colorado," *Colorado Magazine* 13, No. 4 (July 1936).

Hayes, Marita. "D.C. Oakes, Early Colorado Booster," *Colorado Magazine* 31, No. 3 (July 1954).

Hill, Nathaniel P. "Nathaniel Hill Inspects Colorado, Letters Written in 1864," *Colorado Magazine* 34 (April 1957).

Hodder, Hallie Rider. "Crossing the Plains in Wartime," *Colorado Magazine* 10, No. 4 (July 1933).

Lambert, Julia. "Plain Tales of the Plains," *The Trail* 8, No. 12.

Lubers, H.L. "William Bent's Family and the Indians of the Plains," *Colorado Magazine* 13, No. 1 (January 1936).

Mattes, Merrill J. "Article on Seth Ward," in *The Far West and the Rockies Historical Series, 1820–1875* vol. 3, ed. LeRoy R. Hafen.

_______. "The Mountain Men and the Fur Trade," in *The Far West and the Rockies Historical Series, 1820–1875* vol. 3, ed. by LeRoy R. Hafen.

Merrill, Rev. Moses. "Diary," *Nebraska Historical Society Transactions and Reports,* vol. IV.

Oakes, D.C. "The Man Who Wrote the Guide Book," *The Trail* 2, No. 7 (December 1909).

Palmer, H.E. "History of the Powder River Indian Expedition of 1865," *Nebraska Historical Society Publications* vol. II.

Parkhill, Forbes. "Decline and Fall of the Stagecoach Empire," *Westerner's Brand Book* vol. VII.

Parry, Maj. Henry C. "Letters," *Annals of Wyoming* 30, No. 2 (Oct. 1958).

Parsons, William. "Report on the Gold Mines of Colorado, 1858." *Colorado Magazine* 13, No. 6 (November 1936).

_______. "Pike's Peak Fourteen Years Ago, June 1872," *Kansas Magazine* 1, No. 6.

Peck, R.M. "Recollections of Early Times in Kansas Territory," *Kansas State Historical Society Recollections* 8.

Pennock, Ellen. "Incidents in My Life as a Pioneer," *Colorado Magazine* 30, No. 2 (April 1953).

Pratt, Harry E., ed. "Edward J. Lewis, Diary of a Pike's Peak Gold Seeker in 1860," *Colorado Magazine* 14, No. 6 (November 1937).

Purinton, Mrs. Lulu. "Native Sons and Daughters of Nebraska Contest," *Nebraska History Magazine* 18, No. 2 (April–June 1937).

Richardson, Albert D. "Letters on the Pike's Peak Gold Region Written to the Lawrence Republican, May 22, August 25, 1860," Ed. by Louise Barry. *Kansas Historical Society Quarterly* (February 1943).

Rolfe, D.P. "Freighting from Nebraska City," *Nebraska Historical Society Proceedings and Collections* 2nd ser. vol. 5.

Root, George A. and Russell H. Hickman. "Pike's Peak Express Company," *Kansas Historical Society Quarterly* 12, No. 2 (May 1944), No. 4 (November 1944), No. 8 (November 1945); and 14, No. 1 (February 1946).

Sayr, Hal. "Early Central City Theatricals and Other Reminiscences," *Colorado Magazine* 6, No. 2 (March 1929).

Smith, Harriet. "Day Book to Pike's Peak by Ox Wagon," *Annals of Iowa* (Fall 1959). (Now available as a separate book at Denver Public Library, Western History Department.)

Spencer, Otis B. "A Sketch of the Boone–Bent Family," edited by William A. Goff. *Westport Historical Quarterly* 7, No. 4 (March 1973). (In Research Collection 72, Colorado Historical Society Library, Denver.)

Thomas, John J. "Days of the Overland Trail," *The Trail*, Vols. 2 and 10.

Tootle, Mrs. Thomas. "Journey to Denver," edited by Roy E. Coy. *The Museum Graphic* (St. Joseph Museum), 13, No. 2 (Spring 1961).

Wade, Mrs. Noble. "New Lights on Mrs. Lucinda Eubanks," *The Trail* 13, No. 2 (July 1920).

Wildman, Augustus. "The Wildman Letters and Other Documents," in *The Far West and the Rockies Historical Series* vol. 13, ed. by LeRoy R. Hafen.

Willard, James F. "The Tyler Rangers, the Black Hawk Company and the Indian Rising of '64," *Colorado Magazine* 7, No. 4 (July 1930).

Winne, Peter. "Sketches of the Indian War of 1864," *The Trail* 14, No. 11.

Woodward, R.O. "With the Troops in Colorado," *Colorado Magazine* 3, No. 2 (May 1926).

Wynkoop, Edward E. "Edward Wanshear Wynkoop," *Kansas State Historical Society Collections* 13.

Manuscripts

Bent, George. Bent-Hyde Letters. Beineke Rare Books Library, New Haven, Conn.

Binneweiss, W.G. (quoting Walter Ennes). Pamphlet 343, CWA Writers

Project, Garfield and Weld Counties, Document 12. Colorado Historical Society Library, Denver.

Bresee, Floyd Edgar. "Overland Freighting in the Platte Valley, 1850–1870." Master's thesis, University of Nebraska, 1937. Colorado University Library, Western History Collection.

Dailey, John L. "Diary." Manuscript collection, Denver Public Library, Western History Department.

"Dawson Scrapbooks." Colorado Historical Society Library, Denver.

Evans, John. Manuscript P-L 23. Bancroft Library, University of California, Berkeley.

Gerry, Elbridge. Gerry Research Collection No. 264. Colorado Historical Society Library, Denver.

Gill, Mark. Pamphlet 351/1-110, CWA Writers Project, 1933–34, Morgan and Sedgwick Counties. Colorado Historical Society Library, Denver.

Hill, Clifford Clinton. "Wagon Roads in Colorado. Unpublished Master's thesis, appendix. Western History Department, Denver Public Library. Research Collection 663.

Husted, C.R. Bancroft Collection. Western History Collection, Colorado University Library.

Kassler, George W. Manuscript Collection. Colorado Historical Society Library, Denver.

McGrath, Maria Davis. "Real Pioneers of Colorado." Vol. 2 (1934).Colorado Historical Library, Denver.

"On the Overland Trail." Western History Collection, Colorado University Library, Boulder.

Stanton, I.W. Research Collection No. 600. Colorado Historical Society Library, Denver.

"WPA File of Place Names, Interviews and Personalities." Colorado Historical Society Library, Denver.

Wynkoop, Edward W. "Unfinished Colorado History." Manuscript II-20. Colorado Historical Society Library, Denver.

Newspapers

Black Hawk Mining Journal
Boulder Camera
Cheyenne Daily Leader
Denver Post
Denver Republican
Denver Republican and Commonwealth
Frontier Scout
Greeley Tribune
Leavenworth Daily Times
Miners Register
Missouri Democrat
Montana Post (Virginia City)
Rocky Mountain News
St. Joseph Herald

Documents

Indiana State Marriage Records Index, Delaware County.

National Archives. Post Returns and Post Records of Fort Morgan.

U.S. Census, Nebraska Territory, Shorter County and Platte River Settlement, 1860.

U.S. Census, Indiana. Niles Township, Delaware County, 1850, 1860, 1870, 1880.

U.S. Congress. Senate. Joint Committee on the Conduct of the War. *Massacre of the Cheyenne Indians.* 38th Cong., 2nd sess., 1865. Senate Report 142.

U.S. Congress. Senate. Joint Special Committee, appointed under Joint Resolution of March 3, 1865. *Condition of the Indian Tribes.* 39th Cong., 2nd sess., 1867. Senate Report 156.

U.S. Congress. Senate. *Report of the Secretary of War. Communicating in compliance with a resolution of the Senate of February 4, 1867, a copy of the evidence taken at Denver and Fort Lyon, Colorado Territory, by a military commission ordered to inquire into the Sand Creek Massacre, November 1864.* 39th Cong., 2nd sess., 1867. Senate Executive Document 26.

U.S. Congress. Senate. *Claims of Ben Holladay.* 46th Cong., 2nd sess., 1879. Misc. Document 19.

Kappler, G. W. H., ed. *Indian Affairs, Laws and Treaties,* vol. 2. 50th Cong., 2nd sess. Senate Executive Document 319. Washington, GPO, 1904. (Also available at Denver Public Library, Western History Department.)

U.S. War Department. *The War of the Rebellion. A compilation of the Official Records of the Union and Confederate Armies,* four series, 128 vols. Washington: GPO, 1880–1901.

U.S. Department of Interior, Bureau of Indian Affairs. *Report of the Commissioner of Indian Affairs.* Volumes according to year, 1859, 1860, 1861, 1862, 1863, 1864. Washington: GPO, 1852–1866.

INDEX

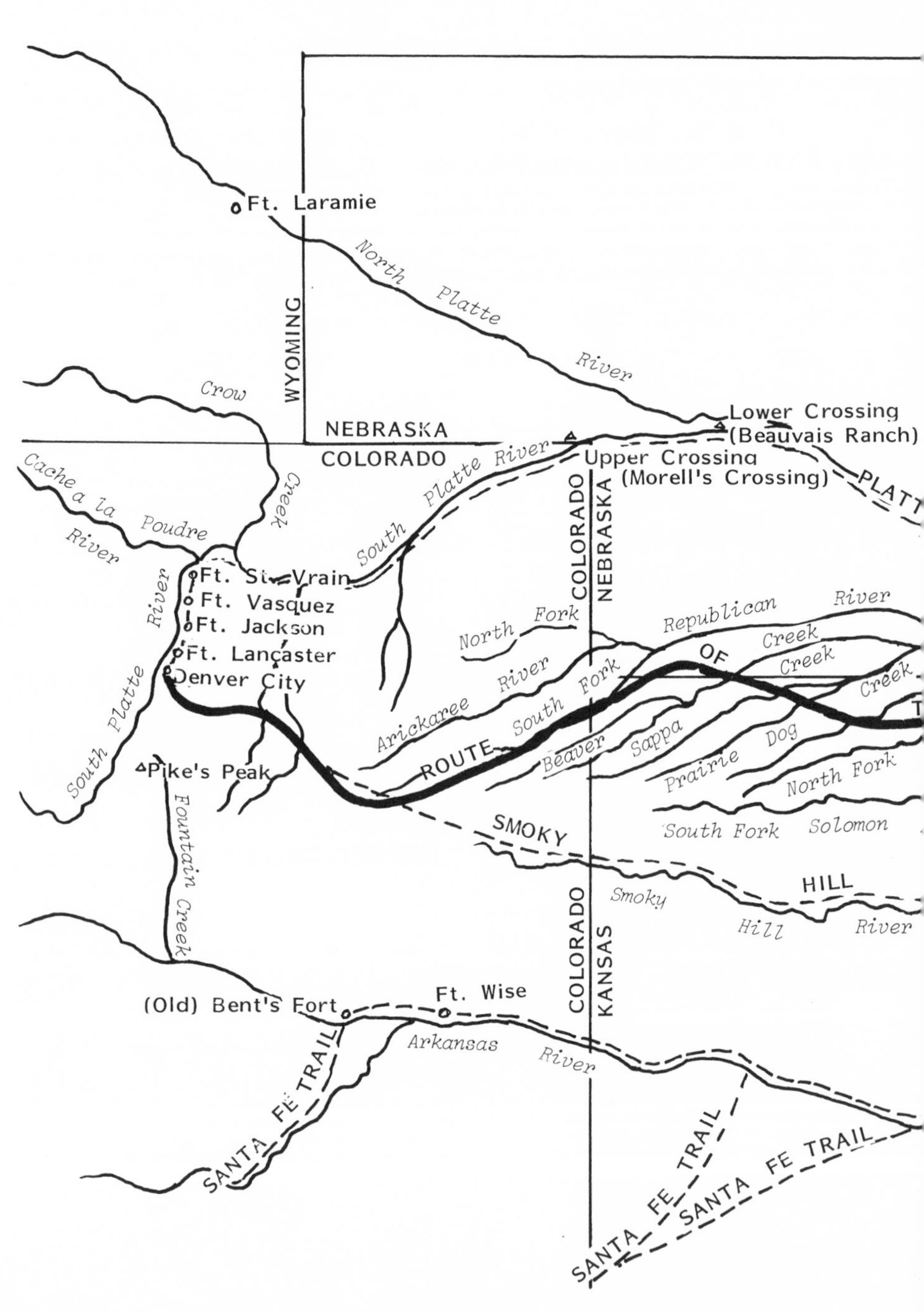
Ft. Laramie
North Platte River
WYOMING
NEBRASKA
COLORADO
Crow Creek
Lower Crossing
(Beauvais Ranch)
Upper Crossing
(Morell's Crossing)
PLATT
Cache a la Poudre River
South Platte River
Ft. St. Vrain
Ft. Vasquez
Ft. Jackson
Ft. Lancaster
Denver City
COLORADO
NEBRASKA
North Fork
Republican River
Creek
Creek
Creek
OF
Arickaree River
South Fork
ROUTE
Beaver
Sappa
Prairie Dog
North Fork
Pike's Peak
SMOKY
South Fork
Solomon
HILL
Smoky Hill River
Fountain Creek
COLORADO
KANSAS
(Old) Bent's Fort
Ft. Wise
Arkansas River
SANTA FE TRAIL
SANTA FE TRAIL
SANTA FE TRAIL

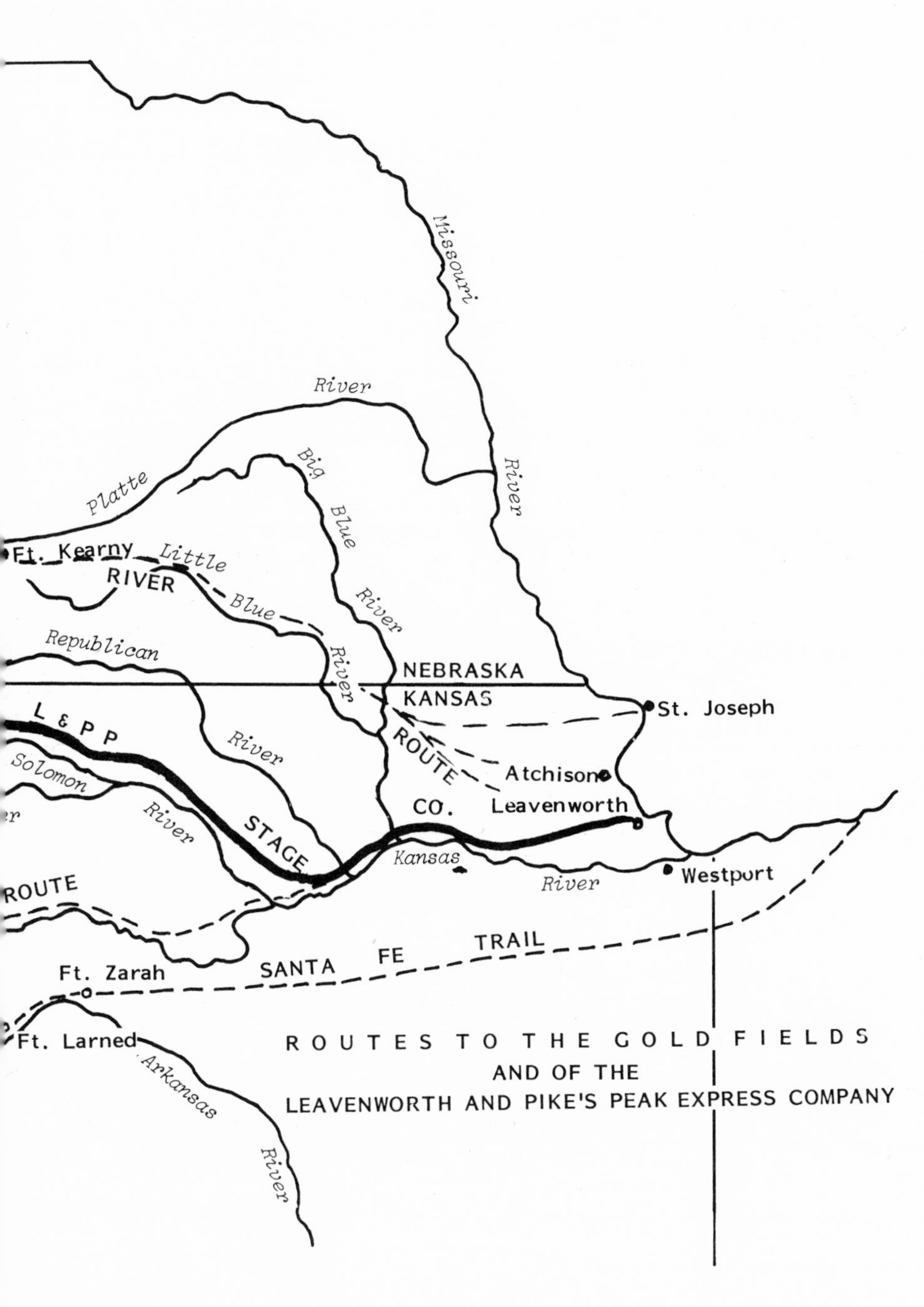

ROUTES TO THE GOLD FIELDS
AND OF THE
LEAVENWORTH AND PIKE'S PEAK EXPRESS COMPANY

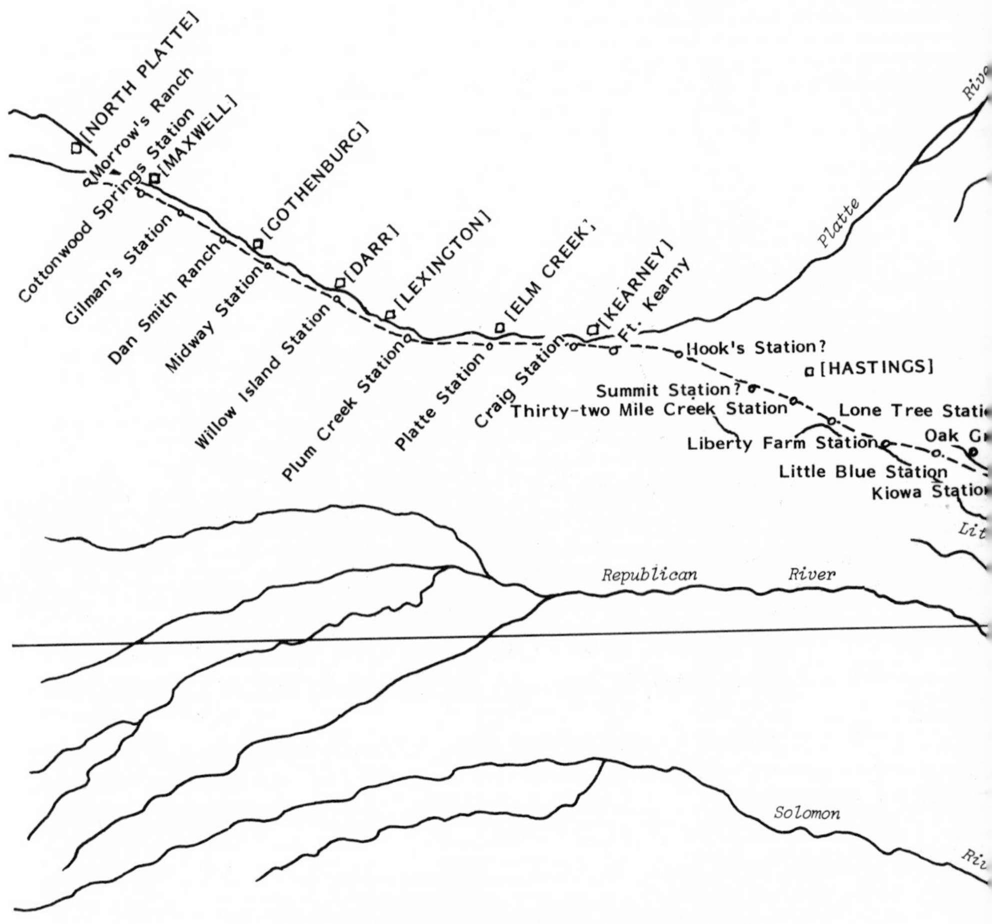

THE OVERLAND STAGE ROUTE
FROM ATCHISON TO NORTH PLATTE

(Locations are approximate)